Praise for *Gentle Baby Care*

"As a new mother, there were many times when I wished my babies came with an instruction manual. Now they do—in the form of Elizabeth Pantley's *Gentle Baby Care*, the best 'baby instruction manual' I've read. Elizabeth guides the new parent through the ups and downs of baby parenthood with her usual nonjudgmental gentleness and warmth. Its easy-to-read format is great for those emergencies when you need information in a hurry. I'll be recommending this book to all of our new parents."

—*Maribeth Doerr, editor-in-chief, StorkNet.com*

"A trusted handbook for parents. It offers practical, well-researched advice on health, safety, and developmental issues as well as lots of gentle support and guidance for parents on the many choices they must make during the first year with a new baby."

—*Joan K. Comeau, Ph.D., director and editor,*
Family Information Services

"Elizabeth Pantley has done it again, providing parents with a valuable tool to help them overcome the challenges that accompany the joys of being a mom or dad. *Gentle Baby Care* puts everything parents need to know at their fingertips in an easy-to-use reference. The book is organized in a way that takes you to the answers you need and refers you to additional topics related to the subject, eliminating the need for busy parents to flip back and forth from index to chapters. Every mother should have two copies of *Gentle Baby Care*—one for herself and one for her caregiver, mother-in-law, or spouse."

—*Maria Bailey, CEO, BSM Media; founder, BlueSuitMom.com,*
Smart Mom Solutions; and host of Mom Talk Radio

"An encyclopedia of child-rearing advice and information, with practical tips on crying, sleep, discipline, baby milestones, and much, much more. Elizabeth's soothing advice will help both new and seasoned parents relate to the newest member of their household!"

—*Betsy Gartrell-Judd, editor, PregnancyandBaby.com*

"An informative and comprehensive guide to responding to your baby's needs with kind and compassionate care and unrivaled sensitivity. Elizabeth Pantley leaves the reader feeling that she respects and supports the uniqueness of each family and its ability to make the choices that suit its own situation, with none of the guilt and judgment associated with most guides—a refreshing and balanced change."

—*Kimberly McIntyre-de Montbrun, mother of four,*
editor of GentleParents.com, and owner of
TwinkleLittleStar.com and PuddleCatchers.com

"At last, the perfect resource guide for new parents. *Gentle Baby Care* is informative, easy to follow, and well organized. Parenting expert Elizabeth Pantley has gathered a wealth of information and valuable resources."

—*Lori Lee Helman, mother of two and owner of*
Mommas Baby (mommasbaby.com)

"*Gentle Baby Care* is an impressive resource guide for every parent new and old! It contains in-depth information that covers baby-care basics plus unique yet equally important topics, such as handling overzealous grandparents, dealing with your baby's crying in a car seat, and keeping your baby quiet during worship services. The added tips from experienced parents are great—tried-and-true ideas from the trenches! Spread the word about this helpful and supportive new resource manual that will benefit every parent and caregiver."

—*Andrea Grace, president, Mommy and Baby Fitness Inc.,*
www.mommyandbabyfitness.com

"The first year of life is filled with worry for many parents, and Elizabeth Pantley offers expert advice for them in a nonjudgmental and, most important, supportive way. This book's format also enables new parents to quickly access vital child-rearing information in their most anxious times. I highly recommend this book to new parents and am envious that I did not have my hands on a copy during my son's first year."

—*Gloria Perez-Walker, founder, Latina Mami*

Gentle Baby Care

Other Books by Elizabeth Pantley

Gentle Baby Care

No-Cry, No-Fuss, No-Worry—Essential Tips for Raising Your Baby

Elizabeth Pantley, author of *The No-Cry Sleep Solution*

Foreword by Dr. Harvey Karp, author of *The Happiest Baby on the Block*

Contemporary Books

Chicago   New York   San Francisco   Lisbon   London   Madrid   Mexico City
Milan   New Delhi   San Juan   Seoul   Singapore   Sydney   Toronto

The McGraw·Hill Companies

Library of Congress Cataloging-in-Publication Data

Pantley, Elizabeth.
    Gentle baby care: no-cry, no-fuss, no-worry—essential tips for raising your baby /
Elizabeth Pantley.—1st ed.
       p.   cm.
    ISBN 0-07-139885-6
    1. Infants—Care—Handbooks, manuals, etc.   I. Title.

RJ61.P222   2003
649'.122—dc22

2003015676

Illustrations on p. 450 copyright © 2002 by Jennifer Kalis

1 2 3 4 5 6 7 8 9 0   AGM/AGM   2 1 0 9 8 7 6 5 4 3

ISBN 0-07-139885-6

Interior design by Nick Panos

McGraw-Hill books are available at special quantity discounts to use as premiums and
sales promotions, or for use in corporate training programs. For more information, please
write to the Director of Special Sales, Professional Publishing, McGraw-Hill, Two Penn
Plaza, New York, NY 10121-2298. Or contact your local bookstore.

This book is printed on acid-free paper.

This book is dedicated to you, Mom, my friend.

If I have one wish, it is that when my children are grown, they will love me

even half as much as I love you.

Contents

· · · · · · · · · · · ·

Foreword

Congratulations on your new baby! You have now joined the long and respected chain of mothers and fathers stretching back to the very beginning of families. In many ways, caring for your new baby will be totally natural and instinctual. Yet, you will certainly have many questions . . . that's normal, too. Although parents today are the most educated in history, in many respects we are also the least experienced.

Parents in the past had a whole network of support at hand. They usually had their parents, grandparents, aunts, and uncles nearby from whom to get help and advice. Also, as they grew up, they had lots of hands-on experience caring for younger siblings, cousins, and neighbors. Their hundreds of hours of tiny-tot training (from diaper duty to burping to rocking a child to sleep) really made them feel prepared for having their own newborn.

But today's parents are different. We often live farther away from our baby-savvy relatives. And, as amazing as it sounds, many moms and dads barely have even held a baby before giving birth and being handed their own little bundle by the nurse. I don't know how much hands-on baby experience you have, but most parents I see in my practice have very little to none. (No wonder new parents sometimes joke that they expect some type of a "shoplifting alarm" to go off when they leave the hospital!)

But, don't worry! Even if you don't know everything about babies, Elizabeth Pantley does. Like her extraordinary book *The No-Cry Sleep Solution*, Elizabeth's *Gentle Baby Care* is a warm, fact-filled, and practical book. Her advice is guided by love and a level head. With her broad experience as a parenting educator and mother of four children, this book is the next best thing to having a wise and experienced friend living next door. I have no doubt that *Gentle Baby Care* will be a valuable addition to your library, whether you are a first-time parent or an old experienced pro.

Harvey Karp, M.D.

Dr. Harvey Karp is an assistant professor of pediatrics at the UCLA School of Medicine, with a private practice in Santa Monica. He is the author of the book and award-winning video entitled *The Happiest Baby on the Block: The New Way to Calm Crying and Help Your Baby Sleep Longer.*

Acknowledgments

I am very grateful for the support of the many people who have made this book possible, and I would like to express my sincere appreciation to:

- Judith McCarthy at McGraw-Hill/Contemporary Books. Thank you for your continued guidance and for always being my advocate.
- Meredith Bernstein of Meredith Bernstein Literary Agency, New York. Thank you for your high-energy enthusiasm and your unwavering belief in my work and support of my efforts.
- Vanessa Sands. Thank you for sharing your insight, your talent, and your friendship.
- Alice Visser-Furray, Carol Dombrovski, and Becky Lauersdorf. Thank you for the many hours you spent on this book and for the many comments, questions, and ideas that you shared.
- My husband, Robert; my mom; and my children, Angela, Vanessa, David, and Coleton. Thank you for all the joy, all the love, and your encouragement and support.
- Maria Bailey, Joan K. Comeau, Maribeth Doerr, Betsy Gartrell-Judd, Andrea Grace, Lori Lee Helman, Kimberly McIntyre-de Montbrun, and Gloria Perez-Walker. Thank you for your enthusiastic and encouraging support.

Allergies and Asthma

· · · · · · · · · · · ·

See also: Colds; Croup; Food Allergies; Solid Foods, introducing

My three-month-old baby is wheezing when she breathes. Could she have asthma?

Learn About It

An infant's airway is very tiny, so just a small amount of swelling can produce that wheezing sound. With young babies, differentiating among a common cold, a respiratory infection, allergies, and asthma can be difficult.

What Symptoms Point to Allergies or Asthma?

While many of the symptoms of colds, infections, allergies, and asthma overlap, looking at the whole list of your baby's symptoms may give you a sense of whether your baby has more than a regular cold. Here are some possible signs of allergies or asthma:

- Runny nose that drips clear and watery
- Coughing, especially at night
- Sniffling
- Sneezing
- Stuffy nose, especially upon waking
- Itchy eyes, ears, or nose
- Watery eyes
- Sore throat
- Difficulty breathing
- Noisy, wheezy breathing
- Skin rash

- Diarrhea
- Cold symptoms that last more than two weeks
- Persistent, chronic ear infections
- An increase in these symptoms after contact with animals or being near plants and flowers
- Family history of allergies or asthma

What About Food Allergies?

The symptoms of food allergies often occur within minutes or hours of ingesting the food to which the baby is allergic. However, a baby with an allergic reaction to the formula he drinks may have daily symptoms that include fussiness, gassiness, and difficulty sleeping—and he is often diagnosed with colic. Breastfed babies with milk allergies suffer symptoms if their mothers are eating dairy products. Additional signs and symptoms of milk allergies include vomiting, diarrhea, abdominal pain, and bloody stools. Do call your doctor if you notice any of these (*see* Food Allergies).

Only a doctor can tell if your child has allergies or asthma, since many of the symptoms resemble those we normally attribute to a cold, respiratory congestion, or other normal childhood conditions such as teething. If you suspect that your child may have either condition, talk to your doctor about your concerns.

For More Information

Websites

American College of Allergy, Asthma & Immunology
allergy.mcg.edu/home.html

American Lung Association
lungusa.org

Attachment Parenting

· · · · · · · · · · · · ·

See also: Baby Carriers; Breastfeeding Your Newborn; Breastfeeding Your Toddler; Co-Sleeping, making it work

I often hear the term attachment parenting, *but I'm not sure exactly what that means or if I am an attachment parent. My baby sleeps with me and I breastfeed, but I also give him a pacifier and use a stroller instead of a sling. Exactly what* is *attachment parenting?*

Learn About It

I have practiced attachment parenting from the time my first baby was born fifteen years ago—before I ever knew the term existed. I'm a firm believer that the attachment parenting approach gives us the most wonderful ways to raise children.

While the basic principles are the same, attachment parenting comes in myriad shapes, sizes, and flavors. It's like vegetarianism: While we understand what people mean when they say they are "vegetarians," there are many different degrees of vegetarianism. Some people don't eat meat, fish, or fowl but do eat eggs and dairy products. Some don't eat meat, fish, fowl, or dairy products, but do eat eggs. A vegan doesn't eat meat, fish, fowl, eggs, or dairy products! Even with all their differences, however, they all fit the description of "vegetarian."

In the same way, no hard-and-fast set of rules makes up attachment parenting, but the heart of this approach is a strong parent-baby connection borne of unconditional nurturing and mutual respect. My colleague and friend Dr. William Sears—lauded as "the father of attachment parenting"—explains attachment parenting as a style of child care based on the seven "Baby *B*s." You can read about this in depth in any of Dr. Sears's books, such as *The Attachment Parenting Book*

(Little, Brown and Company, 2001). To give you an overall picture of what attachment parenting is all about, however, I will summarize Dr. Sears's *B*s for you here.

Birth Bonding

Attachment parents often start defining themselves as such before their baby is even born. They take great interest in the pregnancy and have definite ideas about the early weeks of life as an important time for the connection between baby and parent. Attached parents do everything they can to get off to the right start by carefully weighing birth options, choosing those that are least invasive and enable as much physical closeness in the early hours as possible. From that point on, they focus in on their little one with the eagerness, attentiveness, and, most important, responsiveness that the new relationship deserves.

If the relationship's development is delayed (perhaps by medical complications or adoption, for example), attached parents put extra energy into making up for lost time. They don't dwell on what has been missed; rather, they use whatever starting point they have to build a solid, connected relationship with their baby.

Breastfeeding

Attachment parents are very likely to breastfeed their baby at the start and to continue for a long time. They are aware of the many benefits—both physical and intangible—and are dedicated to successful breastfeeding, even if they get off to a rocky start. They focus on the fact that breastfeeding helps mother and baby connect and enhances a mother's ability to read her baby's cues.

Can a bottlefeeding mother be an attachment parent? *Absolutely!* Remember that these *B*s are ideals, not absolutes. However, the attachment theory does color the way a parent interacts with her baby, regardless of feeding method. Thus, a bottlefeeding attachment mother feeds her baby while holding him in a loving, close embrace, maximizing bodily contact. She is unlikely to use any kind of bottle prop or holder. She uses feeding time to nurture and connect with her baby, making bottlefeeding a pleasant bonding experience for both of them.

Babywearing

Attachment parents understand that babies love and need to be held. They know that the more that babies are held, the more content they are. The more content they are, the less they cry. The less they cry, the more their parents enjoy them. The more their parents enjoy them, the more they're likely to be held. It's a grand circle of a deliberate design: Physical closeness fosters healthy emotional and physical growth. Attachment parents usually have their baby as close as possible—in their arms, on their laps, or in a sling. But bear in mind that this doesn't preclude the use of strollers. Strollers and other baby carriers can be lifesavers. A parent who uses a stroller can be just as much an attachment parent as one who uses a sling! The key is that attachment parents use baby carriers wisely, always making sure that Baby has plenty of contact and cuddles.

Bedding Close to Baby

Attachment parents look upon parenting as a joy-filled twenty-four-hour responsibility. They feel strongly that a baby needs nurturing just as much in the middle of the night as during the day. Especially during the early months, attachment parents stay close to their babies during sleep time, so Baby sleeps either with or close to her parents—with proper safety precautions (*see* Co-Sleeping, making it work).

Parents who have their baby sleep in a crib in a separate room can also be attachment parents. Typically, they use a baby monitor or keep doors open to listen in on their baby. They don't hesitate to go to their little one when he awakens, whether in the morning or the middle of the night.

Belief in the Language Value of Your Baby's Cry

Attachment parents understand that their baby has a limited way of communicating with them. They hear her cry as her only way of calling to them. According to Dr. Sears, "Babies cry to communicate, not to manipulate." Attachment parents react quickly and lovingly to their baby's cries and, very often, to the sounds that precede any cries. In this way, they purposefully build a foundation of trust in the relationship.

Beware of Baby Trainers

Dr. Sears refers to people who create strict rules for the care of babies without regard to a baby's feelings or needs as "baby trainers."

Parents who follow the principles of attachment parenting are naturally suspicious of any advice that does not take their baby's needs or feelings into account or that discounts a parent's basic instincts. The red flag goes up for an attachment parent when she's told, for example, to ignore a baby's cry or to force a baby into a rigid schedule for eating, sleeping, and playing based on convenience to the parent or on some external belief system. Attachment parents know that babyhood lasts a very short time, but the ramifications of babyhood last a lifetime. They also understand that parenting is not a part-time, first-shift-only job to be taken lightly.

Attachment parents are willing to take the long, hard road if it means the best choice for their baby. They tend to put their own needs second to the baby's—yet are pleasantly surprised to find that attachment parenting typically makes the baby years go by much more easily and smoothly. They learn that, instead of being an added burden, attachment parenting helps them *enjoy* babyhood even as they put their baby's physical and emotional well-being ahead of their own.

Balance

Attachment parenting is not about being a martyr, nor about raising a spoiled, indulged child. It is about balance: loving, nurturing, and caring for a child while helping the child grow into a responsible, respectful, delightful, and productive human adult.

Typically, attachment parents arrive at their own parenting philosophy (as individualized as it may be within the confines of attachment parenting) through reading, research, and discussion with others. They tend to evaluate the options and thus take a considered and conscious approach. Perhaps the simplest description is that they follow their own hearts and instincts, which tell them to comfort a crying baby, feed a hungry baby, and stay nearby. These instincts have evolved to ensure the survival of the human race, and they've served it well. Attachment parents are not perfect or noble, nor are their children. These parents simply and wholeheartedly embrace parenting for all that it is and surrender to the natural impulses that keep them close to their babies.

My attachment-parented children are happy, confident, capable, and independent as they grow into their teen years. And every time I get a hug and an "I love you" from one of my teenagers, see one of my older children tend lovingly to their little brother, or notice my children make a right (rather than easy) decision, I am thankful that I've chosen to raise my children using the philosophies commonly referred to as attachment parenting.

For More Information

Books

Granju, Katie Allison, and Betsy Kennedy. *Attachment Parenting: Instinctive Care for Your Baby and Young Child*. New York: Pocket Books, 1999.

Sears, William, and Martha Sears. *The Attachment Parenting Book: A Commonsense Guide to Understanding and Nurturing Your Baby*. Boston: Little, Brown and Company, 2001.

Sears, William, Martha Sears, and Elizabeth Pantley. *The Successful Child: What Parents Can Do to Help Kids Turn Out Well*. Boston: Little, Brown and Company, 2002.

Websites

Attachment Parenting International
attachmentparenting.org

Dr. William Sears
askdrsears.com

The Natural Child Project
naturalchild.org

The Whole Family Attachment Parenting Association
members.tripod.com/~JudyArnall/index.html

Baby Blues

(Postpartum Blues)

· · · · · · · · · · ·

See also: Postpartum Depression; Marriage; Unwanted Advice

> *My baby is a week old. She's healthy and beautiful. My family is ecstatic. My friends are bringing gifts. Everything is so wonderfully perfect—except for me. I'm having horrible mood swings, and I cry at the drop of a hat. I should be so happy, but I'm not. What's wrong with me?*

Learn About It

I remember when I was lying in my hospital bed after the birth of my fourth child, Coleton. I had endured a full day of labor and a difficult delivery (who says the fourth one comes easily?), and I was tired beyond explanation. After the relief of seeing my precious new child came an uncontrollable feeling to close my eyes and sleep. As my husband cradled newborn Coleton, I drifted off; my parting thoughts were, "I can't do this. I don't have the energy. How will I ever take care of a baby?" Happily for me, a few hours of sleep, a supportive family, and lucky genes were all it took to feel normal again. But as many as 80 percent of new mothers experience a case of the baby blues that lasts for weeks after the birth of their baby. This isn't something you can control—there's no place for blame.

The most wonderful and committed mothers, even experienced mothers of more than one child, can get the baby blues. Your baby's birth has set into motion great changes in your body and in your life, and your emotions are reacting in a normal way. Dramatic hormonal shifts occur when a body goes from pregnant to not pregnant in a manner of minutes. Add to this your new title (Mommy!) and the responsibilities that go with it, and your blues are perfectly understandable. You're certainly not alone. This emotional letdown during the first few weeks is common after birth. Just remember that your state of mind has a physical origin and is exacerbated by challenging circumstances—and you and your body will most likely adjust to both soon.

What Are Baby Blues?

The baby blues (also called postpartum blues) are a normal and common part of the postpartum period. These feelings of sadness and fatigue typically begin within a few days of birth and last several weeks or even more. Experts believe that their cause is the rapid change in hormone levels that occurs after the birth of your baby. It is also thought that the sudden, overwhelming responsibility of motherhood combined with family adjustment and lack of sleep have a lot to do with the upheaval of emotions during this time.

How Do I Know if I Have the Baby Blues?

Every woman who experiences postpartum blues does so in a different way. If you are wondering if you have the baby blues, then you're probably dealing with some of the symptoms. The most common symptoms include the ones listed here:

- Anxiety and nervousness
- Sadness or feelings of loss
- Stress and tension
- Impatience or a short temper
- Bouts of crying or tearfulness
- Mood swings
- Difficulty concentrating
- Trouble sleeping or excessive tiredness
- Not wanting to get dressed, go out, or clean up the house

Could It Be More than Just the Baby Blues?

If you are feeling these symptoms to a degree that disrupts your normal level of function, if your baby is more than a few weeks old, or if you have additional symptoms—particularly feelings of resentment or rejection toward your baby or even a temptation to harm him—you may have postpartum depression. *This is a serious illness that requires immediate treatment.* Please read the section on Postpartum Depression and call your doctor as soon as possible. You do not have to feel this way, and safe treatment is available, even if you're breastfeeding.

If you're not sure whether you have the baby blues or postpartum depression, ask your doctor, and don't feel embarrassed. This is a question and a concern that doctors hear often and with good reason.

How Can I Get Rid of the Blues?

While typical baby blues are fairly brief and usually disappear on their own, you can do a few things to help yourself feel better and get through the next few emotional days or weeks:

• **Give yourself time.** Grant yourself permission to take the time you need to become a mother. Pregnancy lasts only nine months, and your baby's actual birth is only a moment—but becoming a mother takes some time. Motherhood is an immense responsibility. In my opinion, it is the most overwhelming, meaningful, incredible, transforming experience of a lifetime. No wonder it produces such emotional and physical change! No other event of this magnitude would ever be taken lightly, so don't feel guilty for treating this time in your life as the very big deal it is. Remind yourself that it's OK (and necessary) to focus on this new aspect of your life and make it your number one priority. Tending to a newborn properly takes time—all the time in his world. So, instead of feeling guilty or conflicted about your new focus, put your heart into getting to know this new little person. The world can wait for a few weeks. And consider as objectively as you can just what you have accomplished: You have formed a new, entire person inside your own body and brought him forth. You have been party to a miracle. Or if you've adopted, you've chosen to invite a miracle into your life and became an instant mother. You deserve a break and some space in which to just exist with your amazing little one, unfettered by outside concerns.

• **Talk to someone who understands.** Talk to a sibling, relative, or friend with young children about what you are feeling. Someone who has experienced the baby blues can help you realize that they *are* temporary, and everything will be fine. A confidante can also serve as a checkpoint who can encourage you to seek help if she perceives that you need it.

• **Reach out and get out.** Aside from informal counseling sessions with acquaintances, simply getting out (if you are physically able and have your doctor's OK) and connecting with people at large can go a long way toward reorienting your perspective. Four walls can close in very quickly, so change the scenery and head to the mall, the park, the library, a coffeehouse—whatever public place you enjoy. You'll feel a growing sense of pride as strangers ooh and aah over your little one. Your baby will enjoy the stimulation and might just reward you with an extra-long nap later!

• **Join a support group.** Joining a support group, either in person or online, can help you sort through your feelings about new motherhood. Chatting with other new mothers can help you understand that you're not alone. Take care to choose a group that aligns with your core beliefs about parenting a baby. As an example, if you are committed to breastfeeding but most other members of the group are bottlefeeding, this may not be the best place for you, since members of the group aren't likely to understand your breastfeeding issues or be able to offer many helpful ideas (*see* "To Locate a Support Group" at the end of this entry). If you have twins, a premature baby, or a baby with special needs, for example, seek out a group for parents with babies like yours. Again, look for a group with your same overall parenting beliefs. The fact that you all have twin babies doesn't mean you will all choose to parent them in the same way, so try to find like-minded new friends.

• **Tell Daddy what he can do to help.** It's very important that your spouse or partner be there for you right now. He may *want* to help you, but he may be unsure of how. There *are* things that he can do for you; show him the accompanying list to help him help you.

Tips for Daddy

- **Understand.** It's critical that your spouse or partner feel that you understand that she is going through a hormonally driven depression that she cannot control—and that she is not "just being grumpy." Tell her you know this is normal and that she'll be feeling better soon. Simply looking over this list and using some of the ideas will tell her a lot about your commitment to (and belief in) her. This in and of itself will be a big help.

- **Let her talk about her feelings.** Knowing she can talk to you about her feelings without being judged or criticized will help her feel much better.

- **Tend to the baby.** Taking your baby for an hour or two every day so Mommy can sleep or take a quiet shower can give her a breath of fresh air. A hint: Have her nurse the baby, then go for a walk or take the baby on an outing. If you stay at home, especially if the baby is fussing, then Mommy will fret instead of rest. A benefit for you is that most babies love to be out and about, and your baby will enjoy this special time with you. To demonstrate your understanding of your important role, tell her that you know this isn't baby-sitting, it's fathering.

- **Step in to protect her.** If she's overwhelmed with visitors, kindly and gently explain to company that she needs a bit of space and a lot of rest. Help her with whatever household duties usually fall to her (or get someone else to help her), and do everything you can to stay on top of yours. Worry about the house's cleanliness or laundry upkeep will do her no good whatsoever. If the grandparents offer to take the baby for a few hours, take them up on it. She probably can't manage most things as well as she usually can, so she'll truly appreciate knowing that you will.

- **Tell her she's beautiful.** Most woman feel depressed about the way they look right after childbirth, because most women still look four months pregnant! After changing so greatly to accommodate a baby's development, a woman's body takes a few months to regain any semblance of normal appearance. Be patient with both her body and her

(continued)

feelings about it. Tell her what an amazing thing she's accomplished. Remind her of the beauty in the strength she's shown. Comment on the way her hair highlights her eyes or how the baby has her perfect lips. Any compliments that acknowledge her unique beauty are sure to be greatly appreciated!

- **Tell her you love the baby.** Daddy, don't be bashful about gushing over the baby. Mommy loves to hear that you are committed to and enraptured with this new little person in your family.

- **Be affectionate, but be patient about sex.** With all that she's struggling with physically and emotionally, weeks may pass before she's ready for sex, even if the doctor gives the OK (*see* Marriage). That doesn't mean she doesn't love you or need you; she just needs a little time to get back to the physical aspects of your sexual relationship.

- **Tell her you love her.** Even when she *isn't* feeling down, she needs to hear this—and right now it's more important for her health and well-being than ever.

- **Get support for you, too.** Becoming a father is a giant step in your life. Open up to a friend about how it feels to be a dad, and do things that you enjoy, too. Taking care of yourself will help you take care of your new family.

• **Accept help from others.** Family and friends typically are very happy to help if you just ask. Very often, people say, "Let me know if I can do anything." And usually, they *mean* it. So go ahead and ask kindly for what you want, whether it's taking your older child to the park, helping you make a meal, or doing some laundry.

• **Get some sleep.** Right now, sleeplessness will enhance your feelings of depression, so take every opportunity to get some shut-eye. Nap when the baby sleeps, go to bed early, and sleep in later in the morning if you can. If you are co-sleeping, take advantage of this special time when you don't have to get up out of bed to tend to your baby.

• **Don't fret about perfection right now.** Household duties are not your top priority now—in fact, nothing aside from getting to know your baby is. Remember that people are coming to see your *baby*, not your *house*, so enjoy sharing your baby with visitors without worrying about a little clutter or dust. Simplify, prioritize, and delegate routine tasks, errands, and obligations.

• **Enjoy your job.** If you work outside the home, then view your time at your job as an opportunity to refresh and prepare yourself to enjoy your baby fully when you are at home. Go ahead, talk about your baby and share pictures with your coworkers. Chances are, they'll love to hear about your new little one. This is a nice and appropriate way of indulging your natural instincts to focus on your baby when you can't be with her.

• **Get into exercising.** *With your doctor's approval*, start exercising slowly with short walks or swims. Exercise will help you feel better in many ways both physical and emotional. Even if you didn't exercise before you had your baby, this is a great time to start. Studies prove that regular exercise helps combat depression, not to mention that it will help you regain your prebaby body much more quickly.

• **Eat healthful foods.** When the body isn't properly nourished, spirits can flag—particularly when the stress of recovery makes more nutritional demands. If you are breastfeeding, a balanced and nourishing diet is especially important for both you and your baby. Healthful foods, eaten in frequent meals, can provide the nutrition you need to combat the baby blues and give you the energy you need to handle your new role. And don't forget to drink water and other healthful fluids, especially if you're nursing! Dehydration can cause fatigue, headaches, and other symptoms that can drag you down.

Parent Tip

"My husband was so wonderful during the time when I had the post-partum blues. He left a nice note for me on the kitchen table every morning and called every day from work just to tell me he loved our baby and me. The little things like that really made me feel so much better."

—Isabelle, mother of Rose (9 months)

• **Take care of yourself.** Parenting a new baby is an enormous responsibility, but things will fall into place for you, and everything will seem easier, given a little time. During this adjustment phase, try to do a few things for yourself. Simple joys like reading a book, painting your nails, going out to lunch with a friend, or pampering yourself and nourishing your spirit in other ways can help you feel happier.

• **Love yourself.** You are amazing: You've become mother to a beautiful new baby. You've played a starring role in the production of an incredible miracle. Be proud of what you've accomplished, and take the time to know and enjoy the strong, capable, multifaceted person you are becoming.

Parent Tip

"In Holland, they have a word for the weeks following the birth of a baby. They're called the 'pink cloud' weeks. When I think back on that newborn period, I remember the 'pink clouds,' not the baby blues."
—**Alice, mother of Patrick (6), Carolyn (4), and twins Rebecca and Thomas (2)**

For More Information

Books

Kendall-Tackett, Kathleen A., and Phyllis Klaus. *The Hidden Feelings of Motherhood: Coping with Stress, Depression, and Burnout.* Oakland, CA: New Harbinger Publications, 2001.

Lim, Robin. *After the Baby's Birth . . . A Woman's Way to Wellness: A Complete Guide for Postpartum Women*, rev. ed. Berkeley, CA: Celestial Arts, 2001.

Placksin, Sally. *Mothering the New Mother: Women's Feelings and Needs After Childbirth, a Support and Resource Guide*, 2nd ed. New York: Newmarket Press, 2000.

Sichel, Deborah, and Jeanne Watson Driscoll. *Women's Moods: What Every Woman Must Know About Hormones, the Brain, and Emotional Health*. New York: Quill, 2000.

Websites

Depression After Delivery, Inc.
depressionafterdelivery.com

Pacific Post Partum Support Society
postpartum.org

To Locate a Support Group

Attachment Parenting International
attachmentparenting.org

La Leche League Groups
lalecheleague.org/WebIndex.html

Postpartum Education for Parents
sbpep.org

Postpartum Support International
chss.iup.edu/postpartum

Suggested Online Support Groups

BabyZone
babyzone.com

GeoParent
geoparent.com

StorkNet
storknet.com/index.html

Baby Bottle Tooth Decay

(Nursing Caries, Infant Caries, Baby-Bottle Mouth, Bottle-Mouth Syndrome)

· · · · · · · · · · · ·

See also: Teething; Toothbrushing

> *A friend of mine had to have her one-year-old daughter's front teeth pulled out. The reason the doctor gave was that her daughter slept with a bottle. My baby sleeps with his bottle, and now I'm terrified that this could happen to him!*

Learn About It

Letting your baby fall asleep every night with a bottle of milk, formula, or juice *does* put him at risk for baby bottle tooth decay (BBTD). When your baby falls asleep with a bottle nipple in his mouth, the liquid continues to drip out and pools around your baby's teeth. A baby who uses a bottle frequently throughout the day for comfort and security, as well as nutrition, also is at risk for BBTD.

What Causes Baby Bottle Tooth Decay?

When milk, juice, formula, and even breastmilk pool around your baby's teeth, the sugars these drinks contain combine with bacteria and create acid that attacks the teeth. Over time, this acid dissolves the tooth enamel and causes cavities, decay, severe pain, and even gum disease. Baby teeth are very important to your child's health and growth—too important to lose and more important than whatever need (Baby's or yours) that sleepy-time bottle satisfies (*see also* Toothbrushing).

How Can I Tell if My Baby Has Baby Bottle Tooth Decay?

Check your baby's teeth frequently for any chalky white spots, white streaks, dark blotches, or lines. The teeth most affected by this disease are toward the front, but since you should check for other types of decay as well, inspect *all* your baby's teeth. Most pediatricians examine a baby's teeth at each well-baby checkup—important because sometimes the decay first shows up on the backside of the front teeth, which can't be seen without a dental mirror. Early detection and treatment have a much better outcome compared to discovery at the first dental appointment. If you notice anything unusual about your baby's teeth, don't hesitate to call a dentist.

Can a Breastfed Baby Get Baby Bottle Tooth Decay?

Liquid doesn't leak from the breast as it does from a bottle; a baby must suck actively for milk to be released. Therefore, a breastfed baby is much less likely to get BBTD. However, a baby who nurses frequently throughout the night can have the liquid pooling effect in the mouth, which might cause the same problem. Keep in mind, though, that the method of delivery is usually the culprit, not the beverage; a bottle that contains anything other than water—including breastmilk—creates the leaking situation and the possibility of BBTD. Play it safe and always brush your baby's teeth before bedtime, particularly if he's eating solids.

How to Prevent Baby Bottle Tooth Decay

Here are some measures you can take to protect your baby's teeth:

- Don't let your baby doze off with a bottle of milk, formula, or juice. If your baby needs a bottle to fall asleep, fill it with water. To

- Putting your baby into (and getting your baby out of) a sling is a breeze. You can even get a sleeping baby in and out of one of these soft carriers without waking her.
- You can carry your baby in a variety of positions.
- Slings are small, lightweight, and easy to transport.
- Slings are wonderful to use when a stroller would be inconvenient, such as up stairs, in large crowds, through narrow aisles, or over rough terrain or when you'll be getting in and out of the car frequently.
- Slings put your baby at the height of people's faces instead of at their knees.
- You can use a sling right up through toddlerhood, when little legs get tired of walking.

An important note about baby slings: They can be confusing to use at first, and your baby can slide out of the bottom if not positioned correctly. Try to find an experienced sling user, a how-to video, or a knowledgeable salesclerk to help you master the art of baby slinging. Your local La Leche League leader may be able to offer pointers, too.

Slings are very much worth the effort. I bought a sling when my second baby, Vanessa, was born. I couldn't figure it out, so I left it in the closet. When my third baby, David, was born, I attended a mother-baby class, learned how to use my sling, and was immediately hooked! I used slings extensively with my third and fourth babies and found them to be a marvelous baby-care tool.

Parent Tip

"I put my newborn in the sling so I could sit in bed at night with my toddler and read books. It kept us all together, my hands free, and gave reading time to *both* boys!"

—Amy, mother of AJ (4) and Ryder (2)

Front Packs

Front pack carriers are similar to slings in use but are more complex in their structure. They have a seat that attaches to the front of you with straps that crisscross behind you; these straps secure the carrier to your body. Here's what you need to know about front packs:

- The benefits of front packs are similar to many of those of slings, such as their light weight and portability and the fact that you can carry your baby while keeping your arms and hands free.
- Some allow you to choose between carrying your baby facing inward toward you or outward, facing the world—which is often fun for older babies.
- Settling the baby into and out of the carrier require more steps than a sling does.
- Moving a sleeping baby into or out of the carrier is difficult, unless the seat unbuckles separately from the harness.
- Front packs are better suited to babies who are strong enough to hold their head upright.

Backpacks

A back carrier is similar to a camping backpack. It has a seat for your baby that attaches to your back with a frame and straps that cross over your shoulders. A few things to know about backpacks:

- They're perfect for an older baby who loves to look around and be carried high on your shoulders.
- Many backpacks have pouches for holding supplies.
- Some models have a canopy for protection from inclement weather or the sun.
- Getting a backpack off and putting it on are typically two-person tasks.
- Backpacks are best for an older baby who can sit up well.
- They're great for an all-day trip, such as hiking, shopping, or visiting an amusement park.

How Do You Decide Which Carrier to Use?

No single baby carrier is perfect for all parents. Every parent has different needs, preferences, and proportions. Many people begin with one type of carrier and move on to another when their babies get older.

First, think about how you plan to use a carrier. Will you use it primarily at home, instead of a stroller while away from home, or both? Do you already have a stroller, or must your carrier fill all your baby-carrying needs? Defining its purpose will help you choose which carrier is best for you. Read the package information (or talk to other parents who own a similar carrier) to learn which purposes it serves best and to determine whether it matches your needs.

The very best way to decide is to try on carriers, either at the store or with a friend who owns one. Actually putting your baby in the carrier will give you the best idea as to fit, but if you are shopping without your baby (or don't have your baby yet), try using a stuffed animal from the toy department.

Parent Tip

"A baby carrier can help new adoptive parents to decline politely those who want to hold your baby while he still needs exclusive Mommy or Daddy contact. The carrier can be especially helpful in difficult situations such as visits to your child's orphanage or former foster parents."*

—**Laurel, mother of Crystal (16 months)**

*This is also an excellent idea for parents who blanch at the thought of their tiny newborn being passed around the room from person to person at a party or gathering.

Points to Consider When Purchasing a Carrier

Before you purchase any type of carrier, consider the following points:

- **Comfort:** Does the carrier feel good to you?
- **Fit for your baby:** Does it seem to suit your baby well?
- **Fit for you:** Does it fit your size and body type? Can you carry the baby without strain?
- **Safety:** Will the baby be secure and well supported?
- **Features:** Does the carrier meet your needs?
- **Usability:** Can you easily get your baby in and out of the carrier? How about putting it on and taking it off? Keep in mind that some models require practice.
- **Construction:** Does the fabric suit your wardrobe, climate, and needs (lightweight for summer, weatherproof for outdoor use)?
- **Care:** Is the carrier machine washable or easy to wipe clean?
- **Flexibility:** Can you carry your baby in various positions?
- **Adjustability:** Can it be tightened or adjusted to fit you when you are at home in indoor clothing or outside wearing a coat? Can you adjust it easily for use by others?
- **Adaptability:** Will it work for your baby now as well as six months from now?
- **Appearance:** Do you like the style? Will you enjoy wearing it?

Babyproofing

. . . .

See also: Co-Sleeping, making it work ("Co-Sleeping Safety Checklist"); Cribs and Cradles ("Cribs and Cradles Safety Checklist"); Emergencies; Sleep, newborn ("Sleep Safety Checklist")

My daughter isn't crawling yet, but I'm wondering if I should start babyproofing the house? What exactly do I need to do?

Learn About It

It probably seems like yesterday that your baby was born, and just that quickly she will be crawling—and then walking—around the house. The job of babyproofing your home is usually more complicated than you expect, so it's never too early to start.

The Golden Rules of Babyproofing

When making sure that your home is a safe place for your baby, keep in mind two rules: First, you can't be too careful or too vigilant. Second, better safe than sorry. Young children are very spontaneous and have little wisdom regarding the dangers of the world, so you must be certain that your home is as safe as possible for your precious child.

Can You Have a Perfectly Babyproofed Home?

No matter how much time and effort you put into your home safety efforts, you can never create an environment that is one hundred percent safe for your baby. The possibilities for a curious and mobile baby to get into trouble are endless, and you can't foresee every possible situation your child will create and the resulting dangers. Bottom line: The most important way to keep your baby safe is constant supervision.

The following checklist will get you started on your safety campaign. Keep in mind, though, that every home is different, and this list is not exhaustive; you'll need to customize it for your own use. The best way to do this is to crawl—yes, *crawl!*—around your house, room by room, and see what hidden hazards need addressing before your ever-curious child finds them. Many department and children's stores offer a wide variety of tools to help make babyproofing easier. As an option, you can hire a child home safety specialist to handle the babyproofing tasks for you. (Check your yellow pages under "Baby Services.")

Safety Checklist for Home Babyproofing

General

☐ Install smoke alarms: one in your kitchen, one in every bedroom, and at least one on every level.

☐ Consider investing in a carbon monoxide detector.

☐ Learn first aid and CPR. Inexpensive and even free classes are available through agencies such as the Red Cross, American Heart Association, YMCA, Boys & Girls Club, and your local fire department or hospital.

☐ Post emergency numbers on your telephones.

☐ Create a home fire escape plan.

☐ Remove guns and weapons, or store them unloaded and dismantled in a locked case.

☐ Remove poisonous plants, or raise them high above your baby's reach. (There are actually many toxic and poisonous plants. A few of the most common are azalea, daffodil bulbs, holly, hydrangea, lilac, lily, mistletoe, philodendron, poinsettia, rhododendron, and tomato plant leaves. For a complete list, consult your pediatrician or poison control center.)

☐ Store flashlights with working batteries in a known place.

☐ Keep a fully stocked first-aid kit (*see* First-Aid Kit).

Electrical

☐ Conceal all electrical sockets with outlet plugs, socket guards, or cord covers.

☐ Keep all wires, cables, and cords organized and secured with child-proof devices and covers.

Doors, Windows, and Cabinets

☐ Put safety locks or grids on all windows.

☐ Put safety latches on closets, cabinets, or drawers that contain hazards.

☐ Remove small pieces from doorstops.

☐ Mount cords for blinds and draperies out of reach, and if you have looped cords, purchase a cord adapter that allows you to split this into two parts to reduce the strangulation hazard that one continuous loop presents.

Bedrooms

☐ Remove choking hazards or dangerous items from dressers and cabinets.

☐ Discard dry-cleaning or clothing bags.

Bathrooms

☐ Lower water temperature to a maximum of 120°F (49°C).

☐ Install toilet lid latches and keep lids closed, or keep bathroom doors closed.

☐ Store electrical appliances, such as hair dryers, out of reach.

☐ Keep medications, toiletries, razors, and other hazards in a locked cabinet.

☐ Put nonskid mats in bathtubs.

☐ Cover bathtub faucets with soft protectors.

☐ Purchase all medications in childproof containers, and keep them out of reach.

Kitchen

☐ Store a working fire extinguisher where it's easily accessible for adults but not for children.

☐ Consider appliance locks for your oven and dishwasher.

☐ Store plastic grocery bags, plastic wrap, knives, scissors, matches, chemicals, and other hazards in locked cabinets.

☐ Use safety guards on stove knobs within a child's reach, or remove these when not in use.

☐ Keep trash in a cabinet with a childproof latch.

Miscellaneous

☐ Use a gate or screen to close off fireplaces.

☐ Install corner guards on sharp furniture edges.

☐ Mount child safety gates at the tops and bottoms of stairs.

☐ Remove glass or fragile breakables from your baby's reach.

☐ Seal off swimming pools, hot tubs, and ponds with locked gates.

☐ Keep the laundry room door closed, and keep lids shut on washer and dryer, or install a childproof latch.

☐ Keep purses and wallets out of your baby's reach.

☐ Install deadbolts, chains, or doorknob covers to prevent your baby from opening doors.

☐ Be cautious when using holiday decorations that are within your baby's reach.

☐ Move pet food, litter boxes, and animal cages out of reach of your baby.

☐ Remember also to keep your things safe *from* your baby—put your valuables, breakables, and important possessions out of reach.

☐ Remember, constant supervision of your baby is the most important safety rule.

Baby-Sitters

. . . .

See also: Baby Carriers; Breastfeeding in Public; Breastfeeding
with Bottlefeeding Supplements; Child Care, choosing; Crying;
Emergencies; First-Aid Kit; Separation Anxiety; Stranger Anxiety

> *I would love to be able to go out for an evening with my partner,
> but I have never left my baby with a baby-sitter. What do I need to
> think about when choosing a baby-sitter, and what instructions do
> I need to give to the baby-sitter?*

Learn About It

Remember when going out for a night on the town used to be spontaneous and carefree? Then you became a parent, and suddenly just going to the movies is a lot more complicated. You worry about finding a competent baby-sitter. You worry about how long your baby will be able to manage between breastfeeds or if she will take a bottle from someone else. You worry about whether she will cry or refuse to sleep. And most of all, you worry about any emergencies that could develop while you are gone.

Of course, you may be excited to go out again, to have time as a couple or time for yourself. And you have every right to enjoy yourself on your evening out. The best way to have a good time is to reduce your level of worry by ensuring that you have a trustworthy baby-sitter who understands what your baby needs and knows the necessary safety and emergency information. You may still worry about your little one, but you can feel confident that she is in good hands. And after you've had your wonderful evening out, you can look forward to arriving home full of excitement at the thought of seeing your precious baby again.

Who Will Be My Baby-Sitter?

When you have a very young, breastfed baby, your best strategy for an evening out is often to take your baby with you in a baby carrier or limit your outings to an hour or two (*see* Baby Carriers; Breastfeeding in Public). But as your baby grows older or if your baby will accept a bottle, there may be occasions when you will leave your baby at home for an evening or afternoon with a trusted baby-sitter.

The general guideline for determining an appropriate age for your baby-sitter is that the younger the baby, the older the sitter. As you know well, taking care of an infant can be demanding. Most twelve- or thirteen-year-olds cannot be expected to handle these demands, much less the demands that an emergency could require.

Before you hire a baby-sitter, check to see how much the sitter expects to be paid per hour. Rates vary widely depending on the area you live in and the age and the experience of the baby-sitter.

Here are some suggestions about where to look for a baby-sitter:

• **Responsible family member:** Your baby's grandparent, aunt, uncle, and older cousin can be fabulous baby-sitters if they live in your area and are willing to baby-sit. Usually there is a built-in level of trust with relatives. Keep in mind that if your relative doesn't know your house or your baby well, it is a good idea to use the list later in this section to help your relative feel confident and also prepared for any emergencies while taking care of your baby.

• **Recommendation from a neighbor, pediatrician, church member, coworker, or friend:** Word of mouth is often an excellent way to find a competent baby-sitter, but you may still want to interview your potential baby-sitter and check references.

• **Advertisement:** You could try to find a baby-sitter through an advertisement in your local newspaper or on a bulletin board at your church, local high school, or doctor's office. When you don't know your potential baby-sitter, it is especially important to ask for and check multiple references, ensuring that your baby-sitter is responsible, reliable, and good with children.

• **Check with an organization or agency:** The local YMCA or your chapter of the American Red Cross might have a list of baby-sitters who have completed their baby-sitting or infant and child CPR course. Or look in the yellow pages under "Baby-Sitting" or "Sitting Services." When you call a company, ask how it chooses its baby-sitters, how the baby-sitters have been screened, what the rate of pay is, and what kind of insurance (if any) the company provides.

• **Baby-sitting co-op:** Some families set up formal or informal baby-sitting co-ops, where a group of parents agree to baby-sit for each other's children. A co-op often works according to a point system: Parents earn points instead of money in return for baby-sitting, and they can exchange their points for baby-sitting services from other parents later. If you are interested in starting a co-op, a wealth of material is available on the Internet to help with structure and basic guidelines.

What Instructions Should I Give the Baby-Sitter?

You'll need some time with your baby-sitter before you go out to ensure that he or she understands what your baby needs and is familiar with basic safety features of your house. Some parents like to have the baby-sitter over the day before they are to go out, to introduce the sitter to their baby and their house. Other parents prefer to have the baby-sitter arrive thirty minutes before they go out, leaving enough time to go through the relevant information.

Either way, keep in mind that you will be giving your baby-sitter a lot of information in a short period of time. It is helpful to have some of the key points written down. One idea is to make a booklet with the necessary information about your baby (routines, how to soothe him when he cries), what to do in case of emergency (emergency contact numbers, basic first-aid instructions), and safety features of your house (location of fire extinguishers, first-aid kit). This booklet will take some time to put together, but it is a useful resource to have in your house for baby-sitters in the years to come, and you can adjust it as needed.

You can use the following list to help you determine what instructions and information you need to give your baby-sitter:

- **Emergency telephone numbers:** List your cell phone or pager number, the name and phone number of your location if the cell phone doesn't work, a neighbor or relative to be contacted when you or your partner can't be reached, and emergency phone numbers for the fire department, ambulance, police, hospital, pediatrician, and poison control. Write down your address and the closest intersection to your home in case emergency services would need that information.

- **Specific information about your baby:** Include the age, weight, and height of your baby; food or medicine allergies; clear instructions for medication to be given and dosage; your baby's eating, sleeping, and playing habits; ideas for how to soothe your baby if he cries; and examples of situations in which you would like to be called.

- **Basic baby safety information:** List the basic safety rules—for example, that your baby needs to be put to sleep on his back, all diaper-changing equipment needs to be within easy reach, the baby should never be left alone on the diaper-changing table, and babies should never be left alone in or near water. Also state what to do in case of emergency (*see* Emergencies; you could copy the list under "Is It an Emergency?" in that entry for your baby-sitter's booklet).

- **Household safety information:** Identify the location of phones, fire extinguishers, smoke detectors, emergency exits and ladders, first-aid box, fuse box, and flashlights. Describe how to open the safety gates, how to lock and unlock the doors, and where you keep the spare keys. Provide instructions on what to say and do when the doorbell or the telephone rings.

- **Household rules:** Give clear rules about whether the baby-sitter is allowed to use the telephone or have visitors over while baby-sitting. Define expectations such as a request for the baby-sitter to stay awake and regularly check the baby and wishes for tidying up toys and dishes that the baby-sitter has used.

- **"Welcome to our home" instructions:** Explain how to operate the TV and VCR, and list food and drinks available for the sitter and the baby. You may wish to purchase a few special snacks or treats just for the evening. Good baby-sitters are worth their weight in gold, so make your sitter feel comfortable and welcome.

While You Are Out

Some parents like to do a "trial" outing the first time they leave their baby with a baby-sitter. If this idea appeals to you, you might go out for only an hour or two, to a place where you can easily be reached. When all goes well, you can gradually increase the length of the time you stay away.

When you are gone for a longer period, you may find it reassuring to call to find out how your baby is doing. If you are out someplace where the ringer on your cell phone or pager needs to be turned off, put the phone on vibration mode and put it in your pocket. That way, you can know when you are being called and, if necessary, leave the venue to make a return call. Or call upon your arrival and provide an emergency telephone number of the business.

It may also be helpful to read this book's entries on Separation Anxiety and Stranger Anxiety. These entries offer ideas for helping your baby adjust to the idea of a few hours without Mommy or Daddy.

And remember to enjoy yourself while you are out!

Back Sleeping

See also: Co-Sleeping, making it work ("Co-Sleeping Safety Checklist"); Cribs and Cradles ("Cribs and Cradles Safety Checklist"); Sudden Infant Death Syndrome (SIDS); Sleep, newborn; Swaddling

I know that my newborn should sleep on her back to reduce the risk of SIDS, but she hates it! When I let her sleep on her tummy, she sleeps longer and better. What should I do?

Learn About It

Studies have proved scientifically that infants who sleep on their backs are less susceptible to Sudden Infant Death Syndrome (SIDS) than those who sleep on their stomachs. This is a statistical percentage: Not every baby who sleeps on her tummy will die of SIDS, and avoiding tummy sleeping is not a 100 percent guarantee against SIDS. However, while a few babies actually benefit from tummy sleeping because of medical issues, back sleeping is safest for most. This is an important issue that you must discuss with your health care provider.

In all my research, I have been unable to pin down any recommendations as to an exact age when belly sleeping is safe, most likely because all babies develop at different rates. However, most researchers imply that once your baby can hold her head up steadily and roll easily from belly to back and back to belly, you can put her to sleep on her back and let her find her own comfortable position. Just always make sure her sleep environment is safe.

Once your doctor confirms that back sleeping is best for your baby, please—for her safety and for your peace of mind—always put her to sleep on her back. If your little one resists this sleep position, try the following measures to encourage back sleeping:

• **Let your baby nap in a car seat, stroller, or infant seat.** Sleeping in any of these will keep your baby slightly curled, rather than flat on a mattress. Many tummy-sleepers enjoy that position much better than flat on their backs. Just be sure to follow all safety precautions, which include keeping your baby nearby. (Manufacturers of all car seats, strollers, and infant seats warn parents never to leave a baby alone in any of these seats.) Also, watch to be sure your baby doesn't become curled too far forward, as this can interfere with proper breathing. To help your baby make the transition to a flat crib, try moving him after he is asleep, gradually changing the stroller to a flat position, or putting him in a rocking cradle.

• **If your baby is a newborn, try swaddling her for sleep** (*see* Swaddling). Being wrapped in a blanket prevents her natural startle reflexes from waking her up.

• **Wait until your baby is in deep sleep before gently turning him over.** You will recognize this stage by your baby's limp limbs and even, steady breathing.

• **Talk to your doctor about the possibility of a compromise: side sleeping.** Ask if a sleeping wedge or tightly rolled baby blanket can be used to hold your baby in this position.

• **Be wary of gimmicks and gadgets.** Although various products are available to keep a baby in the back-sleeping position, the safety of these products has not been tested; at this time, they are not recommended. At this writing, several sleep wraps designed to hold a baby swaddled in a back-sleeping position are just becoming available. Ask your doctor or hospital about these or any other new ideas, and thoroughly investigate them before using them for your baby.

• **Stay firm.** Finally, if you still choose to have your baby sleep on her tummy despite everything you've read, heard, and been told (or if your doctor has approved this position), make certain that the mattress is even, firm, and flat. Check every time you put her to bed that the sheets are smooth and tightly secured. Also, don't put any pillows, blankets, or toys in bed with her. If you still have concerns, ask your doctor or hospital about renting a sophisticated device that monitors a baby's sounds, movement, and breathing.

For Babies Who Sleep on Their Backs

Now that you've gotten your baby to sleep on her back, keep in mind the following:

• Don't let your baby sleep in the exact same position every night and nap. Move her head from one side to the other, and vary her position in the crib or the placement of the crib itself to encourage her to look in all directions. This will prevent the back of your baby's head from becoming flat, a condition called positional plagiocephaly (*see* Flat-Head Syndrome).

• Avoid leaving your baby lying on her back in a stroller, car seat, or swing for long periods during the day. Since she needs to be on her back for sleep, she shouldn't have excessive time during the day on her back also.

• Place your baby on her tummy often when she is awake to encourage head and body movement and physical development of all muscle groups.

Back Sleeping at Day Care

According to some studies, 20 percent of SIDS deaths occur in child-care settings. This may be because not all child-care centers have policies on infant sleep positions; even when they do, not all child-care providers abide by the guidelines of the American Academy of Pediatrics.

You should know that babies who are not used to sleeping on their stomachs are at a particularly high risk for SIDS when placed in this position in a day-care setting. Check on the policies in your child-care center, and be sure that they are placing your baby in the proper sleep position as recommended by your doctor.

Bathing

· · · · · · · · · · · ·

See also: Eczema; Hair Care

The nurses at the birth center helped me give my baby a bath at the hospital. Now that I'm home with my baby, I'm feeling nervous about bath time. She's so incredibly tiny and fragile looking!

Learn About It

Just like many things that are new, the first few experiences of bathing your delicate, wiggly, slippery baby may be rather awkward and can be a real adventure. But don't worry: With a little practice, bath time will become a very special time for both of you. There's nothing quite so special as holding your baby's tiny little body in the bath, and most babies come to love splashing in the tub.

What Kind of Bath?

Commonly, health professionals recommend a sponge bath for your baby until the umbilical cord has fallen off and, if one was done, the circumcision has healed. More and more experts, however, now are saying that bathing your baby in a tub of water right from the start is perfectly acceptable. Regardless of which bathing method you choose for your newborn, the key is to watch the umbilical cord and circumcision areas for any signs of trouble, such as swelling, redness, or discharge, and to respond to these with prompt, proper care.

As for where to bathe your baby, you have several options. You can purchase a small baby tub that sits on your countertop or within a regular bathtub. Or you can place your baby in your kitchen sink on a towel or bath pad. A third choice that many parents enjoy is bathing with their baby in the big tub.

The Sponge Bath

Sponge baths are a great way to start out and perfect for new babies, who really don't get dirty anyway! A sponge bath is also a bit less intimidating if you're nervous about bathing a slippery wet baby. Directions for sponge baths are in the entry on caring for the umbilical cord area (*see* Umbilical Cord Area, "What About Bath Time?").

The Baby Tub Bath

Many parents enjoy using portable bathtubs made especially for babies. They require just a small amount of water and can be raised to a comfortable, back-sparing level. Many of these tubs have an angled back so that your baby can lie comfortably in the tub with his head high above the water level. When shopping for a baby tub, consider some of these features:

- Sturdy, unbendable, unbreakable plastic construction
- A built-in seat with a comfortable, nonskid surface
- A size that fits into your sink or bathtub
- Storage area for shampoo, soap, and washcloth
- A drainage plug for easy emptying

Parent Tip

"From the time our son was born, his daddy has given him his bath. He's now two, and bath time is still 'Daddy time.' They have a blast together, and it's a consistent time for them to bond, since Dad is at work all day. Mommy gets a nice break, too!"

—Sandy, mother of Keegan (2)

The Joys of "Co-Bathing"

Many parents discover that bringing their baby into the big tub with them is a pleasant and enjoyable bonding experience. Infants who are apprehensive about getting into the water are apt to be relaxed and happy if they enter the tub while held in loving arms. A wonderful way to introduce your baby to the bath is to let her enjoy a cuddle while being slowly immersed into the water. An easy way is to have one parent seated in the tub as someone else undresses the baby, covers her with a small cloth, and then hands the baby over to the parent in the water. An alternative is to cover the tub side with a nonskid mat and hold the baby close to your chest as you carefully step into the tub and slowly sit. Yet another choice is to undress your baby, wrap her in a towel, put her in a baby seat next to the tub; get in, then lean over, pick her up, and bring her into the tub with you.

Many co-bathing babies enjoy a breastfeeding session while in the relaxing environment that the bath creates. It is, of course, important that Mommy stay fully alert during the bath so that Baby's face stays above the water.

Older babies love exploring the wonderful world of water play with a parent or big brother or sister alongside. The bath experience becomes one of splashing fun and a real treat at the end of the day. (*Safety note:* Never leave a sibling in charge. Even with the best intentions, a child can become distracted and look away from the baby.)

Parent Tip

"My son has never liked being in the bathtub and especially fussed over having his hair washed. Instead of making it an unpleasant experience, I take him in the shower with me. I put one foot up on the tub spout, sit him astride my leg, and let him nurse while I soap him up, wash his hair, and rinse him. We have no more tears!"*

—Laura, mother of Jackson (10 months)

*Mesh slings are available specifically for showering or swimming. Also, be certain to put a nonskid mat down, and use care when getting in and out of the shower with your baby.

How Often Should Baby Have a Bath?

As long as you are cleaning your baby's bottom with each diaper change and washing his face and hands several times a day, your baby will need a bath only a few times a week. Of course, he'll need a bath after a particularly messy day, such as after a day at the beach, a first experience with finger paints, or one of those ankle-to-waist diaper blowouts. Some parents and babies enjoy a nightly bath as part of the bedtime ritual. If this is the case in your house, use gentle baby soap only every few days. Use plain water in between so that you don't dry out your baby's delicate skin.

Bath Time Safety

Never take your eyes off a baby who is in the bath. Babies can drown in just a few inches of water, and squirmy babies can move faster than you'd expect. Baby bathtub seats are not intended for unsupervised use, and they have been known to tip over. If you have to leave the tub side for any reason—to answer a phone, use the toilet, or tend to another child—scoop your baby up in a towel and take her with you. Drain the tub, since standing water is a potential drowning hazard to your baby as well as older children. Better yet, ask yourself if the need that's calling you away is really so urgent, and don't attend to it until the important business of a baby bath is finished.

Getting Ready for Bath Time

Here are a few things to keep in mind as you get ready to bathe your baby:

- Keep the room warm—around 75°F (24°C)—and free from drafts.
- Have all your supplies within arm's reach: mild baby shampoo, baby soap, towel.
- Lay out a second towel, new diaper, and change of clothes before you get started.

- Fill the tub with bathwater that is warm, not hot. Thoroughly mix the hot and cold water, then check the temperature with your elbow or wrist, or use a baby bath thermometer to keep the temperature of the bathwater between 90°F (32°C) and 100°F (38°C). Remember to check the water temperature from time to time so the water doesn't get too cool during the bath.
- Wash your baby's hair last so she doesn't get chilled during her bath. Or wash her hair and then dry it with a small towel if you plan to keep her in the tub for playtime.

How Should I Bathe My Baby?

There are no exact rules for bathing a baby. Babies don't get all that dirty, so a little splashing in the water is all they need to stay clean. You can do some gentle washing with your hand or a soft baby washcloth, especially in those chubby little creases and folds. You may find that the easiest way to hold your baby is to put your arm under your baby's back and tightly grasp his opposite arm to give full support. Babies are squirmy!

What About After the Bath?

When your baby is clean and fresh and the bathroom is warm and toasty, it's a perfect time for some soft music and a baby massage (*see* Massage).

Bilingualism

See also: Milestones of Development; Reading; Talking

> *I am Mexican, and my husband is American. We live in California near our English-speaking relatives and visit our Spanish-speaking family quite often. We would like our baby to speak both Spanish and English. How can we teach him both languages without confusing him?*

Learn About It

Bilingualism is a perfectly normal feature of life for nearly half the world's population. If you can give your child the gift of fluency in more than one language, by all means do so. Learning your native language is a key to your child's understanding of your culture and, of course, may be essential for communication with your relatives. Furthermore, studies have shown that bilingual children have advantages in school and on standardized tests, and bilingual adults may have better job opportunities in today's world.

How to Raise a Bilingual Child

There are two main approaches to achieving bilingualism:

• **Learning both languages at the same time—one parent, one language (OPOL):** With this approach, each parent *consistently* speaks his or her own native language to the baby. This approach develops "simultaneous bilingualism," and the baby learns both languages at the same time. Early on, a baby who is learning two languages may seem to have a smaller vocabulary than his peers in each language, but the sum of the words the child knows in both languages usually is right on track. (Keep in mind that language acquisition varies widely; *see* Talking.) Your baby may also mix the languages as a result of learning some words in one language and others in the second language. This is quite normal and can be fun to hear; try to tape-record or videotape some of your baby's early language for future enjoyment. A child is usually stronger in one language (usually that of the primary caregiver) but, with the right input, can achieve full fluency in both languages by the age of five.

• **Learning one language first, then adding another—"sequential bilingualism":** The most common approach within this model involves both parents speaking the "minority" language (the one that's less common in their community) to their baby. The child learns the minority language at home and later picks up the language spoken in the community at day care, nursery school, or even grade school. Another sequential approach is for parents to speak only the primary language of the community to a baby until about the age of three. At this age, a child has learned how language works, is cognitively more mature, and will be ready to learn the second language. One or both parents then consistently use a minority language with the child. For either of these approaches it is best if the nonnative speaker of either language has a high level of fluency so that the baby does not become confused by incorrect grammatical structures. Also, most experts recommend that at least one parent speak that parent's native language to the baby because the nursery rhymes and lullabies that are such an important part of a baby's life may be difficult for the nonnative speaker to master.

These are the most common approaches, but families differ and will customize the language process for their own children. Think about these methods, talk with other bilingual families you know, and do your own research to determine which of these works best for you. Or create your own approach based on what you learn!

What Practical Methods Can I Use to Develop Bilingualism?

To learn any language, a baby needs "input"—books, songs, games, and, most important, lots of conversation to label and describe all that Baby sees, hears, and experiences in daily life. The more input the baby receives in each of the target languages, the more fluent he will become in both languages.

The possibilities for increasing your baby's exposure to the target languages are many:

- Order children's books online. Large online retailers sell children's books in most major languages.
- Find a playgroup in which the target language is spoken. If none is available, you could create one if you have friends who speak your language and have children.
- Take extended trips to the country where the minority language is spoken or to the homes of family and friends who speak the language.
- Buy or rent videos and interactive games from companies that promote bilingualism. Babies learn a second language more easily when involved in meaningful activities that require use of that language. Practical usage is the natural way babies learn any language.

Parent Tip

"We gave Carolyn a Dutch doll and an American doll, with the explanation that the Dutch one only understands Dutch, and the American one only understands English. The tea parties around our house are a wonderful exercise in bilingualism! This idea would work equally well with any kind of toy or stuffed animal."

—Alice, mother of Patrick (6), Carolyn (4), and twins Rebecca and Thomas (2)

More Tips

When raising a bilingual child, be sure to encourage a positive attitude toward both languages. Bear in mind that language development occurs naturally in a stress-free environment, and that it is rare for a child to be equally good at both languages. Forcing a child to speak a language according to a specific timetable can backfire; as with any task, when forced, a child may resist. The best approach seems to be to let the child achieve bilingualism at her own pace. If you are working to teach your baby Spanish and she speaks to you in English, just reply in Spanish and continue the conversation. The day will come when she will amaze you with an entirely Spanish conversation or story!

For More Information

Books

Cunningham-Andersson, Una, and Staffan Andersson. *Growing Up with Two Languages: A Practical Guide.* London: Routledge, 1999.

Harding, Edith, and Philip Riley. *The Bilingual Family: A Handbook for Parents.* New York: Cambridge University Press, 1987.

Websites

The Bilingual Baby Company
thebilingualbabyco.com

Fun with Languages Company
funwithlanguages.com

Birthmarks

See also: Rash

> *The skin on my baby's face was clear and perfect when he was born. Now that he's two weeks old, he has a bump with a reddish mark on his forehead. It isn't a bruise, so what is it?*

Learn About It

Your baby may have a "strawberry mark"; the medical term for this is *hemangioma*. It is just one of several common birthmarks. While the term implies that the mark is on your baby at birth (and many of these are), they can also appear in the first few months of your baby's life.

What Are Birthmarks?

Birthmarks are normal skin growths made up of pigmented skin or a concentration of small blood vessels.

What Are the Types of Birthmarks?

Birthmarks come in many varieties:

- **Strawberry mark (hemangioma):** Named for its appearance, this soft, reddish, bumpy birthmark often grows during the first two months and then remains as it is for months or even years. Eventually, it flattens, fades, and typically disappears altogether by the time a child enters school.
- **Stork bite (salmon patch, nevus simplex, macular patch hemangioma):** This is a flat, dull pink spot with an irregular shape that appears over the bridge of the nose, forehead, or upper lip.

This birthmark's uncommon name refers to another common location: the back of the neck, where the fabled stork carried your baby in its beak! Stork bites are sometimes completely gone by the time a child is two years old, but some remain into adulthood. The mark may appear redder when your baby cries or gets cold or hot.

- **Angel kiss:** This is similar to a stork bite, except for the location: the nose or eyelids. The name refers to the saying that an angel kissed your baby before birth!
- **Port wine stain:** This flat, purple and red or maroon mark can appear anywhere on your baby's body.
- **Mongolian spot:** This birthmark is blue and resembles a bruise. Usually a Mongolian spot is found on a baby's lower back or buttocks, but sometimes one appears on the body or arms. Most eventually fade, although some are permanent.
- **Café au lait spot:** This light tan spot—the color of coffee with milk—is usually harmless. The presence of several spots larger than a quarter, however, may be a sign of abnormal cell growth, which your pediatrician can diagnose.
- **Freckles:** Yes, some babies are born with freckles! They may fade or remain as they are.
- **Mole (nevus):** This is the typical birthmark, composed of small, dark clusters of pigmented skin cells that may be raised. Nearly everyone has moles, and they usually appear after birth. Extremely large moles, or any that bleed or itch, should be examined by a doctor.

Should I Do Anything About a Birthmark?

It's a good idea to point out any birthmarks that you discover to your health care provider during routine checkups. Usually, birthmarks are a cosmetic issue only, so typically no treatment is recommended or required. They are marks of uniqueness and distinction that set human individuals apart from one another—so much so that you should record their locations in your child's baby book or medical records.

The only time your pediatrician might be concerned about a birthmark is if it interferes with growth and development, such as one that appears on the eyelid and obscures proper vision or one that is on the nose or throat and affects breathing. Large or prominent birthmarks that dramatically affect appearance and self-esteem can be covered with special cosmetics or even removed with laser procedures. Medical removal is often delayed until your baby is older. The results of these laser treatments are usually very good.

My youngest child, Coleton, has a strawberry mark on his forehead. From experience, I've discovered that the biggest issue for parents of babies with birthmarks is answering an all-too-frequent question: "Oh! Did he get a boo-boo?"

Bottlefeeding

See also: Allergies and Asthma; Baby Bottle Tooth Decay; Breastfeeding with Bottlefeeding Supplements; Breastfeeding Your Newborn; Breastfeeding Your Toddler; Burping; Colic; Spitting Up; Unwanted Advice

I really wanted to breastfeed my son, but it's not working out. I'm going to have to switch to bottlefeeding. What do I need to know?

Learn About It

For a variety of reasons, some women are unable to, or choose not to, breastfeed their babies. Breastfeeding, whenever possible, is the best choice, so congratulations for trying. Bottlefeeding with formula is the alternative. Formula is designed to meet Baby's nutritional needs and can be used as Baby's sole source of liquid nourishment or as a supplement to breastmilk.

The Decision to Bottlefeed Your Baby

The first thing you need to do before switching to bottles and formula is to determine whether this really is the right choice for you. Some women switch to exclusive bottlefeeding early on because the first few weeks of breastfeeding have been difficult for them. Perhaps they have not had the support from a professional, they are misperceiving their situation ("I'm not making enough milk," "It's not rich enough," etc.), or they are experiencing a common but normal adjustment phase that can include sore nipples and engorgement discomfort. Many women later regret that they didn't persist for another few weeks to see if they could have established breastfeeding successfully. Like all worthy endeavors, getting the hang of breastfeeding takes time, patience, and trust in one's body. Once supply is established, a woman's body makes milk in precisely the quantity and nutritional makeup the baby needs at any given time. This rhythm can only be established with time and ample opportunity for the baby to nurse.

There are situations in which breastfeeding is not feasible—for instance, the breasts truly are not able to produce enough milk, or the baby has problems with latching on due to physical abnormalities. However, these instances can be diagnosed only by a lactation counselor and/or pediatrician. These professionals often find ways to remedy the situation so that breastfeeding can continue. The effort is well worth it, given data unearthed by myriad studies.

If you are having a rocky start with breastfeeding (or want to relactate after switching to bottlefeeding), call a lactation consultant, or contact a La Leche League group for help. Another option is to continue to breastfeed for some of baby's feedings and use formula for other feedings (*see* Breastfeeding with Bottlefeeding Supplements).

If you've examined all your options thoroughly and have decided without reservation that bottlefeeding is the best choice for you, then move forward with confidence. All parents and children are unique; you must make the best decisions for *your* child. This is but the first of many situations that will require such focused thought and effort.

Before Bottlefeeding Your Baby with Formula

Parents who bottlefeed must make several decisions about formula type, bottle type, and preparation methods:

• A number of different brands and types of formula are available; ask your health care provider for recommendations. Most babies begin with a cow's milk–based, iron-fortified formula. When allergies are suspected, a soy formula may be given instead. If you think your baby is not responding well to the formula (*see also* Colic; Allergies and Asthma), talk to your pediatrician about switching formulas. *Never give regular cow's milk to a baby under twelve months old, because the composition of cow's milk does not meet a baby's nutritional needs. Among other things, it is low in iron, which is critical for proper development of the brain and nervous system.*

• Formula is sold in three different forms: powdered formula that needs to be prepared with water; concentrated liquid that needs to be diluted (half and half) with water; and ready-to-use formula. Your best choice depends on whether you have more time than money, or vice versa. The powdered formula takes longer to prepare but is much more economical. Many families choose to have the ready-to-use or concentrated formula on hand for traveling and hectic times, and they use the powdered formula for daily bottle preparation. Powder is also convenient for warm-weather outings when you know fresh water will be available.

• Ask your doctor for recommendations regarding sterilization of bottles and nipples. A dishwasher generally sterilizes adequately. Ask your doctor how long you should sterilize your baby's bottle equipment and how old your baby should be before you stop. Typically, after your baby is three to four months old, you can simply wash bottles and nipples with hot, soapy water.

• Check with your doctor about using tap water when mixing formula. In most cases, cold tap water is safe for making a bottle that will be used right away, as long as you run the tap water for about a minute before filling the bottle. Using warm tap water is not recommended because it is possible that lead may leach into the water. When making a number of bottles at once, or in certain areas where the safety of tap water is in question, use cooled boiled water or bottled water (*not distilled*).

• Different types of bottles and nipples are available, and you may have to experiment to find which one your baby likes best.

Baby Is Hungry: How to Bottlefeed Successfully

The following suggestions will get you started with bottle use:

• Always wash your hands thoroughly before preparing formula, and make sure all your equipment is properly cleaned or sterilized. Clean the top of the formula can with hot, soapy water. Use a clean can opener or punch opener, washing these after each use.

• Most parents find it easiest to prepare all of baby's bottles for the day in one session, but be sure to follow your doctor's instructions regarding the safety of your community's tap water; boil and cool the water if necessary. Promptly refrigerate any bottles that will not be used immediately.

• Read the package carefully, and follow the mixing instructions to the letter. Formula ingredients are carefully proportioned to supply the right balance of sodium and other important substances that, in the wrong amounts, can be very dangerous for your rapidly growing baby. Adding too much or too little water can cause serious health problems, as can adding *any* water to premixed formula.

• Some babies enjoy their bottles at room temperature, but others like them slightly warm. Using a microwave to warm up a bottle is not safe. Microwave heating is uneven and can cause hot spots in the liquid that could scald your baby's sensitive mouth tissues. Instead, run the bottle under warm tap water for a few minutes, or put it in a hot (not boiling) pan of water. Be sure to check the formula's temperature by shaking a few drops on your inner wrist; the formula should be at about body temperature.

• Holding Baby in your arms, make sure his head is higher than his tummy. Tilt the bottle so that the milk fills the nipple. If your baby seems to struggle to get milk, the flow is too slow; check to see that the hole of the nipple is not clogged or too small. If baby is spluttering and dribbling milk, the flow is too fast, and you need nipples with smaller holes.

• All babies, whether breast- or bottlefed, benefit from close body contact with their parents. Bottlefeeding parents should pay special attention to this need, as the practice does not afford as many opportunities for skin-to-skin contact as breastfeeding does through its sheer logistics. To compensate, some bottlefeeding parents lift up their shirts while bottlefeeding to simulate this natural way of connecting with a baby. *Never prop your baby's bottle.* Not only does this deprive Baby of needed cuddling, it can also lead to ear infections and to baby bottle tooth decay (*see* Ear Infections; Baby Bottle Tooth Decay).

• As for the amount of formula, here's a rough guide: Your baby will drink two to three ounces of milk each day for each pound of her body weight. Most bottlefed babies want six to eight feedings every day. But this is just an average. Just as with the rest of us, there will be times when your baby is hungrier than usual (for example, during a growth spurt) and other times when she is not as hungry. Follow Baby's cues, and don't force her to drink more than she wants; this can lead to an overweight baby. Likewise, respond to your baby promptly when she cries, and feed her if this is what she's requesting. Don't force her into a schedule. If she still seems hungry after she finishes the bottle, try giving her a little more and adding one more ounce to the bottle next time you feed her.

• Bottlefed babies need to burp and tend to spit up a lot (*see* Burping; Spitting Up). While breastmilk usually does not stain clothing, formula most certainly does, so you'll want to attend promptly to any spit-up on clothing, whether yours or your baby's. You'll also find that the stuff coming out of the other end stains more readily and has much more of an odor than breastmilk-based bowel movements. This is normal.

• Discard any formula left in the bottle at the end of each feeding.

• Your pediatrician can give you specific suggestions about how often you should feed your baby. The most common answer is to let your baby make that decision. Normally, a newborn bottlefed baby wants to feed every two or three hours. Following a rigid four-hour bottlefeeding schedule with a newborn can be dangerous to your baby's growth and development. Most doctors recommend waking a newborn baby who sleeps more than three hours during the day and four hours at night for a bottlefeed. Ask your doctor what you should do if your baby sleeps for long stretches. Remember, strict schedules are not for babies; they are best left to mass-transit systems, students, and the military!

Enjoying the Bottlefeeding Experience

Some mothers report feeling criticized for not breastfeeding, and this feeling spoils the bottlefeeding experience for them. But as with so many other aspects of mothering, feeding your baby is an experience to enjoy. Here are some ways to make the most of the experience:

• After you've made your final decision to bottlefeed your baby part-time or exclusively, put any angst behind you. There is no need to feel defensive or guilty. You love your baby as much as exclusively breast-feeding moms love theirs, and you want the very best for your child. Parenting is among the most extraordinarily complex jobs in the world, and breastfeeding is not the make-or-break definition of good parenting. Your strategy now is to look to the future with the realization that myriad factors are involved in raising a happy, healthy child, and to do your best to be an informed and conscious parent.

• Try to avoid getting involved in a debate with people who are critical of your decision. Come up with a standard response to people who may not understand why you don't exclusively breastfeed your baby, such as, "We've thoroughly researched the topic and made the best choice for our family," or just say, "Thanks for your interest," and change the topic. (*See also* Unwanted Advice.)

• Talk to other parents who bottlefeed, either in your area or through an Internet support group. Ask them about their experiences with bottlefeeding, and share tips and ideas.

• Enjoy the fact that Daddy, siblings, and grandparents can experience feeding Baby and looking into her eyes as she drinks from a bottle.

• Practice as many of the attachment parenting tools as you can with your baby (*see* Attachment Parenting). Attachment parenting methods can be used with bottlefed babies; these tools will help you and your baby develop a unique and wonderful bond that will last a lifetime.

Breastfeeding in Public

· · · · · · · · · · · ·

See also: Restaurants, taking your baby to; Unwanted Advice

I've just mastered breastfeeding my newborn at home, and now it's time for us to venture out. Any ideas on how to best handle breastfeeding in public?

Learn About It

In many parts of the world, the sight of a nursing mother is an ordinary aspect of daily life. In our society, however, some people are still uncomfortable seeing a mother breastfeed in public. Slowly but surely, though, people are coming to see breastfeeding as the natural, normal way of feeding a baby that it is. And thanks to public education campaigns, people are becoming more knowledgeable about the many benefits of breastfeeding.

Your Legal Right to Breastfeed

Society has conditioned many people to view breasts only from a sexual standpoint and not as a body part with a crucial biological function: to feed a baby. The natural default for baby feeding is breastfeeding, not bottlefeeding, yet no one harangues a woman who is feeding her baby from a bottle in a public place. If anyone even suggests that you shouldn't be feeding your baby in public, be aware that you are well within your rights. Keep in mind that it's the onlooker's problem, not yours.

From a legal perspective, you have a right to breastfeed your baby in public anywhere in the United States. Some states have gone so far as to implement specific legislation to that effect to protect the rights of babies and their mothers; these states have set out legal consequences for violations, too. As of this writing, seventeen states have passed laws that say you can breastfeed your baby in any public or private location, and thirteen more exempt breastfeeding from public indecency laws. This may lead you to believe that the act is legal only in states with legislation. The fact is you have a legal right to breastfeed your baby in public even without a specific law. Don't be shy about letting an impolite person know this. For more information about the legal aspects of breastfeeding in public, check out the website of Elizabeth N. Baldwin, an attorney who specializes in this issue: compromisesolutions.com.

In Canada, the Human Rights Code protects women from discrimination on the basis of sex. Breastfeeding in public is not *specifically* labeled as a protected activity, but many people are lobbying to explicitly include breastfeeding under this code.

What About Breastfeeding in Foreign Countries?

When you are outside the United States and Canada, it's best to respect the customs native to the country you are visiting. Even if *you* think you should breastfeed wherever you please, it's important to understand and adhere to local customs. If you don't see other women breastfeeding their babies, then ask around. Talk to a woman with young children, ask a health professional, or do a little research. Once you know what is typically acceptable, then you can proceed confidently without risk of offending anyone, breaking a law, or embarrassing yourself.

Getting Comfortable Breastfeeding in Public

Although you have the *right* to feed your baby in public, there is still the issue of your feelings about doing so. Each woman has her own comfort level. Most women want to find the right balance of pride and modesty—not overly exposing themselves yet feeling comfortable knowing that people are aware that they are breastfeeding. You'll probably need some practice with the particulars, simply because breastfeeding is a function that involves a private part of your anatomy that is normally not exposed in public. Wanting to be discreet doesn't mean that you are embarrassed or ashamed to feed your baby; it simply means that you don't want to cause social discomfort to yourself or others.

The biggest issue for most new mothers is learning how to get settled with your baby modestly. Even a new mother who is breastfeeding with ease at home may fumble and struggle when she perceives that she has an audience; her tension then causes her impatient baby to cry. That only deepens the feeling that all eyes are on her. The reality is that most people are paying attention to their own activities and their own private conversations, by and large ignorant of what's happening with other people. Once you become adept breastfeeding discreetly, you'll be able to comfortably nurse your baby anywhere. All it takes is a little practice.

Parent Tip

"Always remember that what you are doing is necessary, beautiful, and miraculous. Breastfeed your baby with pride."
—**Deborah, mother of Peter (5), Jeremy (3), and Claire (1)**

Tips for Breastfeeding in Public

• Give yourself permission to feel comfortable about nursing your baby in public. Feeding your baby is a natural, normal part of mothering, whether you are at home or out in public.

• Dress for breastfeeding. Wear a shirt or sweater that can be lifted up or unbuttoned from the bottom. When you lift from the bottom, the top portion of your shirt helps cover you from the top, and your baby covers you from the bottom. Whatever portion of your breast is shown while feeding your baby is certainly much less than is shown in the typical television show or magazine or at your local beach or public swimming pool.

- Try a nursing cover-up or a breastfeeding garment with a built-in flap. Many are so beautifully made that even under the most careful scrutiny, they don't look like nursing clothes. Most stores that sell maternity clothing also sell nursing apparel. Even if you don't use these at home, they may help you feel more comfortable when in public.

- Take along a small baby blanket. Some babies are fine with having a blanket thrown over your shoulder and over their heads, but many are very good at pulling off such a blanket. A good alternative is to bring the blanket up from below and tent it around your baby, to cover you as you settle your little one to the breast. The blanket can be loosely placed to create privacy or even removed once you're settled.

- Use your sling as a nursing cover-up. Baby slings are wonderful for nursing your baby on the go because they hold your baby perfectly in the nursing position while providing extra fabric for a screen. Some brands have a "tail" at the end that doubles as an extra blanket to keep the baby from trying to peek out while nursing.

- Feed your baby at the first sign of hunger, because hungry babies aren't quietly patient! If you wait until your baby is crying to be fed, then you may become nervous, and your baby may move about and make the latch-on difficult. Instead, if you nurse him promptly, you can be more relaxed about getting him settled.

- Remember that the alternative to public breastfeeding is usually public crying. Whether you're in a restaurant, at church, or on an airplane, people typically would prefer that you feed your baby rather than let him cry, fuss, or otherwise disrupt the peace. I remember once attending a play with a very antsy two-year-old: my son, David. When I finally settled him on my lap to breastfeed, the gentleman sitting beside me actually said, "Thank you!"

For More Information

Websites

INFACT Canada
infactcanada.ca

La Leche League International
lalecheleague.org

The World Alliance for Breastfeeding Action
waba.org.br

Breastfeeding with Bottlefeeding Supplements

• • • • • • • • • • •

See also: Breastfeeding Your Newborn;
Breastfeeding Your Toddler

My baby is a newborn and exclusively breastfed. I'll be returning to work when she is six months old and plan to pump at work, supplementing with formula if necessary. Either way, I need her to take a bottle. How should I make the transition?

Learn About It

Families have varying reasons as to why their breastfed babies need to take a bottle. Whether it's a full-time need, like returning to work, or occasional separations, many breastfed babies accept a bottle if Mommy is not around.

Combining working and breastfeeding is not always easy, but most mothers who do it say that it is worth every second of effort.

If you know for certain that you'll need your baby to accept a bottle, here are some guidelines to make this effort succeed.

Nipple Confusion

Some young babies adjust just fine to the combination of breastfeeding and bottlefeeding, but some have difficulty and develop "nipple confusion." These babies often prefer a bottle because extracting milk from a bottle is so much easier and faster than from the breast. If you work through the early adjustment period, however, your baby probably will become accustomed to both types of nipples.

When to Introduce a Bottle

Some babies take easily to a bottle; others require more creativity and time to get used to an artificial nipple. You won't know which of these categories your baby falls into until you actually introduce a bottle. Either way, it's important to your ongoing breastfeeding success that you wait to introduce that first bottle until these two milestones occur:

- Breastfeeding is going well. Both you and your baby are comfortable and confident.
- Your milk supply is established, usually when your baby is three to six weeks old. If your baby will have to take a bottle at some point, it's best not to wait too much longer than six weeks to introduce the bottle. Older babies know what they want and might reject the unfamiliar.

How to Start a Baby with a Bottle

The following guidelines will help you and your baby get started with a bottle:

- Plan ahead, and introduce a bottle gradually. At first, you might offer a bottle when your baby is awake but not ravenously hungry. Your baby may be curious enough to sample a few sips, and this is a good way to show what a bottle is all about. If you are breastfeeding, try using pumped milk for this if you can. If you plan to use formula in the bottle over the long term, you can use either breastmilk or formula.

- When offering those first few bottles, avoid your usual breastfeeding chairs and positions. Your baby may be more willing to try something new and different when not presented with his accustomed associations between place/position and breastfeeding.

- Don't push these first sessions too hard. Many babies require a few experimental sessions before they begin to understand that the bottle actually provides food.

- If your baby doesn't like the first bottle offered, try it a few more times. If she still resists, try a different nipple type. There are many options, and you'll find that babies have definite preferences.

• Babies have personal preferences about the temperature of their bottled liquid, too. Some like it at room temperature, while some like it a little warmer. Warming up the *nipple* by running it under warm water before feeding may help your baby accept the bottle.

• Ask your pediatrician to recommend a formula, and do some research on the many options available (*see* Bottlefeeding). *Don't* use regular cow's milk, though, for a baby under a year old. A baby this young can't easily digest its proteins, and you may set up your baby for allergies later in life.

• If you aren't having luck when your baby is awake, try offering a bottle when your baby is sleeping! Just pick him up, hold him in a familiar feeding position, and see if he'll accept the bottle when it's put next to his lips. This may work better if someone other than Mommy tries it out, since your baby knows your scent!

What if Nothing Works?

My youngest child, Coleton, would never accept a bottle, no matter how creative we were in trying to get him interested. Luckily, I work at home, so we didn't need to force the issue with him (and I suspect that if we'd had a reason that *required* him to take a bottle, we would have eventually succeeded). A few times, I had to be gone from the house for several hours, and we discovered ways for him to get some nutrition when I wasn't with him:

• **An eyedropper:** The little eyedropper that often comes with children's medicine can work wonders with a baby who won't accept any nipple other than yours. While it doesn't hold much fluid, a patient and loving caregiver can get the baby to take enough to tide him over. You might also check with your pharmacist for a larger medicine dropper. (Use a clean dropper with no traces of medicine.)

• **A spoon:** A baby spoon is another option for small-dose feeding. Some babies enjoy the novelty of this method.

• **A cup:** An older baby may be able to drink from a cup. A little one needs some time to master this, and you'll have to do most of the "work," but it may be one solution. Look around for different types of baby cups, such as a two-handled sipper cup.

- **Supplemental nursing device:** This is a bottle with a long, thin tube that is handheld or taped to the breast so that a baby who is very tiny, sick, adopted, or unable to suck efficiently can get milk with very little sucking effort. In this way, the baby gets proper nutrition, can learn how to breastfeed, and can stimulate the mother's milk supply. A specialist, such as a lactation consultant, can provide this device.
- **Relax and listen to your baby:** Sometimes our own stress over a negative situation makes it worse. A little patience and a deep breath can do wonders.

Pumping Your Breastmilk

Pumping comes easy to some mothers, who can fill a bottle with very little effort and time. Others struggle to get even a few precious drops. Most women need time to find the right method for them. Talk with other mothers who have pumped or with a lactation consultant who has experience working with mothers who pump.

Breast Pumps

A number of different kinds of breast pumps are available: battery or electric pumps and hand pumps. Some mothers don't buy a pump but rely on manual expression (expressing milk by hand). No single answer is right for all women, so you'll have to experiment to learn what's right for you. High-quality breast pumps can be expensive, but many organizations rent them. There are also a number of moderately priced pumps that work well. (And if you consider the money you are saving from not buying formula, you are still ahead!) You can check with your hospital maternity office, look under "Breastfeeding Supplies and Information" in the yellow pages of your phone book, or peruse a website where people post reviews, such as Epinions.com.

Parent Tip

"I started following my workday schedule a few weeks before I actually started back to work. I pumped and gave my baby a bottle during the time of day when I would be at the office. When I did start work, my baby and my body were both already on our new schedule."

—**Karla, mother of Harrison (10 months)**

Formula

While breastmilk is the best food for babies, many reasons may lead you to give your baby formula. For example, if pumping doesn't succeed, a breastfeeding mother may have the caregiver feed her baby formula. When my second child, Vanessa, was a baby, I worked away from home for a few hours a day. I was never successful at pumping, so when I was at home, I breastfed her, and when I was at work, her grandma or her daddy gave her bottles of formula. Using this method, Vanessa breastfed well into her second year. It worked fine for us and may work for you, too.

For More Information

This section is but a brief overview of breastfeeding with bottlefeeding supplements, and many mothers require much more information. If you have any problems along the way, reach out for help through your hospital's breastfeeding support staff or your local chapter of La Leche League (a worldwide organization for the support of breastfeeding).

Books

Pryor, Gale. *Nursing Mother, Working Mother: The Essential Guide for Breastfeeding and Staying Close to Your Baby After You Return to Work.* Boston: Harvard Common Press, 1997.

See also Breastfeeding Your Newborn ("For More Information").

Websites

Breastfeeding
nursingmother.com

La Leche League International
lalecheleague.org

Breastfeeding Your Newborn

. . . .

See also: Breastfeeding in Public; Breastfeeding with Bottlefeeding Supplements; Breastfeeding Your Toddler

I'm expecting my first baby next month and plan to breastfeed. My doctor recommends it, and it seems like such a natural thing to do. I'm curious, though, about the specific reasons to breastfeed. I also must admit that I'm nervous: How will I know what to do?

Why Breastfeed?

It's wonderful that you're thinking through this topic now. As advanced as science is today, it has yet to discover how to create an artificial food more perfect for baby than Mommy's own milk. The benefits that scientific research has uncovered (and continues to find) are too many to present here in entirety, but here's a partial list:

- Breastmilk contains substances that build your baby's immunities against disease.
- Breastmilk prevents the risk of certain illnesses and infections, which, in turn, can decrease the risk of sudden infant death syndrome (SIDS).
- Breastmilk is a "whole food" that provides all the nutrients your baby requires.
- Breastmilk is easily digested and used efficiently by your baby's body.
- Human milk contains the perfect mix of protein, fats, carbohydrates, and vitamins for human babies, in a form that's more readily absorbed than the additives in formulas.

- The composition of your breastmilk changes according to your baby's changing needs.
- Breastmilk may reduce your baby's chance of developing allergies.
- Breastfed babies are at less risk for obesity later in life.
- Breastfeeding promotes proper tooth, tongue, and jaw growth required for language development.
- Nutrients in breastmilk enhance babies' brain development and actually increase IQ.
- The World Health Organization and the American Academy of Pediatrics (AAP) both recommend breastmilk as the ideal food for the growth and development of babies. The AAP states, "Extensive research, especially in recent years, documents diverse and compelling advantages to infants, mothers, families and society from breastfeeding and the use of human milk for infant feeding. These include health, nutritional, immunologic, developmental, psychological, social, economic, and environmental benefits" (*Breastfeeding and the Use of Human Milk*, RE9729, Work Group on Breastfeeding, 1996–1997).

There are many benefits for you, as well:

- Breastfeeding lowers your risk of osteoporosis and breast and ovarian cancers.
- Breastfeeding is economical and can save you hundreds of dollars over formula.
- Breastfeeding burns about 500 calories each day and may help you return to your prepregnancy weight.
- The act of breastfeeding and the hormones it produces enhance maternal behavior and promote bonding between you and your baby.

All these reasons combine for a very compelling call to follow your instincts and breastfeed your baby. I breastfed all four of my children well into toddlerhood, and from my experience, I must add one more point (and I'm certain other breastfeeding mothers would agree): Breastfeeding is a beautiful experience.

Getting Started

Women have breastfed babies since the beginning of humanity. It's a very natural and normal experience, but that doesn't mean it's always easy! In times past, new mothers were surrounded by other women who had breastfed their own children, and mothers instinctively looked to each other for support and knowledge. Today's new mother may well find herself on her own when starting out with her baby.

After almost nine years of breastfeeding, I can still recall my very first few days at it. They were very difficult. While in the hospital, I rang for a nurse for every single feeding because I couldn't get the hang of it. Luckily, the hospital where I had my children has lactation consultants available to new mothers twenty-four hours a day. By the time we headed home, I felt much more confident about breastfeeding. (I still found plenty of reasons to call their twenty-four-hour hot line for help during the following months.)

Here are some things you can do to help yourself become a successful breastfeeding mother:

- Choose health care professionals who are supportive of breastfeeding and either employ a lactation consultant in their offices or can recommend competent lactation consultants.
- Ask for help. Don't be afraid or embarrassed. Experts in the field understand that getting started can be difficult, and they are eager to help you succeed. This is their purpose, and their job is to assist you. As for modesty, remember that you don't have anything under your shirt that they don't see just about every day.
- Feed your baby frequently and according to his cues. Frequent nursing will stimulate your body to produce more milk and help establish your breastfeeding skills. It will also help you get to know your baby; you'll get very good at reading his cues. In the early weeks, expect to nurse between eight and twelve times in each twenty-four-hour period, at least ten to twenty minutes per side.
- If you have any pain, contact a lactation consultant right away, because something isn't working properly. When your baby is latched on correctly and you are healthy, there should be no discomfort during breastfeeding after the first week or so.

- Although it may seem that you're not producing enough milk, chances are good that you are. How to tell, according to La Leche League (lalecheleague.org):

  > Watch your baby's diapers. She should be wetting at least six to eight cloth diapers (five to six disposables) in each twenty-four-hour period after her third day of life and should regain her birth-weight by week two or three (and steadily thereafter). If you have *any* doubt, call a lactation counselor or your pediatrician.

- Put everything else in your life on hold for a few weeks. Accept help from anyone who offers. Focus on getting to know your new baby as you both gain breastfeeding skills.
- Read a book or two about breastfeeding (and ask Daddy to read a bit, too). Armed with the facts, you're less likely to be misled by well-meaning but ill-advised family members or friends, who unknowingly may pass along incorrect or even dangerous advice. Your own knowledge must be adequate to sift though the barrage of comments and "information" you'll hear from all corners.

What About Daddy?

A father can bond with his baby in many ways, and feeding is just one option. *All* caregiving actions give Daddy a chance to build closeness between him and his baby. Bathing, dressing, cuddling, and carrying all are important aspects of baby care, and all of these promote the relationship between father and child.

Research proves that when the father is supportive of breastfeeding, the mother will find more success. Therefore, it's important that Daddy be informed on the benefits and methods, too. And, as with other issues in parenting, things will go smoother if you are working together.

For More Information

Books

Gotsch, Gwen, and Judy Torgus. *The Womanly Art of Breastfeeding*, 6th rev. ed. New York: Plume, 1997.

Gromada, Karen Kerkhoff. *Mothering Multiples: Breastfeeding & Caring for Twins or More*, rev. ed. Schaumburg, IL: La Leche League International, 1999.

Huggins, Kathleen. *The Nursing Mother's Companion*, 4th ed. Boston: Harvard Common Press, 1999.

Newman, Jack, and Teresa Pitman. *The Ultimate Breastfeeding Book of Answers: The Most Comprehensive Problem-Solution Guide to Breastfeeding from the Foremost Expert in North America*. Roseville, CA: Prima Publishing, 2000.

Sears, Martha, and William Sears. *The Breastfeeding Book: Everything You Need to Know About Nursing Your Child from Birth Through Weaning*. Boston: Little, Brown and Company, 2000.

Websites

Breastfeeding
nursingmother.com

La Leche League International
lalecheleague.org

Breastfeeding Your Toddler

See also: Breastfeeding with Bottlefeeding Supplements;
Breastfeeding Your Newborn

> *I never quite planned this, but my baby just turned one, and we're still breastfeeding. It seems very natural and normal to my husband and me. Is there any reason we should consider weaning?*

Why Breastfeed a Toddler?

In short, there is no "should" or "must" when it comes to weaning your baby. Although many mothers do wean their babies in the first year, the average age of weaning worldwide is around four years old. The American Academy of Pediatrics recommends breastfeeding for at least twelve months and for as long after that as is "mutually desired by mother and baby." The World Health Organization recommends breastfeeding for *at least* two years. The Canadian Paediatric Society endorses breastfeeding for two years or longer.

There are many reasons to continue breastfeeding your toddler:

- The magical health benefits of breastmilk (*see* Breastfeeding Your Newborn) don't disappear just because a baby has passed her first birthday! In fact, some of the ingredients in breastmilk that protect your baby against infection are present in greater amounts in the second year of life than in the first. The benefits of breastmilk will continue to serve your child well into toddlerhood.
- As a toddler becomes more independent, the comforting ritual of nursing can provide a sense of security in your child's rapidly expanding world.

- Breastfeeding can be a lifesaver when toddlers are sick. My own children worked their way through a number of illnesses when they would not eat or drink anything but simply nursed frequently until they felt better again. It prevented dehydration and provided important calories and vitamins needed for recovery—not to mention the wonderful comfort of being held and nursed.
- If you and your baby enjoy the breastfeeding relationship, why stop? There are neither rules about when you should wean nor studies that demonstrate any reason you should. The best time to wean is when both you and your baby are ready.

For More Information

Books for Your Baby

Moen, Cecilia. *Breastmilk Makes My Tummy Yummy.* Sunby, Sweden: Midsummer Press, 1999.

Olsen, Mary. *I'm Made of Mama's Milk.* Portland, OR: Mary Olsen Books, 2002.

Books for You

Bumgarner, Norma J. *Mothering Your Nursing Toddler*, rev. ed. Schaumburg, IL: La Leche League International, 2000.

See also Breastfeeding Your Newborn ("For More Information").

Burping

See also: Bottlefeeding; Colic; Spitting Up; Vomiting

My mother always got mad at my brothers and me for burping after a meal, but here I am encouraging my baby to do the same thing! Seems funny even to ask, but how important is burping, and how do I get my reluctant burper to get rid of those bubbles?

Learn About It

The issue of gas is different for babies than for the rest of us. Since babies can't get up and walk around after a meal, the air they swallow while drinking gets trapped inside and can cause discomfort. So, until your baby is crawling and walking around on her own, helping her move those air bubbles through her body is up to you.

Prevention First

The less air that your baby takes in during feeding, the less she'll need to contend with trapped gas. While you can't eliminate all of it, here are a few tips to reduce the bubbles:

- After a daytime feeding, keep your baby in a rather upright position for half an hour or so by holding him or putting him in a baby seat or swing.
- While breastfeeding, make sure your baby has a good, tight latch and that you are holding him tummy to tummy to minimize the amount of air he takes in.
- If bottlefeeding, try keeping Baby's head higher than his stomach to help the air escape on its own.
- If bottlefeeding, experiment with different types of bottle/nipple combinations. Some are created with curved containers or airtight

inserts to reduce airflow. Different nipples may reduce airflow as well. For example, there are nipples with smaller holes made especially for newborns; these don't let in as much air.

- Hold the bottle nipple down and nearly perpendicular to your baby, so no air gets into the nipple.
- If your baby consistently has a lot of gas, try feeding smaller meals more frequently (*see also* Colic).

How Often Does a Formula-Fed Baby Need to Be Burped?

The typical pattern for burping is in the middle and at the end of each feeding. You can try for a burp after every one to three ounces, or about half the bottle. If your baby doesn't have consistent burps in the middle of her meal, or if she cries when you take away the bottle—thus taking in even more air—then go ahead and skip the midmeal burping. Watch your baby for signs that she needs more or less time being burped.

How Often Does a Breastfed Baby Need to Be Burped?

A breastfed baby may not ever need to be burped. Many don't take in enough air to warrant a burping. Some babies, though, do gulp their feedings, are more prone to gas, or struggle with a mother's very strong milk letdown. In these cases, a postfeeding burp is helpful. You'll get to know your baby soon enough. A breastfed baby who is gulping at feedings, spitting up a lot, or showing signs of discomfort could be responding to an overactive letdown or an overabundant milk supply and does need to be burped. Talk to a lactation consultant or a La Leche League leader about whether this may be an issue for you, and what to do about it.

Try burping your baby during the intermission between the first and second breasts, and again at the end of the feeding, if he's still awake. Attempt to coax a burp for no more than three to four minutes after a feeding. If your baby rarely or never responds with a little belch, then don't feel that you must continue the practice. If at any time your baby seems to act fussy after a meal, try a burp to see if that's the issue.

If you co-sleep with your baby, you most likely won't need to burp him in the middle of the night. Most co-sleeping night feeding is relaxed and slow, so air bubbles aren't an issue. Again, watch your baby. If he feeds and then can't seem to fall asleep easily, then try some gentle burping before sleep.

What Is the Best Way to Burp a Baby?

There is no single right way to burp a baby. All babies are different, so the best frequency and method differs with each one. You'll need to experiment a little to come up with the best answers for your particular little one. No matter which method you use, place a towel, spit-up rag, or cloth diaper under her chin, since food commonly accompanies the air as it comes up. You'll have more than your share of stained shoulders by the time she's six months old. Here are the most common ways to burp a baby:

- **The over-the-shoulder pat:** Hold your baby against your chest with her chin or the upper part of her body over your shoulder. Pat or rub her back.
- **The lap sit:** Place your baby in a sitting position on your lap, one hand supporting her chest and chin. Lean her slightly forward and gently pat or rub. You can even try circling her upper body slightly in a gentle pattern.
- **The tummy roll:** Lay your baby on her tummy across your lap, keeping her head higher than her stomach. Pat or rub her back and bottom gently. You can even jiggle your legs just a bit to help move the gas, which may also comfort her. (Don't shake her roughly, though, as this can be dangerous for a tiny baby, and don't bounce her vigorously, as this can encourage spitting up.)
- **The sling walk:** Place your baby in an upright position in your sling and walk around. A little patting or rubbing can be added but often isn't necessary, since bubbles will naturally make their way to the top. (Remember to put a towel or bib under Baby's chin.)

Car Seat Crying

....

See also: Travel by Car

> *My seven-month-old baby hates her car seat. She cries from the moment we leave the house until we arrive at our destination. Even if she's tired, she won't sleep! Please help!*

Learn About It

While some babies fall asleep almost before you're out of the driveway, others, like your child, won't spend five happy minutes in their car seat. Usually, this is because your baby is used to more freedom of movement and more physical attention than you can provide when she's belted into her seat.

Remember that you and your baby's safety are most important. Parents sometimes take a crying baby out of the car seat, which is extremely dangerous and just makes it even more difficult for the baby to get used to riding in the car seat. Some parents make poor driving decisions when their babies are crying, which puts everyone in the car at risk. Either pull over and calm your baby down, or focus on your driving. Don't try to do both.

The good news is that a few new ideas plus a little time and maturity will help your baby become a happy traveler. (I know, because three of my babies were car seat haters!)

The Trip to Car Seat Happiness

Any one (or more) of the following strategies may help solve your car seat dilemma. If the first one you try fails, choose another one, then another. Eventually, you'll hit upon the right solution for your baby.

- Make sure your baby is healthy. If car seat crying is something new and your baby has been particularly fussy at home, too, your baby may have an ear infection or other illness.
- Bring the car seat in the house, and let your baby sit and play in it. Once it becomes more familiar in the house, he may be happier to sit there in the car.
- Keep a special box of car toys that you'll use only in the car. If these are interesting enough, they may hold your baby's attention.
- Tape or hang toys from the back of the seat your baby is facing, or string an array of lightweight toys from the ceiling, using heavy tape and yarn. Place them just at arm's reach so that your baby can bat at them from the car seat.
- Link a long row of plastic baby chains from one side of the backseat to the other, and clip new toys on the row for each trip.
- Hang a made-for-baby poster on the back of the seat that faces your baby. These are usually black, white, red, and bold primary colors. Some even have pockets so you can change the pictures. (Remember to do this, since the change in scenery is very helpful.)
- Experiment with different types of music in the car. Some babies enjoy lullabies or music tapes made especially for babies and young children; others surprise you by calming down as soon as you play one of your old favorites. Some babies enjoy hearing Mom or Dad sing more than anything else! (For some reason, "Rudolf the Red-Nosed Reindeer" has always been a good choice for us, even out of season.)
- Try "white noise" in the car. You can purchase tapes of nature sounds or even make a recording of your vacuum cleaner.
- Practice with short, pleasant trips when your baby is in a good mood and someone can sit near her and keep her entertained. A few good experiences may help.
- Offer a pacifier or teething toy so your baby has something to suck or chew on.
- Hang a mirror so that your baby can see you (and you can see your baby) while you are driving. Baby stores offer mirrors made especially for this purpose. Your baby may think that you're not there, and just seeing your face will help him feel better.

- Put up a sunshade in the window if you suspect that sunshine in your baby's face may be a problem.
- Try to consolidate trips so that you aren't in the car for long periods and so that you don't have many ins and outs.
- Make sure your baby hasn't outgrown her car seat and that her belts have not become too tight or uncomfortable.
- Try opening a window for some fresh, moving air.
- If all else fails, take the bus!

Car Seats

See also: Car Seat Crying; Travel by Car

I'm pregnant and ready to shop for a car seat. What are my options? How do I choose from so many different kinds?

Learn About It

A car seat is one of the most important pieces of baby equipment you'll need to buy. Not only will you use it many times a day, nearly every day, but also it is crucial to your baby's safety.

Choosing a Type of Car Seat

While the array of choices seems endless, there are really only two basic types of seats to use during the first two years: infant seats and convertible seats. Once you choose a basic style, then you can take the next step and compare options, styles, and prices among the many manufacturers. Here are the definitions of the two styles:

- **Infant car seat:** This is made especially for babies up to twenty pounds. It is rear-facing and designed to hold a tiny baby who can't yet sit independently.
- **Convertible car seat:** A convertible seat is used in the rear-facing position until your baby is old enough and big enough to face the front. Then you can switch it to accommodate the forward-facing position.

The following chart summarizes the major pluses and minuses of these two options.

Pros and Cons of Car Seat Types

	Pros	Cons
Infant car seat	Designed to fit an infant's small body and provides ample support for Baby's head, neck, and back On most models, seat pops out of the base for use as an infant carrier Semi-reclined position works perfectly for a sleeping infant	Only suitable for a baby up to about 20–22 pounds, which for some children is around 4–5 months of age (others can fit these seats until their first birthday, so you'll be buying a second car seat at some point)
Convertible car seat	Will fit a baby up to 3 or 4 years old Can be used in rear-facing and front-facing positions	May not fit a newborn perfectly, since straps and harnesses may not adjust tightly and seat position may be too upright for an infant

Premature Babies and Babies with Special Needs

A third type of car seat is available for babies who weigh less than five pounds, have special needs, or have breathing difficulties that prevent them from sitting safely in a standard car seat. These are called "car beds" and allow a baby to ride in a fully reclined position. The car bed looks like a bassinet and is buckled across the back seat. Most of these can be converted to rear-facing car seats when your baby is able to sit upright.

Car Seat Options

You'll find quite a number of options available as you shop for a car seat. Every family has different preferences, so take your time in making your purchase. The following are some of the standard harnesses available:

- **Five-point harness:** Generally, a five-point harness is considered the best type of harness for an infant. It consists of two straps that go over the baby's shoulders, two that wrap around the lower body, and one that pulls up between the legs. All the straps connect in the center.
- **Overhead shield:** A bar replaces straps across the front of the seat. These usually don't fit an infant tightly and are better suited to older children.
- **T-shield:** This type of shield takes the place of the bottom portion of a harness, replacing the straps with a hard plastic T. Like an overhead shield, this may not be suitable for a small baby. For older babies, some parents find the one-step attachment easier than buckling a five-point harness.

What to Look for in a Car Seat

As you consider the best seat for your family, look through this list to determine which features are important to you.

- **Safety features:** Check out the safety rating of your car seat with *Consumer Reports* or a similar independent agency.
- **Wide straps:** Wider, thicker straps are less apt to twist and tangle.
- **Multiple strap adjustments:** As your baby grows, you'll appreciate the ability to adjust the straps to fit.
- **Easy installation:** Car seats are much easier to install if they have a wider seat-belt path. If you will be moving the car seat between cars, how easy is it to take in and out? You should be able to try the car seat in your car before you buy it, or try it and return it if it doesn't work out. Not all car seats work with all cars.

- **Adjustability:** A baby often falls asleep in the car, so make sure the seat has several positions for reclining.
- **Ease of use:** Try out all the features to determine whether they operate smoothly and easily.
- **Head and neck protection:** If you are buying a seat for a newborn or small baby, look for one with head and neck padding, or purchase a separate cushioned headrest. For an older baby, look for side wings to hold the head up when Baby's sleeping.
- **Fit:** Before you throw away packaging, test the seat to be certain it fits properly in your car.
- **Style:** Look for a color and pattern that harmonizes with your car's interior, if this is important to you.
- **Maintenance:** Is the cover washable and can it be easily removed for cleaning?

What You Need to Know About LATCH

LATCH stands for Lower Anchors and Tethers for CHildren. It is a standardized child restraint system that coordinates the methods of attaching car seats among vehicles and car seats. LATCH increases the safety of car seat use, since studies have shown that over 80 percent of car seats are installed incorrectly. Cars and car seats manufactured after September 2002 are required to meet LATCH regulations and make it easier for all parents to install seats correctly. Some older car seats and cars can be retrofitted to meet the LATCH system.

Regardless of whether your vehicle and car seat operate under the LATCH system, always make sure that you thoroughly read the vehicle and seat instructions. Also, have a specialist double-check your installation. Car seat safety checks often are available through hospitals, police stations, car dealerships, and fire departments. Ensuring your baby's safety is worth the few minutes this takes.

Car Seat Safety Rules

Once you've purchased a car seat, follow these important safety rules:

- Read the manual for your car seat, and follow the instructions exactly.
- Always buckle your baby into the car seat completely and snugly.
- Never leave a baby unattended in a car seat.
- Always place a car seat in the backseat of the car.
- Avoid using old or used car seats. They may no longer be safe, or they may not meet current safety standards.
- Be certain that anyone who takes your baby in a car follows these rules.

For More Information

Website

American Academy of Pediatrics
"Car Safety Seats: A Guide for Families"
aap.org/family/carseatguide.htm

Chicken Pox

(Varicella)

· · · · · · · · · · · · ·

See also: Febrile Seizure; Fever; Immunizations; Rash; Roseola

My baby had a fever for several days, and then he developed a rash. I assumed it was roseola, but now the rash is turning into blisters. My mom says it's chicken pox! Could it be?

Learn About It

It sure sounds like it! While both roseola and chickenpox start out similarly—with a fever —the rash that follows is different. Here's how to tell the difference: A roseola rash is pink and "blanches" (turns white when you press on it); it does not itch. The rash of chicken pox is redder and very itchy. Eventually it turns into pimplelike water blisters that burst and form dry, crusty scabs. Given that your baby's rash is blistering, it's time to call the pediatrician!

Why Should I Call the Doctor?

Call your doctor to confirm your suspicions and find out what treatment the doctor recommends. You also should call your doctor immediately if your baby has any high-risk health issues or if you notice any of the following symptoms, because they may indicate a more serious problem:

- Infection of the blisters
- Vomiting
- Convulsions
- Extreme sleepiness

- Confusion or lack of responsiveness
- Lack of balance

How Can I Help My Baby Feel Better?

Your baby will be sick for up to two weeks with the chicken pox. Here are a few ways you can help your baby feel better:

- While fever is the body's natural response to illness, reducing the fever can help your baby feel better and may prevent a sudden spike in temperature that could cause a seizure (*see* Febrile Seizure). With your health care provider's approval, you can treat fever with acetaminophen (like Infant's Tylenol) or ibuprofen (like Infant's Advil). Some herbal remedies, such as chamomile and valerian, may help reduce fever (*see* Fever). *Never* give a baby with chicken pox aspirin or any medication containing aspirin. This increases the risk of Reye's syndrome, a potentially fatal illness.
- Give your baby frequent baths with baking soda or oatmeal to help soothe itching. You can use regular, dry oatmeal contained in a sock or pillowcase, or purchase an oatmeal bath product like Aveeno at your drugstore.
- Treat your baby's rash with anti-itch cream, such as calamine lotion or Aveeno Anti-Itch Cream. Check with your pediatrician for a product recommendation, as some may be too harsh or cause dry skin.
- Ask your doctor about giving your baby diphenhydramine, an antihistamine used for allergy relief. (This is the active ingredient in Benadryl.)
- Keep your baby's nails very short and smooth, and try to prevent your little one from picking or scratching the sores. This is often best done with distraction; now's the time to allow your baby to watch videos or listen to storybooks.
- Show your baby how to blow on the pox or tap on them when they itch instead of scratching. This can bring some relief and gives your little one a way to deal with that itchy feeling.

Is Chicken Pox Contagious?

Chicken pox is a highly contagious virus. Your baby will be infectious a day or two *before* the rash even appears—before you realize your baby is ill—which is why the disease spreads so easily and quickly among unimmunized children in day-care centers, schools, and families. The illness remains infectious until all of the blisters have crusted. A person can only have chicken pox once, but it will spread easily among children who have never had the virus or have not been immunized.

If your baby has chicken pox, you might get calls from friends who want to bring their children over to pick up the bug. Typically, you'll hear, "They're going to get it eventually, and I'd rather get it over with." But this is never a good idea, since you can neither predict nor control any child's response to the illness. Additionally, chicken pox can be extremely problematic in children who develop complications, as well as in newborns and pregnant women. If your infected baby has been around a pregnant woman or a newborn, make sure to let these families know so that they can consult their doctors. Plus, it's a courtesy to let anyone with children who have been near your baby during the infectious period know that your little one has come down with the chicken pox so they can watch for signs in their children. You might also mention that the incubation period can be as short as eleven days or as long as three weeks.

Your concern should also extend to adults, particularly if they have not been vaccinated or previously exposed.

What Are the Common Complications?

The most common side effect is infection of the blisters. You can help prevent this by bathing your child several times a day and keeping her fingernails very short so that she doesn't scratch, which can burst and infect the blisters. If the pox do become infected, permanent scarring is a real possibility. While rare, chicken pox also can cause pneumonia, which can require hospitalization. In an even smaller percentage, the pox leads to encephalitis (an infection of the brain) or death.

Is There a Vaccine Against Chicken Pox?

A chicken pox vaccine is available. Most doctors recommend it for babies between the ages of twelve and eighteen months. Many school districts require chicken pox vaccinations or valid exemptions. As with all immunizations, learn about its potential risks versus its benefits before you decide whether to have your baby immunized (*see* Immunizations).

The main reasons some parents choose not to vaccinate against chicken pox are that they don't view the disease as a serious risk and that the vaccine doesn't last through adulthood, whereas the actual virus creates a lifelong immunity. They also feel that since 20 percent of children who are vaccinated still get chicken pox, albeit a more mild case, they would rather let nature take its course. Some parents wait until their child is about ten years old to vaccinate if the child has not yet been infected, since the risks of chicken pox complications increase with age.

Parents choose to vaccinate against chicken pox because it can be a long and painful illness, causing up to two weeks of stay-at-home recovery. And while the vaccination isn't foolproof, the very few vaccinated children who do develop the disease tend to have very mild cases. Parents of babies with eczema, asthma, or leukemia often are counseled to vaccinate their children against chicken pox because it's more likely for these children to experience complications.

Because of the risk of complications, both the American Academy of Pediatrics and the Centers for Disease Control and Prevention recommend that babies receive this immunization. Babies with HIV/AIDS, cancer, allergy to gelatin, or any disease of the immune system may not be candidates for the vaccination. Be sure to talk this over with your child's primary-care physician.

Why Is It Called Chicken Pox?

You don't catch this disease from eating chicken or being near chickens. The name *chicken pox* comes from chickpeas, of all things. Supposedly, the blisters of chicken pox resemble chickpeas sitting on the skin.

Child Care, choosing

See also: Attachment Parenting; Babyproofing; Baby-Sitters; Breastfeeding with Bottlefeeding Supplements; Intelligence; Separation Anxiety; Stranger Anxiety

> *My baby girl is due in two months. For financial reasons, I will have to return to work when she is three months old. What kind of child care is best?*

Learn About It

Choosing the right child care for your baby is one of the most important—and difficult—tasks you will undertake as a new parent, and the right answer is different for every family. Give yourself enough time to look into all your potential options, weighing the advantages and disadvantages of each until you come up with a situation you are comfortable with. Leaving your baby with someone else so that you can return to work can be heart wrenching, but when you feel good about your child-care choice, going back to work will be much easier.

What Are My Options?

There are five main child-care options for babies, and numerous variations and combinations within each option. The information that follows can help you compare the advantages and disadvantages of each major form. Additional information is available in the books and websites listed at the end of this entry.

Relative as Care Provider

A grandparent, aunt, uncle, cousin, or another relative takes care of your child in your home or theirs. This is a very popular choice; about

one-fifth of children under the age of six are in the care of relatives
while parents are at work.

Advantages

- Chances are, your relatives naturally love your baby and have her
  best interests in mind.
- Baby may get more one-on-one attention, depending on how
  many children are in the relative's home.
- Your baby isn't exposed to germs from other children, except those
  in the relative's home.
- Care by a relative can be less expensive.
- If your baby stays in your home, there is no morning rush, and she
  can stay in familiar surroundings.
- If your baby is sick, you don't have to stay home from work.
- There may be more flexibility when the parents have an early start
  or a late meeting.

Disadvantages

- The employer-employee relationship can sometimes be awkward
  within a family context.
- Child-rearing beliefs may differ. Ensuring that the relative follows
  your beliefs on major issues like sleep, feeding, attachment parenting, and discipline can sometimes be difficult.
- The relative may have no child-care training and may go purely by
  experience, which may or may not be a good thing.
- Older relatives may not have the energy to take care of a baby,
  especially once she becomes mobile.
- If the relative is sick, the parents will have to take time off work.
- If things don't work out for either party, it may create bad feelings
  in the family.

Nanny, Au Pair, or In-Home Child-Care Provider

Your baby stays in your home while cared for by a live-out or live-in
nanny, au pair, or baby-sitter. Nannies are usually qualified and experienced child-care professionals. Au pairs are generally eighteen- to

twenty-six-year-old foreign women or men who travel specifically to tend children in exchange for the opportunity to live in another country. Au pairs usually have some child-care experience and may be bilingual. Other in-home child-care providers include college students, neighbors with grown children, contacts from a local church—anyone you hire to take care of your baby in your home.

Advantages

- With the caregiver in your home, there's no rush to get Baby ready in the morning.
- Baby remains in familiar surroundings.
- Baby gets one-on-one attention and is not exposed to germs from other children, other than siblings, of course.
- You can hire someone with similar child-rearing beliefs and set up clear guidelines about your expectations.
- When your baby is sick, you don't necessarily have to take time off work.
- There may be flexibility when you work early or late.
- Nannies, in particular, have child-care expertise and often CPR certification.
- Au pairs bring a multicultural perspective to your home.
- If you find the right person, your child can develop a very meaningful and enriching long-term relationship with the caregiver.

Disadvantages

- Even with an interview, reference checks, or the use of an agency, finding just the right person can be difficult.
- There is little governmental regulation, so checking up on how the caregiver relates to or cares for your baby is based on your observation alone. (How do things go when you're not there to watch?)
- A live-in person can interfere with family privacy (especially an au pair, who should be a part of family meals, outings, and vacations).
- The caregiver could quit, leaving the family in the lurch.
- Parents must take time off of work when the caregiver is sick.
- Nannies can be very expensive.
- Au pair agency fees can be high.

- Caretaking skills, experience, English-language proficiency, and cultural adaptability vary widely among au pairs.
- As an employer, you may have to deal with complicated tax and paperwork issues.

Family/Home Day Care

Your baby goes to another family's home, and the caregiver usually has children of her own. Many mothers become caretakers for other people's children to finance their decision to stay at home with their own children. This type of day care should be licensed (but often is not). Guidelines vary per area, but usually, a family day-care home should be responsible for no more than two babies under thirty months or five children under five years old.

Advantages
- Baby spends the time in a home environment.
- As Baby grows, he enjoys "built-in" playmates.
- Typically, the child-to-adult ratio is smaller in a family/home day care than in group day-care settings, so your baby is apt to get more individual attention.
- Baby will be exposed to fewer contagious diseases than in a group setting.
- Generally, this option is moderately expensive, though costs vary widely.
- There may be some flexibility about early or late dropoff or pickup times.

Disadvantages
- Home day cares, even those that are licensed, offer few health and safety guarantees.
- Your application process must be thorough to weed out any unqualified and inexperienced caretakers.
- The provider may subconsciously give her own children more attention than yours.

- Your child will be exposed to germs from the other children in the home.
- If your baby or the caretaker is sick, you will have to take time off work.
- The quality of care can be difficult to assess, and there is little regulatory supervision.

Day-Care Center

Your baby attends a commercial, corporate, or religious day-care center that cares for large groups of children. This center should be state licensed, and it must meet, among other things, strict guidelines on staff/child ratios and health, sanitary, and safety issues. The center may also have accreditation from nonprofit organizations like the National Association for the Education of Young Children (NAEYC), demonstrating that it meets more stringent standards. The best ratios are one adult to three babies, one adult to five toddlers, and one adult to eight preschoolers. This is a popular child-care solution, especially for toddlers and young children; almost one-third of U.S. children under the age of five spend at least some time in a day-care center.

Advantages

- Day-care centers are usually reliable, so parents don't have to worry about an individual caretaker quitting or getting sick, since other caregivers will still be there to cover the spot.
- Most staff members are trained and experienced in child care.
- Because there are multiple caregivers, there is built-in supervision.
- Typically, day-care centers offer a large variety of toys and books.
- As your baby gets older, the curriculum may be more structured, which might be a very stimulating and educational environment for your child.
- Toddlers have plenty of playmates.
- This option can be reasonably priced.

Disadvantages

- Generally, there is a higher baby-to-adult ratio, which is not ideal for a young baby.
- Your baby may be left to cry because staff members are attending to other children or because the center has a policy regarding baby "scheduling."
- Staff turnover and turnaround throughout the day are a concern because most babies do best when they bond with a single caretaker.
- Babies are exposed to numerous contagious illnesses from other children. (While this can be an annoying disadvantage, it may have a positive side. Some studies show that being exposed to germs early in life may help build a child's immune system.)
- When your baby gets sick, you will have to make alternative arrangements.
- Day-care centers usually are less flexible than relatives or home day cares regarding early or late dropoff and pickup times.

Becoming a Stay-at-Home or Work-at-Home Parent

Even if you have decided to return to work after your baby is born, keep the staying-home option open in case you change your mind. Assessing how you are going to feel about returning to work after your baby comes is difficult before the birth. And if staying home with Baby feels right and is financially possible for you, it's well worth considering. If you are returning to work primarily for the income, evaluate the costs of child care, transportation, bottles, a breast pump, work clothes, meals at work, parking, and other expenses; you may find that you won't be making as much in the way of salary as you originally thought. Weigh the intangible benefits, too—like fewer illnesses for Baby, plus convenience, less stress, more family time, and emotional benefits for both of you.

Working at home is another approach to being able to stay at home with your baby. The many options for working at home include telecommuting with your current employer, starting your own business, taking a position that allows at-home work, or taking in other children to watch.

Advantages

- Baby stays with the person she is most attached to—the person who loves her most deeply and passionately: you.
- You're free to raise your baby exactly the way you wish without concern or question from other caregivers.
- You get to experience all of your baby's milestones.
- Breastfeeding is much simpler if the mother stays at home.
- Baby gets all the advantages listed under in-home day care (no rushing, single caretaker, fewer germs).
- Parents don't have to deal with the job-versus-baby guilt that can develop when a parent works away from the baby.
- You can arrange schedules so that parents share Baby's care while each also works outside the home. This can result in lower cost, plus it gives both parents an opportunity to develop a bond with the baby.

Disadvantages

- Parents may lose career momentum if they take a substantial amount of time away from their jobs.
- Feelings of isolation, boredom, or lower self-esteem are possible risks.
- The decision might have financial consequences for the family.
- When parents arrange schedules around shared child care, this choice takes away from their time to be together as a couple.

Combinations

The preceding options represent the most common types of child care available, but many parents find a workable solution by combining them. Some possibilities include part-time work, work from home with a care-taker in the house (mother can take breaks for breastfeeding), a shared family home agreement with another family (you take their baby for half the time, and they take yours for half), or a shared nanny. Also, you can switch arrangements as your baby's and your own needs change. This may seem obvious, but many of us worry so much about our decisions! It's reassuring to know that the decisions you make aren't written in stone.

Parent Tip

"Trust your instincts. The very first child-care provider we had for our daughter seemed wonderful, but I had reservations. However, afraid that we wouldn't find another provider by the time I went back to work, I decided to give her a try anyway. That was the worst decision I ever made as a parent. We left after a particularly bad incident and found someone amazing in her place."

—**Leesa, mother of Kyra (26 months)**

How Can I Decide Which Option Is Best?

Recent studies show that, by far, the most significant factor in how well children do with child care is the *quality* of the child care, not the type. You must invest a lot of time and effort into determining, all things considered, which child-care option would offer the best quality for your baby. To do this, you need to read, ask, observe, check, calculate, think, and only then, decide:

• **Read** more information on the Internet and in books (see the suggestions under "For More Information"). Several websites have printable lists of interview questions and specific factors to consider.

• **Ask** questions of candidates in carefully prepared interviews, and of everyone else you can think of who might know something about child-care options in your area.

• **Observe** how the child-care provider(s) interact with your baby and/or other babies during the interview. If you're bringing your baby to someone else's home or a day-care center, look for how well the place is babyproofed (*see* Babyproofing), how clean it is, and what is available to keep baby entertained.

• **Check** facts, references, accreditation, and licensing. This is the time to find out everything you can so that you confidently trust your child-care provider later.

• **Calculate** which options are financially possible. The least expensive option is not necessarily the best; quality is the most important criterion.

• **Think** about what you want for your baby, for your family, and for yourself. Will you need flexibility? Do you want a child-care solution that doesn't require extra traveling? Do you feel strongly about how much individual attention your baby gets? Do you want your baby's caregiver to be supervised? What issues are most important to you and your baby?

• **Decide** on an option. Make sure you have confirmed when the child care is to start. Once Baby arrives, enjoy every single minute you have with her! Feel confident that you have made the best choice possible for your baby. And remember, if your child-care choice doesn't work out, you can make a change later.

How Do I Keep a Strong Bond with My Baby When I Work?

Many parents worry that their relationship with their baby will suffer once they return to work, but this does not have to be so. Here are some suggestions to maintain the bond:

• Use as many attachment parenting tools as you can (*see* Attachment Parenting). Some working parents like to co-sleep with their babies to make sure they get the physical contact they missed during the day (*see* Co-Sleeping, making it work). Breastfeeding mothers can pump their milk at work; if their baby is close by, they may even be able to leave work to breastfeed (*see also* Breastfeeding with Bottle-feeding Supplements).

• Stay involved with the events in Baby's life when you are not there. Don't rush in and out. Take the time to give the caregiver information or instructions in the morning, and when you return in the afternoon, ask questions. A daily diary is an excellent way to keep track of what your baby is doing. Ask the caregiver to note how well your baby ate and when her diapers were changed. Perhaps more important, have the caregiver jot down a few sentences about Baby's mood, the "tricks" she did, and the games she played. This diary will be a great treasure in later years (*see* Memories).

• Give your baby your undivided attention when you are together. The dishes can wait until Baby is asleep. Try as much as possible to savor the time that you have with your baby. Working parents have a unique understanding of how precious time is, so they typically treasure every moment with their baby!

For More Information

Books

American Red Cross. *Choosing Quality Child Care: How to Be Confident You Make the Right Choice: The American Red Cross Search Guide*, rev. ed. Madison, WI: American Red Cross, Badger Chapter, 2001.

Beauchemin, Cyndi L. *The Daycare Provider's Workbook*. West Linn, OR: TCB Enterprises, 1999.

Douglas, Ann. *The Unofficial Guide to Childcare*. New York: Macmillan, 1998.

Hernan, Frances Anne. *The ABC's of Hiring a Nanny: How to Find a Nanny Without Losing Your Mind*. Olathe, KS: McGavick Field Publishing, 2000.

Websites

BabyCenter.com
babycenter.com/childcare

Child Care Aware
childcareaware.org

National Child Care Information Center
nccic.org/faqs/choosecare.html

Choking

· · · · · · · · · · ·

See also: CPR; Emergencies

I took a CPR class, but I'm not sure if I'd remember the steps to take in an emergency. What should I do if my baby chokes on something?

Caution: The following brief summary is intended to be a refresher for parents who have learned first aid from a qualified professional. These instructions are not intended for use by an untrained person. If you have not taken an infant/child first-aid class, please sign up for one through your local hospital, doctor's office, YMCA, American Heart Association, or American Red Cross. These agencies also provide instruction charts that you can post in your home. Don't risk being uninformed if it ever comes to saving the life of your child or someone else's child.

If you have not taken a first-aid class or if you panic and cannot remember what to do, then call 911 (or your emergency number) and ask for step-by-step instructions.

Choking First Aid for Babies Under One Year Old

The following six steps summarize the procedure to follow if a child under one year old is choking.

Step 1: Determine the Problem
- If your baby can't cry, cough, or breathe, he may be choking. He may make noises, or his skin may look red or blue. If your baby is coughing, allow him to cough; this may dislodge the object. If he is not able to cough, you will need to help clear the airway.

- If another person is nearby, call out, "The baby is choking; call 911."
- If you suspect that an allergic reaction has caused your baby's throat to swell, then call 911 immediately.

Step 2: Give Five Back Blows
- Support your baby's head and neck, and hold him over your arm, keeping the head lower than the body.
- Give five blows to the back between the shoulder blades.

Step 3: Give Five Chest Thrusts
- Turn your baby over on your arm, supporting his head.
- Position two fingers in the center of the chest, one finger width below an imaginary line between the nipples.
- Give five chest thrusts.
- Stop if the baby begins to cough.

Step 4: Check Mouth and Sweep for Objects
- Check in your baby's mouth. If you see something, press down your baby's tongue, and sweep with your finger in an attempt to remove the object. Don't try to grab the object or push it.

Step 5: Call for Help, and Continue Back Blows and Chest Thrusts
- If your baby continues to choke, call 911 or shout, "Help! Call 911." Continue series of blows and thrusts. If you are alone, bring the baby to the phone with you.
- *If your baby is not breathing, follow the CPR instructions on page 141.*

Step 6: Call for Medical Assistance
- After you have removed the object, call 911 or your emergency number to report the incident and describe your baby's condition. Continued coughing, gagging, or wheezing can indicate that additional items are still blocking the airway.

Choking First Aid for Children Ages One to Three

If a child between the ages of one and three is unable to talk, cry, cough, or breathe, follow these five steps, which include the Heimlich maneuver (first aid for choking).

Step 1: Determine the Problem

- If your baby can't talk, cry, cough, or breathe, she may be choking. She may make noises, or her skin may look red or blue. If your baby is coughing, allow her to cough; this may dislodge the object. If she is not able to cough, you will need to help clear the airway.
- If another person is nearby, call out, "The baby is choking; call 911."
- If you suspect that an allergic reaction has caused your baby's throat to swell, call 911 immediately.

Step 2: Begin the Heimlich Maneuver Abdominal Thrusts

- Put your arms around your baby from behind. Place the heel of one hand against the baby's stomach, just over the navel. Put your other hand over your first, and thrust upward several times.

Step 3: Check Mouth and Sweep for Objects

- Check in your baby's mouth. If you see something, press down your baby's tongue, and sweep with your finger in an attempt to remove the object. Don't try to grab the object or push it.

Step 4: Call for Help, and Continue Heimlich Maneuver Abdominal Thrusts

- If your baby continues to choke, call 911 or shout, "Help! Call 911." Continue the series of blows and thrusts. If you are alone, bring the baby to the phone with you.
- *If your baby is not breathing, discontinue the Heimlich maneuver, and follow the CPR instructions on page 142.*

Step 5: Call for Medical Assistance

• After you have removed the object, call 911 or your emergency number to report the incident and describe your baby's condition. Continued coughing, gagging, or wheezing can indicate that additional items are still blocking the airway.

Circumcision Decision

· · · · · · · · · · · ·

See also: Genital Care

We are expecting a baby boy, and we need to decide whether or not to have him circumcised. What are the pros and cons of circumcision?

Learn About It

For some parents, circumcision has a deep religious significance; the procedure is central to establishing a newborn boy's identity. But for many other parents, the circumcision decision has become increasingly difficult. Thirty years ago, up to 90 percent of American newborn baby boys were circumcised; currently, around 60 percent are circumcised. On the West Coast, this figure has gone as low as 40 percent, and in parts of Canada, it is 25 percent and less. Worldwide, the uncircumcised penis is clearly the norm: in 85 percent of the world's male population, the penis is intact (uncircumcised).

Traditionally, many parents turn to the medical profession for advice, but the American Academy of Pediatrics (AAP) has made it clear that there is no right or wrong decision about circumcision. According to the AAP's Task Force on Circumcision (1999):

> Existing scientific evidence demonstrates potential medical benefits of newborn male circumcision; however, these data are not sufficient to recommend routine neonatal circumcision. In the case of circumcision, in which there are potential benefits and risks, yet the procedure is not essential to the child's current well-being, parents should determine what is in the best interest of the child. To make an informed choice, parents of all male infants should be given accurate and unbiased information and be provided the opportunity to discuss this decision.

The changing circumcision statistics and new information leave many parents in a quandary. This decision cannot be made overnight, and you are right to think about, research, and discuss the pros and cons of circumcision well before your baby is born. While this issue occasionally is highly sensationalized and passionately debated in the media, be sure to look as objectively as possible at the procedure, its history, and its potential benefits and risks. In the end, you are the only ones who can make the decision about what is best for your child.

An Explanation of Circumcision

Every physically normal male is born with a foreskin, or prepuce, that covers the glans (tip) of the penis. The inside of this foreskin is a mucous membrane similar to the inside of the cheek, with numerous nerve endings. The foreskin is thought to protect the glans and to keep it moist and clean.

During a circumcision, the physician removes the foreskin surrounding the glans. The procedure is normally performed within the first two weeks of life, because the risks of a circumcision are greater if the baby is more than two months old. There are several different surgical approaches, but the following is typical: The baby is put on his back, and his legs and feet are restrained. Then the foreskin is separated from the glans with a type of forceps (necessary because tight adhesions connect a baby's foreskin with his glans). Clamps hold the foreskin in place, a protective cover is put over the glans, the foreskin is pulled over the cover, and then about one-third to one half of the skin is cut off using a clamp. Antiseptic petroleum jelly may then be put on the penis to prevent irritation and infection. Complications are rare.

A History of Circumcision

So how did circumcision become such a routine procedure in the United States? And why are opinions changing? Circumcision has existed for thousands of years, going back to Egyptian times; it is typically an intricate part of religious faith for Jewish and Muslim families. In the United States, circumcision was not practiced widely, however,

until the late nineteenth century. Around the beginning of the twenti-
eth century, cleanliness became associated with wealth, and a circumcised penis was thought to be cleaner; about 25 percent of men were
circumcised at that point. In the 1930s, the military began requiring
circumcisions because soldiers in the field had little access to water, and
maintaining adequate personal cleanliness was difficult. Studies in the
1940s and 1950s (some of them questionable) showed medical advantages for circumcised men and their partners, and circumcision became
almost universal within the United States.

Circumcision has always carried an element of tradition. When the
father is circumcised, the parents want their son to "be like the father"
(or the brother, or the other boys in the locker room). This is probably
a key reason for the relatively high rates of circumcision in the United
States.

Opinion has started to change, however, and the rate of routine circumcision is decreasing. Recent studies have shown benefits of circumcision as well as risks, and the decision falls fully into the hands of
parents. The charts on the following pages look at arguments for and
against circumcision.

Pain Relief

One recommendation is abundantly clear: An infant undergoing a circumcision should receive pain relief. The ridiculous belief that infants
do not feel pain during circumcision has been completely refuted. The
American Academy of Pediatrics now recommends analgesia (pain
medication) for all circumcisions, as it is "both safe and effective." The
three primary forms of pain relief are a topical numbing cream
(EMLA), a dorsal penile nerve block (a local anesthetic injected into the
penis), and a subcutaneous ring block (also a local anesthetic).

Arguments Favoring (Nonreligious) Circumcision

Argument	Supporting Evidence	Opposing Evidence
Lower chance of urinary tract infection (UTI) in first year of life	Studies show that circumcised boys have a 1 in 1,000 chance of UTI, versus a 1 in 100 chance for uncircumcised boys.	UTIs are rare in boys and are easily treated.
Penile cancer prevention	Cancer of the penis is 3 times more common among uncircumcised men than circumcised men, among whom the disease is virtually nonexistent.	Penile cancer affects only 1 in 100,000 older men and is related to sexual behavior.
Lower risk of sexually transmitted diseases (STDs)	Some studies have shown that the risk of STDs, vaginal disorders in partners, and HIV are lower for circumcised men.	Risk is only slightly lower, and sexual behavior is a much better predictor of the frequency and type of STDs.
Cleanliness	Uncircumcised males risk infection of the foreskin.	Simple education about good hygiene virtually eliminates this risk.
Prevention of a more complicated circumcision later in life	There are sometimes medical reasons for circumcision, such as phimosis (a condition in which foreskin retraction is impossible). Post-infancy circumcisions are painful and carry a higher risk of complications.	Phimosis and other penile conditions requiring circumcision are not very common and not generally considered a valid reason for routine circumcision.

Argument	Supporting Evidence	Opposing Evidence
Belief that a son should "look like" his father	Some people worry that there may be confusion or even psychological problems if the father's penis is circumcised and the son's is not.	Boys won't necessarily "look like" their fathers in all ways anyway. Hair color, eye color, and body shape all may differ, as may the penis.
Worry about being "strange"	In the past, some adult men have requested circumcisions because they have heard from sexual partners that their penises were "strange," they were teased as children, or they felt embarrassed in locker room situations.	The statistics have changed so dramatically that, whatever your decision, your baby is unlikely to be considered "strange" in this regard, no matter what you decide. (In any case, children should be taught to respect individual differences.)

Arguments Favoring an Intact (Uncircumcised) Penis

Argument	Supporting Evidence	Opposing Evidence
Lack of a medical reason for the circumcision	There is no proven medical reason for removing the foreskin. Circumcision interferes with the way nature intended the body to be.	For full-term healthy infants, few risks are entailed in removing the foreskin, while there are some possible medical benefits.
Fear of complications	As with any surgery, risks are involved, including excessive bleeding, infections, and injury to the penis. There are also cosmetic concerns: the foreskin can be cut too long or too short or can heal improperly.	Complications are very rare. This is among the safest of surgical procedures, and cosmetic complaints are rare. The complication rate is thought to be 1 in 200 to 1 in 500.
Pain of the procedure and memory of the pain after the procedure	Studies show infants experience substantial pain from the procedure, as shown by increased heart rate and blood pressure. The "memory" of the pain lasts, as infants circumcised without analgesia have increased sensitivity to vaccinations at four months.	The AAP now recommends that some form of pain relief be used for all circumcisions. Complications from these pain medications are rare.

Argument	Supporting Evidence	Opposing Evidence
Possible risk of conditions that develop because a foreskin is not present.	When the foreskin is removed, the glans can become irritated, causing the opening of the penis to become too small. This may lead to urination difficulties and require surgery. Other possible conditions are tight, painful erections or adhesions and skin tags.	Penile problems developing on a circumcised penis are uncommon.
Worry about decreased sexual sensitivity	The glans might toughen up without its protective cover, and the penis is desensitized.	No study has shown that circumcised men experience less sexual pleasure.
Lack of consent for a potentially life-changing operation	The surgery is performed before the boy has the chance to choose for himself. This argument presumes that subjecting an infant to an unnecessary surgery that will change his body is unfair.	Later in life, circumcisions are more painful and dangerous. Parents have to make many decisions on behalf of their infants; that's the nature of parenthood.
Financial reasons	In some areas, insurance companies or Medicare will not cover the cost of the circumcision (viewing it as an elective procedure).	Costs may be covered by some insurance companies. Check with your provider to verify. The surgery is generally not expensive.

Circumcision Information Checklist

If you do decide to circumcise your son, use the following checklist to make sure everything goes as smoothly as possible:

☐ Have you discussed the issue with your doctor? Make sure you understand exactly what will happen during the operation, what type of pain relief will be used, and what the possible risks are of the surgery and of the analgesia (pain relief).

☐ Have you made sure that the right doctor will perform the surgery? Often your ob–gyn will do the circumcision, but pediatricians also perform the surgery. Especially in an area or hospital that doesn't have a high rate of circumcision, ask about the doctor's experience with circumcisions and the complication rate. If you are unhappy with your doctor's answers to your questions about the surgery or pain relief, or if you don't think your doctor has enough experience with circumcision, find another doctor to do the surgery. You are your child's advocate.

☐ Have you checked with your insurance company as to whether it will cover the surgery? Have you asked about the cost of the procedure?

☐ Have you written your wishes in a birth plan and read the consent form very carefully?

☐ Have you talked to your doctor and read the entry on Genital Care in this book so that you know what to expect as the circumcision wound heals?

Cloth Diapers

. . . .

See also: Diaper Rash; Diapers: Cloth or Disposable?; Rash

I'm due to have my baby in a few months. I'm thinking of using cloth diapers, but aren't they a lot of work?

Learn About It

Cloth diapering actually can be very simple. There are several different ways to diaper a baby in cloth and several reasons why you should consider using cloth diapers.

Why Use Cloth?

Cloth diapers may be gentler on the environment than disposables. A baby can use more than 5,000 disposable diapers from birth through potty training, which makes these the third largest single product in the waste stream after newspapers and beverage containers. This is certainly something to consider when you're making a diapering decision.

Another benefit of cloth diapers is that they can save your family money, especially when the diapers are passed on from one child to another. Depending on the kind of diapers and accessories you purchase, you could save hundreds of dollars.

Cloth diapers also can be beneficial for children who are sensitive to chemicals and other substances or who are prone to diaper rash (although some sensitive-bottomed babies do as well with moisture-wicking disposables). With older babies, another benefit of cloth diapers is that they can ease potty learning because children can tell when they are wet.

113

The bottom line (excuse the pun) with choosing which kind of diapers your family uses is that it's a personal choice. Cloth diapers are a good choice for many families (*see* Diapers: Cloth or Disposable?).

How to Cloth-Diaper Your Baby

The methods used are as unique as the children being diapered. The following outline of the types of cloth diapers and diaper covers most commonly available summarizes the benefits and drawbacks of each. Space doesn't permit a discussion of *every* type here. But if you like one feature of a diaper and not another, you'll find many more kinds on the Internet or through diaper distributors.

Types of Cloth Diapers

There are many types of cloth diapers to choose from. Weigh the benefits and drawbacks of each to select the kind (or kinds) that is right for you.

Flat Diapers. A flat diaper is essentially a big piece of fabric (about the size of a dish towel or slightly larger) that you fold down to fit your baby.

Benefits: Very inexpensive; can be made easily at home; can be folded differently as baby grows; can be passed down to siblings of any size

Drawbacks: Have to be folded before use; need pins, diaper covers, or other product to secure diaper to baby

Prefolds and Diaper-Service-Quality Prefolds. Prefolded diapers are just what they sound like: diapers that are already folded. Diaper-service-quality diapers are rectangular and have extra layers sewn down their middle thirds. They generally come in newborn, regular, and toddler sizes.

Benefits: Already folded and ready for use; very durable; fit most babies very well

Drawbacks: Slightly more expensive than flat diapers; fit only a certain size range; need pins, diaper covers, or other product to secure diaper to baby

Fitted Diapers. Fitted diapers are already sewn to fit the baby. They typically have snaps or Velcro fasteners to secure them and have extra layers of fabric sewn down the middle for absorbency.

Benefits: Very convenient; easy to use; no pins involved

Drawbacks: More expensive; may take longer to dry; may not provide as custom a fit as flat or prefolded diapers

All-in-Ones. A type of fitted diapers, all-in-ones already have a diaper cover sewn onto their outside.

Benefits: Most convenient; easiest to use; no pins involved

Drawbacks: Most expensive; can be bulky; may take longer to dry

All of these diapers can be passed on to younger siblings or resold if still in good condition. All types except the all-in-ones require a cover to contain leaks.

Types of Diaper Covers

Most cloth diapers require some type of diaper cover. To help you choose, review the benefits and drawbacks of each.

Pull-On Plastic Pants. Most people of my generation were covered with pull-on plastic pants. They're plastic, pull-on covers just big enough to cover the diaper area.

Benefits: Inexpensive; easy to use; easy to launder

Drawbacks: Often poor quality; don't last very long; not breathable

Wrap-Style Covers. The many versions of wrap-style covers wrap around the baby and are secured in front with Velcro fasteners or snaps. They can be made out of plastic, nylon, or nylon/taffeta.

> **Benefits:** Can be inexpensive; very easy to use; easy to launder; usually last a very long time; some have "vents" so Baby's bottom gets air

> **Drawbacks:** Slightly more expensive than plastic pants

Other Types. Less popular (but becoming more widely used) are wool, fleece, and some other unusual materials. Untreated wool is naturally waterproof, breathes well, and is not scratchy like a wool sweater. Wool covers come in wrap or pull-on styles and usually require special laundering, but they're worth it since they don't need to be washed very often. Fleece covers are usually wrap style, warm, and good for heavy wetters.

What to Buy

You'll probably need two to three dozen of whatever type of diaper you choose, plus six to eight covers to go with them. A baby who is a heavy wetter may need to wear two diapers at night, so you may want to purchase one or two larger covers as well. Also, you'll need to replace the diapers and covers with bigger ones as the baby grows and as the covers wear out.

How Do I Care for My Cloth Diapers?

Unless you have a special type of diaper cover (like wool), you'll be able to wash the diapers and covers together. Get a diaper pail or garbage can with a lid, and toss the diapers in there as they're dirtied. With a breastfed baby, you won't have much worry about smell; before your breastfed baby starts solids, you won't need to rinse dirty ones, either. For a formula-fed baby or after the baby starts solids, dump the solid part of the bowel movement in the toilet first. You don't need any water in your pail (in fact, it could be a drowning hazard).

When wash time comes, use a gentle detergent and no bleach. Bleach ruins diapers and can be bad for your baby's skin. Do one cold wash or rinse and then a hot wash to kill the germs. Do an extra rinse if your baby has sensitive skin. Most covers can be dried with your diapers, though they'll last longer if they're hung to dry. If you want to get any stains out, hang your diapers out in the sun for a few hours.

Where Do I Buy Cloth Diapers?

Quality diapers are found at many reputable Internet sites, such as greenmountaindiaper.com, borntolove.com, mother-ease.com, and many other such sites. If you buy from these websites, you can support work-at-home moms, too; the sites mentioned are run by moms at home. Many sites have sales and seconds pages. You also can buy diapers and covers in many of the same stores that carry baby clothes and baby supplies.

Colds

See also: Allergies and Asthma; Cough; Croup; Ear Infections; Fever

> *My baby's only a year old, and this is the second time she has come down with a cold. What should I do to help her feel better? How can I prevent her from getting sick again?*

Learn About It

Colds are caused by more than 200 different viruses and are easily transferred from person to person. Babies are more vulnerable to colds because their immune systems are still developing. No matter how healthy your baby is, she'll have her share of colds.

What Are the Symptoms of a Cold?

While we all know what a cold is, some symptoms are similar to other health problems, such as allergies, croup, or flu. If your baby has a common cold, you'll notice a combination of two or more of these particular signs and symptoms:

- Runny nose (discharge begins as clear and thin and may become thick and yellow)
- Sneezing
- Coughing
- Nasal congestion
- Sore throat
- Slight fever
- Watery eyes

• Tiredness
• Lack of appetite

What About Medication?

Cold symptoms are the result of the body's immune response to a cold. For example, we produce extra mucus in the nose and throat to catch and remove the virus, and we cough to remove mucus from the respiratory tract. Because of this, we don't necessarily want to impede the body's natural defense system. For instance, unless the cough is dry, preventing sleep, or making it difficult for a baby to breathe or eat, we don't want to suppress this important function.

The common cold has no cure. All science can offer right now is medicine that relieves the symptoms. Experts recommend that you *never* give your baby over-the-counter medications for colds unless your pediatrician directs you to do so. Then measure and administer these exactly as your doctor advises (*see* Medicine, giving).

The Biggest Problem for Babies: Stuffy Noses

Since young babies drink their food, either by breast or bottle, and find comfort in sucking, a stuffy nose makes your sick baby doubly miserable. Since your baby can't grab a tissue and blow his nose, he'll rely on you to help him clear out enough mucus so he can drink and suck somewhat comfortably. Here are a few tips that can help you help your baby:

• Clear your baby's nose using this two-step process: Squeeze a mist of saline nose drops into your baby's nose. This will thin and loosen the mucus. Then, use a clean rubber bulb syringe and a tissue to gently pull mucus from his nose. (Follow the directions on the bulb syringe package or ask your doctor for a demonstration.)
• Let your baby spend several sessions a day in a room with moist air, by using either a cold-air humidifier or the bathroom shower. (Avoid using a hot-air humidifier because these can pose a burn hazard to your baby or older children.)

Parent Tip

"Turn the shower on in the bathroom, plug the tub, and let the hot water run for a few minutes. Shake a few drops of lavender and eucalyptus oils into the tub, and step into the bathroom with your baby. The steam, along with the soothing and refreshing vapors, does wonders for a stuffy nose and congested lungs. Bring a few books, and spend some quiet play and cuddle time together. Just have lots of soft tissues on hand so you can catch the drips! When the water cools off some, it's the right temperature for a bath. Then your baby can sit in the vapors, and he gets a nice, warm bath, too."*

—Carol, mother of Ben (2)

*Never leave your baby alone in a room with a filled tub.

• Elevate your baby's head during sleep time by raising one end of the mattress or letting her sleep in a stroller, car seat, sling, or your arms. Or let her sleep lying on your chest while you recline in a lounge chair.

How to Help Your Baby Feel Better

Babies tend to be unhappy and fussy when they have colds. They don't feel good, but they don't know why. Try the following ways to help your baby feel better:

• Let your baby rest. Put off running errands, having visitors, or doing anything else that disrupts your baby's quiet recovery time. This also helps *you* stay calm and peaceful so that you can help your baby recover.

• Give lots of fluids. Your baby will feel better and will avoid the dangers of dehydration. If you are breastfeeding, nurse frequently, since breastmilk is a premium fluid. An older baby who usually eats solids may lose her appetite but desire more nursing sessions, for comfort as well as nutrition. If your baby drinks from a bottle or cup, provide lots of breastmilk, formula, juice, and water. For older babies, you can add frozen pops, soup, ice chips, and specially formulated hydration fluids (*see also* Dehydration).

• Treat a fever with acetaminophen (such as Infant's Tylenol), ibuprofen (such as Infant's Advil), or a homeopathic medicine, like belladonna, chamomile, or valerian, with your medical provider's approval. Never give a baby aspirin, since it has been associated with Reye's syndrome, a rare but serious illness. If your baby is comfortable, then a mild fever may not require treatment (*see* Fever).

• Put salve, petroleum jelly, or lip balm on a nose and upper lip that are red or sore from a runny nose. Use a small amount so that you don't further plug your baby's nostrils.

• Keep your baby away from secondhand cigarette smoke. Children who are exposed to cigarette smoke tend to have more frequent colds as well as the related problems of ear infections, bronchitis, pneumonia, and sinus infections.

• Pamper and cuddle. The harder you try to accomplish your regular routine when your baby is sick, the fussier she will be (and the more frustrated *you* will be). Your baby is feeling bad, and the one thing that makes her feel better is your tender loving care. Go ahead and put everything nonessential on hold for a day or two to give your baby some extra nurturing.

• Encourage as much sleep as possible. Do the things that work best to help your baby nap and sleep well, and scale back on any efforts you've been making to encourage sleeping through the night if these disrupt either your sleep or your baby's sleep. Once your baby recovers, you can go back to working toward better sleep, understanding that any sickness will disrupt your baby's developing sleep patterns and take some time to overcome.

• Provide distractions. Older babies often can be distracted from their achy symptoms with a walk outdoors, games, and nonstrenuous activities.

When to Call the Doctor

Most colds peak after the first day or two, begin to subside after four or five days, and then disappear within a week or two. Occasionally, though, a cold will lead to an infection such as strep throat, bronchitis, or an ear infection. These secondary infections require more aggressive treatment than a regular cold, such as the use of a prescribed antibiotic. Following is a list of signs that your baby may be facing an infection or other problem. It's time to call the doctor if you observe any of these signs:

- Your baby is younger than three months old and has *any* cold symptoms.
- Your baby is having difficulty breathing, even after you clear her nose.
- The cold doesn't improve after a week.
- Cold symptoms subside, but other symptoms, such as coughing, appear or linger.
- Your baby seems to have ear pain (such as crying when lying flat).
- Your baby has a sudden or disturbing change in temperament, such as extreme fussiness and crying or sleepiness and lethargy.
- Your baby is refusing fluids.

How to Ward Off Colds

We can't avoid cold viruses completely, but the following tips can help you ward off a few or reduce their efficient spread throughout your family:

- **Be diligent about washing your hands** after changing diapers, blowing your nose, using the toilet, and before handling food or touching your baby. Keep your baby's hands clean, too. And encourage others who hold your baby to wash their hands first. Germs are spread most easily though the touch of hands.
- **Keep your distance from people who are obviously sick with a cold.** Cold germs spread easily and quickly to babies. Be more diligent during the first few months of life, but after that, you don't have

to be obsessive about it. Children gain immunities when they are exposed to and have colds, so you don't have to live in a bubble.

• **Don't share toothbrushes, eating utensils, food, or drinking cups** with other people, and teach your children this important rule from a young age. A soggy cracker passed from hand to hand passes germs along with it, too.

• **Breastfeed your baby for as long as you can.** Breastmilk provides your baby with a tremendous supply of antibodies for good health, among many other benefits.

• **Make sure that you and your family eat right.** Your body will function better and fight off illness more easily if you are nourishing it with a proper diet.

Colic

· · · · · · · · · · · ·

See also: Burping; Crying; Spitting Up; Vomiting

My baby is very fussy and cries a lot, mostly at the end of the day. Does she have colic? Is there a cure?

Learn About It

You may have heard the term *colic* applied to any baby who cries a great deal. Not all crying babies have colic, but all colicky babies cry—and they cry hard. They may stiffen their little bodies or curl up as if in pain. They may cry so hard they don't seem to even know you are there. When babies cry like this, they take in a lot of air, which creates gas and more pain, which makes them cry even more.

Researchers are still unsure of colic's exact cause. Some experts believe that colic is related to the immaturity of a baby's digestive system. Others theorize that a baby's immature nervous system and inability to handle the constant sensory stimulation that surrounds her cause a breakdown by the end of the day, when colic most often occurs.

Dr. Harvey Karp, in his book *The Happiest Baby on the Block* (Bantam Books, 2002), introduces a new theory. He believes that babies are born three months too early and that some babies find their new world too difficult to handle. They yearn for the comforting conditions that occurred in the womb.

Whatever the cause, and it may be a combination of all the theories; colic is among the most exasperating conditions that parents of new babies face. Colic occurs only to newborn babies, up to about four to five months of age. These are some of the symptoms:

- A regular period of nonstop, inconsolable crying, typically late in the day

- Crying bouts that last one to three hours or more
- A healthy and happy disposition at all other times of the day

Can Colic Be Prevented?

Given that we aren't sure what causes colic, we don't know if it can be prevented. Even if you do everything "right" and take all the steps to discourage colic, it still may happen. If you think your baby has colic, talk with your pediatrician and take your baby in for a checkup to rule out any medical cause for your baby's crying. If your baby is given a clean bill of health, then you'll know colic is the culprit in the daily crying bouts.

Since colic occurs in newborns, parents often feel that they are doing something wrong to create the situation. Their vulnerability and lack of experience puts them in the position of questioning their own ability to take care of their baby. Hearing your baby cry with colic and not knowing why it's happening or what to do about it is painful. I know this because one of my four children suffered with colic. Although many years have passed since then (Angela is now fifteen), I remember it vividly. Hearing my baby cry night after night and not knowing how to help her was gut wrenching, heartbreaking, and frustrating. The most important piece of research I discovered was this: *It's not your fault.* Any baby can have colic.

Things That May Help Your Baby

Remember that nothing you do will eliminate colic *completely* until your baby's system is mature and able to settle on its own. That said, experienced parents and professionals can offer ways to help your baby through this time—ask around! I did, and from what I uncovered, I compiled the following suggestions for helping your baby feel better. Look for patterns to your baby's crying; these can provide clues as to which suggestions are most likely to help. Stick with an idea for a few days to see if it helps. Watch for any signs of improvement (not necessarily complete quiet). If the particular course of action doesn't seem to change anything, don't get discouraged, just try something else:

- If breastfeeding, feed on demand (cue feeding), for nutrition as well as comfort, as often as your baby needs a calming influence.
- If breastfeeding, try avoiding foods that may cause gas in your baby. Eliminate one possible cause for a few days, and see if it makes a difference. The most common baby tummy offenders are dairy products, caffeine, cabbage, broccoli, and other gassy vegetables. But don't assume the culprit, if there is one, will be obvious: I know one mother whose baby reacted loudly and consistently after any meal that included eggplant, asparagus, or onions.
- If bottlefeeding, offer more frequent but smaller meals. Experiment with different formulas, with your doctor's approval.
- If bottlefeeding, try different types of bottles and nipples that prevent air from entering your baby as he drinks, such as those with curved bottles or collapsible liners.
- Hold your baby in a more upright position for bottlefeeding and directly after a feeding.
- Experiment with how often and when you burp your baby (*see* Burping).
- Offer meals in a quiet setting.
- If your baby likes a pacifier, offer one.
- Invest in a baby sling or carrier, and use it during colicky periods.
- If the weather's too unpleasant for an outside stroll, bring your stroller in the house and walk your baby around inside.
- Give your baby a warm bath.
- Place a warm towel or wrapped water bottle on Baby's tummy (taking caution that the temperature is warm but not hot).
- Hold your baby with her legs curled up toward her belly.
- Massage your baby's tummy, or give him a full massage (*see* Massage).
- Swaddle your baby in a warm blanket (*see* Swaddling).
- Lay your baby tummy down across your lap, and massage or pat her back.
- Hold your baby in a rocking chair, or put him in a swing.
- Walk with Baby in a quiet, dark room while you hum or sing.
- Try keeping your baby away from highly stimulating situations during the day when possible to prevent sensory overload, and understand that a particularly busy day may mean a fussier evening.

- Lie on your back, lay your baby on top of your tummy, face down, and massage his back. (Transfer your baby to his bed if he falls asleep.)
- Take Baby for a ride in the car.
- Play soothing music, turn on white noise such as a vacuum cleaner or running water, or play a CD of nature sounds.
- As a last resort, ask your doctor about medications available for colic and gas.

Tips for Coping

As difficult as colic is for a baby, it is just as challenging for the parents. This challenge can be especially hard for a mother who has other children to care for, has returned to work, or is suffering from the baby blues or postpartum depression (*see* Baby Blues; Postpartum Depression). Even if everything else in life is perfect, colic is taxing. To take some of the stress out of these colicky times, here are a few things you can do for yourself:

- Know that your baby *will* cry during his colicky time, and while you can do things to make your baby more comfortable, nothing you can do will totally stop the crying. Your baby's crying is *not* a result of anything you've done or not done.
- Plan outings for the times of day when Baby is usually happy, or if outings keep your baby happy, plan them for the colicky times.
- Take advantage of another person's offer to take a turn with the baby, even if it's just so you can take a quiet bath or shower.
- Keep reminding yourself that this problem is only temporary; it will pass.
- Avoid keeping a long to-do list right now; do only what's most important.
- Talk to other parents of colicky babies so you can share ideas and comfort each other.
- If the crying is getting to you and making you tense or angry, put your baby in his crib, or give him to someone else to hold for a while so that you don't accidentally shake or harm your baby. Shaking a baby can cause permanent brain damage,

so if you feel angry (and colic can do that to you), put your baby down.

- Know that babies do not suffer long-term harm from having colic.

When Should I Call the Doctor?

Anytime you are worried about your baby, call your doctor. That goes for anything concerning your precious little one. In the case of colic, be sure to make that call if you notice any of the following signs:

- Your baby's crying is accompanied by vomiting.
- Your baby is not gaining weight.
- The colicky behavior lasts longer than four months.
- Your baby seems to be in pain.
- Your baby has a fever.
- Your baby doesn't want to be held or handled.
- The crying spree isn't limited to one bout in the evening.
- Your baby does not have regular bowel movements or wet diapers.
- You notice other problems that don't appear on the previous list of symptoms.
- Your baby's crying is making you angry or depressed (*see* Postpartum Depression).

For More Information

Books

Karp, Harvey. *The Happiest Baby on the Block*. New York: Bantam Books, 2002.

Sears, William, and Martha Sears. *The Fussy Baby: How to Bring Out the Best in Your High-Need Child*, rev. ed. Schaumburg, IL: La Leche League International, 2002.

Constipation

See also: Allergies and Asthma; Colic; Dehydration; Diarrhea; Solid Foods, introducing

How do I know if my baby is constipated? He hasn't had a poopy diaper in two days, but he's acting normally. Should I be concerned?

Learn About It

Baby poop is a topic no parent ever expects to become a major point of conversation among polite company. Who would ever guess the interest we'd take in our babies' diaper deposits? Oh, but we do . . .

The Definition of Constipation

Contrary to what many people think, constipation is not as much about frequency as it is the pattern and type of movements. Any baby may fuss, grunt, or get red in the face when having a bowel movement. This by itself does not signal constipation.

Constipation is a condition in which stools are hard and dry, and elimination is painful. Another sign that may indicate constipation is a change in normal bowel habits.

Diaper Counting

There is a wide range of "normal" when it comes to babies' bowel movements, but there are some typical patterns. These differ with your baby's diet. Whether he is exclusively breastfed, drinking all or some of his meals as formula, or eating solids will have a direct impact (pardon the pun) on what you find in his diapers.

Breastfed Babies

A newborn breastfed baby typically sports a messy diaper soon after every feeding. The very first poops are meconium, a thick, sticky, dark-colored substance. After the first week, this gradually changes color and texture to a yellow, mustardlike consistency (although variations in color from green to brown also are normal). Because your baby's digestive system is perfectly fashioned to digest breastmilk (and breastmilk is perfectly suited to your infant's nutritional needs and digestive ability), your baby's body quickly and easily breaks it down without much fuss, so there is usually little need to count messy diapers with a breastfed baby.

Bear in mind that every breastfed baby has his own variable poop schedule: Some breastfed babies have five bowel movements a day, while some go two to four days without a stool. On occasion, some breastfed babies don't poop for even longer than that, but when they finally *do* go, they more than make up for lost time! (If your baby is going a longer period between bowel movements, make certain you're seeing a usual amount of wet diapers—around six to eight cloth diapers a day or four to five disposables a day—and that your baby is acting normally. If you have any doubt at all, call your pediatrician.)

If your young baby is wetting his diapers regularly, nursing exclusively and frequently, acting happy and energetic, and growing normally, there's usually little reason to be concerned about how much or how often he messes his diapers.

In an older breastfed baby, you'll probably notice a regular pattern of elimination—perhaps once or twice each day—especially after you introduce solid food. If your baby hasn't had a messy diaper in a while, a little extra breastfeeding usually solves the problem.

Formula-Fed Babies

A newborn baby who is drinking formula will have five to ten stools per day. He will gradually reduce these to about four a day by four or five weeks old. By about two months old, many babies have one messy diaper each day, although it's normal to skip a day or have several in the same day. A formula-fed baby's stools will be pasty and firm, almost like peanut butter, and they will be yellow, brown, or tan, although green, brown, and gray are popular colors as well.

If your baby gets constipated, his stool will get harder and may look like little pebbles. He may not have a stool for three or four days. When this happens, have him checked by your pediatrician, who may talk to you about the type of formula you are using and how often your baby is feeding. Your doctor may recommend a change in formula, number of feedings, or frequency of feedings.

Babies Who Are Eating Solids

When you first start your baby on solid food, you likely will see an immediate change in the type and frequency of her stools, and they will have more odor. Their consistency will change, too, becoming firmer or, occasionally, more runny. As your baby eats more and more solid food, her stools will begin to look more like yours. Keep in mind that certain first foods can cause constipation; if you balance those with non-constipating foods, your baby's elimination pattern may smooth out.

Food That Might Cause Constipation

- Bananas
- Rice cereal
- Applesauce
- Soy
- Cheese

Foods That Make Stool Softer

- Peaches
- Plums
- Prunes or prune juice
- Apricots
- Pears
- Apple juice
- Water
- Breastmilk

Natural Ways to Ease Constipation

Never give a baby any kind of laxative, unless you are directed to do so by a physician. Avoid using corn syrup, as this can harbor minute botulism spores; while insignificant to an adult, these can be dangerous to a baby. Avoid inserting anything into your baby's rectum (as in the old method of using a thermometer to encourage elimination); this can interfere with the normal development of the muscles used in elimination.

There are many natural, gentle ways to help a baby back to her normal schedule of elimination. If your baby is having a hard time passing her stools or it has been a while since she's had a messy diaper, try some of these ideas:

- Give your baby a soothing, warm bath.
- Gently massage your baby's belly.
- Lay your baby on her back and "exercise" her legs, bending them up and down toward her tummy.
- For a baby who is eating solid foods, decrease those that cause constipation, and add those that soften the stool.
- If your baby's hard stools are irritating her rectum, apply some petroleum jelly, diaper ointment, or aloe vera lotion on the outside of her rectum to soothe it.

When to Call the Doctor

Call the doctor if your baby is constipated and you observe any of the following signs:

- Your baby isn't gaining weight and growing.
- Your baby's diapers aren't wet on a regular basis (*see* Dehydration).
- Your baby is acting sick.
- Your baby cries hard when having a bowel movement.
- Your baby's stools are very watery or contain mucus or blood.
- Your baby's stomach is hard or swollen.
- Your baby has repeated bouts of constipation.

Co-Sleeping, making it work

See also: Attachment Parenting; Marriage; Sleep, newborn; Sleep, four months and over

We're expecting our first baby soon and thinking about using a family bed. We've done a lot of research on the whys—and there's lots of information out there. But what about the practical tips? How do we set things up?

Learn About It

The family bed, co-sleeping, shared sleep—no matter what you call it, it means that your baby sleeps with you or very close to you. The family bed is customary the world round and is becoming more and more common in the United States, Canada, and Europe (or perhaps it has always been common but more people are now talking about it). Sharing sleep is very popular with parents (particularly nursing mothers) of young babies who wake throughout the night, since it allows parents to avoid getting up out of bed and traveling up and down a dark hallway. Co-sleeping is popular also with parents of older babies who enjoy the nighttime closeness with their child.

There are as many different styles of family beds as there are families! Here are a few of the typical sleeping arrangements:

- **The family bed:** Parents and baby sleep together in one bed, usually king-sized.
- **Side-by-side:** The child sleeps on a separate mattress or futon on the floor next to the parents' bed.

- **Sidecar:** A cradle or crib is nestled adjacent to the parents' bed, sometimes with one side of the crib removed and the crib tightly secured to the parents' bed.
- **Shared room:** The baby and parents have separate beds in the same room.

The use of these arrangements varies from home to home also. The following sleep situations are common:

- **Shared sleep** means the mother sleeps with the baby during the night and for naps.
- **Part-time shared sleep** is shared sleep for either naps or nighttime only, or for some of both. The baby sleeps in a crib, cradle, or other place at other sleep times.
- **Mom's dual beds** provide one place where Mommy sleeps with the baby and another where she sleeps with her husband. She moves back and forth between beds based on how often the baby wakes up and how tired she is on any given night.
- **Musical beds** are an arrangement with several beds in different rooms; parents and baby shift from place to place depending on each evening's situation.
- **Occasional family bed** is when the baby has her own crib or bed but is welcomed into the parents' bed whenever she has a bad dream, feels sick, or needs some extra cuddle time.
- **Sibling bed** is often a natural follow-up to the family bed. Older children share sleep after they outgrow the need for the parents' bed or the sidecar arrangement.

How to Decide

Every family has different nighttime needs. There is no single best arrangement that works for all babies and parents. Even within a family, there may be several "right" options to choose from. The key is to find the solution that feels right to everyone in *your* family.

It's very important to eliminate your need or desire to satisfy anyone else's perception of what you *should* be doing. In other words, no matter what your in-laws, your neighbors, your pediatrician, or your favorite author says about sleeping arrangements, the only "right" answer is the one that works for the people living in your home.

When to Make Changes

Sleeping situations tend to go through a transformation process throughout the early years of a baby's life. Some families make a conscious decision to co-sleep with their babies until they feel that their children are ready for independent sleeping. Some families make modifications as their babies begin to sleep better at night. Other families move their babies to cribs to accommodate a need for private sleep. The best advice is, go with the flow—and make adjustments according to what works best for you.

Co-Sleeping Safety Checklist

If your baby sleeps with you, either for naps or at nighttime, you should adhere to the following safety guidelines:

☐ Your bed must be absolutely safe for your baby. The best choice is to place the mattress on the floor, making sure there are no crevices that your baby can become wedged in. Make certain your mattress is flat, firm, and smooth. Do not allow your baby to sleep on a soft surface such as a waterbed, sofa, pillow-top mattress, or any other flexible surface.

☐ Make certain that your fitted sheets stay secure and cannot be pulled loose.

☐ If your bed is raised off the floor, use mesh guardrails to prevent Baby from rolling off the bed, and be especially careful that there is no space between the mattress and headboard or footboard. (Some guardrails designed for older children are not safe for babies because they have spaces that could entrap babies.)

☐ If your bed is placed against a wall or against other furniture, check every night to be sure there is no space between the mattress and wall or furniture where Baby could become stuck.

☐ Infants should be placed between their mother and the wall or guardrail. Fathers, siblings, grandparents, and baby-sitters don't have the same instinctual awareness of a baby's location as mothers do. Mothers, pay attention to your own sensitivity to Baby. Your little one should be able to awaken you with a minimum of movement or noise. If you find that you are such a deep sleeper that you only wake when your baby lets out a loud cry, you should seriously consider moving Baby out of your bed, perhaps into a cradle or crib near your bedside.

☐ Use a mattress that is large enough to provide ample room for everyone's movement.

☐ Consider a sidecar arrangement in which Baby's crib or cradle sits directly beside the main bed as one option.

☐ Make certain that the room your baby sleeps in, and any room he might have access to, is child-safe. (Imagine your baby crawling out of bed to explore the house as you sleep. Even if he has not done this yet, you can be certain he eventually will!)

☐ Do not ever sleep with your baby if you have been drinking alcohol, have used any drugs or medications, are an especially sound sleeper, or are suffering from sleep deprivation and find it difficult to awaken.

☐ Do not sleep with your baby if you are a large person, as a parent's excess weight has been determined to pose a risk to baby in a co-sleeping situation. While I cannot give a specific ratio of parent's weight to baby's weight, you can examine how you and Baby settle in next to each other. If Baby rolls toward you, if there is a large dip in the mattress, or if you suspect any other dangerous situation, play it safe and move Baby to a bedside crib or cradle.

☐ Remove all pillows and blankets during the early months. Use extreme caution when adding pillows or blankets as your baby gets older. Dress Baby and yourselves warmly. (A tip for breastfeeding moms: Wear an old turtleneck or T-shirt, cut up the middle to the neckline, as an undershirt for extra warmth.) Keep in mind that body heat will add warmth during the night. Make sure your baby doesn't become overheated.

☐ Do not wear any nightclothes with strings or long ribbons. Don't wear jewelry to bed, and if your hair is long, put it up.

☐ Don't use strong-smelling perfumes or lotions that may affect your baby's delicate senses.

☐ Do not allow pets to sleep in bed with your baby.

☐ Never leave your baby alone in an adult bed unless it is perfectly safe (for example, placing Baby on a mattress on the floor in a childproof room, when you are nearby or listening in with a reliable baby monitor).

☐ As of the writing of this book, there are no proven safety devices for use in protecting a baby in an adult bed. However, as a result of the great number of parents who wish to sleep safely with their babies, a number of new inventions are beginning to appear in baby catalogs and stores. You may want to look into some of these nests, wedges, and cradles.

For More Information

Books

Gordon, Jay, and Maria Goodavage. *Good Nights: The Happy Parents' Guide to the Family Bed (and a Peaceful Night's Sleep)*. New York: Griffin Trade Paperback, 2002.

Pantley, Elizabeth. *The No-Cry Sleep Solution: Gentle Ways to Help Your Baby Sleep Through the Night*. Chicago: McGraw-Hill/Contemporary Books, 2002.

Sears, William. *Nighttime Parenting: How to Get Your Baby and Child to Sleep*, rev. ed. New York: Plume, 1999.

Cough

See also: Allergies and Asthma; Choking; Colds; CPR; Croup;
Emergencies; Fever

How can I tell if my baby's cough is from a cold, an allergy, or something else?

Learn About It

Coughing is a sign of many different types of illnesses or health problems. You often can tell why your baby is coughing based on the sound of the cough and the other signs he may be demonstrating.

When to Be Concerned About Coughing

Coughing sometimes indicates a problem that requires prompt medical attention. Here are two examples of situations when you should be concerned:

- **Your baby is younger than four months old.** Newborn babies don't cough very much. When they do, they require medical evaluation. Call your doctor and explain the situation so that you can learn what to do next.
- **The cough is caused by something caught in your baby's throat.** Did your baby begin coughing directly after eating? Did your baby suddenly start coughing while playing with small toys? Is your baby's face turning red while she coughs? Is the cough sudden and the only sign of a problem? If your baby is coughing and can breathe, don't interfere. Watch carefully to see if the object is coughed up. If your baby cannot breathe or cough, follow standard infant choking procedures (page 101) or CPR (page 141), which include turning your baby

over and delivering blows between the shoulder blades. Call 911 or an emergency service.

• **The coughing is severe and constant.** If your baby is having coughing fits and coughing forcefully, it's important to talk to a doctor and determine what is causing the coughing.

• **The coughing is accompanied by difficulty breathing.** A baby who is having a hard time breathing along with the cough may have croup (*see* Croup) or another virus that requires medical care.

• **The cough is lingering.** If your baby has been coughing for a week or more and the cough just won't go away, call your pediatrician for advice.

• **Your baby has a fever along with a cough.** A combination of fever and cough often signals a virus. It's a good idea to look for other symptoms of illness and call your doctor if you suspect more than a simple cold or flu.

Other Possible Reasons for a Cough

Many common illnesses, such as a cold (*see* Colds) or flu, include coughing among their signs. More complicated health problems, like pneumonia and bronchitis, also are accompanied by coughing. Children who have asthma and allergies cough, too (*see* Allergies and Asthma). When your baby coughs, look for other signs to help determine the reason for her coughing. Listen as your baby coughs, so you can describe it to your doctor: Does the cough sound wet or dry? Rattling, explosive, or barklike? Persistent or occasional? The type and cause of the cough will determine the treatment that your doctor will recommend.

CPR (Cardiopulmonary Resuscitation)

See also: Choking; Emergencies

I've taken a CPR class, but I'm wondering if what I learned applies to babies as well as adults.

Learn About It

Cardiopulmonary resuscitation (CPR) is emergency care given to someone who has stopped breathing. In giving CPR to a child, the specific steps differ according to the child's age, so if you've learned only adult CPR, you need to take a class regarding CPR for children. It's important to learn this procedure in case someone you love stops breathing. You need to prepare yourself for this situation and learn the procedure in advance, because when a child stops breathing, it's too late to learn.

Caution: The following brief summary is intended to be a refresher for parents who have learned CPR from a qualified professional. These instructions do not certify you in CPR and are not intended for use by an untrained person. If you have not taken an infant/child CPR class, please sign up for one through your local hospital, doctor's office, YMCA, American Heart Association, or American Red Cross. These agencies also provide instruction charts that you can post in your home. Don't risk being uninformed if it ever comes to saving the life of your child or someone else's child.

If you have not taken a CPR class, or if you panic and cannot remember how to do CPR, call 911 (or your emergency number) and ask for step-by-step instructions.

CPR for Babies Under One Year Old

The following six steps summarize the procedure to follow if a child under one year old has stopped breathing.

Step 1: Check for Responsiveness

- Shout at the baby, rub his tummy or back, flick the soles of his feet, look, listen, and feel for breathing (place your ear over the baby's mouth). Look for blue skin color, which would indicate lack of oxygen.
- If another person is within hearing distance, yell, "Help! Call 911."

Step 2: Open the Airway

- Lay the baby on his back. Lift his chin gently to tilt the head back.
- Check again for breathing.

Step 3: If Not Breathing, Give Two Breaths

- Cover the baby's mouth and nose with your mouth, and give a gentle one- to two-second puff of breath, until you see his chest rise. Remove your mouth to allow the baby's chest to deflate.
- Repeat. If the baby's chest does not rise, check for a choking obstruction (*see* Choking on page 101).

Step 4: If There Is No Pulse or Heartbeat, Give Chest Compressions

- Check for a pulse or heartbeat by pressing gently on the inside of the upper arm, in the crease of the elbow bend, or on the side of the neck under the jawline or by placing your ear over the left side of the baby's chest. Finding a pulse can be difficult with a baby, so ask your baby's doctor at the next checkup to show you how to do this and practice in advance.
- Position two fingers in the center of the chest, one finger width below an imaginary line between the nipples.
- Give five chest compressions (press down one-half to one inch) as you learned in class. (One and two and three . . .)
- If there is a pulse, continue rescue breathing until Baby is breathing on his own.

Step 5: Repeat
- Repeat the cycle: one breath and five compressions.
- Every minute, check for signs of circulation and breathing.
- If circulation has returned but not breathing, continue giving a breath once every three seconds.
- If breathing has returned, call 911 or your emergency number.

Step 6: Call for Help
- After one minute of CPR, call 911 or yell to another person to make the call. (If you are alone, take the baby to the phone with you.)

CPR for Children Ages One to Three

If a child between the ages of one and three is not breathing, follow these six steps.

Step 1: Check for Responsiveness
- Shout at the baby, rub his tummy or back, flick the soles of his feet, look, listen, and feel for breathing (place your ear over the baby's mouth). Look for blue skin color, which would indicate lack of oxygen.
- If another person is within hearing distance, yell, "Help! Call 911."

Step 2: Open the Airway
- Lay the baby on his back. Lift his chin gently to tilt the head back.
- Check again for breathing.

Step 3: If Not Breathing, Give Two Breaths
- Pinch the baby's nose shut, cover the baby's mouth with your mouth, and give a gentle one- to two-second breath until you see his chest rise. Remove your mouth to allow the baby's chest to deflate.
- Repeat. If the baby's chest does not rise, check for a choking obstruction (*see* Choking on page 103).

Step 4: If There Is No Pulse or Heartbeat, Give Chest Compressions

- Check for a pulse or heartbeat by pressing gently on the inside of the upper arm, in the crease of the elbow bend, or on the side of the neck under the jawline or by placing your ear over the left side of the baby's chest. Finding a pulse can be difficult with a baby, so ask your baby's doctor at the next checkup to show you how to do this and practice in advance.
- Position the heel of one hand in the center of the chest, one finger width below an imaginary line between the nipples.
- Give five chest compressions (press down one to one and a half inches) as you learned in class. (One and two and three . . .)
- If there is a pulse, continue rescue breathing until baby is breathing on his own.

Step 5: Repeat

- Repeat cycle: one breath and five compressions.
- Every minute, check for signs of circulation and breathing.
- If circulation has returned but not breathing, continue giving a breath once every three seconds.
- If breathing has returned, call 911 or your emergency number.

Step 6: Call for Help

- After one minute of CPR, call 911 or yell to another person to make the call. (If you are alone, take the baby to the phone with you.)

Cradle Cap

See also: Bathing; Hair Care; Soft Spots

> *I give my baby a bath every day, and I wash her hair well. Even so, the top of her scalp is covered with crusty patches. What is it, and how can I get rid of it?*

Learn About It

What you are seeing on your baby's head is cradle cap or, if you prefer the fancy scientific name, "seborrheic dermatitis," a type of eczema that is rarely itchy or painful. Many babies have this condition, which is a sign of natural, normal skin growth. It's similar to adult dandruff—annoying, sometimes hard to eliminate, but nothing to be alarmed about. Despite its name, cradle cap is not limited to newborns and sometimes afflicts children long past the cradle years (as old as three).

What Does Cradle Cap Look Like?

Cradle cap can look scaly, crusty, scabby, or oily. It is usually brown, yellow, pink, or reddish and comes off fairly easily when you scrub or comb over it.

Can Cradle Cap Spread to Other Parts of the Body, or to Another Child?

Cradle cap isn't contagious and appears most often on the head. But it *can* spread to, or appear on, other parts of the body, particularly in areas near the eyebrows, nose, ears, neck creases, armpits, and genitals (*see also* Eczema). If your baby has what appears to be cradle cap in places other than the scalp, or if the scalp is heavily covered, make sure to tell your pediatrician. The doctor will need to have a look to rule out infection or a more serious case of eczema that would require medical treatment.

What Are the Causes?

Hormones, yeast, and fungus often are cited as causes of cradle cap. The most commonly noted reason, however, is overproductive sweat glands that have not yet begun to regulate themselves effectively.

How to Get Rid of Cradle Cap

Cradle cap usually disappears on its own, but you can speed the process along. The easiest way is to massage oil (such as baby, vegetable, or mineral oil) onto your baby's head. If you'd like, add a drop or two of lavender for a pleasant fragrance. Let the oil soak for ten minutes to an hour (no harm done if you leave it on longer). Put your baby in the bath, shampoo his hair, and work up a wet lather; use a comb or a baby brush to gently soften, loosen, and remove the flakes. Don't rub too hard, and don't try to get every last little bit out, or you'll just make your baby's head red and tender. Rinse your baby's hair thoroughly. Afterward, brush your baby's hair daily, and repeat the shampooing process every few days.

If you can prevent your baby's head from getting hot and sweaty, this may help, too. Remove your baby's hat when inside the house or in a heated car.

What About Stubborn Flakes That Won't Go Away?

If you've tried the oil and shampoo method every few days for a month or so and the cradle cap isn't going away, talk to your doctor about using an over-the-counter cradle cap, dandruff, or prescription shampoo. If you use any of these, you must be especially careful not to get any into your baby's eyes. Since cradle cap is usually not dangerous, you may want to forgo these products unless your doctor instructs otherwise.

How Can I Prevent Cradle Cap from Coming Back?

The best way to prevent cradle cap from recurring (or from appearing in the first place) is to wash your baby's hair with a mild baby shampoo two or three times a week. Avoid daily washing, as this can dry out the skin and actually create the crusty condition. Whenever you wash your baby's hair, make sure to rinse the shampoo out completely. Brushing your baby's hair with a soft-bristled baby brush every day may help, too.

Crawling

See also: Babyproofing; Milestones of Development; Walking

When will my baby start crawling? He's been scooting and rolling around on the floor for weeks, but he hasn't made any attempts at crawling. How can I help him get started?

Learn About It

It's always exciting when your baby starts to move about on his own. The most interesting thing about crawling, though, is that it's not even considered a developmental milestone. That's because, while many babies begin to crawl when they're between six and ten months old, some perfectly normal babies skip the crawling process altogether. Babies become mobile in many different ways, and the traditional hands-and-knees type of crawling isn't necessarily how your baby will first become mobile. If your little guy has learned how to scoot and roll from one place to another, his unique method may satisfy his need to travel for now, and his next major feat just might be walking.

How to Encourage Your Baby's Movement

Although you shouldn't worry about how or when your baby begins to get mobile, there are some things you can do to encourage your little one's physical development:

• **Give your baby plenty of tummy-time play every day.** Babies need this time to develop strong muscles and learn how to use their arms and legs to move. Don't feel as though you need to put him on his tummy all day long, though, and don't make him stay there if he isn't happy. But do make the effort to encourage ample tummy-time play.

- **Give her tangible motivation.** Place toys just out of your baby's reach. If everything she wants is always at hand, she'll have fewer reasons to try to move. Don't frustrate her, but encourage her by getting down on the floor and cheering her on as she figures out how to make her body get to those toys.

- **Make the floor a fun place to be.** Many babies dislike being on the floor, so they don't get enough time there learning how to use their bodies. You can help your baby enjoy tummy time by surrounding him with an array of interesting toys and by sharing the space with him. As he starts to move around, you can add to the fun by using sofa cushions, boxes, and other obstacles to help him learn how to climb over and around—and eventually pull himself up to standing.

- **Avoid having your baby spend too much time in baby holders.** Devices like swings, bouncers, baby seats, and the like are very helpful in keeping your baby safe and happy while you are otherwise occupied, but use them in moderation. It's more valuable to your baby to have that time to explore what his body can do and how it feels. Try to set up a safe and happy place on the floor whenever possible.

- **Steer clear of baby walkers.** These are proven safety hazards to babies and pose a high risk of accidents. While some people believe that walkers augment the physical development that leads to crawling and walking, research has shown that they actually slow it down.

- **Carry your baby frequently.** Holding your baby in an upright position helps her develop balance and coordination. A baby who is carried for prolonged periods tends to develop good muscle tone in the neck and body and is able to adjust her posture easily in different positions once she becomes mobile.

What if My Baby Isn't Getting Mobile?

Babies demonstrate a wide range of normal when it comes to physical development. Keep watch over your baby's developmental growth, and ask any and all questions you have when you take your baby in for regular well-baby checkups. In addition, if you see any of the following situations, you should discuss them with your doctor:

- Your baby is nearing her first birthday and hasn't found a way to move around when placed on the floor.
- Your baby demonstrates new developmental skills but then stops using them.
- Your baby seems delayed in this area and other skills as well, such as sitting, babbling, and using fine-motor abilities (*see* Milestones of Development).

Protecting Your Newly Mobile Baby

A curious, active, crawling baby can move fast and can get into amazing trouble. Babies have no sense of what things present danger to them; they want to explore everything in sight. At this stage, you'll have to watch your baby like a hawk. It's official: You've entered the phase when babyproofing is extremely important (*see* Babyproofing). Even a few minutes of your turned back can put your baby in a life-threatening situation. So make your home as baby-safe and friendly as possible, and watch your phenomenal little baby meet the world.

Cribs and Cradles

· · · · · · · · · · · ·

See also: Co-Sleeping, making it work

> *When we buy our baby's first crib, what safety features should we look for?*

Learn About It

This is an excellent question. Since your baby will be spending unsupervised time in a crib, it is very important that you know how to create a safe place for your baby. The following checklist will help you to achieve this.

Cribs and Cradles Safety Checklist

☐ Make certain your baby's crib meets all federal safety regulations, voluntary industry standards, and guidelines of the Consumer Product Safety Commission's most recent recommendations (cpsc.gov). Look for a safety certification seal. Avoid using an old or used crib or cradle.

☐ Make sure the mattress fits tightly to the crib or cradle, without gaps on any side. If you can fit more than two fingers between the mattress and side of the crib or cradle, the mattress does not fit properly.

☐ Make certain that your crib sheets fit securely and cannot be pulled loose by your baby, which may create a dangerous tangle of fabric. Do not use plastic mattress covers or any plastic bags near the crib.

☐ Remove any decorative ribbons, bows, or strings. If you use bumper pads, make certain they surround the entire crib and are secured in many places—at a minimum, at each corner and in the middle of each side. Tie securely, and cut off dangling string ties.

☐ Remove bumper pads before your baby is old enough to get up on hands and knees. If your baby can pull himself to stand, make sure the mattress is on the lowest setting. Inspect the area around the crib to make sure no dangers await him if he does climb out of the crib.

☐ Be certain that all screws, bolts, springs, and other hardware and attachments are tightly secured, and check them from time to time. Replace any broken or missing pieces immediately. (Contact the manufacturer for replacement parts.) Make sure your crib or cradle has a sturdy bottom and wide, stable base so that it does not wobble or tilt when your baby moves around. Check to see that all slats are in place, firm, and stable—and that they are spaced no more than 2⅜ inches (60 millimeters) apart.

☐ Corner posts should not extend more than ¹⁄₁₆ inch (1½ millimeters) above the top of the end panel. Don't use a crib with decorative knobs on the corner posts or headboard and footboard designs that present a hazard, such as sharp edges, points, or pieces that can be loosened or removed. Always raise the side rail and lock it into position. Make sure your baby cannot operate the drop-side latches.

☐ Don't hang objects over a sleeping or unattended baby; that includes mobiles and other crib toys. There is a risk of the toy falling on your baby or of your baby reaching up and pulling the toy down into the crib.

☐ If you are using a portable crib, make sure the locking devices are properly and securely locked.

☐ Make sure your baby is within hearing distance of your bed or that you have a reliable baby monitor turned on.

☐ Check the manufacturer's instructions on suggested size and weight limits for any cradle, bassinet, or crib. If there is no tag on the crib, call or write the manufacturer for this information.

☐ Any crib or cradle your baby sleeps in when away from home should meet all the safety requirements in this checklist.

Croup

· · · · · · · · · · · ·

See also: Allergies and Asthma; Colds; Cough; Fever

> *My baby had a cold. Most of his symptoms are gone, but now he has a terrible cough—he sounds like he's barking! What could be causing it? What can I do to get rid of it?*

Learn About It

You've described the exact signs and symptoms of a viral infection called croup. Croup appears after your baby has had a cold. The virus that caused the cold then causes the throat, windpipe, and voice box to swell, which makes your baby's voice sound hoarse and produces that distinct barklike cough.

Can Croup Harm My Baby?

Typically, croup doesn't amount to anything more than an annoyance. But it can be dangerous in a few situations. If any of the following situations are true of your baby, see your doctor immediately:

• **Your baby is a newborn, or very small.** Tiny babies have tiny airways. If these are swollen, your baby can have difficulty breathing, so her condition should be monitored carefully.

• **Your baby's breathing is impaired.** You will know if your baby is struggling to get air if his breathing is very noisy or he is making a high-pitched or whistling noise when he breathes. He may do this a bit during or after crying, but it should go away as soon as your baby calms down. If this type of breathing, known as "stridor," continues when your baby is calm or sleeping, it can be life threatening and demands immediate medical attention. If, in addition to stridor, your baby can't talk or has bluish lips, fingernails, or skin, call 911 or an emergency service for the care he urgently needs.

• **Your baby is having trouble swallowing.** A baby who has difficulty swallowing may begin to drool and become fussy and restless. This may happen along with difficulty breathing.

• **Your baby has a high fever.** If your baby is under three months old, call the doctor if his rectal temperature is over 100.2°F (37.9°C). For babies between three and six months, call if the temperature is over 101°F (38.3°C); for babies older than six months, call if the temperature is over 102°F (38.9°C). (*See* Fever.)

• **Your baby's condition is getting worse instead of better.** If you've tried the treatments listed in the following section for twenty to thirty minutes and your baby shows no signs of improvement, then take him to see a doctor.

What You Can Do to Help Your Baby

• **Keep your baby calm.** Crying exacerbates the problem and will make it even more difficult for your baby to breathe, so do your best to keep your baby peaceful.

• **Let your baby breathe cool air.** Cool air works to reduce swelling, just as ice works on a bruise. If the outside air is cool or even cold, dress your baby for the weather and take her outside to breathe in the fresh air for ten to twenty minutes. An evening walk in the stroller may even put your little one to sleep. If your baby finds her car seat soothing, try taking a drive with the windows open for the cool, fresh air.

• **Provide cool, moist air with a humidifier.** If you have a cool-mist humidifier, set it up in your baby's room. This is especially helpful for sleeping times. Make sure that the equipment and the water inside it are perfectly clean so you don't add bacteria to the air. (Avoid using a heated-air humidifier; they can pose a burn hazard to your baby.)

• **Provide wet, steamy air.** Let the hot water run in a closed bathroom for a while so the air becomes steamy and moist. Bring your baby into the room, and have quiet playtime or cuddle for half an hour or so.

You should see noticeable improvement in the sound and quantity of your baby's coughing and more relaxed breathing. (Never leave a baby alone near a bathtub filled with water.) If you are able to close off your kitchen, you can fill pans or kettles of water and let them boil and fill the room with moisture. There's no harm in letting the pans simmer for a long time while your baby plays nearby. Make sure Baby stays away from the hot pans, and check them often so they don't run dry.

Keep a Close Eye on Your Sleeping Baby

Whenever your baby is sick, be extra vigilant and check on him while he sleeps. You'll want to know immediately if his condition worsens.

Crying

. . . .

See also: Baby Blues; Colic; Postpartum Depression;
Reflux; Shaken-Baby Syndrome; Sleep, newborn;
Sleep, four months and over; Swaddling

I hate hearing my baby cry! What can I do to stop her from crying?

Learn About It

When parents are expecting or awaiting adoption, we dream about our baby-to-be, envisioning those beautiful Hallmark card scenes: a charming baby smiling up at a peaceful mother's face. Before the big day, we read books about how to care for a newborn—how to bathe, feed, and dress her—and then we feel somewhat prepared. A crying baby was never part of that idyllic vision, so this takes us by surprise. But the fact is, all babies cry at one time or another. Some babies cry more than others, but they all do cry. Understanding *why* babies cry can help you get through this phase and respond effectively to your crying baby. So can the list of ideas that follows.

Why Does My Baby Cry?

Simply put, babies cry because they cannot talk. Babies are human beings, and they have needs and desires, just as we do, but they can't express them. Even if they could talk, very often they wouldn't understand why they feel the way they do. They wouldn't understand themselves well enough to articulate their needs. Babies need someone to help them figure it all out. Their cries are the only way they can say, "Help me! Something isn't right here!"

Different Kinds of Cries

As you get to know your baby, you'll become the expert in understanding your own baby's cries in a way that no one else can. In their research, child development professionals have determined that certain types of cries mean certain things. In other words, babies don't cry in exactly the same way every time. (Other child development experts, also known as mothers, have known that for millennia.)

Over time, you'll recognize particular cries as if they were spoken words. In addition to these cry signals, you often can determine why your baby is crying by the situation surrounding the cry. Following are common reasons for Baby's cry and the clues that may tell you what's up:

- **Hunger:** If three or four hours have passed since your baby's last feeding, if he has just woken up, or if he has just had a very full diaper and he begins to cry, he's probably hungry. A feeding will most likely stop the crying.
- **Tiredness:** Look for these signs: decreased activity, losing interest in people and toys, rubbing eyes, looking glazed, and the most obvious: yawning. If you notice any of these in your crying baby, he may just need to sleep. Time for bed!
- **Discomfort:** If a baby is uncomfortable—too wet, hot, cold, squished—he'll typically squirm or arch his back when he cries, as if trying to get away from the source of his discomfort. Try to figure out the source of his distress and solve his problem.
- **Pain:** A cry of pain is sudden and shrill, just like when adults or older children cry out when they get hurt. This type of crying may include long cries followed by a pause during which your baby appears to stop breathing. He then catches his breath and lets out another long cry. Time to check your baby's temperature and undress him for a full-body examination.
- **Overstimulation:** If the room is noisy, people are trying to get your baby's attention, rattles are rattling, music boxes are playing, and your baby suddenly closes her eyes and cries (or turns her head away), she may be trying to shut out all that's going on around her and find some peace. It's time for a quiet, dark room and some peaceful cuddles.

• **Illness:** A sick baby may cry in a weak, moaning way. This is a baby's way of saying, "I feel awful." If your baby seems ill, look for any signs of sickness, and call your health care provider.

• **Frustration:** Your baby is just learning how to control her hands, arms, and feet. She may be trying to get her fingers into her mouth or to reach a particularly interesting toy, but her body isn't cooperating. She cries out of frustration, because she can't accomplish what she wants to do. All she needs is a little help.

• **Loneliness:** If your baby falls asleep feeding, and you place her in her crib, but she wakes soon afterward with a cry, she may be saying that she misses the warmth of your embrace and doesn't like to be alone. That's a simple situation to resolve.

• **Worry or fear:** Your baby suddenly finds himself in the arms of Great Aunt Matilda and can't see you. His previously happy gurgles turn suddenly to crying. He's trying to tell you that he's scared. He doesn't know this new person, and he wants Mommy or Daddy. Explain to Auntie that he needs a little time to warm up to someone new, and try letting the two of them get to know each other while Baby stays in your arms.

• **Boredom:** Your baby has been sitting in his infant seat for twenty minutes while you talk and eat lunch with a friend. He's not tired, hungry, or uncomfortable, but he starts a whiny, fussy cry. He may be saying that he's bored and needs something new to look at or touch. A new position for his seat or a toy to hold may help.

• **Colic:** If your baby cries inconsolably for long periods every day, he may have colic (*see* Colic).

What About Fussy Crying?

There are plenty of times when you can't tell if your baby's crying is directly related to a fixable situation: hunger, a soiled diaper, or a longing to be held. That's when parents get frustrated and nervous. That's when you should take a deep breath and try some of the following cry stoppers:

• **Hold your baby.** No matter the reason for your baby's cry, being held by a warm and comforting person offers a feeling of security and may calm his crying. Babies love to be held in arms, slings, front-pack carriers, and (when they get a little older) backpacks. Physical contact is what they seek and what often soothes them best.

- **Breastfeed your baby.** Nursing your baby is as much for comfort as food. All four of my babies calmed easily when brought to the breast—so much so that my husband has always called it "the secret weapon." And my babies are very typical. Breastfeeding is an important and powerful tool for baby soothing.

- **Provide motion.** Babies enjoy repetitive, rhythmic motion such as rocking, swinging, swaying, jiggling, dancing, or a drive in the car. Many parents instinctually begin to sway with a fussy baby, and for a good reason: It works.

- **Turn on some white noise.** The womb was a very noisy place. Remember the sounds you heard on the Doppler stethoscope? Not so long ago, your baby heard those twenty-four hours a day. Therefore, your baby sometimes can be calmed by "white noise"—noise that is continuous and uniform, such as that of a heartbeat, the rain, static between radio stations, and your vacuum cleaner. Some alarm clocks even have a white-noise function (*see* Sleep, newborn; Sleep, four months and over).

- **Let music soothe your baby.** Soft, peaceful music is a wonderful baby calmer. That's why lullabies have been passed down through the ages. You don't have to be a professional singer to provide your baby with a song; your baby loves to hear your voice. In addition to your own songs, babies usually love to hear any kind of music. Experiment with different types of tunes, since babies have their own favorites that can range from jazz to country to classical, and even rock and rap.

- **Swaddle your baby.** During the first three or four months of life, many babies feel comforted if you can recreate the tightly contained sensation they enjoyed in the womb (*see* Swaddling).

- **Massage your baby.** Babies love to be touched and stroked, so a massage is a wonderful way to calm a fussy baby (*see* Massage). A variation of massage is the baby pat; many babies love a gentle, rhythmic pat on their backs or bottoms.

- **Let your baby have something to suck on.** The most natural pacifier is Mother's breast, but when that isn't an option, a bottle, pacifier, Baby's own fingers, a teething toy, or Daddy's pinkie can work wonders as a means of comfort.
- **Distract your baby.** Sometimes a new activity or change of scenery—maybe a walk outside, a dance with a song, or a splashy bath—can be very helpful in turning a fussy baby into a happy one.

Reading Your Baby's Body Language

Many times, you can avoid the crying altogether by responding right away to your baby's earliest signals of need, such as fussing, stiffening her body, or rooting for the breast. As you get to know your baby and learn her signals, determining what she needs will become easier for you, even before she cries.

Dehydration

See also: Constipation; Diarrhea; Heatstroke; Sunshine; Vomiting

> How can I tell if my baby is dehydrated? She's been sick and not eating or drinking well, so I'm a little concerned.

Learn About It

You are right to be concerned. Sick babies easily can become dehydrated. They lose body fluids through fever, diarrhea, and vomiting, and they often sleep excessively without drinking enough fluids during their brief awake periods. Dehydration is a dangerous state for babies; it can cause shock and even death. That's why the first rule for taking care of a sick baby is to give plenty of fluids.

Reasons That Babies Dehydrate

The most common reason that babies become dehydrated is sickness (most commonly fever, vomiting, and diarrhea). Other situations increase the risk of dehydration, too:

- Hot weather
- Spending time at a high altitude
- Excessive activity
- Asthma or allergy attacks
- Infections
- Not drinking fluids on a regular basis

How to Tell if Your Baby Is Dehydrated

The table on the next page summarizes the signs that can help you decide whether your baby is dehydrated. A dehydrated baby will not necessarily show all of the signs listed, but if two or more are present, your first course of action is to provide fluids. Examine your baby for other signs of illness as well.

What Should I Do if My Baby Is Becoming Dehydrated?

If your baby is displaying the signs listed in the chart under "Severely Dehydrated," *immediately* give fluids while you call a doctor or emergency medical number, or take your baby to the hospital. This is a serious situation that needs medical attention right away.

If your baby is displaying the signs listed under "Mildly Dehydrated," act quickly to rehydrate your baby. Keep in mind that dehydration means your baby has lost not just water, but minerals, electrolytes, and sugars as well, so choose the right fluids for rehydration. Keep in mind that a few sips are not enough. Give your baby something to drink about every ten to fifteen minutes (set a timer). If your baby will drink only a tablespoonful or so, try giving a sip every five minutes until he's feeling a little better, then go to a longer stretch of time.

The following fluids are the best choices for treating dehydration:

- Breastmilk
- Specialty oral rehydration fluids formulated especially for children, such as Pedialyte, Infalyte, and Rehydralyte (refer to instructions on the bottle). If your baby is older than six months and refusing these fluids, you can sweeten their taste with a little sugar, Kool-Aid, or Jell-O powder.

For a breastfed baby who is sick, the best fluid is breastmilk. Even if your baby is well on the way to solid food, experts recommend stepping up the frequency and duration of breastfeeding when your baby isn't feeling well. When my own children were sick as toddlers, they naturally moved toward more frequent breastfeeding as they sought comfort. This worked beautifully to help them recover more quickly and allayed my worries about dehydration.

If your baby is formula-fed, use an oral electrolyte solution in place of formula (in smaller amounts, more frequently than usual feedings)

Indicators of Dehydration

Indicator	Not Dehydrated *Action: Provide normal fluids*	Mildly Dehydrated *Action: Provide immediate and ample fluids*	Severely Dehydrated *Action: Provide fluids and seek immediate medical care*
Wet diapers	Baby's normal output	Dryer than usual; when wet, the color is darker yellow than normal	No wet diapers for 6 or more hours
Soft spot	Normal	Slightly sunken	Very sunken
Energy level	Normal and alert	Less playful than usual	Extreme tiredness, listlessness, weakness, and lethargy
Skin elasticity	Normal; when pinched into a tent, it returns to normal quickly	When pinched into a tent, skin returns to normal slowly	When pinched into a tent, skin stays pinched up or goes back very slowly; hands and feet are cold and clammy
Skin color	Normal	Normal to pale	Blotchy, spotty, or bluish
Mouth and tongue	Moist and normal in color	Dry lips; inside may appear dry	Very dry or sticky
Eyes	Normal	Slightly sunken	Sunken, dry or with dark circles around eyes; no tears when crying (a sign only for older babies, since newborns won't have tears yet)

(continued)

Indicator	Not Dehydrated *Action:* Provide normal fluids	Mildly Dehydrated *Action:* Provide immediate and ample fluids	Severely Dehydrated *Action:* Provide fluids and seek immediate medical care
Cry	Normal	Fussy	Weak or labored
Breastfeeding	Normal	Less frequent or for shorter sessions than usual; fussiness after feeding	Breast engorgement not related to early-morning fullness; weak sucking; no sound of swallowing when Baby is nursing; fussiness during or after feeding

until your baby shows some sign of improvement, then gradually return to your baby's normal formula.

While some drinks are fine for a baby who's feeling under the weather, they are not appropriate for treating dehydration. Do *not* use soda pop, juice, Popsicles, soup, or plain water for a baby who is showing any signs of dehydration. Sports drinks like Gatorade are OK in a pinch for a child who is keeping fluids down fairly well and is not showing signs of dehydration, but the special fluids listed previously are the best. Avoid using homemade hydration drinks made of water, sugar, and salt for babies. Stick with the commercially prepared solutions that have the right combination of ingredients in the right proportions and are made specifically for babies.

How Can I Prevent Dehydration?

You can avoid dehydration by making sure that your baby has plenty of fluids, especially when she's vomiting, having a bout of diarrhea, otherwise sick, or spending time out in the sun or in hot weather.

Diaper Bag

See also: Cloth Diapers; Diaper Rash; Diapers:
Cloth or Disposable?; Rash

*I'm pregnant and trying to do everything I can now to get ready
for my baby. Can you tell me what I need to know about diaper
bags? What should I buy, and what should I put in it?*

Learn About It

I've gone through about ten diaper bags in the last fifteen years. One
thing I've noticed is that with each baby, my diaper bag has gotten
smaller! With my first baby I was ready for anything; I put everything
imaginable into my diaper bag and lugged it all from place to place. I
also continued to carry a purse, so by the time I added coats and a baby,
I needed a U-Haul just to get from the house to the car! By now, I've
reached baby number four, and my diaper bag is ten inches by nine
inches—and it even contains my wallet and cell phone! So, to save you
a few years and an aching back, I'll share what I've learned about this
ever-present baby necessity.

What Kind of Diaper Bag Should I Buy?

Diaper bags have come a long way over the years. Many today are styl-
ish carry-everything bags with compartments for all your belongings.
While there is an endless assortment of choices, there are similarities
among bags, so here are the basic styles:

- **Handheld or over-the-shoulder tote bag:** Many manufacturers
  have designed specialty diaper bags like large tote bags. These have
  two handles and/or a shoulder strap.

165

- **Backpack:** A backpack-style diaper bag functions like any backpack. These have more length than width and tend to have a smaller opening than a tote bag. The advantage to these is that you will be able to have two hands free to tend to your baby or other children, stroller, and anything else. Look for a backpack that is also easy to carry as a tote, since you won't always want to sling it on your back.
- **Other styles:** In addition to the standard diaper bag styles, you can also find diaper bags made as waist packs, stroller attachments, satchels, duffel bags, and more. Don't rush to make a decision, because there is an abundance of styles to choose from.
- **The not-a-diaper-bag diaper bag:** There's no rule that says you must buy a *diaper bag* to use as a diaper bag. A large purse, beach tote, or backpack of any kind can work beautifully. So as you shop, look around at all your options.

All of these bags also come with different inside features. Some have one large open space, and others have lots of compartments and built-ins. The advantage to the compartments is that your bag may tend to be more organized, and it'll be easier to find things. The disadvantage is that the size and shape of the compartments don't always match up to your individual needs.

What Size Diaper Bag?

Diaper bags also come in various sizes. You may find that the best choice is to purchase two bags. This way you can have a small bag for everyday errands and short trips, and a big bag for all-day excursions.

How to Decide Which Bag?

For mothers, a key to choosing the right bag is to take a look at the purse you've been using and pick a diaper bag that has similarities. For example, if you enjoy a purse with lots of compartments, choose a similar style for your diaper bag; if your purse is one open space, lean toward the same type of diaper bag. If your purse is a backpack version, try the same for a diaper bag. Another way to gauge your needs is to examine the luggage, computer cases, and makeup bags that you've enjoyed using and figure out which features most appeal to you about these carriers, then duplicate them in your diaper bag choice.

When shopping for a bag, take along a list of the things you expect to carry in your bag. As you look through various bags, envision the items on your list. In which compartments will you carry which items? Will your things fit in the designed sections—for example, will your wallet fit in the space provided for it?

What to Look for in a Diaper Bag

Once you've thought about what kind of bag to purchase, keep this list handy for your shopping trip. Since you will use your bag nearly every day, being stuck with the wrong choice can be frustrating. Here are a few tips:

- **Fabric:** Is the diaper bag sturdy and durable? Will it hold up to daily use?
- **Washability:** Can it be wiped clean, or is it machine washable?
- **Quality:** Are zippers, snaps, and Velcro openings smooth and well constructed?
- **Straps:** Are the straps adjustable to your size and to your partner's size also? Are they comfortable and easy to adjust?
- **Weight:** Is it lightweight? (A bag that starts out heavy is a burden when filled.)
- **Design:** Will everything you plan to carry fit inside without a lot of extra, wasted space? Will the bag still zip or fasten shut when it's filled with your belongings? If the top is shut with a drawstring, will it shut tight when full?
- **Size:** Will it fit in the bottom of your stroller?
- **Compartments:** Do the number and size of compartments match your needs? Are they logically organized?
- **Changing pad:** Is a changing pad included? Is it big enough for your growing baby without being bulky and hard to fold? Does it

take up too much space inside the bag? (Changing pads that are attached to the bag aren't at all practical.)

- **Accessories:** Does it have the extras you need? Are there extras that you're paying for but will never use?
- **Style:** If both Mommy and Daddy will be carrying the bag, does it have an appealing unisex design? Many adults prefer not to carry a bag covered with pictures of Winnie-the-Pooh and his friends!

Practical Use

As you use your bag, you'll figure out what works best for you. Keep these thoughts in mind:

- Keep your small diaper bag where you normally keep your purse and coat. Stash your big bag in the car so it's ready to go when you are.
- When you return home from a trip, unpack, restock, and put the bag back in the car, or put the small bag on your counter, so that it's ready for your next event. To avoid spills and smells, clean out dirty diapers, used bottles, and old food as soon as you get home.
- If your diaper bag is not babyproofed because it contains plastic bags and small choking hazards, then always keep it out of Baby's reach.
- Store your wallet and keys *inside* the bag, not in an easily accessible outside pouch, where they could fall out or be stolen.
- If you keep valuables in your diaper bag, treat it with the same care you treat your wallet and purse. Thieves know that diaper bags often contain money and credit cards.
- Put your name and phone number on your diaper bag in case it gets left behind on one of your outings.

Diaper Bag Checklist

Your Short-Trip Mini-Bag

☐ Diapers and diaper covers (one for each hour away from home)

☐ Baby wipes or wet washcloths in sandwich bags, or dry washcloths to be wet in a sink elsewhere

☐ Changing pad

☐ Empty bag for wet diapers

☐ Breast pads

☐ Formula and bottles

☐ Sippy cup or boxed juice

☐ Pacifier

☐ Receiving blanket

☐ Toys or teething rings

☐ Baby food, snacks, spoon, bib

☐ Note card with name, address, and emergency numbers

☐ Your cell phone

☐ Your wallet

Your All-Day Diaper Bag

☐ Diapers and diaper covers (one for each hour away from home)

☐ Baby wipes or wet washcloths in sandwich bags

☐ Changing pad

☐ Diaper ointment

☐ Empty bags for wet diapers

☐ Formula and bottles or breast pads

- ☐ Bottle cooler, insulated bottle holder, or thermos
- ☐ Sippy cup or boxed juice
- ☐ Two pacifiers
- ☐ One or two receiving blankets
- ☐ Toys or teething rings
- ☐ Baby books
- ☐ Complete set of Baby's clothes
- ☐ Baby's jacket or sweater
- ☐ Extra shirt for you if Baby spits up
- ☐ Baby food, snacks, spoon, bib
- ☐ Snack for you
- ☐ Note card with name, address, and emergency numbers
- ☐ Sunscreen
- ☐ Water bottle
- ☐ Ibuprofen or acetaminophen for Baby, in a childproof container
- ☐ Aspirin, ibuprofen, acetaminophen, or other medication for you, in a childproof container
- ☐ Money
- ☐ Phone card or change for phone calls
- ☐ Disposable camera
- ☐ Tissues
- ☐ Extra set of keys
- ☐ Sunglasses
- ☐ Hat

- ☐ Band-Aids
- ☐ Disposable placemat
- ☐ Sling or baby carrier
- ☐ Your cell phone
- ☐ Your wallet

Diaper Changing, how-tos of

See also: Cloth Diapers; Diaper Bag; Diaper Changing, resistance to; Diaper Rash; Rash

I'm about to have my first baby, and I suddenly realized that I've never put a diaper on a baby before! What supplies should I buy? What do I need to know about changing a diaper?

Learn About It

The typical baby requires more than 5,000 diaper changes by the time he has learned how to use a potty. At a rate of five minutes per diaper change, this means you'll be spending more than 400 hours engaged in this most basic baby-care activity. While many people focus on the how-to aspects of diapering, I think it's important to first acknowledge and consider the nurturing aspect of changing your baby's diapers.

Diaper Changing as a Parent-Baby Ritual

The position of parent and child during a diaper change is perfect for creating a bonding experience between you. You are leaning over your baby, and your face is at the perfect arm's-length distance for engaging eye contact and communication. What's more, this golden opportunity presents itself many times during each day; no matter how busy you both get, you have a few moments of quiet connection. It's too valuable a ritual to rush the process or treat it as simply maintenance.

Diaper Changing as a Way to Learn About Your Baby

Diapering offers a perfect opportunity for you to truly absorb your baby's cues and signals. You'll learn how Baby's little body works, what tickles him, what causes those tiny goosebumps. As you lift, move, and touch your baby, your hands will learn the map of his body and what's normal for him. This is important because it will enable you to easily decipher any physical changes that need attention.

Diaper Changing as a Way to Develop Trust

Regular diaper changes create rhythm in your baby's world and afford the sense that the world is safe and dependable. They are regular, comfortable, and consistent episodes in days that may not always be predictable. Your loving touches teach your baby that she is valued and loved, and your gentle care teaches her that she is respected.

Diaper Changing as a Learning Experience for Your Baby

Your baby does a lot of learning during diaper changes. It's one of the few times that she actually sees her own body without clothes, when she can feel her complete movements without a wad of diaper between her legs. (Incidentally, that's a good reason to put some naked playtime on the daily agenda.) Diaper-off time is a great chance for her to stretch her limbs and learn how they move.

During changing time, your baby is also a captive audience to your voice, so she can focus on what you are saying and how you are saying it—an important component of language learning. Likewise, for a precious few minutes, *you* are *her* captive audience, so you can focus on what she's saying and how she is saying it—crucial to the growth of your relationship.

Supplies You'll Need

- **A changing place or two:** Given the number of changes you'll be doing, it can be helpful to have one or two standard places for diaper changing. Changing tables are great because they put your baby at a good height for changing and provide convenient storage of supplies. Keep in mind, though, that if Baby's bedroom is upstairs, you'll not want to run up for every diaper change, so a second location downstairs is handy. Of course, if you're comfortable sitting on the floor, you can do a diaper change anywhere, but you'll still want a stash of supplies in your usual changing places.

- **Changing pads or towels:** No matter how careful you are, it seems that half the time, the changing area gets wet or soiled. Since these wet areas are a breeding ground for germs, you'll need to change the surface below your baby anytime there's a leak and at least once a day even if it seems dry.

- **Diapers:** Keep a stack of diapers in each of your changing places. Keep a good supply on hand, but remember that your baby will grow very quickly, so you don't want to be left with a wholesale-sized box in your closet that Baby has outgrown. Remember to stock diaper covers, too, if you are using cloth diapers.

- **Diaper wipes or washcloths:** Remember that you'll be using these on your baby's warm, bare bottom, so *cold* is a bad idea! A wide variety of diaper wipe warmers are available. If you are using cloth wipes, use warm water on them before each change.

- **Diaper rash cream, ointment, or salve:** These don't have to be used at every changing, but if you spot the beginnings of a rash, apply a cream (a zinc oxide–based type provides effective soothing and protection). If you do, that butter-soft bottom will be more comfortable, and the rash will disappear sooner (*see* Diaper Rash).

- **Baby powder:** Powder has become less popular for bottom care in recent years because of safety concerns. It has been known to cause life-threatening episodes—some resulting in death, even though a parent was close by—due to the baby inhaling too much of the powder. If you choose to use powder, be careful of heavily scented varieties; these may offend Baby's delicate senses or cause an allergic reaction. Never use a talc-based powder, as talcum contains particles that are tiny enough to reach the smallest lung spaces, and scientists are still exploring a possible link between talcum and cancer. Many parents swear by plain cornstarch as an inexpensive, gentle, and safe powder.

• **Petroleum jelly:** This makes a great diaper ointment and can be used on dry skin, too.

• **Baby clothes:** Keep at least one change of clothes at your diaper station. Babies tend to spill and spit, and you'll be changing clothes several times a day in the early months.

• **Baby brush or comb and baby toothbrush:** As long as you're here, you might want to fit in a little grooming.

• **Baby fingernail scissors or clippers:** Since you'll have baby barefoot and in a good position for nail care, keep a set of these nearby.

• **Diaper pail:** There's no polite way to say this: diapers stink—particularly if your baby is formula fed or has begun eating solids. And a day's worth of diapers are *really* smelly! Shop around for a diaper pail that seals diapers and their odors off from the rest of the house, and empty it frequently (*see also* Cloth Diapers). Keep a tight lid on the pail to prevent your baby from getting into it. If you use cloth diapers and keep water in the pail, bear in mind that this poses a drowning hazard, so the pail should be sealed with a babyproof lock.

The How-tos of Diaper Changing

You'll want to change your baby frequently to keep her clean and free of diaper rash. Check her diapers often, and change her at the first sign of wetness or mess. Typically, your baby will need to be changed after awakening from sleep, soon after every feeding, and before going down for a nap or nighttime sleep. Make it a habit to do a change before leaving the house; one heel-to-hiney diaper explosion, and you'll appreciate that tip.

Never, ever leave your baby unattended on any raised surface, such as a changing table, sofa, or bed. Even babies who've never rolled before will choose the moment you walk away for their first big twist. Another safety warning: Keep pins, salves, plastic pants, and any other potential dangers out of your baby's reach.

Take a baby-care class before or soon after your baby is born. If you choose to give birth in a hospital, ask about classes that you can attend during your recovery. Also, ask your pediatrician or the hospital nurses to give you a few lessons; they will be happy to do so.

There are no specific rules about diaper changing. And once you've changed a week's worth of diapers, you'll develop your own diapering style. In the meantime, here are the basic steps to get you started:

1. Make sure all your supplies are at hand. Wash your hands.
2. Lay your baby on the changing area, and undress her from the bottom. There's no need to undo the top of her clothing.
3. Undo the diaper, and use the clean top to wipe away most of her bowel movement.
4. Toss the diaper into the diaper pail (which should be within arm's reach).
5. Clean your baby using a clean, wet baby wipe or washcloth. Wash from front to back to prevent transferring bacteria from the anus to the genitals, and take care to clean the folds in your baby's skin. (If you have a baby boy, hold a cloth diaper over his penis, or have one close by, so you and he don't get showered by the ol' fountain of youth.) Dry your baby's skin with a clean towel, or air-dry him for a bit while the two of you talk and play (*see* Genital Care).
6. Place a new diaper under your baby.
7. If you spot any signs of a rash or if your baby is prone to rashes, apply ointment.
8. Put on a new diaper and, if needed, a diaper cover. Make the diaper snug enough so that it won't fall off and so that it catches what it's intended to catch, but ensure that it's not so tight as to completely prevent airflow, which can increase the risk of diaper rash.
9. Dress your baby.
10. Pick up your baby and give him a kiss and a cuddle.
11. Wash your hands with soap and water.

Diaper Changing, resistance to

See also: Diaper Bag; Diaper Changing, how-tos of

> *My child is a bundle of energy. He never wants to lie still to have his diaper changed. He cries, fusses, or crawls away. Such a simple issue turns into a major tug-of-war between us.*

Learn About It

Many active babies could not care less if their diapers are clean. They're too busy to concern themselves with such trivial issues. It may be important to you, but it's just not a priority for your child. Diaper rash or uncomfortable diapers (wrong size or bad fit) can make him dread diaper changes, too, so check to make sure this isn't the issue. Once you're sure all the practical issues are covered, make a few adjustments in this unavoidable process so it becomes more enjoyable.

Take a Deep Breath

Given the number of diapers you've had to change, it's possible that what used to be a pleasant experience for you has gotten to be routine or, even worse, a hassle. When parents approach diaper changing in a brisk, no-nonsense way, it isn't any fun for Baby. Try to reconnect with the bonding experience that diaper changing can be—a moment of calm in your busy day when you can share one-on-one time with your baby. (*See* Diaper Changing, how-tos of.)

Have Some Fun

This is a great time to sing songs, blow tummy raspberries, or do some tickle and play. A fun environment might take the dread out of diaper changes for both of you. A great game that seems to stay fresh for a long time is "hide the diaper." Put a new diaper on your head, on your shoulder, or tucked in your shirt and ask, "Where's the diaper? I can't find it!" Another fun twist is to give the diaper a name and a silly voice, and use it as a puppet. Let the diaper call your child to the changing station, and have it talk to him as you change diapers. For many children, this technique is all you need to solve the problem! If you get tired of making Mister Diaper talk, just remember what it was like before you tried the idea.

Use Distraction

There are a number of fun ideas for special diaper-changing toys. For example, keep a flashlight with your changing supplies, and let your child play with it while you change him. Some very fun kids' flashlights have a button to change the color of the light or the shape of the ray. Call this his "diaper flashlight," and put it away when the change is complete. You may find a different type of special diaper toy that appeals to your little one or even a basket of small but interesting toys. If you reserve these only for diaper time, they can retain their novelty for quite some time. The changing table is a great place to hang a mobile. Young babies enjoying watching it during a change, and with a little practice you can learn to change diapers with colorful creatures dancing in front of your face.

Try a Stand-Up Diaper Change

If your toddler's diaper is just wet (not messy), try letting her stand up while you do a quick change. If you're using cloth diapers, have one leg prepinned shut so you can slide it on like pants, or opt for prefitted diapers that don't require pins.

Diaper Rash

See also: Diaper Changing, how-tos of; Rash

> *My baby has her first diaper rash. I'd like to know why she got it, so we can avoid her getting another. Also, how can we get rid of it?*

Learn About It

Diaper rash, as the name implies, is a rash that appears in the area covered by your baby's diaper. Since a baby's skin is very soft and sensitive, almost every baby has at least one diaper rash during the padded-bottom years. For some babies, it's a rare occurrence, but others seem to have especially sensitive skin that frequently erupts in that telltale shade of painful-looking red. Whether you are dealing with your baby's first rash or a repeat occurrence, the information in this section will help you clear up your little one's tender bottom.

Causes of Diaper Rash

The most common reason for a rash in the diaper area is simply that Baby's delicate skin is surrounded twenty-four hours a day by a diaper—one that is often wet or messy. This creates a warm, moist area that's perfect for irritating that soft-as-butter skin.

Diaper rashes occur regardless of diaper type. All kinds of diapers, whether disposable or cloth, trap moisture. Other factors can contribute to a rashy bottom, including friction, heat, and bacteria.

Preventing Diaper Rash

To reduce the likelihood and frequency of diaper rash, here are the most important preventive measures:

- Change your baby's diaper as soon as it becomes wet or messy.
- With each change, wash your baby's bottom and dry it thoroughly, paying special attention to skin folds and creases.
- Don't scrub your baby's bottom. Using too much pressure when cleaning can lead to skin breakdown. Instead, wipe or pat gently.
- Always wipe from front to back so you don't transfer rectal bacteria to the genital area.
- Don't secure a diaper too tightly. Allow for some air to flow inside.
- Avoid using harsh or perfumed soaps when washing your baby's skin or laundering cloth diapers.
- Rinse cloth diapers thoroughly with very hot water.
- If using diaper covers, avoid plastic and use only breathable fabric types.
- If your baby sleeps through the night and wakes up in the morning with a soaked diaper, apply diaper ointment before putting on your baby's sleep-time diaper each evening.

Treating Diaper Rash

If your baby has a rash now, try the following ideas to clear it up. Follow up by using the prevention strategies in the previous section to help keep your baby rash-free.

- Change your baby frequently.
- After cleaning and drying his bottom, coat it with petroleum jelly or a diaper ointment.
- If your child is in day care, talk to your caregiver about your treatment plan.
- When possible, let your baby go bare-bottomed for a while. Exposing Baby's skin to air is a gentle, natural way to help it to heal.
- Don't use powder that contains talc. Once wet, powder can increase the friction between your baby's skin and the diaper. Also, your baby might inhale some powder, which can be dangerous to his health.
- Experiment with different types of diapers, wipes, and diaper ointments.

Parent Tip

"We found that using a hair dryer on the gentlest setting dries our baby's bottom after bathing and promotes healing of any rash."*

—**Chelsea, mother of Kristin (3) and Jayden (1)**

*Check frequently to be certain it's not too warm, and keep the dryer away from the bathwater and out of Baby's reach.

When to Call the Doctor

A mild diaper rash isn't cause for alarm. There *are* times, however, when you should call your doctor:

- When the rash persists, without improvement, for longer than three or four days
- If the rash spreads beyond the diaper area
- If the rash is bright red or if there are sores or blisters
- If there is a discharge from your baby boy's penis
- If your baby is taking antibiotics
- If your baby has a fever or is acting sick

More than Just Diaper Rash

Various other rashes sometimes are misdiagnosed as "diaper rash." Become familiar with the other types of baby rashes so that you'll know if the one on your baby's bottom requires more extensive remedies (*see* Rash).

Diapers:
Cloth or Disposable?

· · · · · · · · · · · · ·

See also: Cloth Diapers; Diaper Changing, how-tos of

I've been trying to decide which kind of diapers to use for my baby—cloth or disposable. Since I've never diapered a baby before, I have no idea how to choose!

Learn About It

Even experienced parents often struggle with this decision. There are many factors to consider as you make your choice. The following quiz may be of help.

The "Disposable or Cloth Diaper" Quiz

Take this quiz to help you determine which type of diapers would be most suited to you, your baby, and your lifestyle. Add the scores next to your answers. Then consult the information that follows for more insight about your answers.

1. I'm on the go with a busy schedule. Driving from place to place is a big part of my day.

   Always (3)
   Sometimes (1)
   Rarely or never (0)

2. I recycle everything. I even take home pop cans from a day at the park.

   Always (0)
   Sometimes (2)
   Rarely or never (3)

3. This baby is my:

   First (0)
   Second (2)
   Third or more (4)

4. My laundry is caught up; there's not a pile in my house!

   Always (0)
   Sometimes (1)
   Rarely or never (4)

5. My child does (or will) attend day care in a commercial day-care facility.

   Full-time (3)
   Part-time (1)
   Not at all (0)

6. I run out of grocery staples such as bread and milk.

   Often (0)
   Once in a while (1)
   Rarely or never (2)

7. My baby has a disability or health problem that requires I carefully monitor his food intake and wet diapers.

   Yes (0)
   No (2)

8. I live on a very tight budget; every penny counts.

   Very true (0)
   Somewhat true (1)
   Not at all true (2)

9. My time is more valuable than money. I'm too busy.

Always (3)
Sometimes (1)
Rarely or never (0)

10. I'm pretty squeamish. Vomit and cleaning out the toilet make me queasy.

Always (3)
Sometimes (1)
Rarely or never (0)

11. We live in a community with water shortage problems.

Yes (3)
No (0)

12. We live in a large city.

Yes (0)
No (3)

The following scoring guide may help you decide whether cloth or disposable diapers would work best for you. Keep in mind, though, that for any given family, some items from this quiz may carry more weight than others. Looking at each answer more closely, as we will do after the scoring guide, will provide further help as you make this decision. Also, while cloth diapers require an initial investment, you can always buy a few and try out both types before you decide which to use.

Add up your total points: _____

0 to 10 points—Cloth diapers may suit your lifestyle best. Many types and options are available (*see* Cloth Diapers).

10 to 15 points—You may want to combine cloth and disposable for different times of the day and night and for different schedules and activities.

15 or more—Disposable diapers may be your best choice.

Your total score can give you a quick idea of your best diaper choice, but to further analyze this decision, read the information provided below for each question.

1. **I'm on the go with a busy schedule—driving from place to place.** It's a challenge to carry around smelly diapers in your already overfilled diaper bag. If you're already very busy, it might be difficult to add laundering diapers to your schedule.

2. **I recycle everything—I even take home pop cans from a day at the park.** While neither reusable diapers nor disposables are perfect for our environment, current thinking is that cloth diapers have the edge when it comes to environmental concerns. If you are focused on doing your part to save our planet, the use of cloth diapers is one way you can help. Of course, this is just one aspect of a family's commitment to the environment. You can be environmentally conscious and still use disposable diapers, since recycling, reusing, and careful purchasing of all of your household products combine as parts of your effort to protect and conserve our environment.

3. **This baby is my first? Second? Third or more?** It stands to reason that the more children you have in your household, the busier your daily parenting tasks and the higher your laundry pile. The extra task of laundering cloth diapers may be more than you choose to handle. Of course, another option is a diaper service that can do most of the work for you.

4. **My laundry is caught up; there's not a pile in my house!** If stacks of laundry are already taking over your house, you probably don't want to add to the mountain. But again, if you are organized enough to use a diaper service properly, this can be an option for you.

5. **My child does (or will) attend day care in a commercial day-care facility.** Many day-care centers require the use of disposable diapers, since workers don't want to (or can't, due to health-related concerns and restrictions) handle multiple babies' cloth diapers all day long. If your baby is in day care, it's likely that you'll need to use disposables during day-care hours. Of course, you can use cloth at home if you prefer.

6. **I run out of grocery staples such as bread and milk.** There's nothing worse than a poopy diaper in the middle of the night and no more diapers in the sack! If you choose to use disposables, keep a backup supply of cloth on hand in case of emergency.

7. **My baby has a disability or health problem that requires I carefully monitor his food intake and wet diapers.** Discerning wetness in a disposable diaper can be difficult, so if you are monitoring wet diapers, cloth might be the better choice. While you can learn ways to gauge the wetness of a disposable, this takes careful scrutiny and practice.

8. **I live on a very tight budget; every penny counts.** Disposal diapers cost hundreds of dollars more than cloth per year. Many families feel that the convenience is worth the cost, but if you're on a tight budget, it may not be. This is true, of course, only if you do the laundering yourself. When you add the cost of a diaper service, the gap between the two closes.

9. **My time is more valuable than money. I'm too busy.** Some studies show that up to 90 percent of diapers used are disposables. This is most likely because many parents today opt for the convenience of disposable diapers.

10. **I'm pretty squeamish. Vomit and cleaning out the toilet make me queasy.** Using cloth diapers, even with a diaper service, does require more handling of the mess than using disposables. If you're truly bothered by this task, disposables may save your stomach. Keep in mind though, that after the first hundred or so diapers, even the most squeamish among us do toughen up!

11. **We live in a community with water shortage problems.** You'll need to consider the large amount of water required to wash and disinfect cloth diapers. Laundering diapers can use up to 4,000 gallons of water per year. Additionally, if you live in an area plagued by high energy costs, remember that this water must be very hot to sanitize the diapers.

12. **We live in a large city.** Highly populated areas have more landfill-bound trash that they must store or use additional

energy to transport. This may be something to consider in your area. A large city also may be more likely to offer a diaper service.

As with every choice we make, there's no single right answer. Every family must make its own best choice. Looking over this section will help you to make an informed decision when it comes to deciding on the right type of diapers for your family.

Diarrhea

See also: Allergies and Asthma; Constipation;
Dehydration; Solid Foods, introducing

> *How can I tell if my baby has diarrhea? Her stools are normally
> watery, so what constitutes baby diarrhea?*

Learn About It

What you usually find in your baby's diaper *can* look like diarrhea, so
appearance alone is not the way to determine if anything is wrong.
Much depends on what your baby's stools usually look like and what
they look like right now.

How Do I Know if It's Diarrhea?

Look for change—that's your first clue. An increase in the frequency
of bowel movements or a looser or more watery consistency than normal can signal diarrhea. Keep in mind that, if your baby has recently
started solids or if you have changed formulas, these things can affect
your baby's stool as well.

Is your baby acting sick or demonstrating other symptoms along with
runny stools? Also, think about your baby's diet and activities over the
past few days. Has she started a new food? Has she been drinking an
excess of juice or eating lots of fruit? Has she been playing in a place
(such as the beach or someone else's home) where she might have had
access to something she shouldn't have put into her mouth? Has she
taken medication or had an immunization?

What to Do About Diarrhea

If the cause of diarrhea appears to be certain foods or too much juice, try eliminating those items for a few days, and watch your baby for signs of improvement. If the diarrhea is due to a virus or something else that simply must run its course, keeping your baby hydrated is the most important treatment you can administer.

In fact, in the vast majority of cases, the biggest concern with a baby who has diarrhea is dehydration, because when severe, it can be life threatening. A tiny baby can develop dehydration quickly when suffering a bout of diarrhea, so again, the emphasis is on getting fluids into your baby. Don't worry about foods, if he's on solids; right now, concentrate on liquids (*see* Dehydration).

Pampering the Little Bottom

Your baby's little bottom will be very sore from frequent bowel movements, which typically contain more enzymes than usual, and from all the cleaning that accompanies this. Avoid using diaper wipes, since these contain alcohol or other ingredients that can sting. Stick to clean, warm, wet cloths. After cleaning, dry your baby's bottom with either a soft, dry towel or a few minutes of air-drying. Many parents also use a hair dryer, but if you do, use extreme caution and a cool setting; you don't want to overheat or burn your baby. A better choice may be to blow on or fan your baby gently. This is a good time to use petroleum jelly or diaper ointment between changes, as these can help soothe the pain and prevent a rash.

Helping Your Baby Feel Better

Diarrhea signals an illness of some sort, and it's almost a given that your baby doesn't feel well. So a little extra pampering, cuddling, and holding are all in order.

When Should I Call the Doctor?

Most cases of diarrhea clear up within a week. The following guidelines for when to call the doctor are only a general reference. You know your baby, and you should follow your instincts. Anytime you are worried, call your health professional for advice.

Call the doctor if you observe any of the following signs:

- Diarrhea persists longer than a week.
- Your baby is younger than two months old.
- Your baby won't drink any fluids.
- Your baby has any signs of dehydration (*see* Dehydration).
- There is blood, mucus, or pus in your baby's stool.
- Your baby also has a fever or is vomiting.

Discipline

· · · · · · · · · · · ·

See also: Babyproofing

When I look at my sweet, tiny baby, I can't imagine that she'll ever have a tantrum or decorate the walls with her crayons. When will I have to start worrying about discipline?

Learn About It

No matter how wonderful the child, or how great the parents, every child will make her share of mischief. Discipline really isn't about tantrums or writing on the walls. It's about helping your child to make the right choices in life. Discipline doesn't start with the first tantrum; it begins the first day you hold your baby in your arms. Every interaction you have with your baby teaches her something, and it's the cumulative effect of all of your life lessons that will come together as the basis for the person that she will become.

Day-to-Day Discipline in Babyhood

No magic formula exists for raising great children, but a few general philosophies can help you as you begin the incredible journey of parenthood.

Treat Your Baby as You Would Like Her to Treat You and Others

We've all heard the golden rule, "Do unto others as you would have them do unto you." That means, of course, "Treat people the way you would like to be treated." Applying this principle to your interactions with your baby from birth builds a foundation for your baby's views of human relationships. She may not say much while she's young, and her face reveals little of the tremendous and ceaseless learning going on behind it, but make no mistake: She takes in every nuance of your actions. So the principles by which you live—the golden rule and other basic tenets of civilized human interaction—are those she will simply accept as the norm.

As your child grows older, this will have a tremendous impact on how she responds to your teaching and guidance, since trust is a key component of all human relationships. When your baby is honoring you with a world-class tantrum or your one-year-old is still waking you up all night, parenting under this principle can be difficult. But if you treat your child with the respect due to all human beings, whether children or adults, your child will develop the trust and reciprocate the respect that will keep open the doors for learning.

The Decisions You Make for Your Baby Will Affect the Decisions She Makes for Herself

Your baby is unable to make her own choices, which puts you in a very influential position. During babyhood, your child will begin to create her impressions of the world and her place in it. She will begin to formulate her values and ideals. And she will base these in part on the decisions you make for her. So consider carefully the decisions you make.

Remember That the Things You Do Now Set Patterns for the Future

The ways in which you respond to your baby's actions will affect his future behavior. The first time he rips a page out of a storybook, throws his food off the high chair, or hits a playmate, he will absorb your reaction. This memory will become a piece of the information file he is creating to guide his future actions. Because babies do not have good long-term memories, many such situations will occur until he can make proper decisions based on past circumstances. Over time, you will begin to witness situations demonstrating that all the previous lessons you've tried to teach have indeed made their mark.

Always Ask Yourself, "Why?" . . .

When your baby does something that disturbs you, the first thing to do is to consider why she is behaving that way. Imagine that you are your baby for a moment, and examine her reasons for her actions. For example, if your baby slides a stack of paper clips into your DVD player, take a second to figure out why she would do such a thing. When you do, you'll realize that she has watched you slide things into the player, so she's just mimicking your actions—not understanding, of course, that DVDs work just fine, but paper clips don't. By asking why, you've realized that what she did wasn't misbehaving, but rather engaging her developing curiosity about the world.

. . . Then Ask Yourself, "How Can I Teach?"

The next step is to figure out how to teach your baby what she needs to know. Your approach may be as simple as an explanation and demonstration: "We don't put paper clips in here. We put DVDs in here. See? Want to try one?" Over time, and after many such lessons, your baby will begin to apply what she's learning in one area to other areas as well.

Now's the Time for You to Learn, Too

No one is born knowing how to be a parent. The job changes day to day and sometimes seems to require just a little more skill than we have! Now is a good time to read a few parenting books, take a class, or subscribe to magazines for parents. The more you learn, the more prepared you will be to take each new step along with your child's developing personality. Raising your child may well be the most important job of your life. When you are knowledgeable and prepared, it also can be your greatest joy.

For More Information

Pantley, Elizabeth. *Hidden Messages: What Our Words and Actions Are Really Telling Our Children*. Chicago: Contemporary Books, 2000.

————. *Kid Cooperation: How to Stop Yelling, Nagging and Pleading and Get Kids to Cooperate.* Oakland, CA: New Harbinger Publications, Inc., 1996.

————. *Perfect Parenting: The Dictionary of 1,000 Parenting Tips.* Chicago: Contemporary Books, 1998.

Sears, William, Martha Sears, and Elizabeth Pantley. *The Successful Child: What Parents Can Do to Help Kids Turn Out Well.* Boston: Little, Brown and Company, 2002.

Drinking from a Cup

· · · · · · · · · · ·

See also: High Chairs; Homemade Baby Food; Solid Foods, introducing; Vegetarian Baby

My seven-month-old baby is breastfed and just starting on solids. Does he need water or juice? When should I teach him to drink from a cup? If he starts using a cup, will that encourage him to wean from the breast?

Learn About It

You can introduce your baby to a cup anytime after his tongue-thrust reflex disappears and he is able to handle sipping as opposed to sucking—around four months of age. Prior to this, a cup can be used to dribble liquid carefully into a baby's mouth as an option for breastfeeding babies who refuse a bottle and must take a feeding from someone other than Mommy. Most often, however, there is no rush to get a baby to use a cup at a young age, so use your baby's interest and your desire to teach him this new skill as guidelines. Most babies begin to use a cup when they're somewhere between five and ten months old.

Does Drinking from a Cup Mean Weaning?

While drinking from a cup is a helpful and important key to successful weaning, the opposite isn't always the case. Many babies continue to breastfeed or use a bottle long after they begin to use a cup. A young baby, however, can develop nipple confusion or begin early weaning if you use a sipper cup extensively.

The way in which you handle the issue will determine how your baby sees the cup's role in his life. In other words, you can use a cup as little or as much as you'd like. If your goal is to wean your baby from the breast or bottle to the cup, you can move along in that direction. But do examine your goals. If you have no compelling reason to start your baby on a cup, wait.

Keep in mind that sipping from a regular cup (without a sipper spout) doesn't cause nipple confusion or affect weaning in the same ways that sipper cups do. Sippers require sucking, while regular cups do not. So, if weaning isn't your immediate plan, try experimenting with a regular cup first.

Signs That Your Baby Is Ready to Use a Cup

Is your baby ready for a cup? She may be, if she has developed the following skills and interests:

- Can sit without support
- Can hold objects easily in both hands
- Is interested in playing with a cup
- Watches you drink from a cup
- Is curious about drinking from a cup
- Is willing to try drinking from a cup

What Kind of Cup to Use

Of the many cups made especially for babies, many people feel that the best choice for a young, new drinker is a sipper cup (also called a sippy cup or trainer cup). The sippy cup has the following features:

- Small enough for your baby to handle
- Tight-sealing lid with a spout for drinking
- Handles on both sides
- Spill-proof

A sippy cup is a busy parent's best friend, allowing a baby to take a drink along on car trips or to walk about the house without risking a spill on the carpet. As a learning tool, it's great for little ones. If you wait to introduce a cup to an older baby, you can either use a special baby cup or move right on to a regular cup. And remember: Patience, please! Some spilling is only natural.

As for cleaning the lids, I've found that a baby-bottle brush works best. Be sure to pop off the plastic stopper after each use and clean it out thoroughly. Lots of icky germs can live in those hiding places!

Graduating to a Regular Cup

Many babies use sippy cups until they reach preschool age, and your baby can continue to use one whenever it's handy. However, there are two important reasons that you also should teach your baby how to use a regular cup.

While scientific research on the use of sippy cups is rather new, two problems have been noted with excessive and long-term use of these handy cups. The first is that children who walk around with a cup filled with juice all day are continually bathing their teeth in sugar and run the risk of early tooth decay. Even juice diluted with water can activate these sugars in your baby's mouth (*see also* Baby Bottle Tooth Decay). The solution? Give your baby a cup with meals and snacks, and don't allow it to be a constant accessory. Alternatively, put fresh water in that walk-about cup. Many babies enjoy water, and our own bias or lack of knowledge probably leads us to offer juice in the first place.

The second possible problem with overuse of sippy cups is that drinking from these cups requires mouth and tongue movement similar to sucking a bottle or thumb, rather than the more complicated sip-and-swallow action required by drinking from a regular cup. New research suggests that *excessive* use of these cups causes difficulty producing *th* and *st* sounds. The solution is to teach your baby from a young age how to use a regular cup and to balance the use of a sippy cup with practice using a regular cup. Try using the sippy cup when on the go and a small plastic regular drinking cup when at the table.

Careful Use of Cups

If your baby has just learned to walk, beware of letting him wander around with a sippy cup. He could take a spill (pardon the pun) with it in his mouth and damage his teeth. Also, be careful about leaving glasses of alcohol or hot beverages within your little one's reach. If he's like most babies, he will try a sip from any cup he sees.

What to Put in Your Baby's Cup

You can put any liquid suitable for a baby in your child's cup: breast-milk, formula, juice, water, anything your baby likes. (Don't give cow's milk to a baby less than a year old, and wait longer than this if dairy product allergies run in your family.) But whatever you put in the cup, remember that it counts as part of your baby's daily calorie and nutrient intake. Losing track of how much your baby is taking in is easy when you're refilling sippy cups all day long.

What About Juice?

According to research by the American Academy of Pediatrics Committee on Nutrition (published online at aap.org/policy/re0047.html), you should not give juice to your baby until she is at least six months old. Even when she's older, remember that whole fruit delivers more nutritional benefits than juice, so whole fruit is the better choice for children of any age. Relatively speaking, juice contains few nutrients but many calories, so it tends to fill up your baby and take the place of more healthful choices.

When you do give your baby fruit juice, limit the amount to just four to six ounces once a day. Choose 100 percent juice in a variety of flavors, and mix it with some water. Avoid fruit "drinks"; these are mostly sugar and little real fruit. Most babies, especially when encouraged early on, will happily accept a healthful substitute of fresh, cold water.

Weaning from the Breast or Bottle to the Cup

Many parents are interested in introducing a cup to their babies as a first step in weaning from breast or bottle. This works best gradually, over a period of several months. The easiest way to begin is by replacing your baby's least favored feeding of the day with a cup of formula or breastmilk.

Does My Baby Need Water?

If your baby is breastfeeding as the main source of his calories, you don't need to worry about water. Breastmilk contains plenty for Baby. In addition, giving water may fill your baby up and replace necessary breastmilk feedings. A thirsty breastfed baby can just be given extra nursings to quench his thirst and to meet his body's needs for water. However, once your baby weans and gets his calories from solid food, he will need extra water.

Formula-fed babies benefit from some daily water, since the concentration of salt and minerals in formula could put a strain on your baby's kidneys. A small amount of daily water will help his body's processing system.

Tap water may or may not be suitable for your baby. If your neighborhood drinking water has been tested for lead and you live in a newer home, your tap water is probably safe for your baby. However, if you are unsure of the lead content in your water—either from the source or from older pipes in your home—consider purchasing a water filter (the type that's able to filter lead) or buying bottled water.

Since your baby is still tiny and gets water from foods as well as beverages, a few ounces of water a couple of times a day is usually enough. If the weather is hot or your baby is sick, increase the amount of fluids, including water, that you give to your baby.

Ear Infections

See also: Colds; Sleep, newborn; Sleep, four months and over

My baby had a cold, but all her symptoms are gone. Now she has been waking up several times a night and crying out as if she's in pain. She seems better soon after I pick her up. What might be causing this?

Learn About It

Your baby may have an ear infection. Ear infections happen when bacteria and fluid build up in the inner ear. This often occurs after a cold, sinus infection, or other respiratory illness. The fluids get trapped in the ear, causing a throbbing pain that intensifies when your baby is lying down. Ear infections are very common in babies because the space between babies' eardrums and the back of their nose and throat is fairly small, and their ear tubes are wide and horizontal. This gives bacteria from the nose and throat a fast, easy path to the ears.

As babies get older and their ear tubes and immune system mature, they no longer are so susceptible to ear infections. Until then, an untreated ear infection can cause a baby to be fussy and will prevent her from sleeping well.

How to Tell if Your Baby Has an Ear Infection

A baby with an ear infection may exhibit all of the following symptoms, some of them, or even none of them. It's always important to see your pediatrician if you even suspect an ear infection. A gut feeling that something isn't quite right with your baby is justification enough for a call or a visit to the doctor. Listen to your instincts!

The following symptoms *may* indicate an ear infection:

- A sudden change in temperament: more fussiness, crying, and clinginess
- Increased night waking
- Waking up crying as if in pain
- Fever
- Diarrhea
- Reduced appetite or difficulty swallowing (signs include pulling away from the breast or bottle and crying even when hungry)
- Runny nose that continues after a cold
- Drainage from the eye
- Fussiness when lying down that goes away when the baby is upright

The following symptoms almost always indicate an ear infection:

- Frequent pulling, grabbing, or batting at the ears that is not done playfully, but rather with apparent discomfort
- Green, yellow, or white fluid draining from the ear
- An unpleasant odor emanating from the ear
- Signs of difficulty hearing
- Redness or swelling behind or around the ear

What to Do About an Ear Infection

If your baby is exhibiting any of the symptoms listed and you suspect an ear infection, make an appointment with your doctor right away. Seeing your doctor is important because an untreated ear infection can lead to speech difficulties, hearing loss, meningitis, or other complications.

If your baby does have an ear infection, your doctor may suggest some of the following treatments (*but don't try to solve this problem on your own without a doctor's direction*):

- Give a pain reliever—acetaminophen (such as Infant's Tylenol) or ibuprofen (such as Infant's Advil)—or a natural remedy such as chamomile or valerian. (Do not give your baby any aspirin unless a doctor tells you to, as it has been associated with Reye's syndrome, a rare but dangerous illness.)

- Keep your baby's head elevated for sleep. You can do this by raising one end of her mattress (try taping tuna cans under one end), putting her to sleep in a stroller or car seat, or letting her fall asleep in your arms or in a sling.
- Place a warm compress over the affected ear.
- Gently massage around your child's ear to help keep the tube open and reduce pain.
- Keep the ears dry and out of water.
- Offer plenty of liquids.
- Use prescribed eardrops or garlic ear oil drops.
- Administer prescribed antibiotics if other remedies aren't working and if recommended by your doctor.
- Administer an antihistamine and/or a decongestant if the ear infection is related to sinus or nasal congestion.
- Keep your baby home from day care until she is feeling better. (Ear infections are not contagious, although the illnesses that typically precede them are.)
- Avoid taking your baby on an airplane, as the change of air pressure in the cabin during takeoff and landing can greatly increase earache pain.

What About Frequent Ear Infections?

If your baby has repeated ear infections that don't clear up easily, your pediatrician may recommend a more aggressive method of treatment. The most common is to have tiny plastic ear tubes inserted through the eardrum to promote proper drainage. This sometimes reduces the number and severity of infections, but some studies show these are not effective in all cases. It's a good idea to get a second opinion before having anything like this done. Many parents are afraid they may hurt their doctor's feelings by getting a second opinion, but it's standard practice to do so.

Are There Any Homeopathic or Natural Treatments?

As always, you should talk with a professional before giving your baby any remedy, even homeopathic solutions. The following are the most commonly used natural remedies for healing ear infections:

- Echinacea
- Goldenseal
- Chamomile
- Belladonna
- Garlic
- Herbal oil eardrops

Some families find cranial-sacral massage or chiropractic care helpful for a child with recurrent ear infections.

How You Can Reduce the Chance of Ear Infections

While any baby can get an ear infection (and some babies are simply prone to them), you can take a few measures to reduce their likelihood:

- **Prevent the colds and flu that introduce the bacteria into your child's system.** Wash hands (yours and Baby's) frequently. Encourage anyone who holds your baby to wash her hands first, particularly if the adult or anyone in her family has a cold. Keep your baby away from anyone who is obviously sick with a cold or flu.
- **Treat a baby's cold quickly.** Working to reduce the fluid buildup that accompanies colds may prevent the ear infection that typically follows (*see* Colds).
- **Keep your baby away from cigarette smoke.** Just one afternoon spent with secondhand smoke can increase your baby's chances of developing an ear infection.
- **Limit pacifier use.** Some studies have linked frequent pacifier use to an increase in the number of ear infections. This research indicates

that the sucking motion associated with pacifier use hinders proper ear tube function and that a pacifier introduces excess germs into the baby's ears. If your baby has had only one ear infection, I wouldn't worry about this. But if your baby uses a pacifier throughout the day and is suffering from frequent bouts with ear infections, you might want to talk this topic over with your pediatrician.

• **Breastfeed your baby for as long as possible, at least for a minimum of six months.** The antibodies and immune system boosters in breastmilk discourage bacterial growth. In addition, the way your baby drinks from the breast (vigorous sucking and frequent swallowing) helps prevent milk from flowing into the ears. Breastfed babies are far less prone to ear infections than their bottlefed counterparts.

• **Never prop a bottle for your baby, and never leave your baby to sleep with a bottle.** This can cause milk to pool in the mouth and seep into the ear canals. It also may cause decay in your baby's teeth (*see* Baby Bottle Tooth Decay).

Ear Piercing
· · · · · · · · · · ·

> *I've always loved the way baby girls look in earrings. Now that I have my own newborn girl, I'm thinking of having her ears pierced. Is there any danger in having it done at such a young age?*

Learn About It

Parents may want to have their baby's ears pierced for many reasons. Some do so in response to a cultural expectation, in keeping with a family tradition, or as in your case, simply because they like the way it looks. Some parents choose to have their little girl's ears pierced if she doesn't have much hair, so that she looks more feminine. While ears may be pierced at any age, you must be aware of a few safety factors when you are weighing the issue.

Choose the Right Professional

Babies are more delicate than older children and adults, so you have to do everything you can to prevent infection. The first step is to have a doctor, nurse, or experienced professional do the piercing—*not* a teenaged clerk with minimal experience at the mall jewelry shop. In any case, a professional will use clean, disinfected equipment and will sterilize your baby's earlobe before piercing it. It's best to pierce only the lobe, since piercing the cartilage creates greater possibility for infection.

Request That a Piercing Gun Be Used

A one-step piercing instrument places the post in the ear with one quick poke. This avoids additional probing that can increase the chance of infection. A squirmy, crying baby won't do well if the process takes much longer than a moment. Also for that reason, some professionals recommend having two people accomplish the task, if possible—piercing both ears simultaneously.

Use a High-Quality Post

A post made of fourteen-karat gold or hypoallergenic stainless steel will help prevent an allergic reaction to or inflammation from lesser-grade metals. Nickel, for instance, is a common skin irritant.

Give Baby Lots of Comfort

After your baby's ears are pierced, she'll most likely cry from the shock and brief pain of the punctures. Give your baby lots of comfort, including a cuddle and a breastfeed or bottlefeed, until she is settled down.

Make a Commitment to Proper Care

The professional should give you care instructions. Follow these exactly. Usually the instructions will include cleaning the area with a special solution and/or applying an antibiotic ointment several times a day to reduce the chance of infection. You will be instructed to gently rotate the earring several times a day and leave the original post in place for four to six weeks. Make sure that the backing isn't so tight that it squeezes the lobe; this can contribute to infection.

If you don't follow these instructions, your baby's ears are likely to become infected. Should this happen, you'll have to remove the earrings and treat the infection, and the holes most likely will close up during the healing process.

Keep in mind that it will be many years before your child can take care of her own pierced ears. Until then, care will be up to you.

Watch Those Little Hands

As much as possible, keep your baby from touching the earrings. Excessive handling invites infection or injury, such as a tear to the earlobe. In addition, watch that the backing stays secure. An earring and its backing are choking hazards, and you don't want them to accidentally come off and end up in your baby's mouth. Ask for special earring backings that secure tightly to prevent them from falling off.

Watch for Signs of Infection

If your baby's ears become red or have any kind of discharge, rash, swelling, or scab, contact your doctor immediately. She'll need to look at the ears to diagnose and treat the problem, whether it's an allergic reaction or an infection.

Choose the Right Earrings

Stick to post (not hoop) earrings that are tiny and lie flush with the lobe. Avoid earrings with dangling parts, since these will increase the risk of injury.

Is It a Forever Decision?

The pierced holes in children's ears tend to close up more quickly than holes in an adult's ears, so if at any time you or your child decides you don't want the piercing, it's possible that you can let the hole heal and close. This isn't always the case, though, so keep in mind you may be making a lifetime decision for your child.

Eczema

•••••••••••

See also: Allergies and Asthma; Bathing;
Cradle Cap; Hair Care; Rash

> *I've noticed a small, bumpy rash on my baby's cheeks, scalp, and
> arms. It seems to be itchy. What could it be?*

Learn About It

Your baby may have eczema, which often starts out as a red rash that
becomes moist and features pus-filled bumps or turns dry and scaly.
Eczema is a general term used to describe various skin rashes of different origins but similar treatment. Two common types of eczema are
seen in babies:

- **Atopic dermatitis** arises from activity of the body's immune system. It often affects babies who have allergies or babies whose parents have allergies, although the eczema itself isn't necessarily
  caused by an allergy.
- **Contact dermatitis** is a rash that results from skin irritants such as
  soap, laundry detergent, metals, dyes, perfumes, animal dander,
  dust, perspiration, and many more.

What Can Be Done About Eczema?

If your baby gets an eczema rash, it probably will be the first of many;
babies prone to eczema have sensitive skin that may break out with
rashes from time to time. Many babies outgrow the condition. Some,
however, suffer with it throughout childhood and even into adulthood.
If you can determine the causes of your baby's rash, you'll be better able
to control his environment and minimize the flare-ups.

No matter what causes eczema in your baby, here's how to help your baby feel better and his skin heal faster:

• **Use a moisturizing cream once or twice a day.** Dryness exacerbates eczema. Try using moisturizers immediately after a bath, when your baby's skin is still damp to lock in the moisture. Emollients (mixtures of oil, fat, and water) are typically the most helpful. However, be careful which product you use, as many can irritate eczema further. Avoid products with synthetic ingredients, scents, or colors; look for labels that say, "hypoallergenic," "fragrance-free," or, "free of dyes." You might experiment with a homemade lotion of grapeseed or olive oil and water.

• **Avoid harsh soaps.** Use only mild, gentle cleansers on your baby's skin, hair, and clothing. Avoid skin soaps, laundry detergent, and fabric softeners with perfumes or dyes. Wash all new clothing before your baby wears it, and wash new bedding before using it on your baby's bed. Many parents of children prone to eczema put their clothing and bedding through an extra rinse cycle in the wash.

• **Reduce the number and length of baths.** To help prevent dry skin, give only two or three short baths a week. Make sure the water isn't too hot, since extreme temperatures aggravate eczema, and hot water can dehydrate the skin.

• **Keep your baby's nails short.** If your baby scratches the rash, it may spread or become infected. If scratching is a problem during sleep, try putting baby cuffs or mittens on your little one for bedtime. Make sure they are made of soft cotton, since your baby will likely rub these on her scratchy skin. And as with anything your baby has access to, make sure cuffs and mittens are devoid of strings and ornamental doodads that can come off and pose a choking hazard.

• **Avoid common allergens.** If you notice that your baby's rash worsens after contact with specific things like an animal, wool fabric, dust mites, feather comforters, or certain detergents, then avoid these triggers whenever possible.

• **Avoid extremes of temperature.** Hot air and sweating can dehydrate the skin, and cold air can chap it. In either case, the resulting dryness can cause an eczema outbreak.

• **Create a moist-air environment.** Many babies who suffer from eczema are soothed with a cool-mist humidifier that keeps the skin moist and reduces the itchiness. (Avoid hot-air humidifiers because they present a burn hazard.)

• **Use cool compresses.** If your baby's rash is itchy, try placing cool, moist compresses on the affected areas to bring relief and reduce itching.

• **Give your baby an oatmeal bath.** If your baby has an outbreak that is itchy, try using an oatmeal product made especially for dry skin and rashes for a soothing bath. (But remember, keep it short and not too warm.)

• **Dress your baby in cotton clothing.** Light, breathable fabrics, like cotton, are often helpful in preventing eczema.

• **Watch your baby's diet.** Pay attention to your baby's reaction to new foods. If you notice a bout of eczema after she eats certain foods, then avoid feeding them to your baby. Some common triggers are cow's milk, eggs, peanut butter, wheat, soy, citrus, tomatoes, and fish (*see* Solid Foods, introducing).

• **Keep Baby away from cigarette smoke.** Secondhand smoke can irritate your baby's sensitive skin.

• **Breastfeed your baby for as long as possible—six months at the very minimum.** The antibodies that breastmilk contains can help lessen the effects of eczema. As a breastfeeding mother, you can also watch your diet to see if any particular foods seem to make the eczema worse. Since breastmilk is a sterile substance with antibacterial and healing properties and high fat content, some mothers swear by it as a salve! Just apply it over the affected area and let it dry.

• **Don't rush solids.** If your family has a history of eczema, allergies, or asthma, don't start your baby on solids too early. Wait until your baby is six months or older. When you do start solids, carefully monitor your baby's response to each new food (*see* Solid Foods, introducing).

If your baby has frequent or severe eczema, let your pediatrician or a dermatologist take a look at the rash. Your doctor can give you more information about controlling eczema and may prescribe a medicated cream to control the inflammation and itching. Commonly, these creams contain hydrocortisone or a steroid to control itching and inflammation, in an emollient base to keep the skin from drying out. Don't use over-the-counter hydrocortisone creams without your doctor's approval; they may be too potent for your baby's tender skin.

Emergencies

. . . .

See also: Choking; CPR; First-Aid Kit

Now that we have our new baby home, my wife and I have turned into first-class worrywarts! We're so afraid that something is going to happen to our baby and we won't be prepared. How do we determine what's normal and what things we should be concerned about?

Learn About It

It's very common, normal, and even healthy for parents to worry about their babies. What can help reduce some of that worry, though, is having knowledge of what is normal and what constitutes an emergency when it comes to your baby. The following list is a good one to read now to prepare yourself, so that you'll be better able to make decisions if something does happen.

Is It an Emergency?

Call 911 (or your medical emergency number) immediately if your baby:

- Has a blue or gray tint to the lips, skin, or nails
- Has stopped breathing
- Is limp, lethargic, and does not respond to you
- Seems to be struggling for breath and her lips are turning blue
- Has choked or gagged and lost her breath
- Is having a convulsion
- Is unconscious after a fall or accident

Call your doctor, health care professional, or local hospital if your baby:

- Is having difficulty breathing or is making noises with each breath
- Has nostrils that are moving in and out with each breath
- Is breathing rapidly
- Has a high fever (*see* Fever) or is under three months old and has a fever
- Has a temperature below 97°F (36°C)
- Has blood in his stool, urine, or vomit
- Is vomiting repeatedly
- Has discharge, pus, or blood coming from his ears, eyes, umbilical stump, or circumcision site
- Has white patches inside his mouth
- Has a brief convulsion but seems fine afterward
- Has a severe cough or is coughing up blood
- Refuses to eat for two or more feedings in a row
- Is excessively sleepy or lethargic
- Is sick and not having any wet diapers (give fluids immediately)
- Has an unexplained rash or blisters on his skin
- Has a swollen or hard stomach
- Has a sunken soft spot or eye sockets that look sunken (give fluids immediately)
- Has a yellow tint to his skin and/or eyes
- Has a fever with vomiting and seems to be having trouble turning his head or is acting as if he has a stiff neck
- Has a blistering sunburn
- Has not had a bowel moment in three or more days
- Was briefly unconscious or has vomited after a fall or accident
- Is crying inconsolably, and nothing seems to help
- Fell or was dropped from any height
- Shows signs of being dehydrated, such as a dry mouth, dry lips, dry skin, no tears, dark-colored urine, weight loss, or decreased energy
- Displays a significant or rapid worsening of condition

Important note: If there is no sign of any symptom on this list but your instincts still tell you that something is wrong, call a medical professional. It's always better to make the call for advice than to sit and worry.

Eye Color

See also: Eyes, blocked tear ducts; Eyes, crossed

My baby is three weeks old, and her eyes are still an odd grayish-brown color. Since both my husband and I have brown eyes, we're assuming our daughter will have brown eyes also. When will we see her true eye color?

Learn About It

The genes of Mommy and Daddy, grandparents, and even great-grandparents will determine the eventual color of your baby's eyes. Note that your own eyes don't necessarily indicate the genetic tendency you've passed on to your baby. You may have brown eyes, yet you may have passed along a recessive blue-eyed gene that had been passed to you through one of your own parents, who acquired it through one of their parents.

Genes determine the amount of melanin—the brown pigment that's also responsible for skin and hair color—that the iris contains. The more melanin, the darker the eye color. Thus, blue eyes have very little melanin, while dark-brown eyes have the most. Human eyes come in a wide spectrum, from blue and green to hazel, light brown, and dark brown, all due to varying amounts of melanin.

The Color of a Newborn's Eyes

Babies with parents who are Asian, African-American, or dark-complexioned Caucasian usually are born with dark-gray or brown eyes that remain dark, although they typically change hue over time. Babies born of fair-skinned Caucasian parents most often are born with slate-gray or bluish eyes. The combination of parental and grandparental heritage further affects a baby's eye color.

Can Two Brown-Eyed Parents Have a Blue-Eyed Baby?

Actually, it is very common for brown-eyed parents to have a blue-eyed baby. When two parents with similar eye colors have a baby with an entirely different color, someone in the baby's ancestry—grandparents, great-grandparents, or other ancestors—shares Baby's eye color.

When Will My Baby's True Eye Color Be Revealed?

Many babies go through the entire first year with ever-changing, indiscriminate eye color. Blue eyes can become green, hazel, or brown. However, brown eyes won't ever turn blue, since eyes don't lose melanin once it's there. The myriad combinations of human genes provide us with a dazzling variety of human eye colors.

One study demonstrated that eye color can actually take as long as six years to stabilize into a permanent shade. Very often, however, the color in those first-birthday photos is fairly close to what will be listed on your child's driver's license.

Eyes, blocked tear ducts

· · · · · · · · · · ·

See also: Eye Color; Eyes, crossed

My newborn always has a sticky yellow discharge near the corner of her right eye. What is this, and how can I clear it up?

Learn About It

The condition you describe is probably caused by a blocked tear duct and is very common in young babies. A newborn doesn't have tears until about three or four weeks of age. At this age, babies begin to produce normal eye fluid, which is referred to as tears—but this fluid bathes the eyes at all times, not just during crying. Tears normally drain into the nose and down the throat through tear ducts at the inside corners of the eyes. Sometimes a thin membrane covers the nasal opening and obstructs the normal flow. This can happen in one or both eyes.

How Do I Know if My Baby Has a Blocked Tear Duct?

The following signs may indicate a blocked tear duct:

- Tears run down your baby's cheeks even when she's not crying.
- There is a sticky yellow mucus in one or both eyes.
- A crusty discharge causes the eyelids to stick together. (Your baby sometimes wakes up with an eye stuck shut because of the crust.)

What Should I Do About a Blocked Tear Duct?

Your doctor will most likely recommend home treatment as the first step in resolving a blocked tear duct. The following measures are very often all that is needed:

- Keep your baby's eyes clean. Use a warm, moist, clean cotton ball or washcloth to gently wipe the eye whenever you see discharge. Always wipe from the inner corner to the outer eye—from the nose toward the ear.
- Gently massage the tear duct in the inner corner of the eye. Massage inward toward the nose for a minute or so, three or more times each day. Your health care professional can show you how to do this and will let you know how often you should massage the duct.
- If your baby awakens with a crusty coating that prevents an eye from opening, hold a clean, warm, wet compress over the eye to loosen the crust, then wipe it away with a fresh cotton ball or cloth.

With all of these steps, be certain to wash your hands thoroughly before touching your baby's eyes.

What if Home Treatment Doesn't Work?

Most medical professionals continue home treatment until a baby is six to twelve months old. Very often, this is long enough for the tear duct to open. If this treatment doesn't work by the time your baby is six months old, or if your baby is having repeated eye infections from the blockage, your doctor may recommend probing the duct. This is usually done in a doctor's office using local anesthesia in the form of eyedrops. It does hurt, like the pain you feel when you have a shot, and your baby will need to be held very still for the procedure. The good news is that probing successfully opens the duct in 97 percent of cases.

If probing doesn't work the first time, it may have to be repeated, or your baby may need prescription antibiotic ointment or special eye-drops. In rare cases, if this simpler method of treatment doesn't work, a baby may need surgery to place a tube in the duct or create a new tear duct canal. Usually, this is done after a child is older than twelve months old, because it requires general anesthesia.

When Should I Call the Doctor?

If you suspect a blocked tear duct, take your baby to the doctor. The doctor will rule out or confirm your suspicion and recommend a home treatment plan. In addition, you should call your doctor if you observe any of the following signs:

- The lining around your baby's eye looks pink.
- The whites of your baby's eye look red.
- The discharge is frequent and thick.
- Your baby is older than four months old. (This condition generally is limited to newborns, so your older baby may have an eye infection.)

Eyes, crossed

· · · · · · · · · · · · · ·

See also: Eye Color; Eyes, blocked tear ducts

> *Every once in a while, my two-month-old baby looks like he has crossed eyes. Is this normal?*

Learn About It

A newborn's eyes sometimes do look crossed. At times this is just because babies have such wide noses and tiny faces that their eyes appear crossed. And sometimes their eyes really *are* crossed or aren't functioning smoothly together—one eye wanders independently from the other. These things happen because your baby's eye muscles aren't yet coordinated enough to align properly.

When Should My Baby's Eyes Align Properly?

Typically, by the time your baby reaches two or three months of age, this condition disappears. If your baby's eyes still look crossed after two months, even if they appear that way only occasionally, tell your pediatrician. The doctor will give your baby a few routine eye tests and will observe his eye development over your next few visits to be sure that the misalignment clears up on its own.

What if My Older Baby's Eyes Appear Crossed?

If your baby is over three months old and you still notice crossed or wandering eyes, ask your pediatrician whether you should see a pediatric ophthalmologist (eye doctor for children). The eye specialist will test your baby's eyes and determine if treatment is necessary.

What Treatment Is Required for Crossed Eyes?

If your older baby needs treatment for crossed eyes, a condition called strabismus, a number of things can be done. The doctor may prescribe eyedrops or, if your baby has a weak eye that needs strengthening, an eye patch. In some cases, temporary prescription eyeglasses are needed. If these treatments don't succeed, then surgery may improve the baby's vision.

The earlier the treatment starts, the better, since the critical period for human eye development is from birth to age two. A full recovery to normal eyesight is typically possible.

Febrile Seizure
(Febrile Convulsion)

• • • • • • • • • • • • •

See also: Fever

When my niece was a baby, she had a very high fever that caused what the doctor termed a "febrile seizure." It was very frightening, and now whenever my baby has a fever, I'm worried sick that this will happen to him!

Learn About It

Febrile seizures happen in 2 to 5 percent of babies. While this percentage is very small, knowing a bit about febrile seizures can help, should they happen to your baby. This is one of those situations that strike terror in the hearts of parents but don't amount to much in the way of real danger. In most cases, these mysterious seizures are harmless.

What Is a Febrile Seizure?

The term *febrile seizure* refers to a convulsion brought on by a sudden high fever in a baby or young child (*febrile* means feverish). During the seizure, a baby may do one or more of the following:

- Breathe heavily
- Become pale
- Shake or twitch uncontrollably
- Roll his eyes back
- Become rigid
- Become limp
- Lose consciousness

What Should I Do if My Baby Has a Febrile Seizure?

If you see signs of a febrile seizure, respond with the following actions:

- Hold your baby gently or lay him on a flat surface so that he doesn't injure himself.
- Make sure he isn't restricted by clothing or blankets.
- Turn him onto his side so that if he vomits or drools, he won't choke.
- Remove anything he has in his mouth, such as a pacifier or food.
- Do not put anything in your baby's mouth, including fluids.
- If the convulsion lasts more than two or three minutes or is very severe (such as if your baby is having a hard time breathing or is turning blue), call for emergency medical help.
- Once the seizure is over, call your pediatrician immediately, or take your baby to the hospital emergency room.
- Expect your baby to sleep after a convulsion. You can let him sleep, but monitor him carefully, keeping him cool to ward off a recurrence.

If My Baby Has a Seizure, Will He Have Another?

If your baby has had two or more seizures, or if anyone in your immediate family had such seizures during childhood, a recurrence is possible during high fevers. Talk to your doctor about this possibility.

Can I Prevent My Baby from Having a Febrile Seizure?

You cannot always prevent these seizures because their trigger is easy to miss. A sudden spike in body temperature brings on febrile seizures, sometimes when you don't even know that your baby had a fever in the first place. You can sometimes prevent a spike in temperature by treating a baby's fever as soon as you realize that your baby has one. On occasion, a child may display symptoms of possible convulsions by shaking or twitching, giving you a minute to implement some fever-reducing steps, such as bathing him with a cool, wet washcloth (*see* Fever).

You do not necessarily have to treat every single fever aggressively, unless your child or your family has a history of seizures or the fever gets high enough to cause discomfort. Fever in and of itself is an effective and natural biological defense.

For More Information

Websites

Epilepsy Foundation
epilepsyfoundation.org

National Institute of Neurological Disorders and Stroke
ninds.nih.gov/index.htm

Fever

See also: Febrile Seizure

> *My baby feels really hot and seems to have a fever. What's the best way to take her temperature? How do I know if the fever is serious enough that I should call the doctor?*

Learn About It

Fever in a baby indicates that something is happening in the baby's body, since a fever is the body's way of fighting an infection. The first thing to do is to take your baby's temperature and observe her for other signs of illness. Then evaluate your findings to determine if you should call your pediatrician.

Why Does a Baby Get a Fever?

Fever, or a rise in your baby's body temperature above the average normal temperature of 98.6°F (37°C), is a body's natural defense against infection. A feverish baby has a virus or bacteria in her body, and the body is attempting to kill those germs. Fever in and of itself is not a bad thing and has a good reason for happening. However, it can cause your baby to feel awful or lose her appetite. A very high and sudden fever puts your baby at risk for convulsions. These are all reasons we try to lower a baby's high fever.

What Are the Signs of a Fever?

The most obvious sign of fever is heat: your baby feels hot to the touch. You can confirm a fever by taking your baby's temperature (*see* the table on page 229). Other signs can tell you that your baby has a fever, too.

You should take your baby's temperature if she exhibits the following signs:

- Has red cheeks or a flushed face
- Hasn't produced very wet diapers or has urine that's dark yellow
- Isn't eating normally
- Is vomiting
- Has diarrhea or is constipated

How Should I Take Her Temperature?

The three most common methods to take your baby's temperature are to use a thermometer to take the temperature in the baby's rectum, armpit, or ear. When you report the reading, tell your doctor which method you've used. Temperatures can vary by a degree or so among the various methods.

Rectal Temperature

A rectal thermometer yields the most accurate reading. Here's what to do. Coat the end of a rectal thermometer with petroleum jelly. (Check the label on the thermometer to determine if it is rectal or oral. A rectal version has a thicker tip.) Put your baby on her tummy, and gently hold her back down, or place her in the usual diaper-changing position, and have a helper hold her legs up firmly so that she doesn't move suddenly. Insert the bulb end carefully about a half inch (1.25 centimeters) into her rectum. Stop at less than a half inch if you feel any resistance. Hold this position for three minutes, being careful that your baby doesn't move around while the thermometer is in place.

This can be difficult to do with a wiggly, sick baby. If another adult is available, have the adult hold the baby and entertain her while you concentrate on the "business end." Even with help, some people just aren't comfortable or confident using this method; if that's you, then use an alternative.

Axillary Temperature

An axillary temperature is taken in your baby's armpit. This is a fine method for a parent who doesn't want to tackle the rectal approach or as an alternative when your baby has diarrhea and—well, I don't need to explain why, do I? The armpit method is safe, and you can use either a glass or digital thermometer. (Many pediatricians now recommend digital because a glass thermometer poses a risk of breakage and subsequent mercury exposure.) Simply place the thermometer snugly into your baby's bare armpit, holding your baby's arm across his chest for three minutes or until your digital thermometer beeps. Walking, rocking, or nursing your baby during the process will enable you to keep the thermometer where it belongs for the necessary time.

Tympanic Temperature

A tympanic reading is taken in your baby's ear with a specialized ear probe thermometer. This method isn't recommended for babies under three months old; they have such tiny, narrow ear canals that the readings are seldom accurate. For babies older than three months, though, this is the easiest method for taking a quick, accurate temperature. While the device is a bit expensive compared with regular thermometers, you'll most likely use it enough over the next few years to warrant the cost.

To get a tympanic reading, place a new, clean probe cover on the thermometer's probe. (Using a fresh one each time you take the baby's temperature minimizes the risk of introducing germs into the ear.) Gently pull your baby's earlobe down and back; place the end of the thermometer gently inside the car canal, and press the button. You'll get an almost instant reading that is accurate for babies over three months old. Each brand operates a little differently, so read the instructions that come with the thermometer.

At this writing, tympanic thermometers are not as accurate as rectal thermometers, and they must be used precisely to get an accurate reading. If you are not confident about your results or your doctor feels that a very accurate reading is crucial, you may want to do three tests to get an average or do a second test with a rectal thermometer.

What's Considered a High Temperature?

A baby's normal temperature ranges from 97°F (36°C) to 100°F (37.8°C) and can change slightly during the course of a day, often rising in the afternoon and evening. If your child has a fever, it is not necessarily cause for alarm. Just use the following chart—and your gut feeling—to help you determine if a call to the doctor is in order. For future reference, take your baby's temperature a few times when she is well so that you'll have a baseline against which you can compare her temperature when she is sick.

Call the doctor if your baby's temperature reading is higher than the readings in the chart, the fever lasts more than two days, or the symptoms of illness are causing you to worry.

Temperatures Considered "High"

Age of Baby	Rectal Temperature	Axillary Temperature	Tympanic Temperature*
Under 3 months**	100.2°F (37.9°C)	99°F (37.2°C)	100.2°F (37.9°C)
Between 3 and 6 months	101°F (38.3°C)	100.2°F (37.9°C)	101°F (38.3°C)
Between 6 and 12 months	102°F (38.9°C)	101°F (38.3°C)	102°F (38.9°C)

*Due to fluctuating results with an ear probe thermometer, take several readings to determine an accurate temperature.

**A fever in a baby less than three months old is a medical emergency and warrants an immediate call to your doctor.

Observe Your Baby for Other Signs of Illness

Regardless of where your baby's temperature falls on the chart, if you have any doubts or your instincts tell you otherwise, go ahead and make that call to the doctor. Pediatricians' offices are used to—and prepared for—calls from parents with medical questions.

Temperature is not the only gauge for determining how sick your baby is. What's important is how sick she *acts*. Is she eating? Drinking? Playing? If she's acting normally, there is much less cause for concern than if she is lying about listlessly and refusing drinks or food.

Any of the following symptoms should be reported to your child's doctor. Don't hesitate to call your doctor's office at any time, even during the night. If you cannot reach the doctor's office, then call your local hospital emergency room if your baby exhibits the following behavior:

- Is listless, excessively drowsy, or weak
- Has difficulty breathing beyond the typical stuffy nose of a cold
- Has no appetite
- Won't drink any fluids
- Has a rash or spots on her skin
- Appears to have stomach pains
- Seems to have an earache
- Has cried inconsolably, moaned, or whimpered for more than an hour
- Is vomiting
- Has diarrhea
- Has not had many wet diapers
- Seems to have stiffness or pain in the head or neck
- Has swelling of the soft spot on her head or the soft spot looks sunken
- Has a fever that has lasted more than twenty-four hours
- Is getting sicker
- Has a convulsion (*see* Febrile Seizure)

What You Must Do

A great risk of fever is dehydration, since fever causes loss of body fluids. It is extremely important that you keep your baby well hydrated when she is sick with a fever. This is even more critical if she is vomiting or has diarrhea. Dehydration can land your baby in the hospital, so be vigilant and do everything you can to get her to take fluids. Every half hour or so, make certain your baby takes a drink. (You don't have to wake your baby up if she is sleeping, but give plenty of fluids before sleep and upon awakening. If she has slept for a long time, go ahead and wake her to take in some fluids.)

Here are the best fluids for a sick baby (if your baby is new to solids, offer only those items that she has tried before):

- Breastmilk (for both fluids and comfort)
- Formula
- Water
- Diluted fruit juice
- Clear soups
- Popsicles
- Juicy fruits
- Crushed ice
- Hydration fluids specially formulated for babies (available where you purchase baby medicine and formula)

How to Help Your Baby Feel Better

While usually not a cause for worry, a fever can make your baby feel miserable. In addition, the underlying reason for the fever—a cold, flu, or other infection—will cause your baby to be fussy and uncomfortable.

What to Do

- Give plenty of fluids (*see* Dehydration).
- With an OK from your doctor, give your baby acetaminophen (such as Infant's Tylenol) or ibuprofen (such as Infant's Advil). Follow the package directions exactly. Never give a baby aspirin, as

this has been linked with a dangerous condition called Reye's syndrome.

- Ask your doctor about giving your baby a homeopathic medicine, such as belladonna, chamomile, or valerian.
- Dress your baby in light clothing. Cover her with a light blanket if she is cold or shivering.
- Keep the room comfortably cool, perhaps using a fan.
- Give your baby a lukewarm bath. Use just a small amount of water, and let your baby play in the tub. Don't make the water so cool that she shivers, though, and remember that when she is feverish, the water will feel cooler to her than it does to you. (If she's fussy about taking a bath, bring her into the big tub with you or shower with her in your arms.)
- Give your baby a sponge bath or wipe her with wet washcloths.
- Keep her away from siblings or other people to prevent spreading an underlying illness, if it's contagious.
- Take care of yourself: Get lots of fluids, healthful food, and rest so you'll be less likely to catch the illness from your baby and better able to take care of her.

Parent Tip

"My mom taught me to believe in the healing benefits of fresh air. When my babies are feverish, I'll take them out for a short walk. Being outside helps cool them off and distracts them from being sick."

—Colleen, mother of twins Annelise and Emily (18 months)

What Not to Do

- Do *not* give your baby aspirin, as it has been associated with Reye's syndrome, a rare but dangerous illness.

- Do not confine your baby to bed. Allow him to move and play as long as he's comfortable.
- Do not bundle or overwrap your baby. If your baby enjoys being swaddled, use a lightweight blanket and keep the room cooler. Test her body temperature by feeling her ears, her fingers, and the back of her neck. If these are hot, red, or sweaty, she's overwrapped.
- Don't "starve a fever"; sick babies need plenty of liquids, plus food as they desire.
- Do not put alcohol on your baby's skin; this can harm a baby's skin and lungs.
- Don't stress about the fever. If you have concerns or questions, don't hesitate to call your doctor or local hospital for answers.

Fingernail Care

See also: Bathing

> *My baby was born with really long fingernails. Is this typical? How should I cut them?*

Learn About It

It's not unusual for babies to be born with long fingernails. Even if your baby was born with short nails, you'll find that they grow very quickly.

Since babies don't have much control over their hands, they often scratch themselves or others with their flailing movements. For this reason, you should trim your baby's nails frequently—sometimes more than once a week. You don't have to cut them extremely short; just keep them short enough so that your baby doesn't scratch himself.

How Should I Trim My Baby's Nails?

Baby fingernails are very soft and easy to trim. However, many parents are nervous about using scissors or clippers on such an unpredictable and precious little person. Here are some options:

- Trim your baby's nails when he's asleep.
- Try trimming while your baby is strapped into his car seat. (If he's *asleep* in the car seat, all the better!)
- Try trimming nails after a bath when they are softest.
- Have someone else trim your baby's nails while you are breast-feeding or bottlefeeding.
- Use an extra-fine emery board, baby fingernail clippers, or blunt-nosed baby nail scissors.

- This may not be the most mannerly method, but it's probably the most common: Peel the nails with your fingers, or bite them off. (This is easy if you are breastfeeding and nibbling those little fingers anyway.) Just stop using this method when your baby gets to be over a year old, or she may begin biting her own nails. You can keep doing this if your baby sleeps in your arms after nursing, however.
- Make a game of trimming. Have the nail clipper talk and sing as "he" (or "she") clips the nails.
- Play "Where Is Thumbkin?" or "This Little Piggie," and snip as you sing.
- Have a helper distract and entertain your baby while you trim.
- Sit on the floor in front of a mirror or interesting video with your baby in your lap (Baby's back to your front). Keep him secure while reaching around to trim.

No matter what method you use, keep the following tips in mind:

- To avoid cutting your baby's skin, press down on the finger pad as you cut. Tiny newborn nails require extra care to prevent nipping your baby's skin along with the nail.
- Cut your baby's fingernails in a rounded shape so there are no sharp edges.
- Don't feel you have to do all the nails at one time. Trimming a few at a time over the course of a day may be easier.
- For a newborn, consider buying nightwear with foldover mittens that protect your baby from nighttime scratches.

What About Toenails?

A baby's toenails don't grow nearly as fast as fingernails, and since they don't present a scratching hazard, you don't need to worry as much about trimming them. Some babies have very ticklish feet, so hold each foot firmly as you clip. Always cut toenails straight across to avoid ingrown toenails.

A Note About Your Own Fingernails

Many people don't realize how much and how well bacteria thrive under long fingernails. If your own nails are long, take care to clean under your nails every time you wash your hands after using the toilet or changing diapers, so you don't transfer bacteria to your baby when you are breastfeeding, preparing a bottle, or handling pacifiers or toys.

First-Aid Kit

See also: Diaper Bag; Emergencies

> *My medicine cabinet usually holds a bottle of aspirin and a few Band-Aids. Now that I'm a mother, I realize I should stock up on more necessities, but what exactly do I need?*

Learn About It

It is a good idea to keep a complete supply of first-aid items on hand. Keep an eye on expiration dates, make note of things you use, and refresh your stock from time to time. It's important to keep your first-aid supplies in a childproof cabinet, so that your baby or any visiting children can't get to potentially dangerous items. The following checklist will help you choose what you need to purchase.

First-Aid Kit Checklist

☐ Acetaminophen (such as Infant's Tylenol) for infants

☐ Antibacterial cream or herbal salve

☐ Baby nail clippers

☐ Baby nail scissors

☐ Band-Aids

☐ Calamine lotion or hydrocortisone cream

☐ Cotton balls

☐ CPR instructions

- ☐ Decongestant cold medication
- ☐ Ear syringe
- ☐ First-aid booklet
- ☐ Flashlight
- ☐ Gauze
- ☐ Ibuprofen (such as Infant's Advil) for infants
- ☐ Ice pack (reusable dry pack)
- ☐ Ipecac syrup
- ☐ Medical tape
- ☐ Medicine dropper
- ☐ Nasal aspirator
- ☐ Peroxide
- ☐ Petroleum jelly
- ☐ Phone numbers for doctor, hospital, and poison control center
- ☐ Q-Tips
- ☐ Rehydrating/electrolyte solution
- ☐ Rubbing alcohol
- ☐ Safety pins
- ☐ Saline nose drops
- ☐ Thermometer

Flat-Head Syndrome
(Positional Plagiocephaly)

....

See also: Sleep, newborn; Sleep, four months and over;
Soft Spots; Sudden Infant Death Syndrome

*I've heard that if a newborn sleeps on his back all the time—as he
should—his head may become a bit flattened in the back. How I can
prevent this from happening to my baby?*

Learn About It

Scientific research has shown that having newborns sleep on their back
is critical in reducing the risk of SIDS (*see* Sudden Infant Death Syndrome). What's important to know, however, is that if you always place
your baby in this same position, night and day, he could develop a flat
spot on the back of his head. The rate of head growth in the early
months is rapid, and a baby's skull is still soft, so constant pressure in the
same area can cause the bones of the skull and face to shift. This condition is called cranial asymmetry, of which there are three types:

- Plagiocephaly, in which the sides of the child's head are asymmet-
  rical—one side is flatter than the other (the most common type)
- Brachycephaly, in which the back of the head is flat
- Scaphocephaly, in which the child's head is long and narrow

With any of these cranial asymmetry conditions, a baby's face also may
look misaligned: the ears, eyes, jaw, or cheeks may look asymmetrical.

  If you have a sense that your baby might be affected, try sitting with
your baby in front of a mirror and looking at his face and head. Since a

mirror gives a more two-dimensional view, these issues can become more apparent when seen this way.

Does This Condition Affect My Baby's Brain?

A flat spot on the head, when caused by a positional deformity, is mainly a cosmetic problem. Your baby's brain is not affected, and it continues to grow normally. Problems can arise in cases of more severe cranial asymmetry. These are related to the development of the jaw and can affect chewing and eating. Difficulty with vision could also become an issue.

If a child's cranial asymmetry isn't caught and corrected in babyhood, it may lead to issues of self-esteem in later years. That is an important reason to address any concerns now.

How to Prevent Positional Cranial Asymmetry

The following ideas typically are included in a repositioning program for a baby who has a flat spot. Confirm and discuss the exact recommendations for your baby with your doctor. These ideas can also be used to prevent a problem from occurring:

• **Provide ample tummy time when awake.** Since babies should sleep on their back, plenty of playtime on the tummy when your baby is awake is important. Many babies resist this at first, but if you make the floor space interesting by placing an array of toys around your baby and lying there yourself, your baby will start to enjoy this experience. You might also roll up a towel under your baby's chest to lift his face off the floor until he can lift his head and shoulders on his own (*see* Independent Play).

• **Reduce daytime hours spent on the back.** Pay attention to how much time your baby spends on her back in her car seat, infant seat, and swing. Avoid excessive use of these devices, and balance them with plenty of in-arms time, when your baby is held upright with no pressure on the back of her head. Baby carriers and slings are wonderful ways to accomplish this. (Your baby will be happier, too!)

• **Provide head support when your baby is lying on her back.**
Your baby will, of course, lie on her back during the day at times, and
this is fine to a point. However, if your baby has a flat spot, roll up a
towel or use a baby head support under your baby's head and shoulders
to keep the pressure off the flat area. An alternative is to use soft foam
behind your baby's head when she's in a seat during waking hours.

• **Switch positions when bottlefeeding.** Breastfeeding mothers
naturally switch their babies from one side to the other for feeding.
Babies who are fed with bottles should have this same side-to-side
exchange to balance the location and position of their heads during
feeding.

• **Alternate locations of baby's crib or cradle.** While awake in
the crib, whether during the night or day, your baby will look out
toward the interesting sights of his bedroom, not toward a wall. To
encourage your baby to look in both directions, periodically move the
crib to a different location in the bedroom.

• **Alternate sleeping directions within the crib or bed.** Another
way to change the view from the crib (and therefore your baby's preferred position) is to place your baby in different locations in the crib
each night or nap: head at the top, head at the bottom, even head in the
corner. If you are co-sleeping with your baby, move your baby from
side to side during the night; if he sleeps all night without waking, alternate sides each night.

• **Encourage alternate thumb sucking.** A baby who always sucks
her fingers or thumb from the same hand will automatically turn her
head in that direction. Try encouraging your baby to switch sides by
cuffing a sleeve or mitten over the favored hand and helping your baby
get her opposite hand to her mouth.

• **Learn to change diapers from both sides.** Don't always change
your baby's diapers with his head facing the same direction. Routinely
switch sides, and even change him from the bottom when your baby is
lying on a bed or on the floor.

Parent Tip

"Our baby has positional plagiocephaly, and we are doing repositioning therapy during the day. At night, though, we still let him sleep on his back because it can help prevent SIDS. I would rather have a flat-headed baby than no baby at all."

—Desdemona, mother of Mitchell (5 months)

Should You See a Doctor?

If your baby's head appears misshapen, point it out to your doctor. Not every baby with a bit of a flat spot has a problem, so the question is important. Your doctor can confirm if your baby has cranial asymmetry and will discuss the best approach for your baby, which may include the suggestions listed here. If there is no improvement in a few months, then your baby may need treatment with a molding helmet or headband, both of which work in the same way that braces help to straighten teeth.

It is important to address this issue in the first year of life, particularly in the first six months, when your baby is growing rapidly and correction is easiest. Your doctor also should make sure that your baby doesn't have craniosynostosis, a rare but more serious condition that is not caused by sleeping position but is a bone structure issue; this may require surgery to correct. Your doctor should also check to rule out congenital muscular torticollis (CMT), a condition caused when the neck muscles are shorter or tightened on one side. This causes the baby's head to tilt in one direction and may make the baby's head look misshapen. This condition can be corrected with physical therapy, often right at home.

For More Information

Websites

American Cleft Palate–Craniofacial Association
cleftpalate-craniofacial.org

Plagiocephaly.org
plagiocephaly.org

Boppy head supports (Noggin Nest)
boppy.com

Food Allergies

See also: Allergies and Asthma; Colds; Croup; Solid Foods, introducing

I'm allergic to a number of different foods. How do I tell if my baby has food allergies, too?

Learn About It

When a baby has a parent or sibling with food allergies, the baby *does* have a greater chance of having them, too. So be on the lookout for signs of allergies. Infants with food allergies often first show an allergic reaction to formula or, on occasion, to substances in breastmilk.

What Are the Signs of a Food Allergy?

The signs of a food-related allergy can appear soon after a baby eats the food or several hours later. The most common signs may appear individually or several at a time. They include the following reactions:

- Diarrhea
- Vomiting
- Abdominal pain
- Wheezing or difficulty breathing
- Dry, hacking cough
- Rash
- Bloody stools
- Swelling of the tongue or throat
- Extreme fussiness
- Gassiness
- Difficulty sleeping

What Foods Commonly Cause Allergies?

While any food has the potential to cause an allergic reaction, a few foods account for the vast majority of food-related allergies:

- Cow's milk and dairy products
- Eggs
- Nuts
- Fish
- Wheat
- Soy

Ways to Prevent or Control Food Allergies

The following recommendations apply to parents of all babies but most especially to those with a family history of food allergies:

- **Breastfeed your baby** for a minimum of six months—even better, for *at least* twelve months. Breastfeed exclusively, if possible, since babies fed breastmilk are less likely than formula-fed babies to develop food allergies.
- **Control your own diet.** Many substances can pass to your baby in your breastmilk. If your baby is at high risk for allergies or you just wish to avoid finding out if that is the case, you can eliminate from your own diet the highly allergenic foods listed above.
- **Choose baby formula carefully if your baby is bottlefed.** Talk to your doctor about a hypoallergenic formula that's best for your baby's particular needs.
- **Delay the introduction of solid foods until your baby is six months old or older.** Highly allergenic foods can be delayed even longer, until age two or three.
- **Carefully monitor your baby as you introduce solids.** Offer your baby the least allergenic foods first (rice, applesauce, and pears). Introduce new foods one at a time, in small amounts, with a few days between each new exposure—and watch your baby for any signs of food sensitivity. (*See* Solid Foods, introducing.)

For More Information

Website

The Food Allergy & Anaphylaxis Network
foodallergy.org

Genital Care

· · · · · · · · · · · · ·

See also: Bathing; Circumcision Decision;
Diaper Changing, how-tos of

How should I take care of my baby's genital area?

Learn About It

Whether you have a girl or a boy with a circumcised or intact penis,
you need to know how to take care of your baby's external sex organs.
A basic review of the terminology will help, as will an explanation of
how proper care differs depending on the "genital status" of your baby.

Your Newborn Baby Girl's Genital Area

A girl's external genital area is called the vulva, and it consists most vis-
ibly of the outer labia—the two outer lips that conceal the rest of the
vaginal area. Between the outer labia are the inner labia, the lips that
cover the urethral opening (for urine) and the vaginal opening. After
birth, your baby girl's vulva may be red and swollen due to hormones
released just before birth; there may also be a white and occasionally
slightly bloody discharge from the vagina.

Caring for a Baby Girl's Genital Area

- Always wipe from front to back so you avoid carrying bacteria
  from the anus to the vagina.
- Change wet and soiled diapers right away to reduce the risk of irritation or infection of the vulva, urethra, or vagina.
- After a messy bowel movement or during bath time, very gently
  spread your baby's labia and clean the area between the outer and

inner labia with a moist cloth or cotton ball. This is where diaper creams tend to collect. There is no need to clean the normal discharge from your baby's vagina.

- Bubble baths and diaper wipes with perfume or alcohol can irritate the sensitive vulva and vaginal area. If you use soap during a bath (which isn't necessary for *every* bath, since it can be very drying and irritating), make sure that it is a gentle soap formulated for babies. Allow the vulva to air-dry after a bath, or gently dry the area with a towel. Use only nonallergenic wipes for between-bath cleanings and diaper changes.

- Talk to a health professional if your baby girl experiences any of the following: smelly vaginal discharge, blood in the urine or in the vaginal discharge (other than the normal slightly bloody discharge just after birth), or inner labia that seem to "stick" to one another (can lead to labial adhesions).

Your Newborn Baby Boy's Genital Area

A boy's external sex organs are the penis and the testicles. The top of the penis is called the glans, and the skin that covers the glans is the foreskin. If the foreskin was not removed during circumcision, it retracts at about age three. A boy's testicles are protected by a pouch called the scrotum.

Occasionally, one or both testicles fail to descend into the scrotum by the time your baby turns one. If you notice this on your baby, talk to your pediatrician about the possible need for treatment. Some physicians advise bringing the testicle down surgically by eighteen months or so, while others wait longer to see if it descends on its own. Getting it down there is important, since the incidence of testicular cancer is greater in men who have or have had undescended testicles. While the increased risk remains even after surgery, testicular cancer is quite rare even among these men and is treatable with early detection, which is far more possible when both testicles can be reached for regular self-examination.

Many newborn baby boys have swollen scrotums just after birth due to pregnancy hormones. If the swelling continues, talk to a health professional.

Caring for the Intact (Uncircumcised) Penis

The foreskin and the glans are attached to each other in an intact penis, and *it is very important to let the gradual retraction of the foreskin from the glans occur naturally*. The inside of the foreskin is similar to the inside of your cheek. It's a mucous membrane that keeps the glans moist and clean, and all you need to do is wash the penis and the tip of the glans with warm running water as a part of your baby's usual bath. If you force the foreskin to retract by pulling on it, or if you try to clean under the foreskin before it is fully retracted, you may hurt your baby; bleeding and adhesions can result.

As your baby grows, the foreskin will begin to loosen itself; usually by the age of three, it pulls back completely behind the glans. A good rule of thumb is to let your son be the first person to fully retract his own penis. It is normal for a cheesy or white beadlike material to appear as the foreskin gradually retracts. This is just the remnant of cells that have been shed during the separation process. Once your son is older and full retraction is possible, you can teach him how to wash himself with water and a mild soap, just as he does every other body part.

Caring for the Circumcised Penis

Two methods are used in circumcision: the first uses a Plastibell device, and the second uses the Gomco clamp. The Plastibell is a plastic ring placed around the top of the penis that falls off naturally within three to five days. With this type of circumcision, no bandages are necessary. The second method of circumcision uses a Gomco clamp and a gauze dressing, usually soaked in petroleum jelly to prevent the wound from sticking to it. Ask your doctor for instructions about when to change the dressing; you may be advised to change the bandages during every diaper change, or perhaps only forty-eight hours after the circumcision. The following guidelines apply to both types of circumcision:

- Realize that the circumcision site is a sore, open wound. Treat it with the precautions you would use for any open wound. Rinse the area with a drizzle of warm water during every diaper change (but no soap, as that would irritate the wound). Put petroleum jelly on the circumcision line and on the glans to prevent the wound from sticking to the diaper. Some parents use double diapers in the first day or two after circumcision for extra padding and protection of the sore penis.
- Expect your little boy's penis to be red and swollen for the first few days; there may be a yellowish secretion as well. Some babies form a scab that falls off as the wound heals.
- Ask your doctor if you should gently pull the skin behind the circumcision line away from the glans to prevent adhesions. Some doctors recommend that this gentle pulling continue until your baby is fifteen months old, while some don't recommend this practice at all.
- Your baby will be sore after his circumcision, and breastfeeding or bottlefeeding with extra cuddles may help him feel better. Some babies go into a deep sleep after the operation; you may need to wake your baby to feed him.
- After the circumcision site has healed (normally within ten days), the penis needs no special care except for normal cleaning with water and perhaps a mild baby soap during the bath.

When to Call the Doctor

If you see the following conditions, you should call your pediatrician:

- There is more than a quarter-sized circle of blood in your son's diaper.
- Your baby doesn't have a wet diaper within hours after the circumcision, or the urine comes out in dribbles.
- You notice *increasing* redness or swelling, especially after three to five days, or there is a continuing yellow discharge after one week.
- The head of the penis looks black or blue.
- The Plastibell device doesn't fall off after twelve to fourteen days.
- Your baby has a fever or is acting sick.

Grandparents, overzealous

See also: Breastfeeding in Public;
Grandparents, reluctant; Unwanted Advice

> *Help! Since my baby was born, my mother has been over almost every day. She's always giving advice, taking over the baby's care, and bringing armloads of gifts. How can I get her to slow down?*

Learn About It

Let's not talk about your mother for a minute. Instead, think about your baby. Think about the incredible love you feel for your child. Now, imagine that you watch your baby grow from infant to toddler, from toddler to kindergartner, and through the years to the time when your baby isn't a baby any longer. Through the days and nights of everyday life, you pour twenty or more years of this love into your child. Then your child has a baby: your grandchild! Do you want to rush over to your child's home so that you can give advice, help with the baby's care, and bring armloads of gifts? Come on, now, admit it: of course you do! Even though this peek into the future may give you a new insight into what's happening, I know you'll still want more information and some tips on how to handle the situation, so read on!

The Value of the Grand Relationship

For babies lucky enough to have a grandmother or grandfather (or several!), the benefits they'll enjoy from this unique relationship are many. All grandparents are different, of course, and each relationship will have its own special value. Here are some of the common traits of the grand relationship:

- **Unconditional love:** The love between grandparent and grand-child is often total and unconditional. Grandparents have a bond to your baby that encompasses their love for you *and* their love for your child—a multidimensional love that conveys itself to your child with every hug and every smile.
- **Fun without strings:** Grandparents typically bring a special play-fulness to the relationship. They have had their turn raising children and often feel they can relax and enjoy the moments without having to focus on the teaching, setting limits, and enforcing discipline that parenting entails. While parents sometimes view this attitude with concern, most often it's a benefit for children to have a person with whom they can let their hair down and relax.
- **Fun without the stress of time:** Children can enjoy a magical relationship with someone who loves them deeply, has their best interests at heart, and simply enjoys the time they spend together minute by minute. Grandparents often move at a slower pace than parents do. If this is so in your family, your child can enjoy a special lingering quality to the time shared with grandparents—a shady spot under a sturdy tree that has been around a while and provides shelter from the glare of everyday expectations and hectic schedules.
- **A sense of history and ethnicity:** Grandparents are a link to a family's history—a precious source of information and stories about the background, rituals, and eccentricities that weave the rich tapestry of a family. Grandparents can instill a feeling of belonging and teach children about their roots.
- **Respect for and understanding of the aging process:** Children who have a close relationship with grandparents accept aging as normal and natural. From the time the kids are young, they know their grandparents simply as people. This natural relationship helps them accept and appreciate the differences between generations. And as terribly sad as this can be, their relationship eventually teaches them about the circle of life.

Grandparents as Caregivers

A grandparent as full-time caregiver for your child might offer a set of very special benefits. In many families, there's no one else besides you who can love your baby quite as much as Grandma or Grandpa. The absolute trust of this caregiving relationship can't be duplicated with anyone else.

Practical Tips for Relating to Grandparents

As happy as you may be with the wonderful bond between your child and her grandparents, you'll still need some practical ideas for handling the day-to-day issues that may arise. Here are some of the typical problems that occur and ways to help things run smoothly:

• **Different opinions about how you should be raising your child:** Grandparents have raised their children, and you're just getting started, so that makes them feel as if they have the wisdom and knowledge to teach you how you should do the job. Take a deep breath, tell yourself that this is just a sign of their deep love for you and your baby, and read the suggestions in the entry for Unwanted Advice. Parenting has changed with the times, and necessarily so—but don't discount a grandparent's advice without considering it. You just may find a gem of parenting brilliance in a grandparent's outstretched hand.

• **Showering the baby with attention:** If you're concerned about a grandparent who gushes over your little darling as if she were the only baby on Earth, the best advice I can give you is to enjoy it! Your child can benefit tremendously from the attention of someone who thinks your child can do no wrong. It builds your child's self-esteem and gives a feeling of self-worth that can't ever be taken away.

• **Bearing excessive gifts:** A little bit of "spoiling" is a good thing. And letting the grandparents know that you appreciate their generosity is important (and good for your children to model). If you feel that a few too many toys are coming your way, though, you might tactfully suggest that the best gift for your child is the time the grandparents can spend with him. If they are intent on spending their money, you might suggest they lean toward books, educational games, clothing, or the possibility of a college savings account for your child that they can add to on holidays and special occasions.

• **Rules? What rules?** Some grandparents have so much fun with the grandchildren that you can't believe they're the same people who demanded you adhere to a hundred rules when you were growing up— none of which seem to apply to your children. The answer to this issue is to choose your battles wisely, and address those that are most important to you. Battling over a few extra cookies probably isn't worth the friction it would create, but mandatory sunscreen and hat for a day at the beach is an issue worth addressing.

• **Differing expectations:** Whether you think the grandparents spend too much time around your house or don't see the children often enough, you may find that the expectations of the relationship differ by side. Attempting to understand the other person's point of view and encouraging open conversation are the keys to finding the right balance for everyone's needs.

Grandparents, reluctant

· · · · · · · · · · · ·

See also: Breastfeeding in Public;
Grandparents, overzealous; Unwanted Advice

> I'm so disappointed! My baby is five months old, and I thought my
> mom would be so excited about having a grandchild. But she hardly
> ever comes to our house, and she has never offered to baby-sit.
> Doesn't she care?

Learn About It

Chances are, your mother *is* excited about having a grandchild, and
there may be other reasons that she's not as involved as you'd like. Perhaps you and she define a grandparent's role in a baby's life differently.
The following ideas may be helpful as you sort through this situation.

Have a Discussion

As with so many family situations, this is all about expectations. When
expectations clash with reality, misunderstandings occur. So try to find
out what she's thinking, and consider sharing your own feelings. Perhaps she's been so busy that she hasn't considered changing her lifestyle
to include visits with your new baby. Or maybe she has so many other
commitments—work, other grandchildren, an ailing spouse—that her
time is limited and she isn't aware you're feeling left out. In any case,
you can't attempt a resolution without first determining the problem.

Make an Invitation

Perhaps your mother is exercising restraint in a misguided effort not to
intrude. Let your mother know that you'd love to see more of her.

Invite her to spend more time with the baby. If you're comfortable, tell her you'd appreciate her tried-and-true advice and insight. Welcome her into your new life as warmly as you can, and you just might find that an invitation from you is all she needed.

Make It Easy for Her

Your mom may be worried that you'll view her as an on-call baby-sitter if she gets too involved with the baby's life. Let her know that, as much as you enjoy her help, you'd like to leave the baby-sitting arrangements up to her. If she has the time and desire to help, you'd welcome it, but if she prefers to stick to visits, then that would be wonderful, too.

Examine Your Own Actions When Grandma Visits

Pay attention to your responses when your mom visits. Are you so protective of your baby that you hover too much? Do you ever criticize her actions with the baby? Perhaps she misinterprets these actions as meaning that you don't want her over so much. Try to relax a bit and let her handle the baby in her own way. They'll both be fine.

If You Can't Talk About It or Nothing Works...

Sometimes, family dynamics prevent the kind of open communication that might defuse this situation. Or maybe you've tried to talk it out, but your mother's distance is beyond your influence. In this case, make sure to provide grandmother*like* interaction for your child by inviting an older female friend or an aunt or other relative to visit from time to time. Your child will benefit greatly from the wisdom, warmth, and balance offered by the generation before yours. At the same time, the relationship might bring your older friend or relative the satisfaction and joy of a child's love and may satisfy the universal urge she feels to be needed by another person at this time in her life. In other words, if your child's genetic grandparent is distant or reluctant, "choose" a grand-parent for him!

Allow Time for Changes

Remember that bringing a new member into the family requires adjustments by everyone. This little person is brand-new; those around the baby need time to redefine their comfortable places in your life and your family constellation.

Hair Care

· · · · · · · · · · · ·

See also: Bathing; Cradle Cap; Flat-Head Syndrome; Soft Spots

How should I take care of my baby's hair?

Learn About It

Some babies are born with downy peach fuzz covering their heads, some have wisps of feather-soft hair, and some have thick masses of tiny curls. Babies are as unique in their hairstyles as they are in their personalities.

For all their differences, most babies have hair that requires very little care in the first few years. Keeping it clean and brushed is very simple.

Shampooing

Baby hair doesn't get dirty every day, so a daily shampooing is unnecessary. Usually, washing your baby's hair every two to three days is sufficient. Since baby hair and skin are very delicate, a shampoo formulated for babies is best. Baby shampoos won't dry out your baby's hair and skin, and they won't sting those baby blues (or greens or browns) if any suds dribble down his face.

Before you shampoo, if your baby has rather long or curly hair, comb out any tangles with a wide-toothed comb or small brush with coated bristles. Detangle the ends first, then move on to the roots. While you need to take care not to put excess pressure on your baby's soft spots, regular brushing won't do any harm.

As soon as you've washed your baby's hair, dry it with a washcloth or small towel, even if she's not finished with her bath. This way, she won't get chilled from her wet hair.

Parent Tip

"I use a visor when I wash my son's hair. It keeps the water out of his eyes and ears. It's one of the best baby purchases I've made!"

—Kim, mother of Johnny (11 months)

What About Bald Patches?

Baby hair is very fine and often falls out or gets rubbed off in sections. This isn't anything to be concerned about; it's perfectly normal. Some of the hair loss results from a normal hormonal process that causes new-born hair to fall out, making way for baby hair. Some hair loss occurs because your baby spends a lot of time lying on her back, which rubs off the fine hair on the back of her head. If your baby loses a great amount of hair or loses it quickly, let your pediatrician know so that he or she can rule out any medical problems.

Your baby won't have bald spots for very long, since a baby's hair grows back very quickly.

What About African-American Hair?

If your baby has dry, kinky, tightly curled hair, only diligent care will prevent it from getting tangled or nappy. Here are a few tips:

- Look for specialty hair-care products made for African-Americans; many baby shampoos are designed for oilier hair and can create snarls in your baby's hair. (But use extra care so that soap doesn't get in your baby's eyes.)
- Use conditioner or baby oil on your baby's scalp after washing.
- Don't overwash; shampooing once or twice a week is usually plenty. Between washings, use clear water to remove any food or dirt that gets in Baby's hair.
- Rinse the hair from the top down, pouring water over Baby's hair.
- Use a wide-toothed comb to get the tangles out.

- When combing your baby's hair, section it off, using clips to hold the hair. Untangle beginning with the ends and working all the way up to the scalp.
- Keep your baby's hair braided, twisted, or tied up in a ponytail during sleep to prevent it from matting.

The First Haircut

If your baby has long hair, it's important to trim it in the front so pieces don't hang over her eyes, impairing vision. You can trim it yourself, either when your baby is sleeping or with the help of another adult, or take Baby into a salon and have her hair trimmed while you hold her securely on your lap.

Does Your Baby Have Cradle Cap?

If the scalp looks brown or pink and is covered with crusty or oily patches, your baby has a case of cradle cap (*see* Cradle Cap).

Heatstroke

(Sunstroke)

See also: Fever; Sunshine

> *Is there any risk of my baby getting heatstroke this summer? How can I prevent it?*

Learn About It

Heatstroke is caused by overexposure to extreme heat. Babies are at increased risk of heatstroke because their bodies are not able to regulate their internal temperatures, and they are too young to remove their own layers of clothing or to ask for a drink if they feel hot and thirsty. Heatstroke is a life-threatening condition for babies, so it's important that we know the symptoms and how to prevent it.

How Can a Baby Get Heatstroke?

Any situation that causes a baby to become overheated places that baby at risk for heatstroke. Here are some of the most common conditions for this:

- **Being enclosed in a vehicle on a warm day:** Even in an outside temperature of 70°F (21°C), the inside temperature of a closed car can reach a life-threatening level of heat in a matter of minutes.
- **Spending a long time outside in the heat:** Heatstroke is a risk during a day at the beach or an amusement park.
- **Being overdressed for the weather:** We tend to bundle babies more than necessary.

- **Sleeping in a stroller covered with a blanket on a hot day:** When covering your sleeping baby for privacy and sun protection, check that it doesn't become too hot in his "tent."

What Are the Signs of Heatstroke?

If you are in a situation that may put your baby at risk, be alert to any of the following signs of possible heatstroke:

- A sudden rise in body temperature or a temperature over 100°F (38°C)
- Hot, dry skin
- Flushed or pale skin tone
- Rapid pulse
- Vomiting
- Rapid breathing
- Shortness of breath; difficulty breathing
- Sluggishness or nonresponsiveness
- Confusion
- Signs of dehydration (*see* Dehydration)

What Should I Do if My Baby Has Heatstroke?

A baby with heatstroke can lose consciousness quickly or have convulsions, so it's important to act immediately and quickly to cool your baby down.

- If she is in a car seat or stroller, take her out.
- Move her to a cool, shady area.
- Loosen or remove her clothing.
- Spray, dribble, or sponge cool water over your baby's body.
- Fan your baby with a book or magazine.
- Have your baby sip water or breastmilk.
- Call 911 or an emergency service and describe the situation.

- Try to keep your baby calm.
- Do *not* give acetaminophen (Tylenol), ibuprofen (Advil), or aspirin, as these will not lower a temperature brought on by heatstroke.

How Can I Prevent Heatstroke?

- *Never* leave a baby alone in a car. The temperature in a car can escalate rapidly.
- Monitor your baby's temperature when she's bundled in warm clothes and in a car seat—and whenever she is in a hot car, no matter how she is dressed.
- Don't overdress or overbundle your baby. For the first few months, a baby needs about one more light layer of clothing than you do.
- Keep babies under one year old out of direct sunlight, either in a covered stroller, under an umbrella, or in the shade. Do *not* completely drape the stroller with a blanket, because it will impede ventilation and raise the temperature inside.
- When your baby must be in the sun, shield your baby's head, neck, and face with a wide-brimmed hat.
- If Baby will be out in the hot sun, dress him in loose-fitting clothing made of tight-knit fabrics. Long-sleeved shirts and long pants in lightweight fabrics can be used to cover up most of your baby's body.
- During heat wave conditions—defined as more than forty-eight hours of temperatures at 90°F (32°C) or higher, accompanied by high humidity—keep your baby indoors with air conditioning or a fan running.
- Do not take your baby into a hot tub or heated whirlpool.
- Keep your baby well hydrated by offering the breast or a bottle often or making sure your older baby is getting enough water and other fluids (*see* Dehydration).

High Chairs

See also: Baby Carriers; Infant Seats, Swings, Bouncers, and Jumpers

> *We're ready to start feeding our baby solids. What do we need to know about high chairs before we set out to buy one for our baby?*

Learn About It

A high chair represents a fun milestone in your baby's growth, and it is an important purchase because you may use it for several years. The right high chair will be a safe and comfortable place for your baby, easy for you to use, and an attractive piece of furniture to add to your kitchen.

What Are the Choices?

The choices are amazingly numerous. Just browse any store that features baby furniture or toys! The chart that follows compares the five major design types.

What Features Should We Look For?

Before shopping, make a list of features that are important to you, and take this list with you when you shop. Here are a few qualities and features to consider:

- **Construction:** Is it solid, stable, and well made?
- **Adaptable seat:** Can the seat tilt back for a young baby? Can the height be adjusted?
- **Portability:** Can it fold up? Is it lightweight and easy to move?

- **Adjustable straps:** Do the straps easily adjust to fit your growing baby? Do they attach and remove easily?
- **Tray features:** Is the tray wide with a ledge for catching spills? Is it adjustable to accommodate a growing child? Will it work for playtime as well as mealtime?
- **Ease of use:** Can the tray be moved with one hand? Are the moving and adjustable parts easy to work?
- **Washability:** Is the seat vinyl, plastic, and/or removable for washing?
- **Comfort:** Will the seat be comfortable for your baby?
- **Style:** Will the color, fabric, and style look good in your kitchen?
- **Extra features:** Does it feature any extras such as a detachable tray, wheels, or pegs for hanging a bib and washcloth?

Types of High Chairs

Type	Description	Benefits	Negatives
Standard high chair	Baby seat raised on a metal or plastic base	Freestanding; can be moved to different places in the house; tilts back to accommodate young babies; convenient height for feeding a baby; some can be used without the tray as a regular chair	Can take up a lot of room in a small kitchen; Baby is off to the side of the family table; Baby can possibly climb, fall, or slide out
Adjustable chair	A wooden seat with footrest and straps that adjusts to various heights; some have a removable tray	Adjustable in height and depth and can last from babyhood through childhood; allows Baby to sit at the table with you; attractive addition to your kitchen	Not for young babies, best for ages over 6 months; expensive

Type	Description	Benefits	Negatives
Feeding table	A baby seat within a table	Very stable; large table surface; converts to child's table or desk	Can take up a lot of room in a small kitchen; Baby is off to the side of the family table; expensive
Clip-on seat	Fabric seat that clips onto table edge	Great for taking along in a car; allows Baby to sit at the table with you	Not for young babies, best for ages 7–9 months and up; not for glass tables; may not fit some tables
Booster seat	Plastic seat that attaches to a standard kitchen chair	Great for taking in the car; allows Baby to sit at the table with you	Not for young babies, best for ages 7–9 months and up; may not fit all kitchen chairs properly
Harness	A belt with a T-restraint to hold Baby on a standard chair	Great for packing in a suitcase; allows Baby to sit at the table with you	Not for young babies; best for ages 9–10 months and up

How Do We Use a High Chair Safely?

High chair accidents are very common. The majority of these involve a baby climbing out of or falling from a chair. A few important rules can keep your baby safe:

- Follow the installation instructions included with your chair.
- Make certain that all parts are tightened. If it is a folding chair, be sure the locks are securely in place.

- Ensure that the chair is stable. If it is a booster seat, be sure it is tightly secured to the chair.
- Use the straps and harness that come with the seat every time your baby is seated in the chair.
- Never leave your baby unattended when in the high chair.
- Don't place the high chair next to anything that a child could push off from and tip the chair over.
- Don't use a broken chair or one without straps. Don't use an old high chair that is no longer sturdy or doesn't adhere to current safety standards. Some old models may tip over too easily, have no safety strap, or are painted with lead paint.
- Watch out for Baby's hands and feet when moving the tray or other adjustable parts and when deciding where to situate the chair. Make sure Baby can't reach anything dangerous, such as medications, choking hazards, and blind cords.
- Do not let your baby stand in the chair.

Hives

See also: Chicken Pox; Febrile Seizure; Fever; Rash; Roseola

> *About an hour ago, I noticed a rash on my baby's back and thought it was diaper rash. Now it's spreading to her legs and hands, but has disappeared from her back! What is it? Should I take her to the doctor?*

Learn About It

If your baby's rash appears and disappears rapidly and is composed of raised white lumps on a red or pink base, then your baby probably has hives.

What Causes Hives?

Hives are a whole-body hypersensitivity reaction and are quite common. In most cases, hives are not serious. The exact cause of the reaction has quite a few possibilities. Sometimes a thorough review of your baby's last twenty-four hours can uncover the culprit, but don't be surprised if you're left scratching your head in bewilderment. Sometimes it's very difficult to pinpoint the origin. Here are some possible causes:

• **Virus:** Sometimes hives are a sign of a viral infection in your baby's system. If your baby is or has been sick, or if someone who has been in contact with your baby is sick with a virus, then this is possible. Even a baby who doesn't act sick may break out in hives as the only sign of the virus. Bacterial infections such as streptococcus ("strep") also can cause a breakout.

• **Food:** Certain highly allergenic foods can cause hives in your baby. This is true even if your baby has had the food before without a reac-

269

tion. The most common offenders are nuts, shellfish, eggs, berries, wheat, soy, dairy products, and food additives.

- **Irritant:** Babies have sensitive skin, so you can reasonably suspect any new substance that comes in contact with your baby. Soaps, laundry detergents, fabric softeners, lotions, plants, animals, fabrics such as wool—basically anything that touches your baby's skin—may be the source.
- **Insect stings:** Hives can result from the sting of a bee, wasp, fire ant, or hornet or the bite of a mosquito or flea.
- **Heat:** Your baby might have broken out in hives as a result of becoming overheated. This can happen when a baby is overdressed or spends a day in the sun, for example (*see* Heatstroke; Rash).
- **Medication:** Any type of medication can be a potential cause of hives.

What Should I Do About Hives?

The most common treatment for hives is an oral antihistamine, such as Benadryl. This is available at your drugstore, but you should always call your doctor's office for approval and dosage recommendations before you give any medication to your baby. A very mild case of hives may not require any treatment at all. If your baby truly has hives, a dose of antihistamine will cause the hives to disappear very quickly, although they may come back and require additional doses of the medication or a little healing time before they disappear for good.

If your baby's hives are itchy, you can try some of the remedies listed for chicken pox, such as oatmeal baths and calamine lotion (*see* Chicken Pox).

Herbal treatments often are used to combat hives. The following herbs are most commonly used:

- Chickweed (*Stellaria media*) applied as a poultice or added to bathwater
- Herbal teas, such as chamomile, basil, fennel, or tarragon, applied topically
- Aloe vera gel to help relieve itching

As with any treatment (yes, even herbal), check with a medical professional before using these on your baby.

Should I Take My Baby to the Doctor?

If the hives are mild, respond quickly to an herbal remedy or antihistamine treatment in the dose advised by your doctor, and are not accompanied by other symptoms, then you most likely don't need a trip to the doctor. However, call your doctor right away if you observe any of the following signs:

- Your baby has hives all over his body, and they are worsening.
- The hives don't respond to the treatment or medication.
- Your baby's hands, feet, or face is swollen.
- The hives appear to be *under* the skin, rather than on the surface.

If hives are part of a severe allergic reaction, your baby may require additional immediate medication to prevent anaphylactic shock, a dangerous condition that can impair breathing.

Take your baby to the doctor or emergency room or call 911 if you see any of the following conditions:

- Baby is wheezing or having trouble breathing.
- Baby's throat is swollen.
- Baby is extremely weak, lethargic, or dizzy.
- Hives are developing in or around Baby's mouth.
- Baby has persistent vomiting or diarrhea.

How Long Will They Last?

Usually, hives last for a few days and then disappear, although they can last longer. Hives that persist for weeks are called chronic urticaria; while not usually serious, the condition requires a doctor's thorough examination and some lab tests to determine its underlying cause.

How Can I Prevent Hives from Recurring?

If you are lucky enough to figure out what caused the hives in the first place, such as the first experience eating shellfish or a romp with a neighbor's dog, then you can watch to see if the reaction happens again in the same situation. You also can call an allergist to discuss testing for the allergy.

If the hives are linked to an insect bite or sting, ask your doctor or pharmacist about an emergency kit to have on hand in case of another sting.

Homemade Baby Food

See also: Drinking from a Cup; High Chairs;
Solid Foods, introducing; Vegetarian Baby

> *Which is better for my baby: homemade or commercial baby food?*
> *If I do make it, what do I need to know to do it properly?*

Learn About It

Both commercially prepared and homemade baby food can be nutritious choices for your baby, and each has benefits. While properly prepared homemade baby food has the edge when it comes to whole-food nutrition, in today's busy world, commercially prepared foods are necessities in many homes. Like all decisions in parenthood, it's wise to examine the available information and make the best choice for *your* family. The chart summarizes some of the pros and cons for each.

Comparing Costs

Many people assume that homemade baby food is much cheaper than commercial baby food. However, the answer isn't as simple as comparing the price of a sweet potato to that of a jar of prepared sweet potatoes. A big factor is preparation time. If you are going to eat the same foods that you serve your baby, the process is relatively easy. However, you still will need to separate the baby's raw ingredients from yours, unless you are prepared to go without sugar, salt, and spices for a while! And if you don't always eat balanced meals with fresh ingredients, then you'll need to prepare separate dishes for your baby if you want to give him the best possible nutritional start in life.

If you do need to prepare separate dishes, then any accurate cost assessment has to figure in the cost of ingredients; fuel for cooking,

Homemade or Commercially Prepared? Pros and Cons

	Pros	Cons
Homemade baby food	• Control over ingredients • Can be flavored to suit Baby's preferences • Texture can be customized for age of Baby • Can be served when fresh • Usually more economical • Free from additives	• Takes time to prepare • Short shelf life
Commercially prepared baby food	• Saves preparation time • Wide assortment to choose from • Ready to go in single servings • Can keep a large supply on hand	• May contain additives such as salt, sugar, and thickeners • May lose nutritional value from processing and shelf time • May contain more than optimum amounts of sodium and fat

preparing, and dishwashing; storage containers; and leftovers that are thrown away.

If you enjoy cooking and have plenty of time to prepare meals, you may be a perfect homemade baby food cook. However, if you don't spend much time in the kitchen or your calendar is already filled to the maximum, making your own baby food may require more time and effort than you can spare.

Is It Safe for Me to Make My Own Baby Food?

When you stand at the grocery counter and see rows of jars bearing the labels of trusted food manufacturers, you may feel a bit intimidated. You want to feed your baby the most perfect foods for her tiny body. You may wonder, "Can I possibly match up to the quality of food prepared by these manufacturers?" The answer is yes—absolutely! If you follow basic food safety rules, your own baby food will be just as good or better than that sold in baby food jars.

How to Prepare Homemade Baby Food

If you plan to make all of your baby's food, look into a baby food cookbook for preparation tips and recipes. Here are a few of the most important things to remember:

- Be certain that all your cooking utensils, containers, and work surfaces are thoroughly cleaned.
- Wash your hands with soap and hot water before beginning food preparation, anytime you are called away from your task and return to work, or when you cough or sneeze.
- Use the food guide "Food Choices for Your Baby" (*see* Solid Foods, introducing) to determine the foods to prepare for your baby. These guidelines apply to any ingredient used in baby food.
- Thoroughly wash fruits and vegetables, and remove the skins whenever possible.
- Use fresh ingredients, and don't add spices, salt, or sugar.
- Don't allow food to sit out on the counter for long periods during preparation. Keep hot foods hot and cold foods cold.
- Once the food is prepared, don't leave it sitting at room temperature. If you are going to freeze portions, do so promptly.
- When using the microwave, stir the food thoroughly and test for hot spots before serving it to your baby.

Parent Tip

"Filling an ice cube tray and covering it with plastic wrap is a great way to make and freeze single servings. Once they're frozen, pop them from the tray and seal them in containers or clean bags."

—Timea, mother of Daniel (12), Adam (12),
Thomas (5), and Michael (3 months)

- Label all foods with the dates of preparation and freezing. Fresh, pureed foods last for two or three days in the refrigerator and for up to two months in the freezer.
- Never defrost frozen baby food on the counter. Defrost in the refrigerator, in a double boiler, or in the microwave at a low setting. Once it's defrosted, serve it within a day or two. Don't refreeze leftover portions.

Which Is More Nutritious—Commercial Foods or Homemade?

Commercial baby foods sold by major food companies do retain most of the nutrients of whole foods. They are processed and packaged while fresh and dated for your protection.

The nutritional value of homemade baby foods depends on how you prepare them. When prepared improperly, such as boiled or fried or flavored with sugar and salt, they will not be as wholesome as when prepared by steaming, baking, or microwaving without seasoning. You will have control over the nutritional quality of homemade foods, and when prepared correctly, they will meet all your baby's nutritional needs perfectly.

The Missing Nutrient: Iron

Iron is a mineral essential for health. Iron is found in red blood cells, and it carries oxygen from the lungs to the rest of the body. Without oxygen, the body's cells cannot function normally. Babies are born with iron stores that last about five or six months. After that, your baby will get iron from breastmilk or iron-fortified formula and baby cereals. If your baby's diet mainstay is none of these foods, then ask your pediatrician about an iron drop supplement. There are many different kinds of iron supplements, and they should only be taken under medical supervision to prevent an excess of iron in your baby's system. When your baby is eating more solids, you can serve foods regularly that contain iron, such as beef, fish, poultry, beans, dried fruits, whole grains, fortified cereals, and enriched breads.

What About Adult Canned Food?

Some adult canned foods compare favorably in quality and content to the same type of baby food and are less expensive. Some examples are jarred no-sugar-added applesauce, bottled pure juice, canned vegetables (without salt), and canned fruit (without sugar). The differences between these and baby food products are mainly the size of the container and the food's texture. (A food processor or blender comes in handy for breaking down foods like green beans and carrots into manageable mush for your toothless baby.) If your family uses these products, you'll avoid waste, since older family members can eat the balance of the opened container after you feed your baby. Just be sure to read the labels carefully so you are sure to purchase ingredients that are nourishing and appropriate for your baby's delicate but maturing digestive system.

Does My Baby *Have* to Eat Baby Food?

Some parents of healthy babies (particularly those who breastfeed) may decide to skip baby food altogether. They choose to focus on breastmilk as the mainstay for the first year, and they introduce table food that is mashed or cut into tiny pieces for their baby's first solid food. As long as your baby is healthy, thriving, and of normal height and weight, and as long as you are careful to monitor foods that are known to be common allergens and avoid choking hazards, this is a fine option to consider.

For More Information

Books

Kimmel, Martha, David Kimmel, and Suzanne Goldenson. *Mommy Made and Daddy Too: Home Cooking for a Healthy Baby & Toddler.* New York: Bantam Doubleday Dell, 2000.

Yaron, Ruth. *Super Baby Food.* Archbald, PA: F. J. Roberts, 1998.

Immunizations
(Vaccinations)

. . . .

See also: Chicken Pox; Febrile Seizure; Fever

Our baby is due soon, and so many things that I've never even thought about are becoming major decisions in my life! Most recently, our childbirth class had a debate about whether or not to vaccinate our babies. Everyone seems to either have a passionate opinion or to be totally confused. Can you help me sort this out?

Learn About It

Vaccination *is* a much-debated topic. When parents look at the list of recommended vaccinations, they see diseases that sound like they come from the Middle Ages: diphtheria, whooping cough, polio, smallpox, and rubella. And they may wonder why they should worry about such rare and unfamiliar illnesses. What is important to know is that, before vaccines became available in the early 1900s, more than 20 percent of infants died before they ever reached their first birthdays; often the mortality rates were even higher between the ages of one and five. One of the reasons that we no longer have to worry about such statistics, and that these diseases are so rare, is that nearly 80 percent of children in the United States are now immunized against vaccine-preventable diseases.

Having this information doesn't mean you should blindly accept any vaccination offered for your baby. Rather, you should learn about the vaccinations available and make an informed decision about your own baby's immunization program.

Risk Versus Benefits

Just about everything we do in life entails risks. Even simple daily activities, such as driving to the grocery store, carry the potential for disaster. Every day, we must make decisions in which we weigh risk against benefit. We decide, and then we proceed with caution. The real question about vaccinations is not whether they have risks (they do), but if those risks outweigh the benefits. Most authorities on the subject, such as the American Academy of Pediatrics and the Department of Health and Human Services Centers for Disease Control and Prevention, agree that the benefits of immunization far outweigh the risks. Even so, you should do your own research on this topic so that you are comfortable with your choices.

Where Do I Get the Information I Need?

As you search for information on which to base your decision, take care that you review data from *reputable* sources. People who are passionate in their beliefs often manipulate data to make a point (on both sides of any debate). Search out solid validation of your information from a number of sources—second opinions, so to speak. Talk with your pediatrician, head to the library, get on the Internet, and always consider the source and any possible underlying agenda. Once you have the facts, you can review them to arrive at the best decision for your family.

Learn About Future School Requirements

Some state laws prohibit a child from attending school without having received certain immunizations. To stay in school, children must receive additional doses, or boosters, of many of these immunizations. (See the recommended immunization schedule at the end of this topic.)

Some state laws allow for exemptions from the immunization requirements, but there are certain conditions that must be met. Often a physician must certify that a specific immunization is or may be detrimental to a child's health. Another reason that is accepted for exemption in some states is a parent or guardian's religious, philosophical, or personal beliefs objecting to immunization. When you are making decisions about your baby's immunization schedule, it is wise to check into your state's laws regarding immunization requirements, so that you are prepared in advance of your child's first school experience.

Every Family Is Unique

Whether to vaccinate isn't necessarily an all-or-nothing decision. As you learn about available vaccines, you may choose to accept some but not others or to delay a certain vaccination until your baby is older. The key to all of this is to be informed. Don't take the words of a friend or neighbor as certainty without researching them. Talk with your pediatrician, too. The choice to vaccinate your baby is a personal one and should be made only when you have thoroughly educated yourself on this subject and feel confident with your choices.

Where Can We Get Immunizations?

The most common place for your baby's vaccinations is at your pediatrician's office. These are routine and can be done at your well-baby checkups. Local health departments, hospitals, public clinics, and primary-care physicians also may provide immunizations.

Are There Times I Should *Not* Have My Baby Vaccinated?

Sometimes holding off on a particular scheduled vaccination is prudent. Most often, doctors will recommend waiting if your baby's health or history includes the following conditions:

- Currently sick (more than a mild cold)
- Fever
- Any allergies to ingredients in the vaccination
- History of convulsions
- History of severe reactions to previous vaccinations
- Disorder of the immune system or nervous system

Always talk to your doctor or a medical professional if you have concerns about any particular vaccination.

How to Make the Process Easier for Your Baby

There's no way around it: shots hurt. And watching your baby receive them is probably more painful than actually getting them! Here are a few tips that may help you make it easier:

- Expect that your baby will cry from the uncertainty of the situation as much as from the sting of the shot. If you remain calm, your baby may get through this much more easily.
- Distractions work wonders during and immediately after the shot. Point to an interesting picture on the wall, shake a toy, or talk to your baby.
- If you have an older baby, don't say, "This won't hurt," because it will, or "Don't cry," because your baby may need to cry. Instead, show compassion and offer comfort.
- Breastfeed your baby, give him a bottle or pacifier, or hold and cuddle him immediately after the shot until he has calmed down. Don't feel you must rush to get him dressed and out of the office. Your baby and you have both earned a few minutes of calm-down time!

What Are Common Side Effects of Vaccinations?

Serious side effects are rare. A few minor reactions are common and no cause for concern:

- Soreness at the site of the shot
- Slight swelling at the injection site
- Low-grade fever—up to 101°F (38.3°C)—lasting one day
- Fussiness for a day or two

If any of these happen to your baby, give her some extra cuddling, longer breastfeeding sessions, or some ice at the injection site. Ask your doctor about giving your baby acetaminophen (such as Infant's Tylenol) or ibuprofen (such as Infant's Advil). (*See also* Fever.)

The following symptoms are considered normal reactions but warrant a call to the doctor:

- Medium-grade fever—higher than 101°F (38.3°C)
- More than slight swelling at the shot site
- Extreme soreness of the injection site
- Fussiness that lasts more than a day or two
- Nausea
- A slight rash in the area of the injection

The following list shows some reactions that are considered to be severe. If your baby has any of these reactions or if something else is happening that has you concerned, call your doctor immediately or visit your local emergency room. (If symptoms are very sudden or severe, call 911 or your local emergency number.)

- Difficulty breathing or wheezing
- Hives
- Dizziness, limpness, or fainting
- High fever—greater than 105°F (40.6°C)
- Erratic heartbeat
- Convulsions (seizures)
- Constant, inconsolable crying

Write down the reactions you have observed, as well as the date, time, and type of the vaccination.

You should also report adverse reactions to the U.S. Department of Health and Human Services Vaccine Adverse Event Reporting System by phone at 1-800-822-7967 or on the Web at fda.gov/cber/vaers /vaers.htm. This is a national vaccine safety surveillance program. The federal government established this system to collect information from doctors and parents concerning reactions following vaccinations.

Recommended Childhood and Adolescent Immunization Schedule—United States, 2003

Legend: range of recommended ages | catch-up vaccination | preadolescent assessment

Vaccine ▾ / Age ▸	Birth	1 mo	2 mos	4 mos	6 mos	12 mos	15 mos	18 mos	24 mos	4-6 yrs	11-12 yrs	13-18 yrs
Hepatitis B[1]	HepB #1	only if mother HBsAg (–)	HepB #2		HepB #3						HepB series	
Diphtheria, Tetanus, Pertussis[2]			DTaP	DTaP	DTaP		DTaP	DTaP		DTaP	Td	Td
Haemophilus influenzae Type b[3]			Hib	Hib	Hib	Hib	Hib					
Inactivated Polio			IPV	IPV	IPV			IPV		IPV		
Measles, Mumps, Rubella[4]						MMR #1	MMR #1			MMR #2	MMR #2	MMR #2
Varicella[5]						Varicella	Varicella	Varicella			Varicella	
Pneumococcal[6]			PCV	PCV	PCV	PCV	PCV		PCV / PPV	PPV		
Hepatitis A[7]									Hepatitis A series	Hepatitis A series		
Influenza[8]					Influenza (yearly)							

Vaccines below this line are for selected populations

This schedule indicates the recommended ages for routine administration of currently licensed childhood vaccines, as of December 1, 2002, for children through age 18 years. Any dose not given at the recommended age should be given at any subsequent visit when indicated and feasible. ▨ Indicates age groups that warrant special effort to administer those vaccines not previously given. Additional vaccines may be licensed and recommended during the year. Licensed combination vaccines may be used whenever any components of the combination are indicated and the vaccine's other components are not contraindicated. Providers should consult the manufacturers' package inserts for detailed recommendations.

1. **Hepatitis B vaccine (HepB).** All infants should receive the first dose of hepatitis B vaccine soon after birth and before hospital discharge; the first dose may also be given by age 2 months if the infant's mother is HBsAg-negative. Only monovalent HepB can be used for the birth dose. Monovalent or combination vaccine containing HepB may be used to complete the series. Four doses of vaccine may be administered when a birth dose is given. The second dose should be given at least 4 weeks after the first dose, except for combination vaccines which cannot be administered before age 6 weeks. The third dose should be given at least 16 weeks after the first dose and at least 8 weeks after the second dose. The last dose in the vaccination series (third or fourth dose) should not be administered before age 6 months.

   Infants born to HBsAg-positive mothers should receive HepB and 0.5 mL Hepatitis B Immune Globulin (HBIG) within 12 hours of birth at separate sites. The second dose is recommended at age 1–2 months. The last dose in the vaccination series should not be administered before age 6 months. These infants should be tested for HBsAg and anti-HBs at 9–15 months of age.

   Infants born to mothers whose HBsAg status is unknown should receive the first dose of the HepB series within 12 hours of birth. Maternal blood should be drawn as soon as possible to determine the mother's HBsAg status; if the HBsAg test is positive, the infant should receive HBIG as soon as possible (no later than age 1 week). The second dose is recommended at age 1–2 months. The last dose in the vaccination series should not be administered before age 6 months.

2. **Diphtheria and tetanus toxoids and acellular pertussis vaccine (DTaP).** The fourth dose of DTaP may be administered as early as age 12 months, provided 6 months have elapsed since the third dose and the child is unlikely to return at age 15–18 months. Tetanus and diphtheria toxoids (Td) is recommended at age 11–12 years if at least 5 years have elapsed since the last dose of tetanus and diphtheria toxoid-containing vaccine. Subsequent routine Td boosters are recommended every 10 years.

3. *Haemophilus influenzae* **type b (Hib) conjugate vaccine.** Three Hib conjugate vaccines are licensed for infant use. If PRP-OMP (PedvaxHIB® or ComVax® [Merck]) is administered at ages 2 and 4 months, a dose at age 6 months is not required. DTaP/Hib combination products should not be used for primary immunization in infants at ages 2, 4, or 6 months but can be used as boosters following any Hib vaccine.

4. **Measles, mumps, and rubella vaccine (MMR).** The second dose of MMR is recommended routinely at age 4–6 years but may be administered during any visit, provided at least 4 weeks have elapsed since the first dose and that both doses are administered beginning at or after age 12 months. Those who have not previously received the second dose should complete the schedule by the 11- to 12-year-old visit.

5. **Varicella vaccine.** Varicella vaccine is recommended at any visit at or after age 12 months for susceptible children, i.e., those who lack a reliable history of chicken pox. Susceptible persons aged ≥13 years should receive two doses, given at least 4 weeks apart.

6. **Pneumococcal vaccine.** The heptavalent pneumococcal conjugate vaccine (PCV) is recommended for all children age 2–23 months. It is also recommended for certain children age 24–59 months. Pneumococcal polysaccharide vaccine (PPV) is recommended in addition to PCV for certain high-risk groups. See *MMWR* 2000;49(RR-9);1–38.

7. **Hepatitis A vaccine.** Hepatitis A vaccine is recommended for children and adolescents in selected states and regions and for certain high-risk groups; consult your local public health authority. Children and adolescents in these states, regions, and high risk groups who have not been immunized against hepatitis A can begin the hepatitis A vaccination series during any visit. The two doses in the series should be administered at least 6 months apart. See *MMWR* 1999;48(RR-12);1–37.

8. **Influenza vaccine.** Influenza vaccine is recommended annually for children age ≥6 months with certain risk factors (including but not limited to asthma, cardiac disease, sickle cell disease, HIV, diabetes, and household members of persons in groups at high risk; see *MMWR* 2002;51(RR-3);1–31), and can be administered to all others wishing to obtain immunity. In addition, healthy children age 6–23 months are encouraged to receive influenza vaccine if feasible because children in this age group are at substantially increased risk for influenza-related hospitalizations. Children aged ≤12 years should receive vaccine in a dosage appropriate for their age (0.25 mL if age 6–35 months or 0.5 mL if aged ≥3 years). Children aged ≤8 years who are receiving influenza vaccine for the first time should receive two doses separated by at least 4 weeks.

For additional information about vaccines, including precautions and contraindications for immunization and vaccine shortages, please visit the National Immunization Program Website at www.cdc.gov/nip or call the National Immunization Information Hotline at 800-232-2522 (English) or 800-232-0233 (Spanish).

Approved by the Advisory Committee on Immunization Practices (www.cdc.gov/nip/acip), the American Academy of Pediatrics (www.aap.org), and the American Academy of Family Physicians (www.aafp.org).

For More Information

Books

Cave, Stephanie, and Deborah Mitchell. *What Your Doctor May Not Tell You About Children's Vaccinations.* New York: Warner Books, 2001.

Humiston, Sharon G., and Cynthia Good. *Vaccinating Your Child: Questions and Answers for the Concerned Parent.* Atlanta: Peachtree Publishers, 2000.

Romm, Aviva Jill. *Vaccinations: A Thoughtful Parent's Guide: How to Make Safe, Sensible Decisions About the Risks, Benefits, and Alternatives.* Rochester, VT: Healing Arts Press, 2001.

Websites

The American Academy of Pediatrics
aap.org

Department of Health and Human Services Centers for Disease Control and Prevention
cdc.gov/nip

Independent Play

See also: Attachment Parenting; Milestones of
Development; Separation Anxiety; Toys

> *My baby is happy only when I'm playing with her. If I even dare to
> leave the room, she cries as if I've left the country! I'm at home with
> her all day, and I truly enjoy her, but sometimes I feel like her per-
> sonal entertainment director. I'd like her to play by herself from
> time to time so that I can do other things. Am I being selfish?*

Think About It

Simply put, if children love an activity, they will pursue it. And playing with Mommy or Daddy is certainly at the top of any baby's list of
favorite things to do. You should feel honored to hold that spot! Still,
it's not good for either of you if she can't play by herself for short periods of time. Independent play benefits not just you, but her, too: It helps
develop creativity, confidence, patience, attention span, and many more
desirable attributes. So while you get to cross a few things off your to-
do list, she works on her growth and development. Therefore, you don't
need to feel guilty about wanting this for yourself and for your baby, as
long as you maintain balance between solitary and "together" playtime.
Both kinds are important to her development.

The Steps to Independence

Encouraging independent play isn't something you can accomplish
overnight, but there are many steps you can take to gradually help her
toward discovering what a wonderful "playmate" her own imagination
and independence can be. Try these:

- Play peekaboo or a short version of hide-and-seek with your baby. Once she understands that you are still there even when she can't see you, she'll be more comfortable when you leave the room.

- Don't sneak out of the room when she's not looking. When she realizes you're gone, she may panic and forever after worry that you'll disappear if she isn't paying attention—perhaps causing her "Mommy radar" to function even more actively. That said, don't make a big production of your walking away, either. Just casually tell her what you're going to do: "I'm taking this basket to the laundry room," or, "I'm going to get my glasses." Then sing, talk, or hum as you go, so she can still hear your voice even though she can't see you.

- Start off on the floor with your baby and engage her in a favorite toy or activity. Once she's involved, move a few feet away. Sit and watch her; smile or say a few positive words when she looks your way. If she pulls you back, repeat the same process. Over time, move your "observation spot" farther away, and watch for longer periods. When she's comfortable with this, then start your own activity in the same room—such as reading, knitting, cleaning, or doing paperwork. Eventually, you'll be able to cook a meal or do your work while she entertains herself.

- Create and follow a daily routine that includes some short bursts of solo play. For example, set up a regular pattern of playtime while you prepare a meal, pay bills, clean the kitchen, or attend to a few career details—whatever tasks you can accomplish within earshot. Once she is used to this routine, she'll automatically head to her toys at this time of day.

Parent Tip

"My daughter was such a clingy baby I called her my Super Glue Girl. I found that when my friend came for a visit with her three-year-old my baby was so engaged playing with her daughter that she didn't need me as much. I began to arrange more play dates, and this helped her become more independent."

—Shaur-Yun, mother of Natalie (13 months)

• Set aside special playtimes with your daughter. During these periods, give her your undivided attention. Set a timer and explain, "I'm setting the timer for ten minutes, and we can play. When the timer rings, I have to go make dinner." As she gets used to this routine, she'll enjoy your one-on-one playtime and become more relaxed with having you nearby afterward, instead of right by her side.

• Don't feel that you must always play directly with your baby; doing so just heightens her need for you to orchestrate her activities. A better choice is to let the activity move in the direction your child wishes, with your gentle guidance when needed. You may start off putting a puzzle together, but your baby may want to play "pretend" with the pieces. Instead of guiding her back to the puzzle's intended use, go with her inclinations! You might be surprised and delighted at where her creativity takes you both. Then move aside a little, and let her take over on her own.

• As you increase your baby's time in independent play, keep a close watch on her. Go to her and give her your attention *before* she starts to fuss or cry, so she doesn't get any bad feelings about playing alone. She'll learn to trust that you're there when she needs or wants you. If you miss her cues and she begins to get upset or cry, don't mirror her reaction with your response, "Oh, honey, don't cry! It's OK! I'm right here!" She'll only pick up on your tension over the situation. Instead, stay even keeled and cheerful; she'll become calm more easily, too.

• Take advantage of those times when your baby initiates some independent play. This often happens when you least expect it, and you may be missing chances to let her find joy in her own activities. Try not to disturb her if she is involved in a solo activity; your mere presence may break the spell and cause your child to focus on you again.

• Don't push your child away when he's clinging to you. Doing so might amplify his feelings of helplessness. Instead, give him some extra cuddles and then distract him with a fun toy or activity. Once he's happily engaged, you can slowly pry yourself away.

• Set up your baby's play area so that many different toys and activities are in plain sight. A packed toy box is too confusing for a little one to pick from. Instead, take a cue from the typical kindergarten classroom: Line up various toys around the room so that your child can move from one activity to the next, as she desires, without your having to search for things to keep her busy.

• Make certain that your home is thoroughly childproofed. You actually may be *encouraging* clingy behavior by following your baby around and pulling her away from dangerous or delicate items. Do what it takes to keep those items safe for (or from) your baby so you'll feel better about taking your eyes off her for a minute or two. She'll notice the difference when she is free to explore happily and independently.

• Include your baby in your own activities. Little ones love to "help," whether it's sorting laundry, putting away groceries, snapping beans, or washing things. In fact, "Helping Mommy" is a game that often starts out as a team activity and evolves into side-by-side play and work. Look into toys that are miniature versions of household items, such as pots and pans, vacuum cleaners, and such, or provide your child with safe items from your kitchen cabinets. In this way, you can create a situation where your child plays happily near you while you tend to your own activities.

• It bears repeating: Shoot for a balance between independent play and time spent together. Both have important benefits for your baby and for you. A few short years from now, your baby will be a child, and in a blink after that, a teenager. She'll be off on her own, leaving you to wish she'd spend a little more time with you. Enjoy it now!

Infant Seats, Swings, Bouncers, and Jumpers

See also: Attachment Parenting; Baby Carriers; Strollers

What kind of baby entertainment seat should I buy?

Learn About It

There's no doubt that your baby's favorite place in the early months will be in your arms, and a wise and loving parent will indulge that longing (of both Baby and parent) early, often, and whenever possible. When your baby is awake and isn't in your arms, ideally she should be on her tummy learning how to use her muscles and building her strength as she heads toward the independence of crawling.

Sometimes, though, you'll want her nearby but need both hands free for other tasks, and you'll want an option other than placing her on the floor. Baby seats, swings, and the like allow your baby to be in the middle of family activity, watching the goings-on from a safe and comfortable place. Other times, you'll enjoy face-to-face playtime with your baby while she sits in her baby seat, and a bouncer or swing can make a fussy baby very happy. These also are great places for Baby to interact with a sibling who's too young to hold his baby brother or sister. As long as you use these devices judiciously, they can be excellent purchases for the months before your baby begins to sit independently and before she becomes busier crawling than sitting!

Choices in Baby Seats

You certainly don't need every imaginable baby product that's sold. In fact, many of these are useful only for the first six to nine months.

Given that you'll only use them for such a short time, it makes sense to choose wisely. Let's take a look at what you have to choose from.

Infant Seat

An infant seat is a soft little fabric chair that hangs from a metal or plastic frame and often has a rocking, bouncing, or vibrating option. Some features to look for:

- A big seat that won't become too small for your baby before she outgrows the need for it
- A wide, stable, nonslip base
- A removable toy bar that allows you to change the toys that hang from it
- A T-style safety strap to hold your baby securely

Baby Swing

Young babies love movement, and lots of babies enjoy the motion that a swing provides. Many a tired, fussy baby has been soothed by a ride in a baby swing. The biggest risk is overuse—even the fussiest baby shouldn't be left to swing for hours on end! If you choose to purchase a baby swing, look for these features:

- An accessible seat that allows you easy-in, easy-out access, even for a sleeping baby, without struggling to get past crossbars
- A cradle feature that allows your baby to lie flat for sleep, or a seat that tilts back
- Pleasant sound during movement
- Quiet cranking sound, or a battery-operated mechanism
- Secure straps and harness
- Variable speeds so the swing can be adjusted to suit your baby

Parent Tip

"Best-kept secret about baby swings: Some babies hate them! People talk about them like they're the answer to a parent's prayer. Only after I confessed that my son hated his did I find out that I had plenty of company. Sometimes it's good to know from the get-go that there's no guarantee your baby will like a piece of equipment, especially if you're thinking of spending some money on it."
—**Karen, mother of Daniel (12) and Mary (10)**

Jumper

This is a baby seat that's suspended from a long cord hanging from a clamp above a door frame (think baby bungee jumping). As the name implies, the cord is springlike and allows your baby to bounce and jump. This is fun for a baby who is a stable sitter and has full control of his head and neck.

You have a few issues to consider before you buy a doorway jumper. First, it can be used only for a few months, since your baby needs full body control to begin using it and then may grow beyond the jumper's weight limit quickly. The second concern of many doctors is that it allows a baby to use leg, hip, and joint muscles in a way in which they weren't intended, possibly causing harm to a baby's development. Not enough research has been done on this issue, but it does warrant your consideration.

If you use a baby jumper, be certain it is properly installed so that the clamps don't come loose and fall down onto your baby. Make sure that the jumper has an all-around bumper so your baby doesn't hurt himself banging into a door frame. Also, use discretion: Limit your baby's stints in the jumper to short periods and watch out for older siblings.

Stationary Entertainment Center

As a replacement for baby walkers, which have been deemed dangerous to babies' safety and aren't conducive to proper development, manufacturers have developed the stationary entertainment center (such as the Evenflo ExerSaucer). It's basically a baby seat placed within a desk filled with toys and activities. Some offer a bouncing or rocking feature. Babies who aren't yet able to sit independently or crawl do enjoy the benefit of sitting upright, but just like jumpers, these seats put a baby in a body position that's ahead of the baby's developmental ability. When used sparingly, this type of seat can offer a fun diversion for your baby, but do be careful it doesn't take the place of critical floor time or important "in-arms" time.

Parent Tip

"I have always loved holding my babies; there are few things in life so exquisite as a baby in your arms. But as a mother of twins, I know all too well that an infant seat can be a sanity saver for a parent when things get hectic. With my twins, I normally carried one baby in a baby carrier, and the other baby used the infant seat or swing. Then, after a while, I'd switch, so that each baby got plenty of in-arms time."

—**Alice, mother of Patrick (6), Carolyn (4),**
and twins Rebecca and Thomas (2)

The Bottom Line

The best place for your baby is in your arms or on his tummy on the floor. These places provide your baby with the human contact that is so critical to a baby's well-being, along with the opportunity to naturally develop muscles and physical abilities. Of course, infant seats are fine to use for your baby's enjoyment and your convenience! But do be sure to make thoughtful, informed choices about using these devices so that they don't become the default location for your baby's life.

Intelligence

See also: Milestones of Development; Reading; Talking

> *I have read about the importance of intellectual development during the first two years. How do I help my baby learn? What should I teach him?*

Think About It

Babies are remarkable. In the first two years of life, they learn an entire language and an incredible amount of information. Babies are learning all the time, whether we are consciously teaching them or not. They are actively seeking information, and it's up to us to deliver it in ways they can understand and learn from. Both genetics and environment play a part in who your child is and who he becomes, in both his personality and his abilities. The stimulation and learning opportunities you offer during the very important early years are the tools you and your baby use to build his intellectual foundation from the raw material with which he's born.

Believe in Your Baby

Typically, a parent who understands and truly believes that her baby *can* learn will naturally offer many opportunities and experiences in everyday life. So, no matter whether your baby is two days old or two years old, keep these important facts in mind:

• **Babies understand more than you think.** Your little one may not be able to talk, but he has the use of five amazing senses and a rapidly forming brain to process all that input. From birth, babies are built to absorb information, and they do so at an incredible pace. Just witness the astonishing leap from a newborn to a chatterbox two-year-old!

- **Babies learn though observation.** Your baby is watching everything around her, from a gently falling feather to a puppy running past. She is making connections about what she sees to everything else she has ever seen and putting the pieces together to create rules about how things in our world work. She looks for patterns that help her predict how one action follows another.
- **Babies learn through experimentation.** Everything your baby touches provides a lesson in science, mathematics, physics, and more. Your baby's every action gives him further insight into his world.
- **Babies learn by the way we treat them.** Your baby is making daily decisions about life that are crucial to his emotional and intellectual development: Is the world good or bad? Will my needs be met? Are the important things in my life—family, food, shelter—consistent and comforting? Am I capable? Am I valued and loved?

How Your Baby's Brain Works

Your baby's brain contains billions of nerve cells called neurons, which in turn have fibers called dendrites that receive messages from other cells. Most neurons also have axons, which carry messages to other cells. When dendrites connect to axons, synapses are formed; these transmit impulses that control everything that goes on inside your child. Synapses are the basis of intelligence. Just one neuron can connect to 15,000 other brain cells (!), and your baby will make many, many more than he will ever need. Those that aren't used eventually disappear, while those that are used most often will strengthen and stay. In other words, "Use it or lose it"!

So how can you encourage your baby's brain to develop these connections? Easy: Just think of every new experience and every new conversation as forming another connection in the ever more intricate web that is your baby's amazing brain. Every time that experience or a similar one is repeated, the connection is woven a little more strongly. And make no mistake: During the first two years, the brain grows faster than at any other time of life. By the time your baby is an adult, your baby's brain will be four times the size it was at birth!

Language as a Key to Learning

Your baby may not understand every word spoken, but he does understand what you are trying to convey through the pitch and tone of voice and your nonverbal cues. When you pick up your crying baby and hold him close as you croon soft, comforting words, he understands that he is safe and, because he sees you as an extension of himself, whole. You are the source of nourishment, comfort, or a solution to whatever he senses is wrong. For him, it's most likely what we would describe as a "gut feeling"—something we sense instinctively but can't put into words.

This is the single most important thing to remember when your baby cries: He is trying to tell you something but lacks words. When you respond, a connection is made in his brain: He has made a noise with breath and mouth, and something has resulted. He will develop different cries when he realizes that each produces a different response from you. Soon, you will know when he is crying out of hunger, fatigue, pain, or boredom. These are the first steps in the intricate and beautiful dance we call communication (*see* Crying).

Over time, your baby will learn what your words mean and will gradually come to understand the whole of language being spoken around him. Babies understand language much earlier than they can speak it, for various physiological reasons. Despite your baby's verbal silence, however, those synapses are forming and firing, always. You can encourage your baby's intellectual growth by using language in the following ways:

• **Name objects** for your baby as you go through your day. Give everything that your baby sees a name and even a brief description.
• **Narrate your actions.** As you bathe, dress, and play with your baby, describe what you are doing. As your baby watches you make lunch, give a running commentary. He'll love to hear you talk, and he'll

learn so much. The more language your baby hears, the better he will learn it.

• **Simplify.** Use shorter, more specific sentences when you talk to your baby. She is sifting through what you say to focus on the words she knows, so help her out by keeping your language clear and concise. This doesn't mean you should use baby talk, though. Normal everyday language is best for communicating with your baby—with a few baby-talk favorites thrown in for fun!

• **Exaggerate your speech.** Babies enjoy listening to people talk, and that is how they learn. They focus on the sounds, pitch, and tone of words, so don't rush through your paragraphs and leave your baby behind! Balance your normal conversation *around* your baby with exaggerated speech directed *to* your baby.

• **Talk eye to eye.** Your baby learns how to talk not only by listening, but also by watching. You'll often see your baby intently watching your lip and tongue movements as you speak. Encourage this by frequently talking close to your baby's face so that she can see your mouth when you speak.

• **Ask lots of questions.** When you ask questions, your voice naturally rises and becomes more animated. Think of questions as invitations for your baby to respond, even when those responses are coos and babble.

• **Listen to your baby.** You baby will try his turn at conversation, too. The pauses you make allow your baby to process your words and to respond to you as well. At first, this is a movement, a gesture, or a noise that seems to say, "Yes! I hear you." Act as if your baby has said something interesting and respond to his attempt to talk to you, which will encourage more two-way conversation. Remember, he's looking for patterns. Listening to your baby after speaking to him demonstrates the essence of dialogue: One speaker, having said her piece, gives the floor to the other speaker.

• **Encourage your baby's attempts at language.** When your baby begins to make the sounds of language, take advantage of this by playing sound games. Animal noises, alphabet games, and songs, for example, are great ways to encourage sound making. Make a noise, and encourage your baby to repeat. As always, this should be done only as long as both you and your baby are having fun; it shouldn't be a chore.

• **Read to your baby.** The early days of reading together set a tone for your child's future relationship with books, which will be critical to his success in school. In addition, your baby will love hearing your voice and looking at the pictures as you tell a tale (*see* Reading).

All the World's a Classroom

Your baby is an explorer and a scientist. Everything in the whole world is new and exciting. While you may not see it that way, your baby sees a trip to the post office as being just as wonderful as a trip to the zoo. You are your baby's guide through this exciting process of discovery. Stimulate and satisfy your baby's incredible curiosity in these ways:

• **Take your baby with you.** Whenever possible, take your baby along with you when you leave the house. Although many of your trips are routine errands to you, they are new and interesting experiences for your baby, and all the world offers something of interest to your baby.

• **Home is a rich environment for learning.** Your baby will find great interest in what's in the kitchen cabinets, your dresser drawers, and even the laundry basket. As long as she's safe, let her explore. Try to set few restrictions in your babyproofed house, and provide careful, consistent supervision, of course!

• **Show your baby how things work.** Whether it's the simple task of unlocking the door with a key or the more complicated process of building a shelf, your baby will find joy in learning about something new.

• **Provide an assortment of toys.** From the simplest of toys (such as blocks) to more complicated amusements, anything new is exciting to your baby. Keep in mind that nearly *anything* can be a toy to a baby, so look around your house for everyday things that can entertain and teach your little one: spoons, empty boxes, measuring cups—the possibilities are endless (*see* Toys).

• **Involve all her senses.** Provide your little one with things to see, smell, taste, hear, and touch. This will allow her to get those synapses firing in all the parts of her brain for a multisensory learning experience.

- **Let your baby set the pace.** Watch your baby for cues that tell you what's interesting to her, and follow her lead. She may be content to spend twenty minutes folding and unfolding your kitchen towels. Her interest is what tells you that the experience is a worthwhile endeavor.

- **You are your baby's favorite toy!** People are a baby's favorite play toys: you, your partner, your older children, grandparents, friends. Whenever you talk, sing, dance, read, and laugh, you are engaging your baby in very important ways.

You can provide your baby with the enrichment he needs during this critical period of learning in so very many ways. Enjoy this fun, exciting, and ultimately amazing time together with your child.

For More Information

Books

Acredolo, Linda, and Susan Goodwyn. *Baby Minds: Brain-Building Games Your Baby Will Love.* New York: Bantam Doubleday Dell, 2000.

Eliot, Lise. *What's Going on in There?: How the Brain and Mind Develop in the First Five Years of Life.* New York: Bantam Doubleday Dell, 2000.

Staso, William H. *Brain Under Construction.* Santa Maria, CA: Great Beginnings Press, 1997.

Jaundice

See also: Birthmarks; Rash

> *The whites of my newborn's eyes look a little yellow to me. His skin seems kind of yellow, too. Is this normal?*

Learn About It

What you are seeing is a common condition among newborn babies called jaundice. If you look inside your baby's mouth, you may see some yellow coloring in there, too. The level of jaundice will determine what actions you need to take. First, it's helpful to know what is happening in your baby's body that is creating this yellow coloring.

What Causes Jaundice?

Before birth, your baby relied on a high level of red blood cells to get oxygen from Mom's blood. Now that he's "out here" and *breathing* oxygen, his body has to get rid of those excess red blood cells. As the liver breaks these down, it produces bilirubin—a yellowish pigment—and lots of it. Since your baby's liver is immature, it just can't process the glut of bilirubin in his bloodstream. The bilirubin builds up, dissolves into the layer of fat just beneath the skin's surface—and turns your baby yellow! (Some babies look more like they have a suntan, their color being more brown than yellow.) As your newborn's system matures over the first week or two, he will no longer produce this excess of bilirubin.

In rare instances, jaundice results from a slow start to breastfeeding but quickly resolves with frequent nursing. Also, premature or low-birthweight babies are more prone to jaundice than their heavier, full-term counterparts.

What Should I Do About Jaundice?

The first thing to do is mention it to your midwife or doctor. Your health care professional can measure your baby's bilirubin level using a small blood sample from the heel.

What if the Bilirubin Level Is Only Slightly Elevated?

If your baby has a mild case of jaundice, you can help him by feeding him frequently, especially in the early days. Before your milk comes in, your breasts produce colostrum, which has a laxative effect and helps carry away waste. (That's another of the miracle properties of breastmilk.)

The best fluid for your baby is breastmilk, and the second choice is formula. Both are preferred over glucose (sugar) water. Whether you nurse or offer formula, the more diapers you have to change, the better!

What Will Be Done if My Baby's Bilirubin Level Is Too High?

Your health care provider will tell you if your baby's bilirubin level is too high or is rising. A high level of bilirubin must be brought down to prevent complications that can affect the nervous system.

The traditional treatment is for your baby to spend some time under special phototherapy lights. This is difficult in that you will have to be separated from your baby for a few hours or even days. Let your doctor know that you would choose this treatment if it is the *only available* option. Ask about other choices. If your baby must undergo this treatment, ask about ways in which you can be with your baby—for example, by holding your baby's hand and talking to him during treatment.

A new method for delivering phototherapy involves wrapping the baby in a special blanket (called a bili-blanket) embedded with optical fibers that deliver light to your baby's back. Another, newer method relies on a cummerbund-like device that delivers the light therapy. Both of these are good choices because you can hold your baby throughout treatment; sometimes you can even take these devices home with you to treat your baby there. Beyond the obvious and important physical advantages, this is much less expensive than keeping your baby in the hospital.

Some parents think sunlight will have the same effect as phototherapy lights, but it doesn't. In fact, putting a newborn in direct sunlight isn't a good idea because of the danger of sunburn.

In an extremely small percentage of cases, jaundice is severe and doesn't respond well to phototherapy. Your doctor will discuss the options with you if your baby is one of the few affected by this type of jaundice.

When Should I Call the Doctor?

You should let your health care provider know if you observe the following conditions:

- Jaundice is severe (skin or eyes are extremely yellow).
- Jaundice lasts longer than a week.
- Your baby seems excessively sleepy.
- Your jaundiced baby is not feeding every two hours during the day and about every three hours during the night.
- Your baby was premature or is sick and looks jaundiced.

Marriage

· · · · · · · · · · · ·

See also: Baby Blues; Postpartum Depression; Separation Anxiety

I just read that after a baby is born, about half of all couples experience a decline in marital satisfaction. We're about to have our first baby; how can we prevent this from happening to us?

Learn About It

When a baby joins your family, your life changes dramatically. The way you will spend your days—and your nights—will be astonishingly different from before your baby was born. The way you feel about yourself and your place in the world shifts. Your priorities rearrange themselves into new patterns. To keep your marriage strong and loving, you will have to redefine your relationship. You'll best succeed if you and your partner acknowledge and embrace these changes in a new design that includes your roles as mother and father, as well as those of husband and wife.

Communication Is Key

As soon as your baby is born, you'll be whooshed into a whirlwind of change and activity. There will be immediate and dramatic changes to your daily schedule. There will be visitors and gifts, thank-you notes to write, and purchases—big and small—to make. You'll both be learning how to diaper, feed, bathe, and care for a baby, and nobody will be getting any sleep at all. Is it any wonder that your marriage isn't getting the same amount of nurturing as when it was just the two of you?

What's most important during this time is that you talk to each other. Share your feelings about what's going on in your lives, talk about what worries or concerns you, and best of all, don't be afraid to have endless conversations about the wonder and miracle of your precious baby.

Talking to each other will be a key component to keeping your marriage healthy, not just during this time of transition, but for the rest of your lives as well.

Understand That It's Just a Phase

My husband and I have gone through the new-baby phase four times, and it has been a little easier each time. By the time newborn number four joined our family, we could simply look at each other and pass a message between us that said, "I love you with all my heart, but I'm a little distracted right now. Don't worry, I'll be back."

If you find that things are a little odd right now, that's perfectly normal. You're both dealing with this major life change, and it will take a bit before you settle into the new family configuration. If you continue to communicate, you can help each other work through these adjustments and come out on the other end a new family with a strong, loving marriage at the head.

How Intimacy Changes

Typically, if you ask your doctor when you can have sex again, the doctor will say you should wait six weeks after the birth of your baby. Many couples envision a pre-wedding-type waiting period followed by exciting and passionate honeymoon sex. This is often very far from reality.

A woman's physical self undergoes a major change; pregnancy and delivery have an effect on a woman's body like nothing else imaginable. Breastfeeding a new baby every two hours or so, coupled with the fatigue of endless night waking, further shape the purely physical impact of childbearing. Some studies demonstrate that nearly 80 percent of mothers—no matter how deeply they love their husbands—experience a loss of sex drive during the first year of their baby's life, and another 60 percent find that it takes yet another year before they rediscover their pre-baby sexual passion. Many families welcome another pregnancy during this time, further complicating the sexual aspect of their relationship.

These biological effects, though, don't have to signal an end to an exciting and passionate sex life. (Just look around you at all the families with a nest full of children—how do you think they got there?) It does mean that you may need to modify your approach to intimacy, replacing frequent, spontaneous sex with sex that is wonderfully intimate but thoughtfully scheduled.

Make a Commitment to Your Marriage

Once you've passed through the new-baby stage, you'll want to continue to build and maintain a strong marriage. To do this, you must be willing to invest time, effort, and thought. The ideas that follow will help you create and maintain deep meaning and joy in your marriage:

- **Look for the good; overlook the bad.** Make it a habit to ignore little annoying things—dirty socks on the floor, a day-old coffee cup on the counter, worn-out flannel pajamas, an inelegant burp at the dinner table. Choose instead to focus on things that make you smile: the way he rolls on the floor with the baby; the fact that she made your favorite cookies, the peace of knowing someone so well that you *can* wear your worn-out flannels or burp at the table.
- **Give compliments freely and frequently.** Compliments are powerful. They can bring your partner closer to you. Compliments are easy to give; you just have to make the effort to say them. A kind word can bring a smile to your partner's face and lift the mood of the day.
- **Show your appreciation.** Your partner can become your port in the sometimes wild storms of life. He or she may know you better than anyone else in the world—the only one who understands what little things make you most happy. Whenever small favors pass between you, acknowledge them. "Thank you" hugs and "you're welcome" kisses are marvelous ways to stay close, even when days are hectic.
- **Pick your battles.** This is great advice for child rearing—and for marriage as well. Any human relationship has its share of disagreement and conflict. The key to a happy marriage is to decide which issues are worth pursuing and which are better off ignored.

• **Make time for intimacy.** As busy as you may be, as tired as you may get, find the time to stay close to your spouse physically. The foundation for this is the power of touch throughout your days together. Holding hands, hugging, massaging each other's tense shoulders—they're all part of the intimate relationship you have. Every small physical gesture helps to set the stage for more involved overtures when the opportunity presents itself. The more you incorporate these tender actions into your days, the more likely they will extend into your nights in the form of sexual intimacy.

• **Talk . . . and listen, too.** As you work through the years, your marriage will change and shift according to the various milestones in your relationship, such as having children, moving to new homes, and dealing with the challenges that all people face. What's important is keeping the lines of communication open. Talking to each other and truly *listening* to the other's words, hearing the feelings behind the words, will help you two understand one another and stay close.

• **Make time for couple time.** It can be very difficult for your marriage to thrive if you spend all your time being Mommy and Daddy. You need to spend regular time as Husband and Wife, too. This doesn't mean you have to take a two-week vacation in Hawaii (although that might be nice!). Just take small daily snippets of time when you can enjoy uninterrupted conversation or even just quiet companionship. A daily morning walk around the block or a shared cup of tea after your children are in bed might work wonders to reconnect you to each other. And yes, it's quite fine to talk about your baby when you're spending your time together, because, after all, your baby is one of the most important connections you have in your relationship. Sharing the joys that come with having children is one of the things that can keep your marriage close and loving.

When you and your spouse regularly connect in ways that nurture your relationship, you will find that you can maintain a sparkling love between you that will also help you be loving parents.

Massage

See also: Bathing

I've heard that giving my baby a massage would be good for her. What do I need to know about massaging my baby?

Learn About It

Baby massage has been practiced since ancient times. It can be as simple as a gentle rub with lotion after a bath or a more practiced infant massage. The benefits are many for both Baby and parent.

Benefits for Your Baby

- Helps your baby relax
- Stimulates circulation, digestion, and neurological development
- Promotes more restful sleep
- Improves the efficiency of your baby's immune system
- Stimulates your baby's developing nervous system
- Helps relieve pain of colic, gas, illness, and teething
- Promotes healthy weight gain
- Enhances sensory awareness
- Stimulates growth-promoting hormones
- Provides Baby with much-loved touch and connection
- Increases bonding and attachment between Baby and parent
- Provides premature and special-needs babies with immense physiological benefits

Benefits for Parents

- Builds your confidence in baby handling
- Provides you an opportunity to become more competent in reading your baby's cues

- Gives you a special, focused time with your baby
- Deepens the bond between you and your baby
- Provides you with a tool for calming and settling your baby
- Gives parents of premature babies or babies with special needs a way to bond with and help their baby
- Provides parents with an effective way to settle a fussy or colicky baby
- Gives parents a loving way to introduce a sibling to a new baby
- Allows you to enjoy the feel of your baby's miraculous little body

Getting Ready for Baby's Massage

You can massage your baby at any time and in any place. Most babies love to be touched—and most parents love to touch their babies—so anytime you feel like rubbing your baby, you should. In addition to casual touches, you can also plan for a more organized massage as well. A massage is a wonderful way to end a bathing session, begin or end the bedtime ritual, or start the day. Here are some guidelines to prepare for a peaceful baby massage:

- Choose a time when you won't be interrupted or rushed.
- Make sure that your baby isn't too hungry (or too full).
- If your baby is colicky, you may want to choose the time just before crying usually begins.
- Choose a warm room—at least 75°F (23.9°C)—without any drafts. Depending on how warm the room is, you may want to keep Baby covered with a small blanket during the massage, leaving out the body parts that you are massaging.
- Leave your baby in as little clothing as conditions permit—a diaper or nothing at all. (Just keep something handy to cover up that diaper area fast, just in case!)
- If you and your baby would enjoy it, play some soft music, or use the time to talk to and sing to your baby.
- Lay your baby on a soft towel or blanket on the floor or on a bed. A small baby can lie skin-to-skin on your stomach or across your legs.

- Have warm baby lotion or oil ready, if you wish to use one of these. Choose oils made especially for babies, when possible. Avoid nut-based oils, like peanut and almond, to avoid the risk of allergic reactions. And avoid having oils on or next to your baby's face and hands (since they may likely find their way to Baby's mouth!).

Giving Baby a Massage

Here are a few tips on making the massage a pleasant experience:

- Tell your baby what you are doing and ask for permission: "Would you like Mommy to give you a massage?" This sends a message right from a young age that your baby's body belongs to her.
- Always watch your little one for signs of enjoyment (smiles, coos, relaxed posture) or dissatisfaction (turning away, fussing, closing arms, crawling away), and stop if she seems uncomfortable or restless. If your baby is having a colic episode, attempt to calm her with massage before judging her response to the massage. Sometimes babies take a few minutes to adjust, or they may like the massage at first but then have had enough and would like to stop. Respect your baby's signals.
- If you are using oil or lotion, put a bit of it on your hands and rub them together. Never pour anything directly onto your baby.
- Use warm hands when touching your baby.
- Use a gentle touch, but not so light that it tickles your baby—about the same pressure you would use on your eyelids without causing any discomfort. On small areas of your baby's body, use your fingertips. On larger areas, like the back, use the palms of your hands.
- As a general rule, strokes should move from the center of your baby's body outward. For example, when massaging arms, go from shoulders out to hands.
- Keep your movements balanced; if you massage the left arm, then also do the right arm.
- If your baby is a newborn, don't massage near the umbilical cord or the circumcision site (if your baby has been circumcised).

- Don't forget to massage those teeny feet—a delightful experience for any parent!
- Start with a short session at first—no more than about five minutes. Over time, lengthen your massage sessions to twenty or thirty minutes, basing the length of time on your baby's signals of enjoyment.
- Don't massage your baby if she has a fever, has just had an immunization, or is ill.

Read Your Baby's Signals

Very young babies or those who are new to massage are often uncertain about it. Vary the pressure and location of your touch depending on your baby's reactions. Watch your baby's face and body language for feedback. This is a learning experience for both of you.

Parent Tip

"I loved doing massage with all my babies and took a massage class in Sweden. I remember the teacher there recommended giving the massage in a steamy bathroom so our newborns wouldn't get chilled. I played the same music every day when I did the massage, and after a while, they knew that when I turned on that music, they were in for a treat!"

—Alice, mother of Patrick (6), Carolyn (4), and twins Rebecca and Thomas (2)

What About Siblings?

Here's a wonderful experience for your older child and baby alike: teach big brother or sister how to massage the baby. This can create a special bond between them and can promote soft and gentle touches. Massage time for your baby is often a perfect time to massage your older child, too. As your baby gets a little older, he'll probably want his turn at massaging his older sibling. Few things are more special for a parent than watching siblings treat each other with gentle loving care, and this kind of ritual is perfect for encouraging sibling attachment.

At What Age Should Massage Begin?

You can, and should, massage a child of any age from newborn to adulthood. Children learn much about the power of gentle touch. My son David knows how wonderful a massage can be, and when he was eight years old, he gave me a nightly back massage throughout my pregnancy with his baby brother. (Yes, *every* night—isn't that sweet?) All of my older children love to be rubbed; there's something very special about spending a little time giving your teenager a back rub or foot massage. It maintains a beautiful parent-child connection throughout a lifetime.

What About Baby Massage Classes?

Many hospitals and private organizations offer baby massage classes. These are beneficial because a certified Infant Massage Instructor can show you all the how-tos, step by step. An instructor can give you a hands-on demonstration and answer your questions to help you feel confident in this very gentle and soothing art. Remember that massage and touch are an experience that is exclusive between the parent and baby. The instructor will help you learn how to read your baby and how to use the art of massage.

Parent Tip

"My husband gives our daughter her nightly bath and massage as a way of connecting with her after he's been away at work all day. It's a special time for both of them, and I get an hour for myself."

—Olga, mother of Eugenia (14 months)

For More Information

Books

Heller, Sharon. *The Vital Touch: How Intimate Contact with Your Baby Leads to Happier, Healthier Development.* New York: Henry Holt, 1997.

McClure, Vimala Schneider. *Infant Massage: A Handbook for Loving Parents.* New York: Bantam Doubleday Dell, 2000.

Websites

The International Association of Infant Massage
iaim-us.com

Touch Research Institutes
miami.edu/touch-research/home.html

Medicine, giving

. . . .

My baby has an infection, and the doctor has prescribed antibiotics. The baby doesn't like the taste of the medicine, and it's a major battle every four hours. Any tips on giving medicine to a squirmy, uncooperative baby?

Learn About It

Giving a baby medicine *can* be a challenge. After all, babies are used to eating or drinking only things that taste good, and they can't understand the reason for putting something in their mouth that doesn't taste yummy. This is an important and possibly lifesaving reflex; without it, babies would sample any number of dangerous liquids. Given the need for medicines to improve our children's health, we must be persistent and creative as we encourage our babies to swallow the yucky stuff.

Why Medicine?

A baby's sickness breaks a parent's heart. Naturally, we reach for medicines as a way to soothe as fast as possible. Sometimes, however, it's better to use time, patience, and loving care. For a variety of reasons, experts advise parents not to get into the habit of giving their children medication at the sign of every ache or sniffle. Before administering any medication, ask your doctor a few questions:

- Is this medication necessary for recovery? Are there any other options?
- What exactly is the drug for? Will it fight the illness, make my baby feel better, or both?
- How will I know if my baby is reacting adversely to this drug?

315

Tricks of the Trade

After you have verified the need for the medicine, you have to figure out how to get your baby to accept it. Based on experience, here are some tips that can help you with that challenge:

- Have the right attitude. Once you've determined that the medication is not optional, don't treat it as though it is. The medicine is necessary, may help your baby feel better, and will heal her illness, so convey this to your baby in your words and actions.
- Prepare the medication—measuring or mixing—before you pick your baby up. That way, you can measure accurately.
- Have juice or milk ready for a chaser, or be ready to breastfeed your baby.
- If the medicine has a bad taste, try letting your baby suck on an ice cube or Popsicle in advance to numb the tongue.
- Try giving medicine while your baby is in a high chair or baby seat.
- A syringe or vitamin dropper (available from your pharmacy) allows you to squirt medicine into your baby's mouth easily. Squirt the fluid into the inside cheek to prevent choking.
- Try to get your baby's attention with a song, toy, or a peek outside, then sneak the medicine into his mouth while he's distracted.

Parent Tip

"A spoon full of sugar—from Mommy's special spoon—helps the medicine go down. We gave our children a small amount of applesauce or yogurt mixed with [already measured] medicine on a regular silver tablespoon and told them it was 'Mommy's special spoon.' This allowed us to administer antibiotics and pain reliever without a fuss."*

—Becky, mother of Joshua (13), Karissa (11),
Sarah (5), and Melissa (2)

*Ask your doctor or pharmacist first to be sure the medication can be mixed with food.

- If your baby usually spits out the medicine after you put it in, gently hold her lips together until she swallows.
- Ask your pharmacist if you can mix the medication with juice or yogurt. If so, mix it with just a small amount so that you can be sure that all the medication is taken.

A Few Important Rules

Besides convincing your baby to swallow the medicine, you have to take precautions to ensure safe use of all medicines. Whenever your baby needs medicine, be sure to follow these guidelines:

- Babies are not miniature adults, so half of an adult dose may be harmful to your child. Don't self-prescribe over-the-counter medications. Instead, read package instructions carefully or check with your doctor for dosage information.
- Read the label on all medications—even those prescribed by your doctor.
- Don't use kitchen flatware tablespoons or teaspoons for measuring. Instead, use a measuring spoon, syringe, dropper, or medicine spoon. You can get these at your pharmacy, and often a measuring device comes free with your baby's prescription.
- Wash the medicine dropper or measuring cup thoroughly after each use.
- Always watch for side effects, such as a rash or fever, and report them immediately to your doctor.
- Give your child all doses for as long as your prescription dictates.
- Make sure all medicines in your home have childproof caps that are sealed tightly.
- Give medications only when truly necessary. Not every sniffle requires medication.

Memories

· · · · · · · · · · · ·

My baby is already six months old. The time has gone by so fast! I've taken lots of pictures, but I haven't been very organized about it. How can I best capture the memories of my child's babyhood?

Learn About It

There is something extraordinary about babyhood. The wonder of a new life, the innocence of your sleeping infant, that gummy smile that lights up your baby's face, the first attempt at walking—all these moments and a thousand more are precious but so fleeting. Any experienced parent will tell you that time flies by; before you know it, your baby will be waving good-bye on his first day of kindergarten. Soon after that, you'll be shopping for a cap and gown. You don't want to forget this special time in your baby's life; luckily, there are a variety of ways to preserve these early years for posterity.

Photographs

Cameras—traditional or digital—remain parents' primary tool for preserving memories. Most families start taking photos in the hospital and continue to be camera enthusiasts throughout the baby period. Here are some tips for improving the quality of your photographs:

- Take plenty of close-ups to show your baby's personality, expressions, and emotions. Your baby should fill *at least* a third of the photograph, and the background should be simple so that attention focuses on your baby's face.

• Back up to tell a story. Sometimes the surroundings help explain something about your baby, providing context for the expressions and actions in the photo. For example, if you want to show how much your baby loves books, take a photo of him from a distance that shows him "reading," completely surrounded by his book collection.

• Capture a wide range of your baby's feelings: not every photograph has to be of a smiling baby. In fact, the ones in which your baby is serious, crying, frustrated, or intensely concentrating may be funnier, more interesting, and more telling of his actual personality than a posed "say cheese" smile (although those first posing cheesy smiles can be adorable!).

• Vary the perspective of the photos. Get down and take a photograph at his eye level, or stand on a chair for a bird's-eye view.

• Run for the camera when your baby does something funny, like wrapping himself up in toilet paper (after checking, of course, to make sure your baby is safe). Put a single-use camera in the diaper bag for unexpected special or funny moments when you are out.

• Try these professional tips: Use a higher-speed film (400 or 800) because babies move so quickly that getting a clear action photo can be difficult. Unless you need to blow up the photo to poster size, you won't notice the slightly grainier texture of the higher-speed films. Try using a flash outdoors to eliminate dark shadows. Use a red-eye retouching pen to get rid of red eyes on photographs.

• Record a "day in the life" of your baby, snapping pictures at all the key moments, starting with his first feeding of the day and going all the way through to when he is asleep in bed at night.

• Contrast the different generations. Take a picture of your baby's hand in Daddy's, or a close-up of Great-Grandmom holding your baby skin to skin, butter-soft innocence against weathered experience.

• Take lots of pictures and get duplicates. Yes, you will have hundreds of photos that you don't want to use, but these photos can be put in boxes and saved for a rainy-day toddler craft activity or a school project later.

• Get professional photographs taken from time to time. Large photos taken by an expert in children's photography become treasured peeks back in time. Ask for recommendations from friends, and look at photographer portfolios, policies, and prices before deciding where to have a photographic session.

• Consider storing negatives separate from the photographs, in a metal fireproof box, as a backup in case photos are lost or damaged.

Writing

A picture may be worth a thousand words, but it can't tell funny stories or convey your baby's emerging personality. If you want to remember your child's baby years—and pass these memories on to future generations—then write them down. Many people are intimidated by the prospect of writing, but the truth is that you are an expert writer when it comes to your baby. After all, you know your baby better than anyone else and can describe his or her characteristics, likes and dislikes, and the special moments you have shared together.

Here are some suggestions for preserving memories through the written word:

• **Keep a diary.** Don't worry about spelling, handwriting, or writing style; you can fix those things later if you want to. Instead, jot down interesting developments in your baby's life or even just the ups and downs of being a parent. This diary can even be the raw material for stories you write about your baby when you have the chance.

• **Jot down your baby's first words and early sentences.** Even just scratching these on a notepad preserves them forever. Here's one of my favorites, said by my now-thirteen-year-old daughter, Vanessa, when she was three and a half: "Mommy, do you know you are loved dearly? Yes. I love you dearly. That means more than the whole world and Japan and July and August. And that's more than a million!" (I'm glad I wrote that one down, and you'll be glad when you capture your baby's first gems, too!)

• **Do a once-a-year journal entry.** Pick a month when life is usually rather settled, and put the journal entry at the top of the priority list. Record the most important developments in your baby's life that year. More important, try to create a "picture in words" of exactly who your baby is at that moment in time. Describe Baby's personality, likes and dislikes, ups and downs, reactions and relationships. Each year, you will probably end up writing three or four pages of perfectly sized little nuggets for you and your child to later read and enjoy. If you do this for the next eighteen years, you will have an extraordinary gift to give your adult child. A lovely tool for this project is *The Book of Birthday Letters* by Bobbi Conner (Andrews McMeel Publishing, 2000).

• **Write about your own childhood,** and ask your parents and grandparents to do the same. After a baby is born, family history and old memories seem so much more important. What does your mother remember about your baby years? What does your grandfather remember about your mother's childhood? How have you changed or remained the same? All these things create a picture of your family's history and will be wonderful for you and your baby to read many years from now.

Scrapbooking

The relatively new phenomenon of scrapbooking has replaced sewing as America's number one hobby. It combines the two primary memory tools—photographs and writing—and adds a healthy dose of creativity and some excellent photo safety techniques to boot. If you are interested in scrapbooking, you'll find a wealth of information on the Internet and in books (see the suggestions under "For More Information"). Message boards for scrapbooking enthusiasts and local scrapbooking groups abound. By participating in these, you can exchange ideas, look at page layouts, and meet interesting people in the process.

Videotaping

Home videos can be appallingly boring or incredibly interesting. You certainly will want to record some of the key moments of your baby's life, but you don't want forty-five minutes of your baby in the bathtub! The key is to keep your videos snappy and fun. Here's how:

Parent Tip

"When your baby receives a book as a gift, ask the person who gives the book to write a little message inside the front cover, including your child's name, date, and the occasion. It's a wonderful memory that your child will cherish someday."

—Sarah, mother of Ryan (4) and Audrey (1)

- Tell a story about your baby, with a beginning, a middle, and an end. If you are taping his first birthday, start with some video of his cake and birthday presents. Then show baby jumping up and down with excitement at his new little toy. Don't tape him unwrapping every single package. Take a few shots of his birthday guests, and finish up with a few seconds of your exhausted little one-year-old, asleep in his bed.

- Don't talk too much during the recording. You can always edit in titles later. It's better to capture the chatter of the people on screen than to always narrate from behind the camera.

- Take short clips, about thirty seconds each, unless something dramatic is happening. There is nothing wrong with turning your video recorder on and off!

- Don't use the zoom button unless necessary because it makes for a shaky picture. Instead, zoom occasionally, a bit at a time, or just get closer.

- Get a video-editing program for your computer (you may need a video capture card as well). Price and quality vary widely, so investigate carefully. You can create interesting and fun videotapes of your baby with these programs.

Other Ways to Remember the Baby Years

Excellent baby books are available in which you can record all major developments in your baby's life and even glue in a lock of your baby's hair or create a hand- and footprint of your newborn. You may also want to keep a few of your baby's very favorite clothes—even if they are worn out—because every time you see that precious little sweater, your heart will melt at the memory of how cute your baby looked in it.

Enjoy the Special Moments

Finally, don't be so busy preserving memories that your forget to make them. Take a deep breath and savor that feeling when your baby's sweet little hands grasp at your chest while he breastfeeds. Enjoy the feeling of having him cuddled up in your arms for a book, and absorb the delightful moment when he finally manages to crawl. Even without photos, writing, scrapbooking, or video, these special moments stay in a parent's memory forever.

For More Information

Books

Editors of *Memory Makers* Magazine. *Baby Scrapbooks: Ideas, Tips, and Techniques for Baby Scrapbooks.* Denver: Satellite Press, 2000.

Jane, Lisa, and Rick Staudt. *How to Photograph Children: Secrets for Capturing Childhood's Magic Moments.* New York: Abbeville Press, 2001.

Ledoux, Denis. *The Photo Scribe: A Writing Guide: How to Write the Stories Behind Your Photographs.* Lisbon Falls, ME: Soleil Press, 1999.

Milestones of Development

. . . .

See also: Crawling; Intelligence; Talking; Walking

How do I know if my baby is developing normally?

Learn About It

Babies grow and develop at their own pace, and as any parent of multiple children can tell you, babies are all very different from one another. There's a wide range of "normal" when it comes to babies.

My own four children reached developmental milestones very differently from each other and from other babies. As an example, one of my children talked a blue streak at twelve months, while another one's entire vocabulary on her second birthday was "uh-uh." One took tentative first steps at fourteen months, while another took off running at ten months. As I look at them now—all walking, running, and talking—those milestones seem insignificant. Baby Uh-Uh now has superior verbal and academic skills and is considering a future career in law or politics. By the time our fourth baby joined our family, I no longer worried about when he would roll over, crawl, walk, or talk. I was able to relax and enjoy each step along the way, knowing that some children move quickly ahead in some areas but take their time catching up in others.

Try to keep that in mind as you look at the following list of developmental milestones. Also keep in mind that if your baby was born prematurely, his development might be more in line with his adjusted age (that is, the age he would be now if he had been born on his due date).

If you have a baby with special needs, such as those of Down's syndrome, he may be slower than shown on this chart in learning new skills.

Although checking your baby's performance against this list every month can be fun, remember that your baby is an individual with her own innate timetable. Be aware that "average" or "typical" is not the same as "normal." For example, the average baby walks at about twelve months of age, but it is normal for a child to reach this milestone at anywhere from seven to eighteen months! Baby milestones usually follow each other in a certain order, but that can vary while still being in the realm of what is normal. For example, many babies crawl before they walk, but some never crawl at all. And some babies become so intent on mastering one particular skill that they all but abandon other areas of development for a time.

While keeping all of this in mind, pay attention to your baby's development. Relax about the details, but watch for steady progress in whatever direction or order your unique little one takes. The operative word is *steady*. Most parents enjoy looking ahead to what's coming in the way of their baby's changes and growth, and a general idea of what should be happening is helpful. The following list, which shows the milestones that most babies achieve at each age, can help you keep tabs as Baby evolves from newborn to toddler. If you have any concerns or questions about your baby's development, talk to your pediatrician.

Parent Tip

"One experienced mom said to me, 'Stop wishing for the next big milestone and enjoy the developmental stage your baby is in right now. They change so quickly.' It is the best parenting advice I've received!"
—**Robbi, mother of Elly (10 months)**

By 1 Month Old

- Lifts head up slightly for brief periods when lying on tummy
- Looks at faces with interest
- Focuses on objects that are 6–12 inches from face
- Sometimes turns toward sounds or voices
- May startle at loud sounds
- Shows a preference for black-and-white or high-contrast patterns
- Communicates needs with noises, cries, and body language
- Sleeps 16–18 hours per day, distributed over 6–7 sleep periods

By 2 Months Old

- Lifts head at a 45-degree angle for a few minutes when lying on tummy
- Follows an object with eyes when it's about 6 inches away
- Smiles
- Makes cooing noises
- Communicates needs with coos, noises, cries, and body language
- Shows a preference for black-and-white or high-contrast patterns

By 3 Months Old

- Lifts head at a 45-degree angle when lying on tummy
- May lift head and chest when lying on tummy
- Holds head steady when held upright
- Prefers high-contrast primary colors
- Brings hand up to mouth
- Reaches for toys
- Bats at toys
- Follows objects past midline (from side to side)
- Recognizes familiar people
- Smiles at people
- Kicks legs for fun
- Coos, squeals, and makes vowel sounds such as *ah*, *eh*, or *oo*
- Communicates needs with coos, noises, cries, and body language
- Takes 3 naps of 5–6 hours total
- Sleeps 10–11 hours at night (with several awakenings)

By 4 Months Old
- Lifts head at a 90-degree angle when lying on tummy
- Sits with support
- Babbles and makes noises
- Mouths toys
- Laughs
- Focuses on tiny objects
- Holds a rattle or small toy
- Shows interest in own hands and feet
- Recognizes family members
- Communicates needs with coos, babbles, noises, cries, and body language

By 5 Months Old
- Raises upper body on straight arms when lying on stomach
- Rolls over
- Holds head steady when being held upright
- Sits with support
- Brings toy to mouth
- Pays attention to small objects
- Makes a variety of sounds
- Reaches for toys
- Distinguishes between bold colors

By 6 Months Old
- Sits with some support
- Rolls over in both directions
- Reaches for toys
- Picks up small objects
- Brings toys to mouth
- Makes sounds with two syllables
- Makes some jabbering consonant sounds like *ba*, *ma*, *da*, and *ga*
- Pays attention when called by name
- Takes 2 naps of 3–4 hours total
- Sleeps 10–11 hours at night (with several awakenings)

By 7 Months Old
- Imitates some sounds
- Sits without support
- Shifts body around by squirming, scooting, rolling, or otherwise propelling self on stomach or back
- Moves a toy from hand to hand
- Holds 2 objects simultaneously
- Makes consonant sounds (*f, v, th, s, sh, z, m, n*)
- Imitates sounds
- Begins to demonstrate separation and stranger anxiety
- Has full-color vision; is able to see at longer distances
- Pays attention when people talk

By 8 Months Old
- Sits well without support
- Stands when supported
- Shifts body around by squirming, scooting, rolling, propelling self on stomach, or crawling
- Babbles, combines vowels and consonants, strings sounds together (like *ma-ma* and *da-da*)
- Participates in baby games like peekaboo
- Waves bye-bye when prompted
- Chews on toys
- Looks for a toy that is dropped, or drops toys intentionally
- Makes needs known with specific sounds or cries

By 9 Months Old
- Stands when holding onto something for support
- Shows determination when wanting something
- Looks for a toy that is dropped or hidden
- Holds toys in both hands
- Participates actively in play
- Takes 2 naps of 2½–4 hours total
- Sleeps 11–12 hours at night (with several awakenings)

By 10 Months Old

- Pushes from lying on stomach to sitting
- Sits down from a standing position
- Stands with support
- Climbs up stairs
- Begins using dialogue (you talk, she babbles, you talk, she babbles)
- Produces sounds that vary in volume, pitch, and rate
- Understands some of what other people are saying
- Gets upset if a toy is taken away or frustrated at own physical limitations
- Transfers toys from hand to hand
- Picks up small objects between thumb and finger
- Likes to explore
- Uses furniture or props to pull up to a standing position or cruise along furniture

By 11 Months Old

- Calls parents by name: Ma-ma, Da-da
- Understands simple concepts like "no" and "bye-bye"
- Cruises furniture or walks with help
- Puts objects in and out of containers
- Produces wordlike sounds that vary in volume, pitch, and rate
- Uses a few simple words
- Responds to music by moving, dancing, and bouncing
- Follows simple one-step instructions
- Shows interest in books and pictures

By 12 Months Old

- Moves body easily; gets up and down from standing to sitting
- Walks with help or by pushing objects; begins walking independently
- Points, gestures, or makes sounds or first words to make needs known
- Understands and responds to simple instructions

- Knows some body parts by name if taught
- Takes 1 or 2 naps of 2–3 hours total
- Sleeps 11–12 hours at night (with several awakenings)
- Likes to explore and is curious
- Bangs toys together
- Understands what "no" means but doesn't always respond
- "Helps" when getting dressed by extending arm or leg
- Shows interest in mirrors and can recognize self
- Shows interest in books; may recognize favorites
- Gives a kiss and hug when asked

Moving

See also: Babyproofing; Discipline; Memories; Separation Anxiety; Sleep, newborn; Sleep, four months and over; Travel by Airplane; Travel by Car; Visiting Other People's Homes with Your Baby

We have bought a new house, and I am panicking about how the move will go with my sixteen-month-old daughter. How will I ever manage to get everything packed when she keeps me so busy? What can I do to make moving day as smooth as possible? How can I help her settle in to the new house?

Learn About It

Moving is considered one of the most stressful human experiences, and parenting a baby or toddler is a challenge all its own. Stress, disruption, and emotional swings are normal during a move, and babies thrive in a calm and stable atmosphere with clear routines. The combination can seem completely overwhelming to everyone in the family, including your baby. Yet, with careful planning and the right approach, you may be pleasantly surprised at how well your baby does with the move to your new home.

How to Move Successfully

The first thing to remember is that your baby will take her cues from you. If you are frazzled, stressed, and upset, your baby will pick up on that mood and mirror it—or at least be confused about all that is going on. If you can remain calm and upbeat, your baby probably will adjust remarkably well to the hustle of the move.

So how do you remain calm and upbeat when you feel as if your entire world is being turned upside down? Try thinking of your move as three different phases: before the move, during the move, and after the move. Then plan carefully for each phase.

Preparing for the Move

As you prepare for the move, there is much you can do to lay the groundwork for a smooth transition:

• Packing is the central feature of preparation. Begin with the nonessential areas, like linen closets and storage rooms. Gradually move on to the more central areas of the house. Leave the baby's room, toy area, and kitchen until last to minimize interruption of your baby's routines.

• Babies love boxes. To prevent your baby from unpacking your boxes faster than you can pack them, give her a box of her own and some items to "pack" (and then "unpack"). Toys, plastic plates and cups, and stuffed animals work well, and Baby will have a lot of fun filling and emptying her box. Another idea is to create a tunnel, train, car, or little house with some of the empty boxes—another few hours of entertainment!

• Your baby will still need your undivided attention many times throughout the day. You may as well accept that in advance so that you and your baby don't get frustrated with one another. Taking a break will be good for both of you: Go for a walk, or just cuddle up for a book together. You can share baby duty with your partner when he or she is home, or you might ask a family member or friend to take care of your baby for a few hours so that both of you can work uninterrupted. You could even hire a baby-sitter, perhaps a neighboring teen, to take care of your baby in your house while you pack, bringing her to you when she needs to breastfeed or cuddle with Mommy or Daddy.

• Some parents with young children feel that paying movers to pack up their household—thus avoiding weeks of stress with packing and boxes—is well worth the money. Depending on the type of move and the area, hiring a moving company may be an affordable option.

• While decluttering is an essential dimension of every move, don't throw away too much of what is familiar to Baby. She may not notice a few missing stuffed animals, but she might become upset to discover that her crib, changing table, and mobile have all somehow disappeared in the move. You can get rid of these things later, after your baby has settled into the new house.

• Always be mindful of safety, no matter how much chaos you have around you. Be very careful with medications, vitamins, chemicals, and the like, clearly marking their boxes and making sure that Baby cannot possibly get into them. Keep your house babyproofed until the last minute. When you do pack your babyproofing items, mark the box clearly so you can quickly access it in the new house, since your baby will be anxious to explore her new surroundings. Also, while plastic bins with tight lids might seem a good way to transport toys and clothes, they can pose a suffocation hazard to babies.

• Don't forget to take pictures of your home before you leave. Photos of the front of the house, garden, living room, kitchen, and, of course, Baby's room will be fun to look at later. Your baby won't remember the house, but it will probably always have a special place in your heart as your first home with your baby. Photos of the park where Baby played and of little friends in the neighborhood are nice to have, too.

• Talk to your baby about what is happening. Explain that you are going to make a new home together and how nice it is going to be. An infant may have no clue what you are saying, but she will love the reassuring tone of voice; it may help calm *you* down, too! For an older baby, you might write a "book" about your move to explain what is going to happen, using poster board or very heavy paper. Start with pictures of the family in the old house, then glue in a picture of a moving truck (perhaps from a magazine or the Internet) and boxes, and finish with pictures of your new house. If you have pets, be sure to include them in your book, so the baby doesn't think they are going to be left behind. You can bind the book together with heavy tape, and it just may become a "family bestseller"!

Parent Tip

"When we moved, I sent a box of my baby's toys by mail in advance to the new house. That way, when we got to our unfamiliar surroundings, he had his very familiar toys."

—**Sarah, mother of Ryan (4) and Audrey (1)**

During the Move

On the day of the move, the following suggestions will help you balance the demands of moving with the responsibilities of parenting:

- There are three ways to take care of Baby on the actual moving day. You can carry a very young baby around in a sling or baby carrier throughout the day, as long as you leave the heavy lifting duties to other people. For an older baby, it may be more practical to arrange for a trusted family member or friend to baby-sit. Last, you might have others do the moving while you go to someone else's house for the day with the baby. With so much activity in your house, the potential for danger is simply too great for a marginally attended, mobile baby.

- Be sure to have an "emergency bag" ready with whatever items you need to get your baby to sleep that evening: diapers, wipes, pajamas, books, lovey (comfort object), pacifiers, and essential food and drink supplies. If you don't co-sleep, you might pack a T-shirt you have worn for a few days to be used at Baby's bedtime, so that she will have the familiar and reassuring smell of Mommy right next to her when she goes to sleep in an unfamiliar location.

- If you have to travel any distance to your new home, check out the suggestions in the sections on traveling (*see* Travel by Airplane; Travel by Car) to help make your trip more peaceful.

- Your top priority upon arrival in your new home should be getting the kitchen unpacked enough to prepare an easy meal for your baby and yourselves. Then move on to create some semblance of order in your baby's room or sleeping area. Don't forget some basic babyproofing: Put covers on electrical sockets, and ensure that dangerous boxes are out of reach (*see* Babyproofing).

• In general, the best plan is to keep the content of Baby's room the same in the new house as it was in the old, though most babies don't mind new wallpaper, curtains, and decorations. You might leave Baby a little present on her bed—a stuffed animal, book, or toy—to celebrate moving to the new house.

• If your baby has not been with you for the day and you are introducing her to her new home, give her your undivided attention as she explores her new home for the first time—and don't forget to take some pictures or video!

Settling In

The first few weeks in your new home will be rather chaotic, but there's much you can do to help your baby settle in peacefully:

• For Baby's sake, stick to routines as much as possible. Feed her normal meals at normal times, let her nap when she usually naps, and if she gets a bath, a book, and a song before going to bed, continue to provide exactly that.

• Get unpacked as soon as possible, but take time to let Baby—and yourself—settle into the new house and neighborhood. Go for walks to the park, join a playgroup (both are great ways to meet other parents), or just create a comfy corner in your new house where you and your baby can "escape" and enjoy each other's company.

• Your baby may have an adjustment period of several weeks or more in the new house, especially if he is sensitive to new situations. He may have sleeping problems and be more demanding and irritable than normal. Older babies may have more tantrums and fussiness. All of this is normal and requires patience and understanding on your part.

• If the changes become a pattern and lead to longer-term sleep or behavior issues, read the entries for Sleep, newborn; Sleep, four months and over; Discipline. Also, note that your baby may have to relearn basic rules of the house (like using paper to scribble on instead of walls and using cushions to jump on instead of tables).

When the Going Gets Tough

There will be difficult days before, during, and after a move. After all, moving is stressful on parents and babies. Go easy on yourself; very few people would win the Best Parent of the Month award during a move! Sometimes the best tack to take when you are completely overwhelmed is to drop everything and take a walk, go to the park, or head out to a restaurant. You'll come back refreshed and ready for a new start. And, of course, there is the "this, too, shall pass" approach. Soon you and your baby will drive up to your house, and you will hear, "Home, Mama, home!" At that moment you will think to yourself, finally, "Yes, this is home." Home, sweet home.

Music

See also: Colic; Crying; Intelligence; Reading; Talking

I've heard that babies like music and that music is good for their development, but I can't carry a tune. How can I best bring music into my baby's life?

Learn About It

For hundreds of years, mothers have crooned their babies to sleep with lullabies, fathers have sung nursery rhymes to their toddlers, and families have made folk music a part of everyday life. Why? Because music is calming, music facilitates language development, and most of all, music is enjoyable for both parents and children. It is clear that the more music your baby hears and the more "musical" connections her brain makes (*see* Intelligence), the more music will play a role in her later life.

Music and Your Newborn

Studies have shown that even within the womb, a baby responds to music and melody. Hearing is fully developed by the third trimester, and when a fetus hears a tune over and over again, she will recognize—and feel comforted by—that tune after her birth. If classical music is played for premature babies, their heart rates slow down and their breathing steadies, showing that the music helps to relieve stress. For your upset baby, music can serve the very practical purpose of calming her down. Your baby doesn't care whether you are completely tone deaf or an opera star, as long as she hears the comforting sound of your voice. Here are some ideas for how to introduce your newborn to singing and music:

• When your baby is upset, hold her close to you, sing to her, and dance and sway with the music. The combination of close body contact, movement, and music can do wonders to soothe a crying baby.

• Try singing and listening to a variety of different types of music to see how your baby reacts. When she is upset or sleepy, she may respond to lullabies. When she is cheerful, she may love to dance to your favorite rock song with you. When she is quiet and alert, she may like to listen to classical music.

• Sing the songs or lullabies you remember from your childhood; you may find yourself tearing up as you do. If you don't remember the words to the songs, check out a book from the library—or, even better, ask your mother or father. Recorded music has its place, of course, but be sure to also give your baby the gift of your own experience with music.

• Use music to let your baby know what is happening and to establish comforting routines:

  · Put on the same calming music every time you prepare to give your baby a massage.
  · Sing the same lullaby every night as you put your baby to bed.
  · Keep a fun cassette in the car and sing along so that your baby learns it is fun to go places in the car.
  · When you are about to change her diaper, turn on the musical mobile near the changing table.
  · Put on some music during your baby's bath.
  · Play your favorite songs during the "fussy hour" when you have to prepare dinner and your baby needs attention.

• Enjoy music yourself. Not only is music comforting for your baby, it is also very calming for you. Whether you are singing a song to your crying baby or dancing around the kitchen trying to soothe a colicky newborn, music can help soothe your jangled nerves as well as your baby's.

Music and the Older Baby

As your baby grows, you will delight in seeing how she begins to rock, wiggle, bob, and dance to the music she hears. All babies have an instinctive sense of rhythm and a love of music, so music should be a part of your everyday life. Here are some ways in which you can nurture your older baby's relationship with music:

• Play simple games with your baby that involve both music and movement: Patty-Cake (clap your baby's hands), This Little Piggy (wiggle her little toes), or Ride a Cock Horse to Banbury Cross (jiggle her on your lap). (You can find the words in any Mother Goose book of nursery rhymes.) Or hide a music box in the room and go "hunting" for the sound of the music. When she is a bit older, play Ring-Around-the-Rosie or London Bridge.

• Dance and sing with your baby. Have a daily dance session in the living room where both of you wiggle to the beat of some lively music. (This is a great way to fit in your own daily exercise program.) Create your own lyrics to a favorite song, with your baby's name in it (for example, "You are my Thomas, my little Thomas, you make me happy when skies are gray" to the tune of "You Are My Sunshine"). Soon your baby will be singing right along with you.

• Let your baby play with musical instruments. You can make them yourself. To make a shaker, fill a small plastic bottle with beans or popcorn kernels (make sure the lid is glued and tightened securely to prevent a choking hazard). Make a drum out of an empty oatmeal container, or use a pie pan and a spoon to tap out the rhythm to a song. Of course, you can also buy xylophones, tambourines, harmonicas, and other instruments for your baby. But be warned: Babies can make a *lot* of noise with these instruments (which is why aunts and uncles delight in buying these for their *siblings'* children!).

• Find a "music and movement" playgroup for your baby, in which both you and your baby can learn about music and have fun with other babies and parents. Some cities also have musical concerts in parks for families with young children, and your baby might find these fascinating.

• Get "read and sing" books for your baby. The Raffi Songs to Read books (*Five Little Ducks, Baby Beluga,* and many others) are excellent.

Any song book with animals also will be a hit, as babies love to point, sing, and dance—and moo—to the tune of songs like "Old MacDonald Had a Farm."

For More Information

Books

Campbell, Don, and Joseph Pearce. *The Mozart Effect for Children: Awakening Your Child's Mind, Health, and Creativity with Music.* New York: Quill, 2002.

Ortiz, John M. *Nurturing Your Child with Music: How Sound Awareness Creates Happy, Smart, and Confident Children.* Hillsboro, OR: Beyond Words Publishing Company, 1999.

Naps

. . . .

See also: Sleep, newborn; Sleep, four months and over; Swaddling

I'm starting to wonder if my baby's poor napping schedule affects his nighttime sleep. He doesn't ever nap for more than an hour, yet he doesn't sleep well at night either. Is there a connection?

Learn About It

There is a definite correlation between the length and the quality of naps and nighttime sleep. Conversely, night sleep affects naps, so it can be a vicious circle. Improving your baby's daily nap routine can help him feel happier, grow better, be less fussy, and sleep better at night. (Having a little time for yourself can also help *you* to be less cranky.)

When Should Your Baby Nap?

The timing of your baby's naps is important, since a nap that occurs late in the day will prevent your baby from being tired when bedtime approaches. Researchers have discovered that certain times of the day coincide with a baby's biological clock. These optimum periods balance sleep and wake time to affect nighttime sleep in the most positive way.

All babies are different, but generally, the best nap times are:

- If Baby takes three naps: midmorning/early afternoon/early evening
- If Baby takes two naps: midmorning/early afternoon
- If Baby takes one nap: early afternoon

Typical Napping Schedule

Age	Number of Naps	Hours of Naptime
4 months	3	4–6
6 months	2	3–4
9 months	2	2½–4
12 months	1–2	2–3
2 years*	1	1–2
3 years*	1	1–1½

*Some children no longer need naps after turning two but will have an earlier bedtime.

How Much Naptime Does Your Baby Need?

Babies differ in their napping needs. Some naturally need less or more than is typical, but look at the preceding chart for a general guide that applies to most babies.

Watch for Signs of Tiredness

Tired babies fall asleep easily, and your baby will give you signals that he is ready for a nap. If he isn't tired, he'll resist sleep. And if you miss his signals, he can easily become *overtired* and will then be unable to fall asleep.

Once you determine a good nap schedule for your baby, use those times as a guideline, but use your baby's sleep signals as the main cue for naptime. If you spot these signals, don't begin a lengthy prenap routine, just get your tired little one off to bed! Your baby may demonstrate one or more of these signs of being tired and ready to nap:

- Reducing his level of activity
- Becoming quiet
- Losing interest in playtime
- Rubbing his eyes
- Looking glazed or unfocused
- Fussing or crying
- Yawning
- Lying down or slumping in his seat
- Caressing a lovey or blanket
- Asking for a pacifier or bottle or to nurse
- Dreamily sucking a thumb or finger

The Nap Routine

Once you have created a nap schedule that works with your baby's daily periods of alertness and tiredness, follow a simple but specific nap routine. Your baby will be comfortable if there is a predictable pattern to his day, and he may come to predict when his naptime approaches. For example, he may begin to recognize that after lunch and storytime comes naptime. In addition, if you include relaxing activities in your nap routine, such as massage, rocking, white noise, or soft music, these activities can help to prepare your baby for sleep.

Tips for the Reluctant Napper

If your baby hasn't been a very good napper and you're working to create a nap routine, the following ideas may help you encourage your baby to actually sleep when you think he should sleep. Don't try everything on the list; just choose the ideas that sound like they may work for your baby, and include them in your daily nap routine.

- Use consistent white noise during naps. You can use a bubbling fish tank, a fan/heater (taking care that it gets neither too hot nor too cold), a recording of nature sounds, or a white-noise sound clock. This creates a very strong sleep cue and blocks out household noises that may wake your baby.

- Bring your stroller in the house, and walk your baby around until she falls asleep. Even simply rolling the stroller back and forth over a "lump" like a doorway jamb can work. If your baby sleeps only a short time and starts to wake, you can often walk or bounce her back to sleep. Once she gets used to taking a longer nap, you can make the transition to her bed.

- If your baby is younger than five months old, try swaddling him for sleep (*see* Swaddling) or letting him sleep in a moving cradle or swing.

- Make sure the room is dark during sleep. Cover the windows any way you can—even with a piece of cardboard or aluminum foil. Some babies are very sensitive to light, and it prevents them from falling asleep or wakes them up after a short period of sleep.

- If your baby gets upset with just the mention of naptime, change your approach. Some older babies are so intent on learning about the world that they hate to stop even for a minute! Instead of announcing, "Naptime," say, "It's quiet time," and lie down with your baby, read a book, listen to a peaceful tape, turn on your white noise, give a bottle, or nurse him. If your little one is tired, he'll surely fall asleep. If not, the "quiet time" will work wonders to take the edge off—for both of you.

- Try lying down with your baby in a quiet, dark room and pretending to be asleep yourself. Once she's sleeping soundly, you can get up (that is, if you're not sleeping too!). If you *do* fall asleep, it's because your body needs that sleep. Enjoy the nap!

- If you've tried for fifteen or twenty minutes to get your baby to nap and she is still wide awake, then she's not tired enough to sleep. Let her get up and play for an hour or so. Tire her out with activity, then try again when she shows signs of being tired.

For More Information

Book

Pantley, Elizabeth. *The No-Cry Sleep Solution: Gentle Ways to Help Your Baby Sleep Through the Night.* Chicago: Contemporary Books, 2002.

Newborn Clothing

See also: Baby Carriers; Bathing; Car Seats; Cloth Diapers; Cribs and Cradles; Diaper Bag; Diaper Changing, how-tos of; Infant Seats, Swings, Bouncers, and Jumpers; Swaddling; Toys

My baby is due next month, and I'm wondering what clothes I need for her layette. I've been shopping, and there's a tremendous amount of baby clothes to choose from.

Learn About It

Many of us will remember the fun we had dressing up baby dolls when we were young. And dressing up a real baby can be even more fun; tears may come to your eyes when you see your baby in that darling outfit you're picking now. Indeed, dressing up your baby and showing her off is one of the privileges of being a parent. But beware: Babies don't care about their clothes in the same way you do, and three minutes after you put on that expensive new outfit, your baby may spit up all over her pretty dress, or the contents of her diaper may leak into those cute jeans.

For your baby, there are only two standards for baby clothes: Are they comfortable? And are they easy to get into and out of when a change is required? You may quickly adopt your baby's way of looking at her clothes after she is born, saving the fancy outfits for special occasions.

Some Tips

When buying your baby's new clothes, think about these general tips:

• Buy mostly clothes that will be too big for your newborn baby. She will grow very fast, the clothes may shrink, bigger clothes tend to be more comfortable, and you may get some newborn-sized clothes as gifts. Remember also that often children's clothes tend to run small, so that most three-month-old babies will fit into clothes that are tagged "6–9 months." It is nice, though, to have one or two things that will fit your newborn well (especially for the first photos).

• Look for comfortable fabrics (cotton), easy-to-wash items (if you can't put it in the washer and dryer at normal temperatures, forget it), and easy-to-put-on items (no tiny buttons or tricky zippers). Check to see if there are snaps around the diaper area for easy access. Items that go over the head should have loose neck openings or neck snaps. Babies don't like tight clothing being pulled over their heads.

• Buy only the basics before your baby is born. You don't know exactly what her weight will be, what her complexion will be, how fast she will grow, or what type of clothing you will get as gifts. You will need to wash these basic items with baby-friendly laundry detergent before your baby wears them, but if you buy "dress-up" outfits before your baby is born, you might want to keep the tags on (and the sales slips handy) until you know your baby's size and needs. And don't forget that going shopping for baby clothes is also great fun *after* your baby is born.

• Think about the season in which your baby will be born. If you have a winter baby, you will want to layer your baby in thin, loose clothes when you go out. (Layers are warmer and more comfortable than thick sweaters.) If you have a summer baby, you will need short-sleeved, snap-at-the-crotch outfits and some lightweight long-sleeved tops and pants, as it is important that your baby does not get overheated and is protected from the sun. If your baby is born in the spring or autumn, buy mostly for the season ahead, and layer or strip according to the weather. Receiving blankets are also great to have when you need to warm up or cool down a baby; swaddling a baby not only helps her to feel secure, it also keeps her warm. And when the weather is too hot, the blanket is easy to remove.

• Think about borrowing newborn clothes from friends or buying clothes from secondhand shops. The dressier, high-quality newborn clothes get very little wear and tear, and hand-me-downs are often in excellent condition.

• After your baby has outgrown the clothes, you may want to lend them to another parent with a newborn child, but keep one or two really special outfits, like the outfit your baby wore on the way home from the hospital, apart in a "precious memories" bag. You may later want to use the outfit for another child or eventually a grandchild, make a memory quilt from the material, or even give the outfit to your baby when she gets older so she can dress up her baby in it.

Newborn Clothing Checklist

☐ 4–6 one-piece sleepers (nightgowns), size 3–6 months, flame resistant (federal standards require this for sleepers): The drawstring bottoms are great for easy access at night, but when baby gets older (and more active), you'll want to remove the drawstrings or use footed sleepers instead.

☐ 4–6 snap-at-the-crotch undershirts, size 3–6 months: On a hot summer day, the colorful undershirts make great daytime outfits as well.

☐ 3–4 pairs of booties or socks: These need to be loose enough so your baby can easily wiggle her toes, but snug around the ankles so she can't kick them off. It is a good idea to carry an extra pair in the diaper bag, as it always seems to be when you are out that the baby manages to lose a sock.

☐ 4–6 stretchies with feet (one-piece daytime wear outfits) *or* 4–6 rompers (snap-at-the-crotch daytime outfits), depending on the season, size 3–6 months: If you have a winter baby, you will need more stretchies, though a summer baby should also have 2–3 stretchies for the occasional cool or windy day.

☐ 1–2 season-appropriate hats: A summer baby will need a lightweight sun hat with a brim, and a winter baby will need a warmer hat to cover his ears.

☐ 2–3 easily washable bibs: The bibs will protect your baby's outfits from spit-up for at least a little while.

☐ 1 going-home outfit, size 0–3 months: This is the one you'll want to take pictures in and, of course, save for the future, when you will be amazed that your baby was ever that tiny.

Pacifiers

· · · · · · · · · · ·

See also: Breastfeeding Your Newborn; Colic; Crying; Sleep, newborn; Sleep, four months and over; Thumb Sucking

> *My baby is two months old and a little breastfeeding wonder girl. In fact, she seems to want to nurse constantly, and if she is not breastfeeding, she is crying. She's as chubby as can be, so I know she's getting enough milk. Would it be OK to give her a pacifier?*

Learn About It

Babies are born with an instinctive need to suck. After all, it is only through sucking that babies can get milk and therefore ensure their survival. But for many babies, sucking is more than just an "I'm hungry" urge. Sucking is also soothing. It stimulates nerve endings in babies' mouths, and calms babies as they focus on the steady rhythm of the sucking. Plus, it helps develop the jaw muscles. Given the pleasant associations a baby makes with the action, it's no small wonder that sucking becomes a comfort ritual for babies.

Of course, your baby may be very happy to fill all her sucking needs at your breast, and for many mother-baby teams, this works out well and the baby never needs a pacifier. Some babies, however, have a greater urge to suck than others, and some may reject the breast because they feel no hunger but fuss because they still want or need to suck to comfort themselves. Still other babies—for instance, twins, babies close in age, and those with high needs or colic—can make life very challenging for the tired mother. The pacifier, *when used correctly*, might give both Mother and Baby a way to cope with this essential instinct when it goes beyond the bounds of survival. Note that I wrote "might." That's because, ultimately, the *baby* will decide whether to accept this "artificial nipple"; many babies do not. And some parents decide not to offer their baby a pacifier. The decision on whether to use a pacifier and when is different in all families.

When Can I Introduce the Pacifier?

A pacifier (or bottle nipple) requires your baby to use different mouth and tongue muscles than those needed for breastfeeding. If your baby tries to suck on your breast the way she has learned to suck on the pacifier, she may become frustrated and refuse to nurse. Therefore, if for some reason your baby is in the hospital nursery instead of rooming in with you, make sure that she is not given a pacifier unless a doctor specifically recommends it (as is occasionally the case with premature babies who still need to develop their sucking reflexes). After you are home, wait until you are certain that both you and your baby are confident in your breastfeeding relationship before using a pacifier. Normally your baby should be at least four weeks old before you even consider a pacifier. Until then, you can give your baby your clean finger to suck on if you need a break from pacifying your baby at your breast.

If your baby has any of the following problems, do not introduce a pacifier. Instead, turn to a lactation consultant or a health professional for help in these situations:

- Your baby doesn't seem to be growing well or has too few wet diapers.
- Your baby has trouble latching on.
- Your baby sucks incorrectly, leading to sore, painful breasts.
- You are worried about your milk supply.
- Your baby fusses while drinking at the breast.

If your baby is bottlefed, then there should be no problem with introducing a pacifier when you are ready to do so.

How Should a Pacifier Be Used?

To pacify means to "allay the agitation of or to soothe," and a pacifier can do exactly that for a baby. But before popping a pacifier in your baby's mouth, you first need to figure out what is making her so agitated (*see* Crying). Babies cry to communicate all kinds of things, not just "I want to suck." Try the techniques mentioned in the crying section first, then use the pacifier only as a last resort. It is especially important to make sure that your baby continues to get enough nourishment from breastmilk or formula, because pacifiers occasionally satisfy a baby's sucking urge to the point where they don't take in enough food.

That said, pacifiers are excellent for situations such as car seat crying, in a church service or other situation when crying would be awkward, or as an alternative for a colicky baby. Sometimes you can just see the relief and relaxation on a baby's face when she begins to suck. You don't need to feel like you are doing something wrong when you use a pacifier sensibly. Problems with pacifier use develop only when parents get in the habit of thinking that the problem is "baby crying" and the solution is "pacifier popping." The risk is twofold: first, that continuous pacifier use can replace the nurturing and cuddling so necessary for your baby's optimum emotional and psychological development, and second, that it can create an intense habit that is very difficult to curb when a baby gets older.

What Kind of Pacifier Should I Buy?

Here are the issues to consider when buying pacifiers:

- Is it a sturdy, one-piece pacifier with no possibility of a piece breaking off?
- Are there ventilation holes to prevent saliva from collecting behind the base of the pacifier, possibly leading to a rash?
- Is the pacifier the right size for your baby? The age range should be marked on the package.
- Is the pacifier dishwasher safe?
- Is there an expiration date, or is the package dusty? You don't want a pacifier that has been on the store shelves for a long time. The nipples age and could be hard, gummy, or cracked. This can pose a choking hazard should pieces fall off or erode.

When you have found pacifiers that meet all these requirements, buy a variety of nipple shapes, and test to see which ones your baby likes best. Orthodontic pacifiers have not been proved to have any advantage over other types of pacifiers, so your baby's preference is what's most important.

What Health and Safety Issues Are Involved with Pacifier Use?

As with all things you give your baby, there are certain guidelines to keep your baby safe and healthy when using pacifiers:

• Every day, you should check the pacifiers your baby uses, tugging on the nipple to look for any weaknesses or potential tears. If you have any doubts about the pacifier, throw it away. Keep a few spare ones around so you aren't tempted to use a questionable pacifier.

• Don't put the pacifier on a string, cord, or ribbon. This presents a strangulation risk. Even if the string is too short to go around your baby's neck, it could get wrapped around a hand or a finger and cut off circulation. If your baby is constantly losing her pacifier in her crib, put several of them in the crib in hopes that she will be able to find one on her own during the night.

• Never make your own pacifier with a bottle nipple. This can be very dangerous for your baby.

• Don't dip the pacifier in sugar water or honey. Honey is dangerous for babies under the age of one, and sugar can lead to tooth decay.

• If the pacifier falls to the ground, rinse it off with hot water. If it falls outside, wash it in the dishwasher or use hot, soapy water. Putting the dropped pacifier in your mouth to clean it is not a great idea because your mouth bacteria will be passed on to your baby. (However, most moms have admitted to doing this in emergency situations.)

• Boil brand-new pacifiers before using them. (Make sure they are completely cool before giving them to your baby.) After using them, wash them in the dishwasher; bacteria breed on pacifiers.

What Are the Risks of Pacifier Use?

In addition to the possible breastfeeding and nurturing problems already discussed as a possible result of continuous pacifier use, you should be aware of a few other potential risks:

• If pacifier use is prolonged, dental problems can develop, resulting in an overbite where the upper front teeth protrude over the lower front teeth. (Check for an overbite by rubbing your finger along your baby's teeth, or ask your pediatrician or dentist.) Some dentists do prefer a pacifier to a thumb; they reason that if problems develop, the pacifier can be taken away but the thumb can't.

• Studies have indicated an increased susceptibility to ear infections among babies who constantly suck on a pacifier. When pacifier use is limited to sleeping times, the risk decreases.

• Sleeping problems can develop if your baby always uses the pacifier to fall asleep. When sucking is associated with sleeping, every time she wakes up and finds the pacifier has fallen out of her mouth, she will cry for you to put it back in. For suggestions on how to deal with this, *see* Sleep, newborn; Sleep, four months and over.

• Speech delays and even social difficulties can develop if your baby has a pacifier in her mouth all the time once she begins to talk. She may not learn to form words correctly, and her speech may be distorted or unclear.

When and How Should I Wean My Baby off the Pacifier?

Some doctors advise limiting pacifiers to nighttime use after six months of age and weaning the baby from them completely at age one as an oral health preventive measure, with the argument that the baby will become more attached to the pacifier as he gets older. Others advise, in the absence of developing dental or speech problems, that you can wait until your child is two or three years old (or older), when you can use an incentive chart or distraction. In the end, the decision is yours. You know your child better than any doctor does. When no medical issues are involved, only you can accurately assess what role the pacifier is playing in your child's life and how you can best wean her from it.

Here are a few ideas for getting the process going when you're ready to start weaning:

- Use distraction as your chief weapon during the day. When your baby starts to fuss for a pacifier, sing a song, offer a toy, or go for a walk to get your child focused on something other than her sucking urge.
- Gradually reduce your baby's use by keeping the pacifiers in the crib or only in certain areas of the house. Some families have a rule like "no pacifiers downstairs" or "only in your car seat."
- Give your baby an alternative to help soothe her when she feels upset or tired. A cuddle, blanket, stuffed animal, or favorite toy may comfort your baby instead of the pacifier.

Pediatrician, choosing

· · · · · · · · · · · ·

See also: Immunizations; Milestones of Development

We are awaiting the birth of our adopted baby, and we're wondering when we should select a doctor for her care and how to go about making that decision.

Learn About It

Choosing your baby's doctor several months before her expected arrival is a good idea. This way, you won't feel rushed and can take the time to make the right decision. During the first few years of life, your baby will have frequent visits for routine checkups and illness, so selecting a health care professional you trust is important.

Decide Which Type of Health Care Provider

Different types of health care professionals are qualified to care for your baby:

- **Pediatrician:** This is a medical doctor with specialized training in caring for children from birth through adolescence.
- **Family physician or general medical practitioner (GMP):** This type of physician is educated and trained in family practice—medical care that covers every member of the family for well and sick care. You may already have a family physician for your own health care.
- **Nurse practitioner (NP):** This is a registered nurse (RN) with advanced education and training. Nurse practitioners often work in partnership with a licensed physician.

Once you've determined what type of professional you would like to consider, find prospective doctors through these sources:

- Recommendations from friends who have children
- Your obstetrician
- Your local hospital's referral service
- Medical schools and medical directories
- The American Board of Pediatrics (abp.org)

Determine Your Insurance Company's Requirements

Check out the rules of your insurance policy before choosing your baby's doctor. You may have to designate your baby's doctor for your health insurance carrier, or you may be required to have your selection approved in advance. Many health plans have strict rules about which doctors you can visit, so it's important to determine if your choice of primary care physician also decides which specialists and which hospitals you will be able to use if your baby should need specialized care. Often, these choices are linked together by the rules of a health plan.

Consider Your Parenting Philosophy

Choose a doctor who has a similar philosophy with regard to important parenting issues, since most parents turn to their pediatrician for advice and guidance on more than just health-related issues. While this similarity in outlook is not crucial, it certainly makes for a more complete and enjoyable relationship that allows open conversation and precludes the need to avoid topics on which you disagree. A like-thinking pediatrician understands your starting point when advising a particular course of action and is more likely to prescribe actions that suit your ideals. An easy way to find out a doctor's opinion is to ask open questions, such as, "What are your recommendations about breastfeeding and bottlefeeding?" Here are just a few of the important topics you should consider:

- **Feeding:** Does the doctor support your goals for breastfeeding, bottlefeeding, and weaning?
- **Sleep:** What is the doctor's opinion on sleep-related issues, such as co-sleeping and letting babies cry themselves to sleep? Are the doctor's views similar to yours?
- **Immunizations:** Will the doctor provide you with ample information to make decisions about various vaccinations? Do the doctor's standard recommendations suit you?
- **Discipline:** Does the doctor believe in the same approach toward discipline as yours?

Take the Time to Interview Prospective Doctors

Most medical professionals are happy to provide a brief interview meeting at no charge. This gives you an opportunity to meet the doctor and ask questions. Here are a few tips to make this a productive event:

- Make an appointment.
- Arrive early and observe the waiting room, staff, and other patients. Is the staff helpful? Is the atmosphere child-friendly? Is the office clean and tidy? How long do people wait for their appointments?
- Be prepared with a brief list of questions.
- Stick to your most important topics.
- Refrain from small talk or lengthy explanations.
- Remember that your main purpose is to listen, not to talk.

Before Your Interview

If you do a little research and handle the technical details before your appointment, you can use your time with the doctor to obtain answers to your most important questions. You can obtain information about a doctor, such as certifications and residency background, from the following sources:

- American Board of Pediatrics (abp.org)
- American Academy of Pediatrics (aap.org)
- American Medical Association (ama-assn.org)
- Royal College of Physicians and Surgeons of Canada (rcpsc .medical.org)
- Your local hospital referral office
- Your health insurance company

You often can get information from a receptionist or secretary at the doctor's office. First, ask for a brochure or other written information about the doctor and the practice, or ask if the office has a website with general information. If the following information isn't covered, then call the office and ask these questions:

- What is the background and experience of the doctor? (Asking the doctor this question during your upcoming appointment may well take up a large portion of your meeting.)
- What are the office hours? Are there evening or weekend hours?
- How is billing handled?
- What insurance is accepted?
- What are your after-hours and emergency procedures?
- What hospitals is the doctor affiliated with?
- How do you handle questions by telephone?
- Will our doctor personally see us for every scheduled appointment?
- If our doctor is unavailable, who will see us?
- How many doctors share this office?
- Do you have a special waiting room or a separate entrance for sick children, or how do you separate them from others?
- Do you have a lactation specialist in the office? If not, can you recommend one?

Interview Questions

Arrive at your appointment to interview a medical professional with your list of questions. Don't ask about issues that sound good but don't really matter to you; the meeting likely will be short, maybe five to fifteen minutes (ask in advance how much time you will have). Stay focused on your own priorities. Relax and be friendly, but stay on track. Here is an assortment of sample questions to help you create your own list:

- Can you explain how we will work together during our baby's first year?
- Will you examine our baby at the hospital (or at our home) directly after birth?
- What is your typical advice to new parents about . . .
  - Circumcision?
  - Breastfeeding?
  - Bottlefeeding?
  - Sleeping through the night?
  - Immunizations?
- Can we come to you with questions about nonmedical issues, like feeding or behavior?
- What do we need to know about our newborn's health and care?

After Your Interview

To make your final decision, consider the answers to these questions:

- Is the office conveniently located for you?
- How long did you have to wait in the waiting room?
- Did you feel good about the office and staff?
- Did the doctor listen thoughtfully to your questions?
- How willingly and thoroughly did the doctor answer questions?
- What was the doctor's attitude when answering them?
- Do you feel comfortable with the doctor's specific child-rearing philosophy?
- Did you feel that you could freely ask questions?
- Did the doctor appear knowledgeable and current with information and advice?
- Would you feel comfortable bringing your baby to this person for care?
- Would you feel confident having this doctor handle an emergency with your child?

Pets

· · · · · · · · · · · ·

See also: Babyproofing ("Safety Checklist for Home Babyproofing")

Our dog has been our only "baby" for the past three years. Soon we'll be bringing a new human baby into our family. How should we introduce the two of them?

Learn About It

Typical pet owners devote a great deal of time to their pets, lavishing them with the attention and affection befitting any member of the family. When it's time to welcome a brand-new (human) member to the family, pet-owning parents typically hope that pet and baby become fast friends and enjoy a fun, safe, healthy relationship. Here are a few tips on how to introduce your pet to your new baby.

Plan Ahead

Before you bring your baby home, prepare your pet, if you can:

• Have your pet spend some time around babies and children. If you don't have family or friends with children, take your pet to a park or school playground during the casual after-school or weekend hours, where your pet can become familiar with the scents, actions, and sounds of children.
• Let your pet sniff and explore the baby's room, toys, and clothes.
• Think about how your daily schedule may change and try to work those changes into your pet's day *before* baby arrives.
• Have your pet bathed and checked for fleas, worms, and other parasites. Make sure all vaccinations are up-to-date.

- If your pet now sleeps in your bed, it's wise to move him out now. If you plan to have your baby sleep with you, your pet must not be part of the family bed for your baby's safety. A pet nuzzling up to a tiny baby for cuddling could end up snuggling over her face. Even if you don't plan to bring your baby into your bed, she may wind up there anyway, so to prevent a struggle with an unhappy pet later, make the change now. (You can always invite your pet back after Baby gets older.)

- Reduce the amount of time and attention that you give your pet before the birth. No matter how much you love the animal in your house, your new baby will take up a tremendous amount of your time and energy; helping your pet adjust to the new constraints on your time will help you both later. Further, if you start changes *now*, your pet won't blame the baby for the reduced attention from you.

- Once your baby is born, have someone bring home a few articles of Baby's clothing (even a wet diaper) from the hospital, so your pet can get acquainted with Baby through his keen sense of smell.

- If your pet isn't trained to understand the commands *No*, *Down*, and *Off*, do that training now. These commands will be important when your pet is around your baby and when visitors come to meet your baby. If your dog has any behavior problems, now is the time to take him to a trainer.

Bringing Baby Home

When the big day arrives and you're ready to bring your baby into the house for the first time, a few tips can help your pet understand the importance and permanence of this new little family member:

- If your dog typically jumps up on you when you enter the house, have someone put him on a leash and restrain him when you walk in the door with the baby. This way you can introduce the two with a pleasant, loving attitude, without disciplining your pet for jumping.

- Think about how your pet typically responds to a visitor. If he's always excited to meet someone new, then you can carry your baby into the house and make a fuss over the introduction. If your pet is typically wary of strangers, consider having someone else walk in the door with the baby the first time while you reassure your pet as he meets the baby.

• Make the first contacts between the two a positive experience. Praise and a few treats will go a long way.

Parent Tip

"You can prepare your baby for contact with pets by teaching her the word *gentle* from the beginning. Stroke her face as you say it. By the time she becomes mobile, she'll know what gentleness is. Then you can work with her on developing the motor skills to perfect her gentle touch."

—Laurel, mother of Crystal (16 months)

New Routines for Everyone

Once your baby has joined the family, and the introductions are complete, you'll want to encourage a safe and happy friendship between your pet and baby. Keep these tips in mind:

• If your pet is a dog, try to work a daily walk into your schedule. The baby will love a walk outside in his sling or stroller, and your dog will enjoy it, too. (It's also great exercise for you.)

• Praise your pet whenever he is gentle around the baby. This will encourage a desire to protect your baby.

• If your dog, or any other pet, shows any signs of possession regarding his food, treats, or toys—such as growling—break him of it now, before your baby starts to crawl and begins picking up and playing with your dog's food or toys. Practice taking away your dog's food dish, bone, or toy when he's eating or playing. Discourage any negative response. Make him sit and wait. Then give it back with praise. (Well before your baby starts crawling, consider putting the dog's food and water where Baby can't get to them.)

- Remember that animals can be unpredictable. No matter how much you trust your pet, and no matter how well trained your pet is, you need to be especially careful around the baby. Even an unintentional jump, scratch, or nibble can harm an infant. Never, ever leave your baby alone with a pet.

- It's OK to put your pet second to your baby. It's important that your pet know that his position is lower in the "pack" than the baby. If your pet is a dog, remember that dogs are remarkably adaptable and yours will do fine once he learns his adjusted place in the pack. In fact, he'll be more comfortable when he's certain of that. Eventually, he may become your baby's favorite playmate and protector.

Postpartum Depression
(PPD, Postpartum Distress, or Postnatal Depression)

. . . .

See also: Baby Blues; Marriage; Sleep, newborn;
Sleep, four months and over; Unwanted Advice

> I know it's normal to have the "baby blues" right after you have a
> baby, but my son is six weeks old. I thought everything would be
> wonderful by now and I would be so in love with my baby. I
> thought mothering would come easily. It's not that way at all! I
> can't sleep, even when he's sleeping. I feel hollow inside, like the
> real me is gone. Sometimes I cry for hours; other times, I feel angry
> enough to explode. Life feels like an endless amusement park ride,
> and sometimes I just want to get off. Why am I such a terrible
> mother?

Learn About It

You're *not* a terrible mother! You are a mother who is suffering from a
condition known as postpartum depression (PPD), a condition that is
treatable. While as many as 80 percent of mothers experience a temporary and mild condition referred to as the baby blues, up to 15 percent of women have the more severe reaction you're experiencing.
Having PPD doesn't mean that you have done something wrong or that
something is wrong with you; it is an illness, and it can be cured. Once
you learn more about what's causing your despondent emotions and
take some steps toward treatment, you'll be on the road to finding yourself again and enjoying your baby.

What Is Postpartum Depression?

PPD is a medical condition, a specific type of depression that occurs within the first few months after childbirth. It is caused by the biochemical and hormonal changes that happen in the body after pregnancy and birth—nothing that is within your control.

What Are the Symptoms of Postpartum Depression?

While PPD affects all women differently, a few typical symptoms can help your physician make the diagnosis. You probably are not experiencing *everything* on the following list, and the degree of symptoms may range from mild to severe. However, if a number of these apply to you, you may be suffering from PPD. Symptoms of postpartum depression may include but are not limited to the following:

- Feeling hopeless, worthless, or inadequate
- Frequent crying or tearfulness
- Insomnia or sleepiness
- Lack of energy
- Loss of pleasure in activities you normally enjoy
- Difficulty doing typical daily chores
- Loss of appetite
- Feelings of sadness and despair
- Feelings of guilt, panic, or confusion
- Feelings of anger or anxiety
- Extreme mood swings
- Memory loss
- Overconcern for Baby
- Fear of "losing control"
- Lack of interest in sex
- Worry that you may hurt your baby
- A desire to escape from your baby or your family
- Withdrawal from social circles and routines
- Thoughts about hurting yourself

If you suffer from extreme degrees of any of these symptoms, particularly thoughts about hurting yourself or your baby, or if you have additional physical symptoms such as hallucinations, confusion, or paranoia, then please call a doctor today. *Now.* Your condition requires immediate medical care. If you can't make the call, then please talk to your partner, your mother or father, a sibling, or a close friend, and ask that person to help you arrange for help. Do this for yourself and for your baby. If you can't talk about it, rip this page out and hand it to someone close to you. It's that important. *You do not have to feel this way.*

What Can a Doctor Do About Postpartum Depression?

As with any form of depression, help is available and only as far away as your health care provider. Contact your ob/gyn or midwife to start with, if that's most comfortable for you. Either professional can help you get the care you need from someone with experience in dealing with this condition. In the longer term, it's important that your therapy take place with a professional who has experience in treating PPD; the malady is different from other forms of depression, and it is very specifically related to your role as a new mother.

Parent Tip

"In the time it takes you to read this chapter, you could set up an appointment with a doctor. Remember, this is a medical problem, and it can be serious. For your sake, for your baby, and for all those who love you, you must make that call. With help, you will regain your life and your perspective."

—Vanessa, mother of Kimmy (12), Tyler (10),
Rachel (5), and Zachary (3)

A visit to a doctor for the symptoms you're feeling is nothing to fear. Your condition is something your doctor has seen before, so you need not feel at all self-conscious. As for treatment, there are a variety of options, depending on how severe your symptoms are. Your doctor will evaluate your condition and may suggest medication, such as antidepressants. (Make sure to tell the doctor if you are breastfeeding so the proper medication can be prescribed.) In addition, your doctor will tell you that therapy and support are critical for recovery.

What Can I Do About PPD?

The first step you can take is to understand that you have an illness that requires action on your part so you can heal. Forgive me for repeating this, but it is important: Take that first step and call a doctor. In addition, the following things can help you begin to feel better right away:

- **Talk to someone.** Whom do you trust? Whom do you feel comfortable talking to? This person might be your spouse or partner, your mother, your sister or brother, or a friend. Sharing your feelings with someone who cares about you can really help. Even if you feel you can't talk specifically about PPD, just discuss your feelings and your new role as a mother and its effects on you.
- **Read books about baby care and parenting.** Knowledge is power. Reading may help you feel more confident, which in turn will help you feel more in control of your situation. It will also give you the knowledge you'll need to ward off the unwanted advice or criticism that can come your way during the early months of parenting, which can be especially hard to take when you are feeling depressed (*see also* Unwanted Advice).
- **Join a support group.** PPD support groups allow mothers who are dealing with depression to talk with others who have similar feelings. A list at the end of this entry can help you find a group in your area. You might also call your health care provider, your local hospital, or your church for information. While PPD support groups are an

excellent choice, any group for new mothers in which you can share your feelings about motherhood can help you feel better about yourself. Choose your support group with care, as you'll want to be around people who support your parenting decisions. A group whose members criticize or question your mothering choices will make you feel worse, not better. Conversely, spending your time with like-minded people will boost your self-confidence and help you feel more confident as a mother. This idea shouldn't be seen as a cure, but rather one part of the process of recovery.

- **Accept help from others.** If anyone offers to help you—whether it is to take your baby for a walk, cook a meal, or drive your older kids to sports practice—accept! Learn to say yes. You don't have to do everything to be a good mother. It's natural for human beings to lean on each other, so go ahead and do a little more leaning.

- **Get some extra sleep.** Put your efforts to get your baby to sleep through the night on hold right now; this will come in time. Forget about the clock. Just sleep—both of you—whenever you can. Extra sleep will help you feel better.

- **Relax your standards.** This is not the time to worry about a spotless house, gourmet meals, the corporate ladder, or your manicure. Try to stick to the basics and concentrate on yourself and your baby.

- **Get some fresh air.** When possible, put your baby in the sling or the stroller, and take a walk. The exercise and open spaces will help you feel more energized. Try to work a daily stroll into your schedule. If you have older children, walk them to school. If the weather isn't suitable for outdoor walking, then drive to a shopping mall for an indoor walk.

- **Feed yourself healthful foods.** You can eat properly without much effort. Focus on fresh fruits and vegetables and on simple but nutritious meals. Eat frequently. Going long stretches without food wreaks havoc on your system. Simple snacks like an apple with peanut butter, a bagel, or yogurt with cottage cheese are easy to prepare and prevent your blood sugar from dipping and adding to your feelings of depression. Continue to take vitamins, and drink plenty of water.

• **Love yourself.** You are going to be OK. Take it one step at a time—but do take steps (such as those outlined in this section). With help and time, you'll develop a refreshing and healthy outlook on your new role as a mother.

For More Information

Books

Bennett, Shoshana S., and Pec Indman. *Beyond the Blues: A Guide to Understanding and Treating Prenatal and Postpartum Depression.* San Jose, CA: Moodswings Press, 2002.

Kleiman, Karen R., and Valerie D. Raskin. *This Isn't What I Expected: Overcoming Postpartum Depression.* New York: Bantam Books, 1994.

Websites

Depression After Delivery, Inc.
depressionafterdelivery.com

Pacific Post Partum Support Society
postpartum.org

Support Groups

La Leche League
lalecheleague.org/WebIndex.html

Postpartum Education for Parents
sbpep.org

Postpartum Support International
postpartum.net

Rash

· · · · · · · · · · · ·

See also: Chicken Pox; Diaper Rash; Eczema;
Fever; Hives; Roseola; Thrush

My baby has a rash. What could it be?

Learn About It

That butter-soft skin you so love about your baby is very sensitive and
can easily develop rashes. The Rash Reference Chart at the end of this
entry can help you decipher what's happening with your baby's skin. In
addition to the major reasons for baby rashes that are listed and refer-
enced separately, your baby might develop heat rash, friction rash, a rash
caused by a bacterial infection, or newborn acne.

Heat Rash (Prickly Heat, Miliaria)

A heat rash appears suddenly as a red, pimply rash in the creases and
folds of your baby's skin. It often occurs when your baby has been
bundled too warmly or during the hot summer months. This rash usually clears up quickly. You often can prevent heat rash by dressing your
baby for the weather so that he is neither too hot nor too cold. The
best way to tell if your baby is too hot is to feel your baby's tummy,
ears, neck, and fingers. These areas provide a good indication of his
body temperature.

Friction Rash (Intertrigo)

Babies are delightfully chubby, but some of that chub can cause a rash
where it contacts other chub. The most common place for this type of
rash is between the tummy and thighs or between those soft skin folds.

To prevent and treat this type of rash, try to keep your baby's skin dry. You also can protect the folds in your baby's skin with diaper ointment, baby powder, or petroleum jelly.

Bacterial Infection (Impetigo)

If your baby's rash is blistery, crusty, or scabby, it may be caused by bacteria. This type of rash can occur when your baby's immune system is challenged with an illness such as a cold or when the skin is broken by a scratch. It is important to keep the area clean and dry, since bacteria of all types thrive in moist areas. Contact your pediatrician if you think your baby has impetigo, because treatment usually requires a prescribed antibiotic.

Newborn Acne (Milia, Miliaria)

Babies are born with smooth, clear skin, but around the second to fourth week, some develop facial rashes that look a lot like teenage acne. The rash can have tiny red, yellow, or white dots or red blotches. At work are the hormones in your baby's body, which cause an overproduction of skin oil. The oil glands and pores then become clogged, creating that pimply look.

This isn't considered a medical problem, simply a cosmetic issue, and will clear up within a few weeks. All you need to do is wash gently with water or a mild baby soap once or twice a day. The newborn type of acne doesn't usually scar, and soon your baby's skin will be silky smooth again.

Determining the Type of Rash

The chart that follows will help you analyze your baby's rash.

Rash Reference Chart

Name	Description	Location	Cause	Treatment
Bacterial infection (impetigo)	Blistery, crusty, or scabby; sometimes with pus or discharge	Common on the hands, mouth, and nose, but can be all over the body	Bacterial infection	*See* Rash ("Bacterial Infection")
Chicken pox	Red and very itchy; eventually turns into pimplelike blisters that burst and form dry, crusty scabs	All over the body	A highly contagious virus	*See* Chicken Pox
Cradle cap	Brown, yellow, pink or reddish; scaly, crusty, scabby, or oily	Most often on the head; *can* appear on eyebrows, nose, ears, neck, armpits, and genitals	Natural, normal skin growth	*See* Cradle Cap
Diaper rash	Flat, red or pink; may have blisters	In the diaper area	The warm, moist environment under a diaper	*See* Diaper Rash
Eczema	Starts as a red rash, possibly becoming moist with pus-filled bumps or turning dry and scaly and itchy	Typically forehead, face, arms, legs, scalp, and neck but can cover the whole body	An activity of the body's immune system; allergic reaction to something eaten or touched	*See* Eczema
Friction rash (intertrigo)	Usually pink to brown	In creases and folds of skin	Rubbing of skin	*See* Rash ("Friction Rash")
Heat rash (miliaria)	Red, pimply	In creases and folds of skin	Overdressing; hot weather	*See* Rash ("Heat Rash")

(continued)

Name	Description	Location	Cause	Treatment
Hives	Appears and disappears rapidly; raised white lumps on a red or pink base	Whole body	Hypersensitivity reaction to something eaten or touched or a reaction to a virus	*See* Hives
Newborn acne (milia/miliaria)	Tiny yellow, red, or white dots	Face	Clogged oil glands	*See* Rash ("Newborn Acne")
Roseola	Pink; blanches (turns white when you press on it); does not itch; preceded by fever	All over the body	Viral infection	*See* Roseola
Thrush (candida)	White spots in mouth with red diaper rash	Baby's mouth and diaper area and mother's nipples	Yeast infection	*See* Thrush

Reading

See also: Attachment Parenting; Bilingualism; Intelligence; Talking

Our pediatrician told me that I should start reading to my baby. Why? It's not like my little one understands the words. Is reading really all that important for babies?

Learn About It

Very few questions in parenting have a black-and-white, no-contest answer, but this is one of them. *Yes, reading to your baby is very important.* Early reading creates the foundation for all of your child's future learning, no matter the age, no matter the topic. You do your baby a tremendous service by introducing him to books early in life and by making books a part of your baby's everyday routine.

The Many Values of Reading to Your Baby

Research has shown clearly that reading aloud to all children—from newborn babies to teenagers—has numerous positive effects. Here are some of the ways your baby benefits when you read aloud to him or her:

• **Reading aloud to your baby promotes bonding.** Cuddling up with your baby to read a book tells your baby that you love him, that you want to give him your undivided attention, and that reading is fun and enjoyable. Your baby soon begins to associate the feeling of warmth, security, and pleasure with the experience of reading. This leads not only to a positive relationship with books, but also to a closer bond between you and your child.

• **Reading aloud has a soothing and calming effect.** A baby treasures no sound more than that of Mommy's or Daddy's voice. Even to us adults, there is something eminently peaceful about a "read-aloud voice." Hearing *your* read-aloud voice soothes your baby and helps her to wind down and relax. Your book-reading sessions can be like a calm oasis for your baby and for you in the midst of a sometimes hectic life.

• **Reading aloud exposes your baby to the rhythms and sounds of language.** Every time your baby listens to you reading, he learns more about language: sentence structures, rhymes, and patterns. And he learns that his parent's voice is connected somehow to the words on the page. All these things are immensely beneficial for your baby's developing verbal and intellectual skills (*see* Intelligence). Even baby books with just one or two words per page can help your baby learn language and the connection it has with the written word.

• **Reading aloud expands your baby's vocabulary.** Babies learn the meaning of words by hearing them used in a meaningful context over and over again. Picture books can provide the perfect opportunity for your baby to learn the names of things and, soon, to reproduce those words. And if you don't yet know, you soon will learn that babies love to hear their favorite books read over and over again! (*See* Talking.)

• **Reading aloud increases your baby's attention span.** Listening is an acquired skill, and the earlier parents begin reading to their baby, the sooner the baby will learn to stay focused on listening to the book. On average, babies have attention spans of only three or four minutes. With daily reading sessions, however, this attention span will gradually grow until your baby will be begging you for "one more book, please."

• **Reading aloud develops imagination and empathy.** The stories you read expose your baby to a new world full of wonder, excitement, happiness, and tears. As your baby grows into toddlerhood, she gradually absorbs the range of human experiences and emotions that books can portray. Eventually, this leads to a richer imagination and a greater understanding of how others think and feel.

• **Reading aloud can help your baby understand the situations or feelings he experiences.** New situations—a trip to the dentist, a new baby-sitter, a lost teddy bear, a move to a new house—can be very stressful or even frightening for an older baby. One of the best ways to help your baby feel confident and secure is to read a book together that explores the new situation or describes the emotions Baby is experiencing.

• **Reading aloud is the key for later reading success.** The U.S. Department of Education's report *Becoming a Nation of Readers* states, "The single most important activity for building the knowledge required for eventual success in reading is reading aloud to children." It is not an overstatement to say that if you want your children to do well in school, start reading to them daily from a very young age.

How to Develop a "Read-Aloud Culture" in Your Family

To help you achieve these benefits of reading to your child, here are some tips on how to make reading a part of Baby's everyday life:

• **Build reading aloud into your schedule from the very beginning.** After breakfast, before bedtime, after naps, and during a bath are all good times for a book-reading session. In the beginning, build multiple short reading sessions into your day. As your baby grows older and develops a longer attention span, schedule several longer reading sessions. View these reading sessions as part of daily life—every bit as essential as eating and sleeping.

• **Look forward to your read-aloud sessions.** Not only do you get a chance to bond with your baby, you also get to sit down and relax. Your baby—who has an amazing ability to read body language—will sense that you are enjoying this special time together.

• **Realize that reading aloud is a learning process for both parent and baby.** Very few parents are instinctively good at reading aloud. At first, you may stumble over words and feel silly reading aloud to an infant. But practice makes perfect. Try to vary the tone of your voice and keep your baby entertained with facial expressions and even funny noises as you read. Soon, you will feel more comfortable with reading aloud, and in the process, your baby will have developed listening skills and an increased attention span. Even parents who are not good readers themselves can read simple books to their children, and by increasing the length and complexity of books over the years, they can even improve their own reading skills.

• **Have many books in your home.** Libraries give parents a fantastic opportunity to expose their children to a wide variety of books, and your public library should play an essential role in your child's life. I make a monthly trip to our library and fill a box with nearly fifty books at each visit. I always shudder to see a parent in the library coaxing a child to choose "just one book." It's an effort not to remind the parent that library books are free! For babies, book *ownership* also is important. Babies thrive on familiarity and often like to have the same book read repeatedly. They also tend to chew, throw, and tear books; most libraries are fairly tolerant of this with board books, but it is better if you can let Baby play with your own books rather than the library's. Consider buying books for your baby as an investment in the child's future—one of the best you can make. Also, ask relatives and friends to sometimes give your baby books (instead of toys) for special occasions like holidays, birthdays, and rites of passage. If they sign their name in the book, along with a little message, the book becomes a special memento of an important person in your baby's life. And don't forget to look for books at yard sales and library cast-off sales; you can find some excellent books at giveaway prices.

• **Give your baby easy access to books.** Put books everywhere your baby goes: a box near his toys, a low shelf in his room, a basket in the kitchen, under the coffee table, and next to the diaper-changing area. Your baby will become much more attached to books if he gets lots of opportunities to handle them. Yes, the books will be mouthed—babies put objects in their mouths to try to understand what they are—so start out with sturdy board or plastic baby books for unsupervised playtime. After your baby is a year old, he will need exposure to traditional books, too. You can expect some books to end up in your "book hospital," but with patience and training, your baby will be handling books like a pro within a very short period.

• **Take "emergency" books with you.** Before you go out, make sure you have diapers, wipes, a change of clothes—and books! Whether you are waiting in a doctor's office, standing in the checkout line, or having coffee at a neighbor's house, books are fun for your baby to look at and will keep him entertained. Plus, your baby will develop the habit of taking books along everywhere and, in no time at all, will be reading on the school bus!

• **Don't push your baby into reading himself.** Most experts believe it is unnecessary to start a baby on a learning-to-read program. There is no hurry for learning to read; the important thing when your child is a baby is developing a love for books. The truth is, a well-read-to child will develop many reading skills naturally. Don't discourage your baby, either. If your little one is asking about words and letters, then do encourage this enthusiasm and interest. Many older babies enjoy word and letter games. Just follow your child's lead.

• **Read a book on the topic of reading aloud.** Several excellent books are available that discuss at length the advantages of reading aloud to children, give tips on how to do it successfully, and list specific recommendations for books at each age level. See "For More Information" for a list of some of my favorites.

• **Finally, read for yourself.** Most things in life are taught by example; so, too, is reading. Babies who see that reading is an enjoyable and consistent part of their parents' daily life will conclude that reading is important, valuable, and pleasant for themselves as well.

What to Read to Your Baby

In recommending books for you to read to your baby, the most important suggestion is that you read books that *you* like. When you enjoy them yourself, your baby enjoys the time, too. Borrow books from the library, and see which ones you and your baby like before buying your own copies. As your baby grows and you get more familiar with the range of children's books available, you will develop a good sense of what your baby likes. Here are some general guidelines to help you get started:

• For newborns, the type of book is not as important as the fact that your baby is hearing your voice and beginning to associate your read-aloud voice with the object called a book. Nursery rhymes are an excellent choice. Young babies are also more drawn to black-and-white contrast, bright primary colors, and simple bold pictures rather than complicated artwork, so choose some of these for your little one.

• As babies grow, they will begin to manipulate books. Your baby will grab, mouth, throw, stack, rip, and talk to them. Eventually, he'll learn how to turn the pages. This is a natural and healthy sign that your baby is interested in books. When you are reading, try offering a teething ring or a small plastic baby book to distract him from his "target book," but don't worry if he seems to think books are a food group. This is a good time for the board, cloth, and bath books that are widely available. Don't forget to read traditional books to your baby, though, and occasionally let Baby handle the books under supervision. Now's the time to begin teaching your child to respect books.

• By nine to twelve months old, your baby will become interested in books with photos or realistic pictures of familiar objects, books with songs, lift-the-flap books, and touch-and-feel books. In artwork, realism is better than abstraction when your baby is young. You can also make a book with photos of your baby's favorite people and things; you might add a little story, as well.

• Around his first birthday, your baby will love to hear simple stories. Don't feel glued to the text on the page; you can describe the pictures in words you think your baby will understand, and then talk about the story with your baby. Describe the characters or situations: "See the elephant. He has a long nose, doesn't he? That is called a trunk. And the elephant is so big! The mouse there is small, and the elephant is big." Once your baby is familiar with the book, you can start reading the words, too, or even do a little of both.

• Be patient. Some babies are slow to warm up to books. You may go through the whole first year wondering if your baby is *ever* going to really pay attention when you read. Slow starters often explode onto the book scene, though; suddenly, your formerly uninterested child will be *asking* you to read not just one book but piles of them! You may even find your slow starter growing into the bookworm of the family.

• Finally, here are some of the basic read-aloud "rules" that experts recommend:

- You may want to say the title and author of the book before you start reading. Soon your baby will recognize books by their titles.
- Read at the right pace. The most common mistake parents make is reading too quickly. But pace yourself according to your child's interest. If your baby is turning the page before you're done, speed up a bit, or drop the rest of the section and go on to the next page.
- Don't force the book-reading sessions. If your baby has had enough, move on to something else and try again later.
- Many babies love to have the same book read many times in one sitting. Be patient with this; the book's familiarity makes your baby feel comfortable and secure and helps her digest the information she's learning.

Helping your child find the joy in reading should be a fun and rewarding aspect of parenting. And it is well worth the time and effort you invest.

For More Information

Books

Hunt, Gladys. *Honey for a Child's Heart: The Imaginative Use of Books in Family Life*, 4th ed. Grand Rapids, MI: Zondervan Publishing House, 2002.

Trelease, Jim. *The Read-Aloud Handbook*, 5th ed. New York: Penguin Books, 2001.

Reflux

(Gastroesophageal Reflux Disease, GER, GERD)

. . . .

See also: Burping; Colic; Spitting Up; Vomiting

My baby is very fussy after eating and spits up after every meal. I've heard about a condition called gastroesophageal reflux. What exactly is it? How do I know if my baby has it? What can I do about it, if she does?

Learn About It

The word *gastroesophageal* refers to the stomach and esophagus. *Reflux* means to return or flow back. With gastroesophageal reflux, the stomach's contents flow back up into the esophagus. Reflux in an adult produces heartburn. Reflux in a baby is caused by an immature digestive system; almost all babies with reflux outgrow the problem around their first birthday.

Spitting up frequently, particularly after meals, is a common symptom of reflux. However, not every baby who spits up has reflux, and not every baby with reflux experiences this symptom. You'll need to look at several aspects of your baby's health to determine if he does have reflux. A baby won't demonstrate all of them, but signs of possible reflux include the following:

- Regular spitting up or frequent forceful vomiting
- Difficulty feeding or refusing feeding even when hungry
- Excessive feeding
- Guzzling or frantic swallowing
- Crying that appears to be a sign of pain
- Persistent, frequent night waking

- Waking in the night with a burst of crying
- Fussiness and crying after eating
- Increased fussing or crying when lying on back
- Decreased fussiness when held upright or when lying on stomach
- Squirming or back arching after feeding
- Frequent colds or recurrent coughing or wheezing
- Spitting up when straining to pass a bowel movement
- Frequent hiccups
- Sinus and nasal congestion
- Slow weight gain and growth
- A family history of reflux

If your baby shows some of these signs, talk to your doctor about the possibility of reflux. Many of these signs can also signal other issues, such as a breastfeeding mother's overactive letdown reflex or overabundant milk supply, so you'll need to contemplate the information in this section and talk them over with your lactation consultant or medical provider. If your doctor confirms your suspicion of reflux, he or she may suggest some of these remedies:

- Breastfeed exclusively, if possible, since breastfed babies experience less severe reflux than formula-fed babies.
- Offer frequent, small meals as opposed to fewer, larger feedings.
- Feed your baby in a more upright position. When lying to nurse, raise Baby's head on your arm.
- Hold your baby upright for thirty to sixty minutes after feeding. Carrying your baby in a sling or front pack is a wonderful way to accomplish this.
- Burp your baby more frequently (*see* Burping).
- Have a supervised period of tummy-down time with your baby on a thirty-degree angle, head up, after feeding. (Remember that most babies should *sleep* on their backs. According to the American Academy of Pediatrics, this even includes most babies with reflux. If your baby has severe reflux, talk to your doctor about an alternative, such as side sleeping.)

- Prevent your baby from sitting and slumping over (such as in an infant seat) directly after eating.
- Elevate the head of your baby's bed. Use a higher setting on the crib mattress at the head, place something stable under the legs of the bed or crib, place a block of wood or a few books under the mattress, or use a crib elevation wedge available through baby product distributors.
- For a formula-fed baby, try switching formula to a different type or a thicker variety, such as those that contain a rice thickener. Experiment with different bottle types and nipple styles to reduce excess air intake.
- For a breastfed baby, give frequent, smaller feedings. If your baby is ready for solid food, add a small serving of rice cereal after nursing.
- If you are breastfeeding, try eliminating foods from your diet that are known to create refluxlike symptoms in your baby. These include milk products, gassy vegetables, and vitamin supplements.
- Avoid putting pressure on your baby's stomach by dressing him in clothing or diapers that are tight around his belly.
- Make feeding times peaceful and relaxing.
- Avoid letting your baby cry for any length of time, as crying can make reflux worse. Carry your baby as much as possible to decrease her crying and keep her calm. (*See* Crying.)
- For ideas and companionship, join a support group of families who are dealing with reflux. You can find these through your local hospital or online.

If reflux is severe and these solutions don't seem to help, talk to your doctor about medical remedies, such as using an antacid created especially for babies with reflux.

For More Information

Website
The GERD Information Resource Center
gerd.com

Crib Wedges

Our Kids, Inc.
baby-be-safe.com

Pedicraft
pedicraft.com/reflux.html

Restaurants, taking your baby to

· · · · · · · · · · · ·

See also: Breastfeeding in Public; Travel by Airplane; Travel by Car; Visiting Other People's Homes with Your Baby

We used to eat out frequently. Now that we have our baby, we've only been out a couple of times, and I didn't enjoy either experience. Do we have to give up eating at restaurants now?

Learn About It

Most likely, if you didn't enjoy eating out with your baby, it's because you were expecting your normal dining experience. With a baby along, though, you'll have to redefine your idea of "normal," just as with any other component of your prebaby life. With a little planning, practice, and perspective, you'll find that your baby can be an enjoyable dining partner.

Choosing the Restaurant

Say good-bye to the days of choosing a restaurant based on its fine cuisine, except on occasions when you are dining with adults only. The right choice of restaurant can mean the difference between an enjoyable event and an unpleasant one. Choose an establishment with the following features:

• **Prepared to accommodate children:** Call ahead and ask if they have a children's menu and high chairs. If the answer is "yes" to both, then the restaurant is probably a good choice.

• **Family friendly:** A noisy environment with other children around will allow you to relax about your baby's coos, squeals, and cries. A hushed restaurant (one with candles and tablecloths) will amplify every one of your baby's noises, and you'll be a nervous wreck.

• **Uncrowded:** If you have to wait forever for your food to be served, you'll be dealing with fussiness before you're done. If you choose a popular restaurant, go before the rush hour.

• **Menu with a few typical kid-food choices:** If you are planning to feed your older baby there, look for a restaurant that serves some of her familiar choices. Many times a parent is surprised to find that the grilled cheese sandwich she ordered turns out to be a gourmet version—and I don't know many babies who relish Swiss cheese on sourdough.

Preparing the Baby for the Event

Unless your baby can fall asleep anywhere, plan a restaurant excursion for right after your baby's nap. If you have a newborn who can still sleep anywhere, it won't matter what time you go. Just bring in your car seat, stroller, or portable baby seat for her to sleep in, unless you're comfortable and practiced at having a meal with her in your arms.

Try not to arrive at the restaurant when your baby is starving. If you do, though, take along a snack to tide her over until the meal is served. You also can ask your server to bring something to the table for your little one. Most are happy to bring some crackers or cheese even before they take your order, if you request it. If you are visiting a quick-service restaurant, the food will arrive fast enough to suit your baby and you.

Food for Baby

You have a number of options for your baby's meal. For example, you can ask for an extra plate and share pieces from your own meal (obviously, this works if you order something that your baby likes as well). If you have more than one child along, you can order a meal for them to share. Another option that many parents don't think of is to create your *own* entrees. You can determine what ingredients the kitchen has in stock by looking over the menu. Then simply ask for a few things in a polite way: "Do you think I could get a slice of tomato, a piece of avocado, and some cheese for my baby?" Most servers are happy to work with you. If you've planned ahead and brought an empty sipper cup, you can ask your server to fill it with milk or juice.

Don't be too worried about what your baby actually eats. As long as she's happy, just enjoy your own meal. I've watched many parents ruin their own mealtime by nagging and begging their children to eat the entire time they are at a restaurant. Don't fret so. Simply pack up whatever she doesn't eat in a doggy bag—frequently, that will be almost the entire meal, albeit in a messier pile than when it was first served.

Taking What You Need

You can enhance your restaurant experience by taking along a few things:

- A bib (an extra large one with a catchall pocket at the bottom)
- Your baby's sippy cup, spoon, and bowl
- A washcloth or wet wipes in a plastic bag for after-meal cleanup
- A change of clothes for your baby in case of spills

Keeping Your Baby Happy

What seems like a short time to you can be an eternity to your baby. While you may be interested in the food, your baby won't be. If she's at the stage of crawling, cruising, or walking, then sitting quietly in one seat for an hour or more can be torture for her! The following ideas can help you keep your baby happy for an extended period:

- Take along an assortment of quiet toys for your baby to play with, or go to a restaurant that offers a child's meal with a special prize.
- Ask for crackers or bread to be served as soon as you are seated so that your baby has something to eat (and play with!) while you are waiting for your meal to be served.

- Relax! It's perfectly fine for your baby to play with her crackers instead of eat them, or stack up the little jelly packets, or fill a plate with sprinkles of salt and pepper. If these activities keep her happy and quiet, then go ahead and let her play.

- After you've ordered your food, you might want or need to take your baby for a walk. Keep in mind other people's desires for a quiet meal, but go ahead and take a stroll down the hallway or outside or make a trip to the restroom. This is usually a great distraction for little ones.

- A coffee cup filled with ice, along with a spoon for stirring, makes a great toy. Just make sure that the ice pieces aren't the size of a choking hazard, since a few will likely make it into your baby's mouth.

- Order food that your baby likes, but don't worry about how much she actually eats. A little smearing and mashing make for a quiet, happy baby while you eat your own meal.

- Don't stay long after you've eaten, unless your baby seems content. Long postmeal conversations tend to invite fussy, disruptive behavior from babies.

- If your baby has made a mess at the table (or beneath it), remember to leave a bigger tip for the server who has to clean it all up!

Roseola

(Baby Measles, Roseola Infantum, Three-Day Fever)

. . . .

See also: Chicken Pox; Febrile Seizure; Fever; Hives; Rash

> *My baby has had a fever for the last three days, and I thought she had the flu. Now she's getting a rash on her body and neck! What's happening?*

Learn About It

Your baby probably has roseola, a common virus that affects babies and toddlers. It most often begins with a fever, typically between 100°F and 105°F (38°C and 41°C). After a few days to a week, a pink rash appears, which lasts one to three days. Roseola is different from some other rashes in that it will "blanch," or turn white when you press on it. (A way to determine if a rash blanches is to roll a clear glass over the rash, pressing gently.) Your baby might act very tired and irritable and may have decreased appetite, a runny nose, and/or a mild case of diarrhea.

Are There Any Risks?

Roseola is a fairly mild viral infection. The biggest risk to a small number of children is the possibility of a febrile convulsion brought on by the high fever, particularly if the temperature rises quickly (*see* Febrile Seizure).

Do I Need to Take My Baby to the Doctor?

Anytime your baby is ill and you have concerns, you should call your doctor. While your baby's symptoms may appear to be related to roseola, you could be mistaken, so rely on your pediatrician's experience and expertise. Your doctor knows your baby, can judge if an office visit is necessary, and can give you advice specifically for your situation.

How Do We Get Rid of the Virus?

No medication or treatment exists specifically for roseola. It is a virus and, as such, must run its course and disappear on its own. Treatment, then, is palliative, meaning you just do your best to keep your baby comfortable. Because the fever is the worst part of this virus, handle your baby's fever in the usual ways:

- Keep her cool by dressing her lightly.
- With your doctor's approval, give your baby acetaminophen (such as Infant's Tylenol), ibuprofen (such as Infant's Advil), or an herbal remedy (such as chamomile or valerian). Do *not* give your baby aspirin, as it has been associated with Reye's syndrome, a rare but dangerous illness.
- Give your baby a sponge bath or tub bath, or wipe her with wet washcloths.
- Be certain your baby has plenty of liquids—especially breastmilk, formula, and water—to prevent dehydration and provide the nutrition required for recovery.
- For more important information, *see* Fever.

Is It Contagious?

Roseola affects only children up to about age three, among whom it is contagious. The incubation period (from infection to symptoms) is one to two weeks. Your baby may be contagious during the entire course of the virus, so keep him away from other young children until he is back to normal.

Separation Anxiety

· · · · · · · · · · · ·

See also: Attachment Parenting; Independent Play; Stranger Anxiety

> *My baby is happy only when I'm within arm's reach. If I dare to leave the room, she cries as if I've left the country! I can't even so much as take a shower these days, let alone leave the house without her. My mother-in-law says it's because I've spoiled her. Is she right? Have I made her so clingy?*

Learn About It

Nothing you've done has "made" your baby develop separation anxiety. It's a perfectly normal and important developmental adaptation. Nearly all children experience separation anxiety between the ages of seven and eighteen months. Some have more intense reactions than others, and for some, the stage lasts longer than for others, but almost all babies have it to some degree.

The development of separation anxiety demonstrates that your baby has formed a healthy, loving attachment to you. It is a beautiful sign that your baby associates pleasure, comfort, and security with your presence. It also indicates that your baby is developing intellectually (in other words, she's smart!). She has learned she can affect her world when she makes her needs known, and she doesn't have to passively accept a situation that makes her uncomfortable. She doesn't know enough about the world yet to understand that when you leave her, you'll always come back. She also realizes that she is safest, happiest, and best cared for by you, so her reluctance to part makes perfect sense—especially when viewed from a survival standpoint. Put another way, you are her source of nourishment, both physical and emotional, so her attachment to you is her means of survival. And when she reaches a certain level of intellectual maturity, she realizes this.

This stage, like so many others in childhood, will pass. In time, your baby will learn that she *can* separate from you, that you will return, and that everything will be OK between those two points in time. Much of this learning is based on trust, which, for every human being young or old, takes time to build.

How Do I Know if My Baby Has Separation Anxiety?

Separation anxiety is pretty easy to spot, and you're probably reading this topic because you've identified it in your baby. The following behaviors are typical of a baby with normal separation anxiety:

- Clinginess
- Crying when a parent is out of sight
- Strong preference for only one parent (which may change from one to the other!)
- Fear of strangers (*see also* Stranger Anxiety)
- Waking at night and crying for a parent
- Easily comforted in a parent's embrace

How You Can Help Your Baby with Separation Anxiety

Eventually children outgrow separation anxiety. Until then, you can help your baby cope:

- Allow your baby to be a baby. It's perfectly OK—even wonderful—for your baby to be so attached to you and to desire your constant companionship. Congratulations, Mommy or Daddy: It's evidence that the bond you've worked so hard to create is holding. Politely ignore those who tell you otherwise.
- Don't worry about spoiling your baby with your love, since quite the opposite will happen. The more that you meet your baby's attach-

ment needs during babyhood, the more confident and secure he will grow up to be.

• Minimize separations when possible. It's perfectly acceptable for now—better, in fact—to avoid situations that would have you separate from your baby. All too soon, your baby will move past this phase and on to the next developmental milestone.

• Give your baby lessons in object permanence. As your baby learns that things continue to exist even when she can't see them, she'll feel better about letting you out of her sight. Games like peekaboo and hide-and-seek will help her understand this phenomenon.

• Practice with quick, safe separations. Throughout the day, create situations of brief separation. When you go into another room, whistle, sing, or talk to your baby so he knows you're still there, even though he can't see you.

• When you have to leave your baby, don't sneak away. It may seem easier than dealing with a tearful good-bye, but it will just cause constant worry that you're going to disappear without warning at any given moment. The result? Even *more* clinginess and diminished trust in your relationship.

• Tell your baby what to expect. If you are going to the store and leaving your baby at home with Grandma, explain where you are going, and tell when you'll be back. Eventually, your baby will understand your explanations.

• Don't rush the parting, but don't prolong it, either. Give your baby ample time to process your leave-taking, but don't drag it out and make it more painful for both of you.

• Express a positive attitude when leaving. If you're off to work or an evening out, leave with a smile. Your baby will absorb your emotions, so if you're nervous about leaving her, she'll be nervous as well. Your confidence will help alleviate her fears.

• Leave your baby with familiar people. If you must leave your baby with a new caregiver, try to arrange a few visits when you'll all be together before you leave the two of them alone for the first time.

• Invite distractions. If you're leaving your baby with a caregiver or relative, encourage that person to get your baby involved with playtime as you leave. Say a quick good-bye, and let your baby be distracted by an interesting activity.

• Allow your baby the separation that he initiates. If he crawls off to another room, don't rush after him. Listen and peek, of course, to make sure that he's safe, but let him know it's fine to go off exploring on his own.

• Encourage your baby's relationship with a special toy, if she seems to have one. These are called "transitional objects" or lovies. They can be a comfort to babies when they are separated from their parents. Many babies adopt blankets or soft toys as loveys, holding them to ease any pain of separation. The lovey becomes a friend and represents security in the face of change.

• Don't take it personally. Many babies go through a stage of attaching themselves to one parent or the other. The other parent, as well as grandparents, siblings, and friends, can find this difficult to accept. Try to reassure them that it's just a temporary and normal phase of development, and with a little time and gentle patience, it will pass.

Shaken-Baby Syndrome

(Pediatric Traumatic Brain Injury, Whiplash Shaken Infant Syndrome)

See also: Baby Blues; Colic; Crying; Discipline; Postpartum Depression; Reflux; Sleep, newborn; Sleep, four months and over

I've heard that shaking a baby is dangerous and can cause permanent harm. What can you tell me about this?

Learn About It

You are referring to shaken-baby syndrome, which is when vigorous shaking causes brain damage that can lead to seizures, blindness, developmental disabilities, brain damage, coma, and even death. A baby's head and neck are delicate. The neck muscles are weak, and the brain and blood vessels are tenuous. While a baby isn't too fragile for everyday care, significant trauma can be caused with forceful shaking, jerking, or jolting.

How Does This Happen?

It is an extremely rare person who intentionally harms a baby. Most cases of shaken-baby syndrome occur when an adult becomes angry and frustrated with a baby and loses control. The most common triggers for this are incessant crying, temper tantrums, toileting problems, or frequent, persistent night waking. While these issues are common parenting problems, adults without help or training sometimes lose control and shake a child in anger and frustration.

How Is Shaken-Baby Syndrome Diagnosed?

This syndrome is difficult to diagnose unless someone describes the situation that caused the signs and symptoms. However, certain signs, such as bleeding in the eyes or brain hematoma (collection of blood on the brain), can prompt a medical professional to make the diagnosis.

What Are the Signs of Shaken-Baby Syndrome?

The following signs can indicate shaken-baby syndrome:

- Seizures
- Breathing difficulty
- Vomiting
- Loss of consciousness
- Bleeding in the retina of the eyes
- Increased head size due to excess fluid
- Lethargy

Is There a Cure for Shaken-Baby Syndrome?

While immediate medical care can reduce the medical repercussions of violent shaking, many children suffer irreparable permanent damage from the incident, such as hearing loss, vision impairments, and developmental disorders.

How Can Caregivers Prevent Shaken-Baby Syndrome?

The most important prevention method is to explain the syndrome to all the people who care for your baby, including baby-sitters, day-care providers, siblings, and grandparents. Remember (and remind these people) that, while everyone feels frustrated at times when caring for a baby, that frustration should *never* take physical form.

Instead, if you become angry, frustrated, or feel pushed beyond your limits of patience with a baby for any reason, you should stop whatever you are doing, and put the baby down in a safe place (such as a crib) in a closed room. Let him cry if necessary while you calm yourself down. If you are unable to regain your composure within a few minutes, call someone else for help. Don't return to the baby in your frazzled state.

If you find that your baby's frequent crying continually makes you angry, read the suggestions in this book under the topic of Crying. If frequent, persistent night waking is a problem, read the ideas under Sleep, newborn; Sleep, four months and over. If you feel that your emotions are too intense, inappropriate, or just a bit out of whack, read the topics of Baby Blues; Postpartum Depression.

If you continue to feel routinely frustrated by your baby's actions, then *please* talk to someone about how you feel. This person can be your partner, your parent, a friend, your doctor, a religious leader, or a counselor—anyone who can help you talk through your difficulty (or get you the help you need) so you can gain control of your feelings during this difficult time. If you suspect someone you know is at risk of shaking or otherwise harming his or her baby, please share this information with him or her.

It bears repeating: No matter how upset you get, *never, ever shake a baby*.

Shoes

See also: Milestones of Development; Walking

> *My baby has just started walking. It drives my mother-in-law crazy that I let him run around barefoot. She says his feet need support and wants me to put him in a pair of those rigid, high-top shoes like the bronzed ones she has sitting on her mantel from when my husband was a baby. Would my little boy benefit from a pair of these?*

Learn About It

Grandmothers often give good advice based on experience, but in this case, recommendations on babies' footwear have changed quite a bit from what they were twenty years ago. Since then, we've discovered that children's feet develop best when unhindered by rigid supportive shoes. The best footwear for your baby is actually none at all!

The bones in a baby's tiny feet are still developing, and they are quite pliable. Walking barefoot allows babies' bones and joints to move freely. As your beginning walker makes his way around the house, he will make total use of his muscles and toes to grip the floor. This will give him more stability and better control. Moreover, strong ankles and properly developed foot bones affect your baby's entire body, especially his pelvis and backbone.

When it's cold in the house, invest in skid-free socks or soft booties to keep your baby's feet warm without putting too much barrier between his feet and the floor.

When Does a Baby Need Shoes?

It's best to let your little one spend a good amount of his walking time without shoes. However, shoes do have an important role: When your baby is walking outside or in public places, they provide necessary protection.

Keep the weather in mind when shoe shopping. Babies need sturdier, warmer shoes for wet, cold winter weather and lighter-weight shoes for summer. Avoid sandals for new walkers, though. Sandals rarely have the proper fit for developing balance and coordination.

The choice of baby's first shoes is an important one. These guidelines may help:

• **Size:** Make sure your baby's shoes fit perfectly. Shoes that are too small can cramp growing feet and prevent optimum development, and shoes that are too big will hinder balance and stride. Look for shoes that slip on easily and have a finger-width space between the toes and the tip. They should allow plenty of wiggle room without being so big as to slip off his heel as he walks. When a baby is standing, there should be no areas where the shoe is putting pressure on the feet. Baby shoes are sold in different widths, so check the sides of your baby's feet to make sure the width is correct, too. If you're unsure how to decide on the correct size, go to a children's shoe store or large department store, and have the salesperson measure your baby's feet and show you how to choose a shoe with a proper fit.

• **Shape:** This is important, too. Your baby's first shoes should surround his little feet to keep them in as natural a position as possible to provide stability and protection without restriction. Boots, pointy-toed dress shoes, and party shoes with heels may look cute but aren't a good choice, since they confine the feet in unnatural positions.

• **Material:** The more flexible the material, the better. Soft, breathable material, such as leather, is a good choice. The shoe should allow freedom of movement while protecting against injury. Look for non-skid bottoms that promote traction, as opposed to slick, smooth bottoms that will encourage falls. Mini versions of your favorite athletic shoes are often a good bet.

• **Function:** Think about the fact that you will be taking your baby's shoes on and off frequently. This will be easier if the shoes have Velcro closures or zippers rather than laces or buckles. Some parents prefer shoes with laces since they can provide a more customized fit. But as your little one begins to learn how to get dressed, he'll appreciate having some shoes he can remove or replace on his own.

- **Fit:** Babies' feet grow at an incredibly fast rate, and it's easy to put a too-small shoe on your baby without realizing it. Check your baby's shoe fit every few weeks. You'll be very surprised to see how quickly those little feet grow!

Parent Tip

"When shopping for shoes, trace around your child's stockinged foot on a piece of paper. Cut it out and take it with you to slip inside the shoe. It saves the hassle of wrestling every pair onto your child to try."*

—Sarah, mother of Ryan (4) and Audrey (1)

*When you find a shoe you like, always double-check for proper fit with the real, live foot!

Avoid Hand-Me-Down Shoes

Buying new shoes every few months can be expensive, but don't try to cut corners by using hand-me-down or secondhand shoes. Once shoes have been worn for a while, they mold to the wearer's foot, changing the fit from the original design. The exception to this rule is a pair of party shoes that were worn once or twice and still look brand-new, if you intend to use them for a special occasion, not daily.

What About Socks?

Babies can't tell us when their socks are too tight, so check to be sure that all socks have a comfortable fit and don't bind or restrict the toes. Opt for socks in a natural fabric like cotton so that air can circulate around your baby's feet.

Sleep, newborn

See also: Attachment Parenting; Co-Sleeping, making it work; Cribs and Cradles; Naps; Sleep, four months and over; Swaddling

How do I get my two-month-old to sleep through the night? My sister's eight-month-old sleeps all night, but my baby is up every two hours!

Learn About It

How wonderful to have a newborn! New babies bring so much wonder, joy, and love to your family. But unavoidably, as you've discovered, they bring sleeplessness as well. Newborn babies have very different sleep needs than older babies, and their frequent waking is a biological necessity. Their tiny bodies need nourishment every few hours. A few more months should pass before you even begin to think about all-night sleep.

Night Feedings

Many pediatricians recommend that newborns not be left to sleep longer than three or four hours without feeding. For the vast majority of babies, this isn't an issue; they wake far more frequently than that. It helps if you recognize that your baby's night waking isn't a mere inconvenience but an important aspect of a child's early growth and development.

Although young babies require night feedings, you shouldn't automatically assume that any time your baby makes a peep, a feeding is necessary. It will take some intuition and observation, but you can learn when you should pick your baby up for a night feeding and when you can let her go back to sleep on her own.

Babies make many sleeping sounds, from grunts to whimpers to out-right cries, and these noises don't always signal awakening or a need to eat. These are what I call "sleeping noises," and your baby is nearly or even totally asleep during these episodes. When my son Coleton was a newborn, he slept beside me, and I automatically put him to the breast whenever he made a noise, even the littlest sniff. Until I came to real-ize that, on many of those occasions, he wasn't even awake, I woke him myself and actually reinforced his night-waking episodes, making them a habit. You can avoid this situation with your baby. When your baby makes noises during the night, listen and watch carefully. You will soon learn to differentiate between sleeping sounds and awake-and-hungry sounds, so you can let your sleeping baby sleep!

If you determine that your baby is really awake and hungry, even if less than three or four hours have passed since her last feeding, feed her as quickly as possible. When you respond immediately to her hunger cues, she will most likely fall back to sleep easily. But, if you let her cry escalate, she will wake herself up totally, and it will take longer for her to go back to sleep. Not to mention that *you* will then be wide-awake, too!

Help Your Baby Distinguish Day from Night

Your newborn will sleep about sixteen to eighteen hours every day, and it will take a while before most of those sleep hours occur at night. You can help your baby distinguish between nighttime sleep and daytime sleep and thus encourage sleep for longer periods at night.

If your baby naps well in a lit room where he can hear the noises of the day, you can take advantage of this by placing a bassinet or cradle in the main area of your home. Conversely, make nighttime sleep dark and quiet. This will begin the process of helping your baby reorganize sleep hours into short naps during the day and long stretches of sleep at night. If you have a baby who takes extremely long naps during the day but is up frequently at night, try waking your baby from his long nap and then putting him to bed earlier. You can also help your baby tell the differ-ence between day naps and night sleep by using a nightly bath and a change into sleeping pajamas to signal the transition between the two.

Watch for Signs of Tiredness

One way to encourage good sleep is to get familiar with your baby's sleepy signals and put her down to sleep as soon as she seems tired. A baby who is encouraged to stay awake when her body is craving sleep is typically unhappy. Over time, this pattern develops into sleep deprivation, which further complicates your baby's developing sleep maturity. Learn to read your baby's sleepy signs:

- Quieting down of motion and noises
- Losing interest in people and toys
- Looking unfocused and "glazed"
- Yawning
- Fussing

Practice reading her sleepy signs, and put her to bed as soon as you realize that she's tired.

Try Creating a Womblike Environment

Newborn babies often sleep better and longer when you reproduce the conditions of the womb. Here are some ways to do this:

- Swaddle your baby for sleep (*see* Swaddling). This helps your baby feel snug and secure.
- Use white noise. Some options are a ticking clock, a bubbling fish tank, or a recording of nature sounds. You can also purchase recordings that reproduce the heartbeat sounds of the womb especially for newborns. These are often sold through catalogs and stores that feature maternity or baby goods.
- Try using movement to soothe your baby by putting him in a rocking cradle, a bouncy baby seat, a swing, a baby hammock, or a crib with a vibrating motion attachment.
- Bring your stroller into the house. Walk your baby around for naps until he falls asleep. (You can even do this in a small apartment. Just roll back and forth, over a "lump" like a doorway; this is often relaxing for a baby.) When your baby falls asleep, park him near you. If he starts to

move about or make noises, walk and bounce him. Once he gets used to taking a longer nap, you can make the transition to a bed or crib.

Make Yourself Comfortable

As much as we adore our little bundles, it's a rare parent who enjoys getting up with a baby over and over again, night after night. However, since your baby *will* be waking you up, you may as well make yourself as comfortable as possible. A comfy bed or chair, a footrest, a nursing pillow, a bottle of water, a book to read, or anything else that helps you enjoy these night interludes will be helpful.

Create a nighttime environment that is peaceful and comfortable. Relax, if you can, about night wakings right now. Being stressed or frustrated about having to get up won't change a thing, and it interferes with your own rest—it's easier to go back to sleep if you aren't feeling annoyed. The situation will improve day by day. And before you know it, your little newborn won't be so little anymore. She'll be walking and talking and getting into everything in sight—during the day—and sleeping peacefully all night long.

Sleep Safety Checklist

☐ Put your healthy baby to sleep on his back (*see* Back Sleeping). However, a few babies have conditions that require that they sleep on their sides or tummies. Be sure to talk to a doctor about which sleep position is best for your baby.

☐ Keep your baby warm, but not too warm. Keep the bedroom at a comfortable sleeping temperature, usually between 65°F and 72°F (18°C to 22°C). Be careful not to overheat your baby. If your newborn comes home from the hospital wearing a hat, ask your doctor if Baby should wear it to sleep and for how long, since a hat could contribute to overheating.

☐ Do not use blankets or comforters under or over your baby. These can entangle your baby or become a suffocation hazard. Instead, when the temperature warrants, dress your baby in warm sleeper pajamas layered with an undershirt.

☐ Dress your baby in flame-resistant and snug-fitting sleepwear, not oversized, loose-fitting cotton or cotton blend clothing. Billowy or cotton fabrics pose a burn hazard in case of fire or even a close encounter with your stove or fireplace.

☐ Do not allow your baby to sleep on a soft sleeping surface such as a pillow, sofa, waterbed, beanbag chair, pillow-top mattress, foam pad, sheepskin, featherbed, or any other soft and flexible surface. Your baby should sleep only on a firm, flat mattress, with a smooth, wrinkle-free sheet that stays securely fastened around the mattress.

☐ Do not leave stuffed toys or pillows in bed with your baby. You may leave a small, safe toy with a baby more than four months old who can roll over and lift and move his head easily.

☐ Keep night-lights, lamps, and all electrical items away from where Baby sleeps.

☐ Make sure you have a working smoke detector in Baby's sleeping room, and check it as often as the manufacturer suggests.

☐ Do not put a baby to sleep near a window, window blinds, cords, or draperies.

☐ Do not allow anyone to smoke around your baby. This holds true whether your baby is asleep or awake. Babies exposed to smoke face an increased risk of SIDS, as well as other health complications, such as asthma.

☐ If your baby is sick or feverish, call your doctor or hospital promptly.

☐ Keep your baby's regular appointments for well-baby checkups.

☐ Never shake or hit your baby.

☐ Never tie a pacifier to your baby with a string, ribbon, or cord. Any of these can become wound around your baby's finger, hand, or neck.

☐ Follow all safety precautions when your baby is sleeping away from home, whether in a car seat, stroller, or unfamiliar place.

☐ Never leave a baby unattended while in a stroller, baby seat, swing, or car seat.

☐ Never leave a pet with access to a sleeping baby.

☐ Learn how to perform infant CPR. Be sure that all other caregivers for your baby are also trained in infant CPR. (*See* CPR.)

☐ Keep your baby's sleep environment clean. Wash bedding often.

☐ If your child spends time with a child-care provider, baby-sitter, grandparent, or anyone else, insist that safety guidelines be followed in that environment also.

☐ Breastfeed your baby whenever possible, since breastmilk prevents the risk of certain illnesses and infections, which, in turn, can decrease the risk of SIDS and other health conditions.

For More Information

Books

Karp, Harvey. *The Happiest Baby on the Block*. New York: Bantam Books, 2002.

Pantley, Elizabeth. *The No-Cry Sleep Solution: Gentle Ways to Help Your Baby Sleep Through the Night*. Chicago: Contemporary Books, 2002.

Sleep, four months and over

· · · · · · · · · · · ·

See also: Attachment Parenting; Co-Sleeping, making it work;
Cribs and Cradles ("Cribs and Cradles Safety Checklist");
Naps; Sleep, newborn; Swaddling

*I know it takes time for babies to be mature enough to sleep
through the night, but are there any things I can do to speed the
process along?*

Learn About It

You are right that it takes time for a baby's sleep maturity to develop.
This process begins at about six to nine weeks of age, but it is not until
about nine to ten months or later that a baby's sleep begins to resemble
an adult pattern of sleep. While patience is certainly the most important component during the waiting period, there are things that you
can do to help your baby sleep better.

What Are Realistic Expectations for Baby Sleep?

The medical definition of "sleeping through the night" refers to a five-
hour stretch, typically from midnight to 5:00 A.M. Most babies awaken
two to three times a night up to six months and once or twice a night
up to one year. Some awaken once a night from one to two years old.
A baby is considered to be sleeping through the night when she sleeps
five consecutive hours. While this may not be *your* definition of sleeping through the night, it is the reasonable yardstick by which we meas-

ure babies' sleep. Once a baby reaches this milestone, even longer stretches of sleep become possible.

Why Your Baby Wakes Up Throughout the Night

Brief awakenings during sleep (night waking) are a normal part of human sleep, regardless of age. Babies have more frequent night awakenings than do adults. However, a baby who requires nighttime care every hour or two is involving a parent in all his brief awakening periods. The baby makes a "sleep association," wherein he associates certain things with falling asleep and believes he *needs* these things to fall asleep. It is with the intent of breaking this association that the cry-it-out process was developed. The good news for babies is that research has uncovered numerous alternatives to crying it out—ways to slowly and lovingly help your baby create new falling-to-sleep associations.

Is There a Sleep Problem?

The first thing to consider is whether your baby's wakeful ways and the coping strategies you employ are upsetting to *you*. Or does the problem lie more in the perceptions of those around you? Put another way, your baby's sleep habits need changing only if *you* feel they're a problem. If you, your baby, and your spouse are content with the way things are— even if your baby is waking ten times a night—then relax and let nature take its course. If, however, you feel you'd like to make some changes, then the remaining tips in this section highlight a few ideas to encourage your baby toward better sleep. If these don't seem to be enough and if your baby's night waking is frequent and troublesome to you, I'd like to refer you to my book *The No-Cry Sleep Solution*, which offers many more solutions and a specific plan for improving your baby's sleep (*see* "For More Information" at the end of this entry).

Tips for Better Sleep

Think of the following list of ideas as a menu. You won't want (or need) to follow every single suggestion. Just pick and choose those that sound right for you and your baby. And be patient. Sleep changes don't happen overnight; they happen over *many* overnights!

- **Fill your baby's tummy during the day.** Make sure your baby is getting enough to eat during the day, especially if your baby is exclusively breastfed or formula fed. Some babies get in the habit of nursing or drinking bottles all through the night, taking in an inordinate percentage of their daily calories then. To sleep longer at night, such babies need to tip the feeding scales toward daytime.
- **Develop a bedtime routine.** A routine for the hour before bedtime is a crucial way to cue and prepare your baby for sleep. The hour before bed should be peaceful. Include any of the following activities that you enjoy and that help soothe and quiet your baby:

  - Warm, calm bath
  - Massage
  - Reading books
  - Singing songs
  - Playing soft music
  - Taking a walk
  - Rocking
  - Breastfeeding
  - Bottlefeeding

- **Establish an early bedtime.** Many people put their babies to bed much too late, often hoping that if baby is "really tired," he will sleep better. This often backfires because baby becomes overtired and then finds it difficult to relax for sleep. A baby's biological clock is preset for an early bedtime. When parents work with that time, a baby falls asleep more easily and stays asleep more peacefully. Most babies sleep better and *longer* with an earlier bedtime, often as early as 6:30 or 7:00 P.M. It is helpful if you establish your baby's bedtime and plan for it by beginning your prebed routine an hour before, when possible.

• **Let your baby take regular daily naps.** Up until age three or four, naps are an important part of keeping your baby happy and well rested. The best naps are at least an hour long. Catnaps can take the edge off, but since the sleep cycle is not fully completed, they may just make your baby fussier in the long run (*see* Naps).

• **Learn to read your baby's tired signs.** As babies grow, their sleep needs change. What used to work may no longer work. Try to figure out your baby's new rhythm. If you put Baby down for sleep when he is truly tired, he will fight sleep less! Here are some of the ways that babies tell us they are tired:

- Becoming mellow and quiet
- Losing interest in people and play
- Looking unfocused
- Lying down or slumping when seated
- Fussing and crying
- Yawning

• **Make your baby's nighttime environment conducive to sleep.** The right situation can help your baby sleep better and longer. Here are a few components to consider:

- Most babies sleep better when the room is dark, so cover the windows, and don't turn on lights during night wakings. Use only a tiny night-light.
- Make certain there are no loud or sharp noises when Baby is asleep.
- Use white noise to mask sounds (options include a ticking clock, a bubbling fish tank, or a recording of nature sounds). This drowns out noise that may otherwise wake your baby and creates a very strong sleep cue. Additional advantages are that you can use your white noise when away from home to create a

familiar sleep environment, and white noise can help an early riser to sleep longer, as it can mask outside noises that wake a baby.

- Incorporate some tire-the-baby-out time—running, jumping, laughing—before your bedtime routine of winding down with book reading, storytelling, breast- or bottlefeeding, and quiet cuddles. The active period can help your baby be ready for sleep.
- When your baby wakes in the night, do not talk or play. Say only, "Shhhh" or, "Night, night." Don't give in to your baby's desire for a nighttime play session.

• **Discover your baby's sleep associations, and gradually change them.** It's possible that your baby has created an association with certain things and concluded they are required for sleep. The most common are breastfeeding, bottlefeeding, using a pacifier, or having a parent hold and rock him to sleep. If you note that your baby relies on any of these for every nap, bedtime, and night waking, then you'll most likely need to modify these actions before your baby will begin to be able to put himself back to sleep during the night. The best way to approach this is with gradual changes. Make an effort to shorten the duration and type of aid that you offer your baby in the middle of the night. You may need to substitute back patting, rubbing, or soft words for a long breastfeeding session or a full bottle. These modifications take time and a double dose of patience, but nearly all babies will respond with longer sleep stretches once parents decide to make the effort.

• **Be patient with your baby.** Please keep in mind that it's a rare baby who can be put into a crib wide awake and then fall asleep peacefully! The vast majority of children need some parenting before sleep until about age three or four. Don't feel there is anything wrong with you or your baby if your little one needs some "help" getting settled for sleep. It is natural for a baby to need some parental soothing before sleep. And it is a very special, beautiful, bonding time that should be cherished.

For More Information

See also Sleep, newborn ("Sleep Safety Checklist").

Books

Pantley, Elizabeth. *The No-Cry Sleep Solution: Gentle Ways to Help Your Baby Sleep Through the Night.* Chicago: Contemporary Books, 2002.

Sears, William. *Nighttime Parenting: How to Get Your Baby and Child to Sleep*, rev. ed. New York: Plume, 1999.

Snoring and Sleep Apnea

See also: Colds; Sleep, newborn; Sleep, four months and over

> *My baby is a very restless, noisy sleeper. He snores, snorts, and breathes through his mouth. He doesn't have a cold or allergies, so what could this be?*

Learn About It

Your baby may be suffering from sleep apnea. *Apnea* means "absence of breath." The most disturbing symptom of this sleep disorder is that the sleeper actually stops breathing for up to thirty seconds, occasionally longer, after which the intake of breath causes a loud noise. This is very frightening for a parent to witness and should be taken very seriously, but in general, it is not life threatening and can be treated. Up to 10 percent of children have significant sleep apnea. The main causes include a narrow throat or airway, enlarged tonsils or lymph nodes, obesity, and facial abnormalities. Additional symptoms that may appear in older children are daytime sleepiness, nightmares, bed-wetting, sleep terrors, sleepwalking, profuse sweating while asleep, and morning headaches.

Not every child who snores has sleep apnea. However, if snoring is loud or is combined with the other symptoms, apnea could be the problem. Conversely, not all children with narrow airways, enlarged tonsils, facial abnormalities, or excess weight have sleep apnea.

Untreated apnea can cause heart problems and high blood pressure, in addition to significant sleep deprivation. Studies have been unable to link sleep apnea to the incidence of SIDS.

What Is the Cure?

The most common remedy for childhood sleep apnea is removal or reduction of the tonsils or adenoids. Other typical treatments are enlarging the air passage, holding the passage open during sleep, or (when the condition is caused by obesity) weight loss. As always, before you proceed with any of these options, it is wise to get at least two professional opinions.

Checking Baby for Sleep Apnea

All parents should check their sleeping babies from time to time. In a quiet room, your baby's breathing should be barely audible; it should be through the nose and appear effortless and regular. (This does not hold true if your baby has a cold or stuffy nose, but it's important to know that children with sleep apnea often have exaggerated symptoms when they have colds.)

If your baby's breathing during sleep is though the mouth, loud, or accompanied by snores or wheezing, if Baby appears to be struggling to breathe, or if you witness a pause in breathing, get professional advice. Talk to your pediatrician; an ear, nose, and throat specialist; or a sleep disorders clinic about the possibility of sleep apnea. If your baby is a newborn, these signs can be extremely serious and should be reported immediately.

Soft Spots

(Fontanels)

· · · · · · · · · · · ·

See also: Hair Care

What do I need to know about protecting the soft spot on my baby's head? I can actually see it moving up and down in time with his heartbeat, and it makes me a little nervous about how vulnerable this area must be.

Learn About It

While you do have to be thoughtful about preventing falls or sharp blows, your baby's brain is actually well protected by a very tough membrane that is surrounded by the hard bones of his skull. Your baby's head can tolerate everyday care, such as washing or hair brushing, and even the occasional scary but inevitable bump.

Why Do Babies Have Soft Spots?

Your baby actually has two soft spots. The most noticeable one is in the front middle of the head and is shaped like a diamond. The second is more toward the back of the head and is triangular. These are called "fontanels." Their size varies widely, and their purpose is to provide the flexibility needed for your baby's head to move through the birth canal (thank goodness!). The soft spots also allow for the rapid growth of your baby's brain during the first year of life.

When Do the Soft Spots Disappear?

As your baby grows, the fontanels will become smaller and smaller. The one toward the back of the head will disappear first, usually by six months of age. The larger, more obvious spot on the top of the head will vanish by about eighteen months—longer than most people realize. We typically think of soft spots as a trait of newborn babies, but an older baby *does* have soft spots; the hair just makes the spots less noticeable.

Should I Worry About a Soft Spot That Moves or Changes Shape?

It is normal to see your baby's pulse through the soft spot. It is also normal to see it bulge just a bit when your baby cries.

The soft spot can provide warning signs of sickness. For example, a baby who is dehydrated has a sunken soft spot; other illnesses can cause the fontanels to bulge. These may be signs of danger, and you should provide your baby with fluids and call your pediatrician or emergency medical center immediately. If you have any concerns about your baby's soft spot, call your health provider with your questions.

Solid Foods, introducing

See also: Allergies and Asthma; Food Allergies; High Chairs;
Homemade Baby Food; Vegetarian Baby

My mother says she fed me solids when I was two months old. My sister started feeding her baby solid food when he was four months old. My five-month-old baby is healthy and growing well on breast-milk alone, so I'm confused. When should I give my baby solid foods? How important is solid food at this age? When I do begin, what kind of food should I start with?

Learn About It

There's no hurry to introduce your baby to solid foods. In the past, parents were told to consider solid food when their babies reached four months of age. Research over the past few years, however, has demonstrated that breastmilk, formula, or a combination of the two provides your baby with everything she needs for the first six to nine months of life—even up to twelve months in some cases.

Even when you first introduce solid foods, you should view them as a complement to a main diet of breastmilk or formula—a sort of "side dish." When Baby is ready, you'll gradually increase the amount and variety of solid food over a period of several months.

Why Wait to Introduce Solid Food?

Waiting a while before introducing your baby to solid food is prudent for a number of reasons, including the fact that it's not nutritionally necessary. Here are just a few other reasons:

- Babies younger than four months of age have a strong tongue-thrust reflex. This causes a baby to push any foreign substance (even food!) out of the mouth; it's a built-in reflex that helps prevent your baby from choking. Waiting until your baby is well over four months of age will make your first feeding sessions more successful.
- In the early months, a baby is very good at sucking and swallowing but not at *chewing* and swallowing. Therefore, solids just get moved randomly around in a baby's mouth and are not processed properly.
- A young baby's digestive system is immature. It doesn't filter solid food properly, and this can result in spitting up, constipation, diarrhea, or food allergies. This is why parents with food allergies themselves should wait longer—sometimes even a full year—to introduce solids to their babies. If this is your situation, ask your pediatrician for advice.
- Solids displace breastmilk in an infant's menu, thus substituting an inferior food for a superior food. Early feeding of solids can reduce a mother's milk supply and begin the weaning process earlier than necessary or desired.
- Contrary to common thought, solid foods don't help a baby to sleep through the night, so this isn't a good reason to hurry solids.
- Young babies cannot communicate when they have had enough to eat in the ways older babies can. Therefore, younger babies are more at risk of overfeeding.
- The American Academy of Pediatrics (AAP), in its policy statement on breastfeeding, published the following remarks with regard to introducing solid foods to breastfed babies:

  - "Exclusive breastfeeding is ideal nutrition and sufficient to support optimal growth and development for approximately the first six months after birth."
  - "Gradual introduction of iron-enriched solid foods in the second half of the first year should complement the breastmilk diet."
  - "It is recommended that breastfeeding continue for at least 12 months, and thereafter for as long as mutually desired."
  - "In the first six months, water, juice, and other foods are generally unnecessary for breastfed infants."

How Do I Know When to Start My Baby on Solids?

Every baby is different. Babies begin solids at different times, but eventually all children eat table food, so relax about this particular milestone. A few months pass by fast, so don't feel pressured to make a quick decision. Here are a few signs that your baby might be ready for the new experience of eating solid food:

- Your baby weighs at least thirteen pounds and has doubled her birth weight.
- Your baby can hold his head up well and sit up steadily with support. It's simple physics: Eating while lying down isn't very effective (and can be dangerous).
- Your baby has outgrown the tongue-thrust reflex, described earlier. You can tell this has happened when you first offer your baby a taste of food and some of it actually stays in your baby's mouth and is swallowed. A little one who still has the reflex will push the spoon and the food right out of her mouth with her tongue.
- Your baby seems persistently hungry, even after a feeding.
- Your baby is very interested in the food that you are eating and may even make chewing motions or try to grab some of your dinner from you.
- You baby is ready and willing when you offer a spoonful of baby food.
- Your pediatrician gives the OK to start feeding your baby solid food.

The First Feeding: What's for Dinner?

While many babies eagerly accept any new food of a soupy consistency, it's smart to take the introduction of solid food a little more carefully. Certain foods can provoke allergies in babies, so choose those first foods carefully. Watch for any signs of allergic reactions, and introduce new foods one at a time so you can trace the source of any problems.

The best first food for your baby is an iron-fortified, single-grain baby cereal. The most popular grain is rice because it is easy on your baby's delicate digestive system and is less likely to aggravate allergies. Powdered, boxed cereal that is made especially for babies is a good choice to begin with. You can mix it with breastmilk or formula to make a very thin, watery consistency. For other popular first-food choices, see the list later in this entry, under "Food Choices for Your Baby."

The recommended type and consistency of first foods differ based on your baby's age. A four-month-old baby requires a more watery consistency and more basic items than would a baby who is twelve months old. The twelve-month-old could easily tolerate a wider range of first-food options and a thicker texture.

Parent Tip

"Little ones need their food cut up into bite-sized portions. For a time, I used the usual way of doing this: a fork and knife. Then I realized I could do this many-times-a-day task much faster and easier with scissors. I had a pair always ready to go in my kitchen, set aside for this purpose. I would simply run it through the dishwasher like any other utensil. This tip saved a great deal of time and did the job much better than a knife and fork ever could."

—Lilly, mother of Lisa and Lori (now both grown-up)

What Goes in Must Go Out

To spare you the surprise, I'll tell you that your baby's diaper deposits will change in consistency and color when your baby's diet expands. Bright, intensely colored foods will color your baby's stool a similar hue. Rice, bananas, and applesauce—common first foods—can cause constipation, so watch how these affect your baby. Babies who eat these foods in small amounts balanced with lots of breastmilk or formula probably will do fine. If constipation occurs, remedy this by balancing foods that constipate with foods that add fiber, such as prunes or peaches. (See the ideas under "Food Choices for Your Baby," and remember to add foods one at a time.)

Watching for Allergic Reactions

After the introduction of each new food, take a day or two to watch for any allergic reactions before you offer another new food. Also, keep in mind that, if allergies run in either parent's family, your baby is more likely to have allergies. Be very careful about feeding your baby the foods listed under "Foods to Avoid," as they include the most common source of food allergies. Remember, though, that *any* food has a potential for allergic reaction.

Here are the signs that your baby might have food allergies or may not be ready for a certain food:

- Vomiting or increased spitting up
- Rash or hives
- Diarrhea or loose, watery stools
- Constipation
- Wheezing, coughing, or difficulty breathing
- Stomachache
- Excessive gas or bloating
- Runny nose and watery eyes
- Fussiness
- Swelling of the face, hands, or feet
- Frequent ear infections

If you notice any of these symptoms, or even something that's not on the list but seems suspicious to you, always call your doctor and explain your observations.

Keeping Baby's Food Safe

Food poisoning is even more of a concern for babies than for adults. Babies can become severely ill from contaminated food, so follow these guidelines carefully:

- Always check for expiration dates on baby food that you purchase.
- Store unopened jars of baby food at room temperature. Jars that have been opened must be refrigerated.
- Clean off the tops of baby food jars before opening them.
- Don't use a previously unopened jar of baby food if the vacuum-sealed top has popped up.
- If you mix dry cereal with liquid, serve it to your baby immediately. Don't save leftovers.
- If you feed your baby directly from the jar, don't save the leftovers. They have been mixed with your baby's saliva and can spoil. If your baby typically eats less than a full jar, then spoon it into a separate bowl before serving. Refrigerate the rest for another meal.
- Read the labels on baby foods to be aware of ingredients as well as serving and storing instructions.
- When preparing homemade baby food, review the instructions for safe preparation and storage (*see* Homemade Baby Food).

Food Choices for Your Baby

All your baby's first foods should be very smooth and liquid. As your baby gets used to eating, you can gradually change the texture, making it thicker and chunkier. Of course, if you are starting solids with an older baby, you have a little more flexibility. The following list provides general guidelines for choosing foods. Please note that it does not include every possible food; also, some foods can be prepared in different ways, so they fit in several categories.

Step 1: Introduce Solids—Pureed Foods

Rice baby cereal, iron-fortified
Pureed bananas

Step 2: Explore New Tastes—Smooth, Creamy Foods

Applesauce
Pears
Barley baby cereal
Soft, ripe avocados
Mashed ripe bananas
Plums

Step 3: Expand the Menu—Foods with More Texture

Baby oatmeal cereal
Sweet potatoes
Mashed white potatoes
Soft, cooked carrots
Squash
Mixed cereals
Plain yogurt
Peaches

Step 4: Add Different Textures and Flavors

Mashed peas
Green beans
Soft-cooked pasta
Cheerios or other dry cereal (except hard cereal shaped in balls)
Toasted bread or bagels
Zucchini
Soft, ripe cantaloupe or other melon
Natural soft cheese
Broccoli

Step 5: Venture into Table Foods

Chicken and turkey
Beef
Pancakes
Cottage cheese
Graham crackers

Pudding
Soup
Rice cakes
Beans
Cantaloupe

Foods to Avoid

During Baby's first year, you should avoid the following foods (due to their potential for allergic reaction, their choking hazard, or their low nutritional value):

- Eggs
- Cow's or goat's milk and milk products
- Wheat
- Nut butters (including peanut butter)
- Seafood
- Citrus fruits and juices (like orange, grapefruit, and lemon)
- Soy products
- Raw strawberries (cooked berries are usually fine)
- Honey or corn syrup
- Tomatoes
- Vegetables that contain high levels of nitrates, such as beets, turnips, collard greens, dark green kale, and spinach (safe when sold as commercial baby food, however, because of their processing)
- Fruit juice (opt for healthier liquids instead: breastmilk, formula, and water)
- Soft breads, such as white, unless toasted (these can form a pasty glob in a child's mouth)
- Salt (unnecessary and possibly unhealthful)
- Sugar
- Artificial colors and flavors

In addition, avoid the following foods during the first three years (most because of their choking hazard):

- Nuts
- Hot dogs (unless skinned and cut lengthwise, then across, in tiny, noncircular pieces)
- Hard candy
- Chewy candy, such as caramel
- Gum
- Grapes (unless peeled and sliced into slivers)
- Raw carrots
- Celery
- Peanut butter by the spoonful (OK when it's spread thinly in a sandwich)
- Popcorn
- Unpasteurized juice
- Chunks of apple, pear, or peach unless very soft
- Raisins
- Meat with bones
- Caffeine (found in coffee, tea, cola drinks, chocolate, and cocoa products)
- Bacon, unless very crisp

First-Feeding How-Tos

View the first few weeks during which your baby is eating solid foods as an experiment and a prelude of things to come. At the beginning, most babies wear more of their food than they eat!

- Your baby's first few "meals" will amount to only a teaspoon or two of food. The purpose is not to fill Baby up but to offer the new experience and get your baby started on the way to eating solid food.
- Use a soft, padded baby spoon. The tiny size and flexible surface allow a much more pleasant experience, since your baby will likely suck and chew on the spoon along with the food.
- Single-ingredient foods are best for the first few months. This way, you can monitor your baby's likes and dislikes and watch for possible allergies (*see* Food Allergies).

- Your baby may turn up his nose at certain foods, but don't take that no to be permanent. You can offer the food again a week or so later and see if he reacts differently.

- Your baby's appetite will differ from one meal to the next and from one day to the next, so rather than watching the clock, watch your baby for cues that she's full. If your baby refuses to open up for the next bite, turns her head away, or starts playing with her toys, she is probably full. Forcing food after a baby has a full tummy discourages your child from listening to her own hunger and fullness cues and can start a child on the road to a lifetime of overeating.

- Don't restrict your baby's food intake because he looks chubby to you. If you are concerned about your baby's weight, then talk to your pediatrician before you make any attempts to change your baby's diet.

- Expect those first meals to be messy. Prepare yourself with an oversized bib (consider one even for yourself!), washable high chair, plastic dish with suction cups that will keep the dish on the tray, and splatter mat on the floor.

- Your baby's food doesn't have to be heated. Room temperature is fine for little ones. If you *do* warm up your baby's food, always stir it thoroughly and taste some yourself before feeding it to your baby.

- Continue to breastfeed or provide formula before or after solid meals for a while until your baby is very comfortable with eating regular food. Some time will pass before your baby is taking in enough variety and quantity for a healthful diet; in the meantime, breastmilk and formula provide important vitamins, iron, carbohydrates, and protein that are necessary for growth and development.

- Begin finger foods when your baby has experience eating chunky foods, and always supervise your baby during mealtimes.

- During the transition to solid food, ask your pediatrician whether he or she recommends vitamin, iron, or fluoride supplements.

- Adult dietary guidelines are not appropriate for infants and toddlers, so don't assume your baby should be eating what you view as a healthy diet for yourself. Remember too that you want to view the whole picture of your baby's diet; a cookie now and then won't do any harm as long as your baby's overall diet is healthy.

• Unless your pediatrician tells you otherwise, let your baby take the lead in deciding how much to eat. Your role is to offer healthful food choices. Neither force your baby to eat nor restrict your baby's food intake. If you feel your baby is too thin or too heavy, talk to your pediatrician about your concerns.

• Use the following chart to keep track of the new foods that you offer to your baby. If you jot down your baby's reaction (liked it or didn't) and any possible allergic responses, you can use the information as a handy reference for yourself and, if allergies are detected, for your pediatrician as well.

Solid Foods Allergy and Preference Chart

Food	Date 1	Response	Reaction	Date 2	Response	Reaction
Rice						
Bananas						
Applesauce						
Pears						
Barley						
Avocados						
Plums						
Oatmeal						
Sweet potatoes						
White potatoes						
Carrots						
Squash						
Mixed cereal						
Yogurt						
Peaches						
Peas						
Green beans						
Pasta						

Food	Date 1	Response	Reaction	Date 2	Response	Reaction
Dry cereal						
Bagels						
Zucchini						
Cantaloupe						
Cheese						
Broccoli						
Chicken/turkey						
Beef						
Pancakes						
Cottage cheese						
Graham crackers						
Pudding						
Rice cakes						
Beans						
Other:						
Other:						
Other:						
Other:						

Spitting Up

See also: Burping; Colic; Reflux; Vomiting

> *My four-week-old baby spits up after almost every meal. Is this normal?*

Learn About It

Nearly half of all babies spit up frequently in their first three to four months of life. Consequently, almost half of all new parents have stains on their shoulders! For most babies, spitting up is simply a nuisance, a sign of an immature and developing digestive system. Spitting up is very different from vomiting, which signals illness (*see* Vomiting). Your baby won't show any concern over spitting up; he'll carry on as if it didn't happen. By the time your baby begins to sit up and crawl, he'll no longer be spitting up.

How You Can Control Spitting Up

If your baby's spit-up is minimal, you don't need to worry about it. If there's a little more than you'd like to deal with or it seems to disturb your baby, the following tips may help you reduce the amount of spitting up:

- Get those air bubbles under control by following the ideas listed in the entry for Burping.
- Feed your baby smaller, more frequent meals.
- Make feeding time calm and peaceful.
- Hold your baby upright for thirty minutes or so after feeding, or let her sit upright in a baby seat.
- Avoid jiggling your baby too much immediately after a meal.

- Elevate the head of the crib a bit by taping wood blocks or tuna cans under the front legs or placing books under the mattress (make certain your mattress still fits properly into the crib).
- Avoid letting your baby cry, as the added air intake can increase the amount that your baby spits up.
- If excessive spitting up persists and you are bottlefeeding, you may need to try a different formula. If you are breastfeeding, you may have an overly strong letdown reflex or an overabundant milk supply. Talk to a lactation consultant if you suspect either of these may be an issue.

How Do I Know if It's More than Normal Spitting Up?

Sometimes, spitting up may be a sign of something more than normal baby behavior. The following signs may indicate a cold, virus, or other illness or a more severe form of spitting up called gastroesophageal reflux (*see* Reflux, where there is a list of reflux signs). If you notice any of the following conditions, call your doctor:

- Fever
- Congestion
- Vomiting that increases in frequency and amount
- Vomit that looks green, brown, or red
- Inconsolable crying
- Projectile vomiting
- Excessive sleepiness
- Failure to gain weight
- Coughing or gagging during feeding
- Change in amount of normal stool or urine (fewer wet or messy diapers)

For a young baby, it is always important to call your doctor if you suspect illness.

Stranger Anxiety

See also: Attachment Parenting; Independent Play; Separation Anxiety

> *My baby used to be so outgoing and smile at everyone. Suddenly, she clings to me and cries if a stranger even so much as says hello! What happened to my confident baby?*

Learn About It

Your baby has reached an important milestone in human development. She is demonstrating that you've done a great job taking care of her: She knows she can trust you, and her affection for you is deep and healthy. Stranger anxiety, as your baby is experiencing, is a testimony to the strength of her attachment to you. So it's not something to be worried about, it's actually something to celebrate!

At What Age Does Stranger Anxiety Normally Appear?

Attachment and bonding, two components of stranger and separation anxiety, begin to develop right from birth. A newborn enters the world with no understanding of the people in it. During months one through six, your baby learns general rules about people. In most cases, those rules demonstrate that people respond to your baby's needs with the things he requires to survive and thrive. Between months six and nine, a baby begins to differentiate among people. He begins to identify familiar people, and everyone else becomes a "stranger." Babies respond differently to this revelation. Some display curiosity and caution, and others an intense aversion to anyone beyond the most familiar circle of family. Both of these reactions are normal; so are most variations of these two extremes.

How Long Does Stranger Anxiety Last?

In most cases, stranger anxiety appears sometime after six months of age and can last as long as three years. Most often, stranger anxiety peaks at between twelve and eighteen months, then tapers off. The leap from stranger anxiety to social butterfly isn't an overnight event; it is a process. Your baby may first seem rather moody—sometimes accepting a new person as friend, other times hiding his face in your shoulder if a person so much as tries to engage him in conversation. Over time, your baby will begin to learn that talking to new people is a safe, and usually fun, thing to do, and he'll welcome meeting new people. But keep in mind that this takes longer for some children than others, and your patience is most important as he works through this stage in life.

What Can I Do to Help My Baby Through This Stage of Development?

Although separation anxiety is normal and healthy and may linger for quite some time, it's still a good idea to help your baby move through this phase. Life is just more fun if your baby can learn to be comfortable with new people. Try these ideas:

• When introducing your baby to new people, hold her securely in your arms. The safety of your embrace will help her feel more comfortable with the unknown.

• Respect your baby's fear. Don't pressure him into interacting with, or being held by, a person he's not sure of. Pressuring him will often backfire; your baby will cry and cling to you all the more. This might even *increase* his fear the next time he faces a close encounter with a stranger. Your respect for Baby's fear is also the first lesson in teaching your baby self-protection. You do this by showing that you respect his emotions and by giving him permission to make choices in situations regarding his body.

• Keep in mind that, although you may be very familiar with aunts, uncles, or grandparents, if your baby hasn't seen much of these people, he will categorize them as "stranger." This isn't a judgment of your family members, just an indication that your baby doesn't know them well. The toughest challenge is helping these people understand that a little time and patience are necessary to help your baby become more comfortable with them.

• Use distraction to help ease your baby's fears and the "stranger's" feeling of offense. A good way to take the edge off the situation is with a simple statement such as, "It takes her a few minutes to warm up to someone she doesn't know well." Then launch into an unrelated topic, giving your baby a chance to regroup and watch this new person without being the center of attention.

• Allow your baby to initiate contact and set the pace for interaction with new people. If you consistently follow this pattern, your baby will feel some control over the situation and will be more likely to respond in positive ways when meeting her next new friend.

Strollers

· · · · · · · · · · · ·

See also: Baby Carriers; Car Seats

My baby is due next month, so I decided to buy a stroller. It seemed like a simple enough quest, but when I arrived at the store, I discovered about a million different kinds! I am in shock. How do I choose from so many styles, patterns, and types? I don't even know where to begin.

Learn About It

A stroller is an important purchase, since most of us parents use it frequently, and most keep using it into their children's third year. A wrong choice becomes a constant irritation in your life, but the right choice becomes as comfortable as an old shoe.

So Many Choices

When my oldest child was a baby, there were basically two choices: folding umbrella stroller and standard (usually blue). Now, shopping for a stroller is like choosing a new toy for the baby; the choices are seemingly endless.

Here are my basic rules for stroller shopping:

- Shop when you have plenty of time. Don't rush the decision.
- Make a list of features important to you, and take it with you when you shop.
- Take the baby along during his "good mood" part of the day so you can test-drive candidates completely.
- Don't compromise. Plenty of places sell strollers, and the right one is worth the wait.

The following chart will give you some basic information to help you through the maze of stroller shopping.

Types of Strollers

Name	Description	Best Use	Benefits	Negatives
Compact and umbrella	Lightweight, easy-to-fold portable stroller	Keeping in the car and for traveling	Light and easy to carry or tote; great for very short trips (such as picking up an older sibling from school)	Angle and size usually unsuitable for a newborn; best for babies at least 4 months old; not sturdy enough to carry a baby, diaper bag, and other carry-alongs; less room and less comfortable for bigger baby than standard stroller; typically does not allow child to lie down flat; can tip easily when loaded
Single standard	Ordinary stroller: a baby seat on wheels	Everyday use	Light enough to pick up, yet offers convenient storage and comfort features	May be too big to carry easily in a smaller car or to travel with
Double standard (2 in a row)	Similar to a single stroller but with a second seat behind the first	Everyday use for 2 babies or for 1 baby plus lots of supplies and shopping bags	Absolutely necessary for any family with 2 or more little ones or for a 1-child family planning on adding another baby soon	Can be cumbersome and heavy to fold and lift; typically, only 1 seat reclines fully for naps

Name	Description	Best Use	Benefits	Negatives
Double standard (2 abreast)	Similar to a single stroller but adds a second seat alongside the first	Everyday use for 2 babies	Alternative to the front-and-back double; both seats fully recline	Too wide to maneuver easily through some store aisles, crowded places, narrow sidewalks, or doorways (measure before purchasing)
Triple plus	Specially made strollers with 3 or more seats	Everyday use for 3 or more little ones	Necessary for any family with triplets or 3 very close in age	At nearly 5 feet long, a challenge to maneuver; uphill pushing difficult; not all seats recline; short on storage space; expensive
Sport (jogger)— single, double, or multiple	Sturdy, well-balanced stroller with large tires	Jogging, speed-walking, or strolling over bumpy terrain	Great for moving fast or covering rough ground such as grass, gravel, or sand	Tri-wheel system makes steering and turning difficult; tiny infants don't fit the seat well; older children often resist the seat's reclining position; not easily transportable
Travel systems	Combination infant car seat and stroller base	Everyday use of car seat portion for the first 3–6 months; everyday use of stroller thereafter	Purchase covers 2 needs; car seat snaps securely into stroller and may snap into grocery carts also	Typically large and heavy; car seat is rear-facing infant seat; some stroller seats don't fit older babies; although Baby in seat is much heavier than Baby in arms, parents tend to overuse the carrier

(continued)

Name	Description	Best Use	Benefits	Negatives
Carriage (buggy)	Basket-type traditional buggy	Ideal for newborns and younger infants	Allows Baby to recline to a horizontal position; can also be used as a mobile crib	By 3 or 4 months of age, most babies outgrow this option
Rolling car seat base (mobility base)	Frame that allows you to use your car seat as a stroller	Less expensive alternative to travel system; ideal for disabled children in specialized car seats	Light and very compact; folds totally flat	Ride not smooth; difficult to steer; not as stable as regular stroller; works only with custom or specialized seats
Convertible car seat/stroller	Car seat with stroller wheels and handle that retract into carrier unit	Everyday use for the first 3 months	Helpful for families who travel frequently by plane, bus, or train	Odd-looking stroller; Baby sits very low to ground; no storage
Nonstroller options	Alternatives such as a sling, front pack, or backpack to complement your stroller or to use exclusively during early months	Everyday use for young babies	Lightweight; easy to take along; comforting to Baby; keeps both hands free but Baby close to you; promotes bonding; some types facilitate discreet breastfeeding	Difficult to use for extended periods when Baby gets heavier; no storage or limited storage

Features to Consider

Before shopping, make a list of features that are important to you. Take this list with you when you shop. Here are a few features to consider:

- **Reclining seat:** No matter the age of your baby, there will be times when your little one will sleep on the go. Make sure the seat reclines adequately and easily. Some strollers offer only a semi-reclining option, so determine if this would be adequate for your baby's naps in the stroller.

- **Comfortable handle height and style:** Make sure the handle is at a good height for you and is wide enough for a good steering grip. If another person will also use the stroller, look for a model with an adjustable handle height or one that feels comfortable to both of you.

- **Swiveling wheels:** Few things in stroller land are more frustrating than a stroller that wants to go right when you want to go left! (Think shopping cart with one inoperative wheel.) Make sure that the wheels swivel smoothly in all directions. Sometimes the baby's weight distribution affects how smoothly the wheels swivel in front or back, so be sure to test strollers with Baby in the seat.

- **Parking brake:** Can you apply the brakes easily and quickly, even with your baby (or Baby's sibling) in your arms?

- **Storage:** The last thing you want to do is push a stroller while carrying an armload of stuff, so look for plenty of storage. Most strollers have large under-the-seat baskets. Some offer behind-the-seat pouches, cupholders, and other storage options as well. Look for removable options, such as cup trays.

- **Removable seat liner:** A good stroller will last a few years, but you'll need to clean the seat cushion. A removable pad is the best choice.

- **Weather canopy:** A weather canopy protects your baby from the sun and rain (and from overly friendly strangers). If you anticipate lots of foul-weather use, look for a stroller with a plastic rain shield option.

- **Carriage mode:** If you are pregnant, have an infant, or think you might try for another baby, look for a stroller that converts to a carriage configuration. Most do this with a special pad insert that creates a buggy pocket that conserves warmth and protects from wind and drafts. Many have handles that reverse so you can push with the baby facing toward you.

Test-Drive Your Stroller

Before you make a purchase decision, test-drive a few strollers. If you plan to buy one over the Internet, try out the various models in a local store. As you put your baby into a stroller for a test drive and wheel around the aisles of the store, consider these points:

- Is it easy to get your baby into and out of the stroller?
- Are the harnesses and straps easy to use? Do they fit your baby? Are they adjustable?
- Is the handle a comfortable height, or can it adjust to your height?
- Is the handle wide enough for a comfortable grip?
- Do your feet kick into the wheels or frame when you're walking quickly?
- Does it steer easily? Can you steer it with one hand? (The other may be holding baby gear or the baby who won't sit in your wonderful new stroller.)
- Do the wheels rotate easily as you turn?
- Roll backward a few feet and then forward. Do the wheels adapt easily, or do you have to struggle to straighten them out?
- Does the seat back fold down quietly, smoothly, and easily to accommodate a sleeping baby without waking him?
- Can you fold and unfold the stroller easily? Can you do this with your baby in your arms?
- With a multipurpose or travel system stroller, can you easily switch the various pieces?
- Can you pick up the stroller, as you will when you pack it in the car?
- Is the color and style something you'll enjoy looking at for the next few years?
- Does it have all the features on your wish list? (See the previous list under "Features to Consider.")

Sudden Infant Death Syndrome (SIDS)

(Cot Death, Crib Death)

. . . .

See also: Back Sleeping; Co-Sleeping, making it work ("Co-Sleeping Safety Checklist"); Cribs and Cradles ("Cribs and Cradles Safety Checklist"); Sleep, newborn; Sleep, four months and over

Every time my newborn sleeps more than a few hours, I wake up in a panic. I have to feel his chest to make sure he's breathing. I'm terribly frightened he might die of SIDS. I'd like more information about this topic.

Learn About It

Sudden infant death syndrome (SIDS) will not affect the vast majority of families, but even still, you aren't alone in your fear. SIDS is among the main concerns of all parents of newborns because it is the sudden, unpredictable, unexplained death of a baby during sleep. In most cases, the baby seems healthy and is between the ages of one and four months.

After thirty years of research, scientists still cannot find a definite cause for SIDS, or a way to predict or prevent it. Researchers have discovered certain strategies that appear to reduce the risk, however, and I have incorporated those items into this book's safety information. Take the time to review the checklists that apply to your baby's sleep environment.

The Most Important Rule: Back to Sleep

Many studies have proved conclusively that babies who sleep on their backs are less susceptible to SIDS than those who sleep on their stomachs. *Face up is the recommended sleep position for most healthy, full-term infants.* Once your doctor confirms that back sleeping is best for your baby, your best approach for reducing the risk of SIDS is to always put Baby to sleep on her back—sunny side up. (For more information and tips on how to help your baby if she prefers tummy-sleeping to change to sleeping on her back, *see* Back Sleeping.)

More Safety Information

You'll find additional safety information and current recommendations for reducing the risk of SIDS in the "Sleep Safety Checklist" (*see* Sleep, newborn), the "Co-Sleeping Safety Checklist" (*see* Co-Sleeping, making it work), and the "Cribs and Cradles Safety Checklist" (*see* Cribs and Cradles).

For More Information

Websites

National Sudden Infant Death Syndrome Resource Center
sidscenter.org

Sudden Infant Death Syndrome Alliance
sidsalliance.org

Sunshine

· · · · · · · · · · ·

See also: Dehydration; Heatstroke; Swimming

> *My baby is only three months old, and summer is just starting. I'd love to enjoy some beach time with her, but I'm wondering about her being out in the sun at such a young age. Is this OK?*

Learn About It

Babies have very delicate skin, so they are especially vulnerable to the dangerous effects of the sun. Babies burn much more easily than adults, and sun damage done during childhood can affect skin health for a lifetime. You can take your baby outside, but you would be wise to take precautions to protect her from the sun.

Protecting Your Baby's Delicate Skin

While protecting your baby from the sun is important, it's unrealistic to think that you'll never be outside with your baby on a sunny day! Here's how to keep your baby safe while enjoying the outdoors:

• Keep her out of direct sunlight, particularly when the sun's rays are the strongest, between 10:00 A.M. and 4:00 P.M. Sit under a tree or umbrella or in the shade of a building, or put your baby in her stroller with the canopy over her head.

• Put a wide-brimmed hat on your little one whenever you're out in the sun. Your baby will get used to wearing a hat if you start when she is little. If your baby is older and resists keeping a hat on, you'll need to use your powers of persuasion and distraction to keep the hat where it belongs.

• Professionals often recommend dressing your baby in a long-sleeved shirt and long pants; these can be lightweight as long as the material is tightly woven. You can determine how much sun will come through clothes by holding them up to a bright light. The tighter the weave, the less light—including sunlight—that will come through the fabric. This approach can be tricky because she may get warmer dressed this way. Pay attention to how your baby feels and looks, and if you put her in shorts, be extra vigilant about the time she spends in the sun.

• Consider adding sunglasses with UV protection to your baby's summer wardrobe.

What About Sunscreen?

In general, avoid using sunscreen on a baby younger than six months old. There are exceptions, however, and you should defer to common sense. For example, if you want to let your baby explore the beach, but hot weather prevents you from keeping all of her skin covered, it is fine to use a small amount of sunscreen on the areas not covered. (Be careful not to put lotion around her eyes, and keep the lotion away from her hands, since they may end up in her mouth.) Slight exposure to sunscreen is better than damaging, painful exposure to the sun.

With babies older than six months, always use sunscreen when going out into the sun. First, test a patch of sunscreen at home and wait for a few hours, or even overnight, to be sure your baby doesn't have an allergic reaction to the lotion. Read the label on your sunscreen to determine how often it needs to be reapplied. Its effectiveness does wear off.

Choose sunscreen formulated especially for children. Read the label to make sure the lotion protects against both UVA and UVB rays. Sunscreen should have an SPF (sun protection factor) of at least 15 and should be waterproof if your baby is going to be getting wet. If your child is fair skinned, you are going to be spending a long time outside, or you just want more sun protection, opt for a much higher SPF. Alternatives to typical sunscreens include nonchemical varieties available in health food and body lotion stores, and zinc oxide (good for the face and shoulders).

More Sun Facts

Sun protection isn't just for summer days at the beach. Keep in mind that sand, water, concrete, and snow all reflect the sun's rays, making them even more potent. And don't forget that the sun's ultraviolet rays are almost as strong on a cloudy day as on a sunny one.

When you're outside, you'll also want to keep an eye on your baby to make sure she doesn't develop heat exhaustion. You can protect her by keeping her in shady areas and having her stay well hydrated (*see* Heatstroke).

What if My Baby Does Get Sunburned?

Even with the best planning, sometimes we get caught off guard. If you notice that your baby has become bright pink or red from the sun, here's what to do:

- Immediately get your baby out of the sun.
- Keep your baby well hydrated with breastmilk, water, or juice.
- Give your baby a bath in a few inches of lukewarm water, and let her play and splash, or wipe her with a cool, wet cloth.
- If your baby is younger than six months old, call your pediatrician and describe the extent of the burn. If your baby is older than six months, call the doctor if you notice blisters, pain, or fever.
- Keep her out of the sun until the burn has healed.

Vitamin D, the Sunshine Vitamin

We get vitamin D from certain foods, such as milk, eggs, and fish. Breastfed babies receive small amounts of vitamin D from breastmilk, in a form that is easily absorbed and used by your baby's body. (Even so, some pediatricians suggest vitamin A and D drops for breastfed babies, particularly in communities where there is little sunshine.) Formula-fed babies receive vitamin D from most formulas, since they are enriched with this vitamin. Our bodies also make vitamin D when we are exposed to sunlight. You don't have to put your baby at risk for sunburn to provide the benefits of sunlight. As little as ten to twenty minutes a day in the outdoors is often enough for a baby's body to produce adequate vitamin D.

Swaddling

See also: Baby Carriers; Colic

My newborn sometimes gets fussy at night, and my friend told me that swaddling might calm her and help her sleep better. Is it a good idea? How do I do it?

Learn About It

The practice of swaddling babies dates back centuries and is still common in many cultures. Swaddling involves wrapping a baby securely from shoulders to feet with a small blanket. There are many good reasons to swaddle an infant.

The Benefits of Swaddling

- Swaddling can be a great way to soothe and calm a fussy baby. It is thought that being tightly enwrapped gives a feeling of security, similar to being in the womb.
- The newborn cannot regulate his temperature as well as an adult, so swaddling keeps Baby's body warm. (Just make sure your baby doesn't become overheated.)
- Swaddling often helps a young baby sleep longer because it prevents the "startle reflex" that can cause babies to wake up.
- Swaddling can help a baby focus on breastfeeding, by keeping arms and legs out of the way.
- Swaddling prevents a newborn baby, who can't quite control his movements yet, from scratching himself with his nails.
- A swaddled baby is easy to carry and hold—an adorable, compact little package.

How to Swaddle Your Baby

Once you've done it a few times, swaddling becomes easy. You'll need a blanket that's not too much bigger than your newborn; a square receiving blanket is the perfect size. Its fabric should be lightweight and breathable but still warm, like cotton. Try swaddling a few times when your baby is happy so that you're not struggling with a fussy or rigid baby, or practice swaddling a doll or stuffed animal. Everybody's method is a little bit different, but follow the illustrations on the next page and these basic directions:

1. On a stable surface (such as a bed or clean floor), lay the blanket out in front of you so it's shaped like a diamond. Fold down the top corner. Place Baby in the middle of the blanket with Baby's head lying on top of the folded corner.
2. Hold Baby's right arm down against Baby's body. Pull the left corner of the blanket across Baby and over the right arm so that it's snug but not too tight. Tuck this corner under Baby's body on the other side.
3. Bring Baby's left arm to his side, and bring the blanket's bottom corner up and tuck it under Baby's left shoulder.
4. Pull the upper edge of the blanket down over the left shoulder, and bring the right corner across Baby, keeping both of Baby's arms down against his body.
5. Pull the tail of the blanket around Baby like a belt, and tuck it in where it fits to prevent the blanket from unwrapping, or simply hold or position Baby so the blanket remains snug.

A veteran parent, a nurse, or your doctor can give you a swaddling demonstration if you can't seem to get it right. The process can seem complicated, but once you've seen it done a few times, you'll get the hang of it. And both you and your baby should enjoy the calming results.

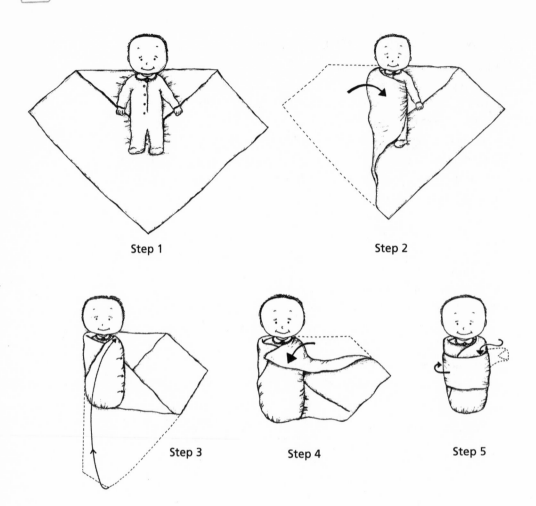

Step 1

Step 2

Step 3

Step 4

Step 5

Swaddling Options

Some babies need to adjust to swaddling if it's new to them. If your baby doesn't respond well to the first try, give her a few opportunities to get comfortable with it before you abandon the idea. If your baby doesn't seem to like swaddling, try leaving her arms free, and just swaddle the rest of her body. In any case, the blanket should fit snugly but not tightly. A blanket that is too tight could impede circulation or cause discomfort. Also watch to be sure your baby doesn't become overheated.

If you can't seem to get the hang of swaddling with a receiving blanket, you can find a number of swaddling products online. The options include blankets with Velcro ends that stick together.

The Age for Swaddling

Swaddling usually works well for babies from newborn to about three or four months of age. However, babies who are used to swaddling may enjoy it for even a little longer.

For More Information

Book

Karp, Harvey. *The Happiest Baby on the Block*. New York: Bantam, 2002.

Website

Dr. Harvey Karp's Website
thehappiestbaby.com

Swimming

· · · · · · · · · · ·

See also: Heatstroke; Sunshine

> *Our local public pool offers swimming classes for parents with babies. This sounds like fun, but I'm wondering: Is this something I can do safely with my eight-month-old baby?*

Learn About It

Swimming classes can be fun to share with your baby and with other parent-baby pairs. The term *class* in this context shouldn't mean that your baby will "learn" anything. Until a child is over four years old, any swim program should be viewed as simply a pleasurable way to introduce your baby to the fun of being in the water.

At What Age Can You Take a Baby in a Pool?

As long as the water and weather are warm enough, you can take any baby over a few weeks old into a pool while in your arms. The younger the baby, of course, the more closely you'll need to monitor the reaction to the water, and the more careful you'll need to be about the chill that can occur when wet skin hits cooler air. Keep in mind that your baby will chill before you do. If your baby is shivering or his lips look blue, he should have been out of the water some time ago. Quickly wrap him up and warm him.

How Can I Make Our Swimming Experience Safe?

The one most important rule for swimming with a young baby is to always keep her in your arms when she's in or near the water. *Always.*

How Can I Help My Baby Enjoy His First Swimming Experiences?

When taking your baby for a swim, make sure he isn't hungry or tired so that he and you can both enjoy the water. Avoid taking a swim immediately after your baby has been fed.

Very young babies don't really need any floats or swimming aids, since they will not be out of your arms at any time (right?). If you decide to let your older baby float around in a baby boat or swim ring, always keep in mind that these are not designed for safety or protection; you should keep your hands and eyes on your baby at all times.

Follow your baby's lead. If he seems happy and curious, then move him around in the water. If he seems nervous or frightened, don't push him beyond his comfort zone. Some babies take time to warm up to the idea of a big body of water, even if they love to splash in the bathtub at home. Some babies take numerous trips to the pool or beach before they're even willing to get wet. Be patient!

How Do I Choose a Class?

Ideally, look for an instructor who has knowledge of child development in addition to swimming. A teacher like this can gear the class activities to the proper developmental abilities of the babies in the group. It's important to work with a teacher who understands children and can be sensitive to a baby's fear or uncertainty of the water. The teacher shouldn't expect babies to do more than what they are comfortable doing—even if that means just dangling their feet in the water for the first few lessons, or even just looking at the pool from a deck chair!

What Should Your Baby Wear?

At the beach, your baby can wear a diaper, bathing suit, or birthday suit—whatever you and Baby are comfortable with. Many parents keep their babies in a T-shirt to protect against the sun. If your baby is a walker, you might want to invest in some water socks or pool shoes to protect little feet against sand, rocks, and shells and to prevent slipping while walking poolside. If you are in a pool, disposable or reusable swim diapers are a great option. These don't swell up like a sponge, but they do retain the unmentionables that other swimmers would rather not see floating in the water!

Protect Your Baby from the Sun and Chemicals

If your swimming extravaganza is taking place outside, be certain that you protect your baby from the sun with a hat and (if the baby is older than six months) sunscreen. This is very important, since the sun's rays are magnified when reflected off the water (*see* Sunshine).

Be cautious about immersing your baby in a pool that has a high level of chlorine. This chemical may irritate a baby's delicate skin.

Après Swim

Remember, just like you, your baby will probably be ravenous after a swim, so plan to feed him soon after you're out of the water. A breastfeed, bottlefeed, or snack will keep your baby happy. And a snuggly feed after a swim is extra warm and cozy for both Mom and Baby.

An Important Warning

No matter how many swim classes your baby has had, no matter what your baby's comfort and skill levels while in the water, and no matter what kind of swimming float your baby is wearing, *you should never leave your baby unattended while in or near water—not for even a second.* Babies are unpredictable. They easily can fall into the water and drown even in water just a few inches deep. Swimming lessons for babies have nothing whatsoever to do with reducing the risk of water hazards. As a matter of fact, they can *increase* the risk of water accidents when parents are lulled into thinking their baby is safer because of the swimming lessons. Also, swimming lessons, if they are successful, dispel your baby's natural wariness about water and make it more likely for a baby to explore on his own if given but a second. You are many years away from watching your child swim independently while you sit on the beach in a lounge chair.

Talking
(Language Development)

See also: Bilingualism; Milestones of Development; Walking

My baby is almost a year old. She babbles all day long, but I can't understand a single word she says. My niece is just a few months older, and she's starting to put words together in short sentences! Should I be concerned? Does this mean that my niece is smarter than my daughter? How do I help my baby learn to talk?

Learn About It

One of the most exciting aspects of the early years is watching your child grow from a newborn baby into a walking, talking toddler. We marvel at and celebrate each and every milestone along the way. Often, though, we get caught up in comparing our babies with every other baby in town or every baby chart that lists *when*, *what*, and *how*. The reality is that, when it comes to learning to talk, the range of "normal" is extremely wide. My own four children started to talk at vastly different ages and varying degrees. One daughter didn't talk until she turned two, while another was using sentences around her first birthday. One of my sons added new words and phrases carefully, one at a time, and the other spouted paragraphs before his second birthday. Now all four talk a blue streak, and our house is never quiet!

The best way to gauge your baby's language development is to pay attention to your little one's *individual* progress. In other words, don't compare your baby to any other; each baby is unique! As Baby grows, ask yourself if he's making regular progress. Often you'll see major jumps in progress over a few months, and sometimes you won't see too much change, but it's those regular and progressive developmental steps that are most important. What's important is that your child is generally moving forward. Your pediatrician will ask you about your child's language development at well-baby checkups. If at any time you don't see overall progress in your baby's speech habits, or if your baby seems to regress in language skills or appears not to hear or understand people, ask your pediatrician to do an evaluation.

Language is as much about understanding as it is about talking. As a baby begins to understand more of what is being said, the baby will take more steps toward mastering language use.

The Steps of Language Development

Babies begin to talk at very different ages, but most of them follow a predictable pattern of language acquisition. Use the following list to track your little one's progress, keeping in mind that this pattern isn't an exact sequence. Your baby may skip around a little. Regardless of any chart, if you are concerned at any time about your baby's progress, talk with your pediatrician.

With these cautions in mind, look for the following signs of progress:

- Crying, whimpering, and making noises to get your attention
- Cooing (vowel sounds, like *ah*, *eh*, or *oo*)
- Active listening (looking at you when you talk)
- Jabbering (consonant sounds like *ba*, *ma*, *da*, or *ga*)
- Producing sounds that vary in volume, pitch, and rate
- Responding to her own name by looking at you
- Stringing sounds together (like *ma-ma* or *da-da*)
- Beginning to take turns—the start of dialogue (you talk, she babbles, you talk, she babbles)
- Attaching real words to real things (calling *you* Mama—a wonderful moment!)
- Making wordlike sounds by combining vowel and consonant sounds (gibberish or babbling)
- Using sounds and gestures to get a point across, such as pointing to things of interest and asking questions with words or sounds ("Uh? Uh?")
- Understanding what other people are saying

- Making appropriate gestures (waving bye-bye); beginning simple signs, if child is deaf
- Following simple one- or two-step directions ("Go get your book.")
- Pointing to things as you verbally label them ("Where is the bird? Where is my nose?")
- Building a collection of regularly used real words (mispronunciation and replacing more difficult sounds with easy, familiar ones are normal in this stage of language development)
- Making simple two-word sentences
- Repeating words or phrases she hears
- Stringing words together to make clumsy, yet understandable, sentences ("Me go up chair.")
- Using simple, correct sentences
- Joining thoughts together to make understandable paragraphs

Encouraging Language Development

While children learn to talk on their own schedules, you can support and nudge that schedule with your own actions. Here are some ways to boost your little one's language skills:

- Talk to your baby incessantly. Narrate your daily activities. ("I'm cutting beans into little pieces. I'm putting the beans into a bowl. It's a big bowl.")
- Ask lots of questions. ("Do you like beans? Do you see the green beans?")
- Use simple words and expressive, exaggerated language, but avoid using baby talk.
- Play sound games, such as giving animal noises to all your baby's toys or pictures in books.
- Name things your baby is looking at. Start with a simple label and expand the idea. ("That's a tree. It's a big tree. It's a green maple tree.")
- Sing songs and recite simple rhymes, such as "The Itsy, Bitsy Spider" and "Old MacDonald Had a Farm."

- Expand on your baby's use of words. (If Baby says, "Mama," you say, "Here's Mama. Mama loves you.")
- Encourage your baby to look at your face when you talk. (Get down to Baby's level, and look eye to eye.)
- Read to your baby *often*. Use baby books with bright pictures and simple text. Follow your baby's lead. You can read the text, talk about the pictures, sing about the story, make up your own story, or simply point to objects and name them.
- Respond to your baby's babbles with real words, and expand the thought. ("Baa-baa? Blanket? You want your blanket? Here's your blanket!")
- Encourage two-way conversation by letting your baby babble and responding with questions and comments.
- Make puppets, toys, or everyday objects talk and sing to your baby.

For More Information

Books

Acredolo, Linda, Susan Goodwyn, Douglas Abrams, and Robin Hansen. *Baby Signs: How to Talk with Your Baby Before Your Baby Can Talk*, rev. ed. Chicago: Contemporary Books, 2002.

Ward, Sally. *Babytalk: Strengthen Your Child's Ability to Listen, Understand, and Communicate*. New York: Ballantine Books, 2001.

Tantrums

· · · · · · · · · · · ·

See also: Discipline

I can hardly believe it, but my ten-month-old son had a temper tantrum! What have I done wrong? What's going on?

Learn About It

A baby's first tantrum usually does take parents by surprise. Your baby can really shock you by shrieking, stamping, hitting, or making his whole body go stiff. But don't take it personally. Baby tantrums aren't about anything you've done wrong, and they aren't really about *temper*, either—your baby isn't old enough for that. The ways you'll respond to your baby's behavior when he is older are different from the way you should respond now.

Why Babies Have Tantrums and What You Can Do About It

A baby tantrum is an abrupt and sudden loss of emotional control. Various factors bring on tantrums, and if you can identify the trigger, then you can help your baby calm down—and perhaps even avoid the tantrum in the first place. In addition, if you see these emotional outbursts for what they really are, you'll be able to stay calm. The chart on the next page summarizes the common reasons why babies have tantrums and ways to solve the problem.

Tantrums: Causes and Solutions

Reason for Tantrum	Possible Solution
Overtiredness	Provide quiet activity or settle Baby down to sleep
Hunger	Give Baby a snack, a breastfeed, a bottle, or something to drink
Frustration	Help Baby achieve goal or remove source of frustration; distract Baby
Fear, anxiety	Hold and cuddle Baby; remove Baby from difficult situation; breastfeed
Inability to communicate	Try to figure out what Baby wants; calmly encourage Baby to show you
Resistance to change	Allow a few minutes for Baby to adjust
Overstimulation	Move Baby to a quiet place

How to Prevent Baby Tantrums

Often, you can prevent babies from losing control of their emotions if you prevent the situations that lead up to this. Here are some things to keep in mind:

- When your baby is tired, put him down for a nap or to sleep.
- Feed your baby frequently. Babies have small tummies and need regular nourishment.
- Give your baby toys that are geared to her age and ability level.

- Warn your baby before changing activities. ("One more swing, then we're going home.")
- Be patient when putting your baby in an unfamiliar environment or when introducing your baby to new people.
- Help your baby learn new skills, such as climbing stairs or working puzzles.
- Keep your expectations realistic; don't expect more than your baby is capable of.
- As much as possible, keep a regular and predictable schedule.
- When your baby is overly emotional, keep yourself as calm as possible.
- Use a soothing tone of voice and gentle touch to help your baby calm down. Your baby can't do it all alone but needs your help.

Teething

See also: Baby Bottle Tooth Decay; Toothbrushing

> *My baby is almost a year old, and she doesn't have any teeth yet! My friend's one-year-old has a whole mouthful. Should I be concerned?*

Learn About It

Actually, your baby *does* have teeth. They began forming even before birth but just haven't cut through the gums yet. Believe it or not, some babies are actually born with that first tooth already above the gum. Many others, like your daughter, wait to show off that first pearly white until after they blow out their first birthday candle. If your one-year-old doesn't have teeth yet, she probably is showing some early signs of teething, and that first tooth should be along very soon.

The Order of Teeth to Come

No matter when your baby starts teething, teeth typically come in a predictable pattern. Not all children are typical, however. Some pop teeth in their own random order, which is neither good nor bad—just different. For most babies, however, teeth appear according to the schedule shown in the diagram. (As with *any* blanket statements about a group as diverse as children, keep in mind that your baby may do things differently.)

What Are the Signs of Teething?

Babies often show signs of teething weeks before a tooth emerges. Some babies experience extreme teething symptoms, while in others,

Typical Teeth Order for Primary Teeth

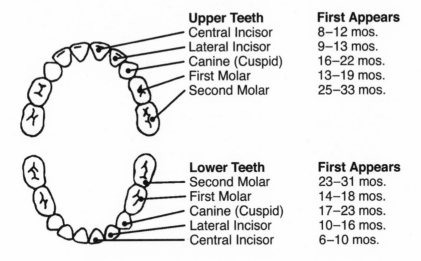

Upper Teeth	First Appears
Central Incisor	8–12 mos.
Lateral Incisor	9–13 mos.
Canine (Cuspid)	16–22 mos.
First Molar	13–19 mos.
Second Molar	25–33 mos.

Lower Teeth	First Appears
Second Molar	23–31 mos.
First Molar	14–18 mos.
Canine (Cuspid)	17–23 mos.
Lateral Incisor	10–16 mos.
Central Incisor	6–10 mos.

that first white tip takes a parent by surprise. A number of typical signs can tell you that your baby is expecting a tooth to erupt:

- Fussiness
- Drooling
- Runny nose
- Rash on the chin or around the mouth
- Biting and mouthing everything
- Red cheeks
- Difficulty falling asleep or staying asleep
- Rejecting the breast or bottle
- Increased need to suck
- Swollen, discolored gums
- Softer-than-usual bowel movements

Some parents report a slight fever, diarrhea, vomiting, or a diaper rash with teething. Since these signs may signal an infection or virus, however, you should always report them to your doctor.

How to Help Your Teething Baby Feel Better

If you suspect that your baby is teething, here are some ways you can help relieve the discomfort:

- Give Baby a clean, wet, cool washcloth to chew on. You can even chill this in the refrigerator if your baby likes it colder.
- Let Baby chew on a teething ring, either at room temperature or chilled in the refrigerator. (Never put teething rings in the freezer: they become too hard and can crack.) If your baby uses a pacifier, try chilling it, and see how your baby likes it.
- Frequently and gently pat Baby's chin dry.
- Offer a sip of cold water.
- Rub Baby's gums with a clean, wet finger.
- For an older teething baby, make frozen treats from apple juice, orange juice, or yogurt. Just fill a small paper cup, a shape-sorter toy piece, or an ice-cube tray, and use a small plastic spoon for a stick. Or purchase frozen pop molds from the housewares department of your local store.
- Using a toothbrush made especially for a baby, clean and massage the gums.
- Dab petroleum jelly or a gentle salve on Baby's dry chin in the drool area to help prevent rash.
- Breastfeed often, for comfort as well as nutrition.
- Offer commercially available teething biscuits, but always supervise your baby as she mouths these. Small pieces can come loose and pose a choking hazard. For the same reason, don't offer hard foods like carrot sticks, apples, or bagels to teething babies.

Over-the-counter teething pain reliever ointments can be quite potent. (Put a dab on your lip, and you'll notice a tingly, numbing feeling.) The ointments also wash out of the mouth quickly, so they don't bring lasting relief. Therefore, use these sparingly and only with your doctor's OK.

If your baby is having a very hard time and is struggling with teething pain, check with your pediatrician about using a pain reliever made especially for teething babies. It's best not to give your baby over-the-counter pain relievers, even herbal remedies, until you've consulted with your doctor. Also ask your doctor about homeopathic teething tablets and tinctures.

Take Care of Your Baby's Teeth

From the time that first tooth appears, proper care is important. As soon as your baby has a tooth, have your pediatrician inspect your baby's mouth. The American Academy of Pediatric Dentists recommends visiting a dentist soon after the first tooth erupts or by the first birthday. However, some dentists and pediatricians feel that waiting until your child is two or even three years old is fine, especially if your pediatrician is checking your baby's teeth. Talk to your own doctor or dentist about the timing for your baby.

Even before your baby's gummy smile turns into a toothy one, read the entries in this book on Toothbrushing and Baby Bottle Tooth Decay. You'll learn just what to do to keep that amazing new smile in healthy, sparkling condition.

For More Information

Websites

American Academy of Pediatric Dentistry
aapd.org

American Dental Association
ada.org

The Canadian Dental Association
cda-adc.ca

Television

See also: Intelligence; Reading; Toys

> So much television programming is aimed at young children. Much of it appears to be educational, teaching the ABCs and life skills. I never much thought about it until I had my baby, but now I'm wondering: When is it appropriate to introduce my baby to television, and what do I need to know about this topic?

Learn About It

The answer to your question isn't simple. A great deal of research has been done on the effects of television on children's lives. The first step in making your decision is to get the facts. Because nearly all of us have one or more TVs in our home, and since most of us watch some TV nearly every day, I warn you that most of this research tells us things that we really don't want to know but need to know!

Once you've researched the topic a bit, the next step is to think about what you've learned and make a conscious decision as to if and how TV will fit into your baby's life. In a nutshell, here's what you need to know:

• Experts suspect that babies younger than two years old view TV as a confusing array of colors, images, and noises. They don't understand much of the content. Since the average TV scene lasts five to eight seconds, your baby or toddler doesn't have enough time to digest what's happening: Just when your little one starts to understand a scene, it changes!

• Cartoons and many children's shows are filled with images of violence. If you find this hard to believe, surf the TV on Saturday morning. The realism portrayed in today's cartoons has moved light-years beyond the Bugs Bunny type of violence. Many children's shows are almost animated versions of adult action films. Research shows that exposure to this type of programming increases the risk of aggressive behavior and desensitizes children to violence.

• Babies and toddlers have a very literal view of the world. They can't yet tell the difference between real and pretend, and they interpret what they see on TV as true life. Research has demonstrated that many young children believe that TV characters actually live inside the TV set! This can confuse young children's understanding of the world and get in the way of their learning what's right or wrong. It can paint a picture of a frightening, unstable, and bewildering world. Although this may be close to the truth, your little one does not yet have the faculties to put what he sees into proper perspective.

• Television watching can be addictive. The more children watch, the more they want to watch. Even toddlers can become drawn to the set. Once they have become addicted, turning off the TV can become a daily battle. Children who watch TV excessively often become passive and lose their natural creativity. They eventually have a hard time keeping themselves busy, and they lose valuable time that should be dedicated to play—the foundation of a healthy childhood and the primary way in which very young children learn.

• Parents sometimes unwittingly begin to use TV more and more as a way to keep their children happy and quiet. It takes strong will and dedication to avoid the easy route provided by this free and easy—yet sometimes dangerous—baby-sitter.

• Children experience unparalleled physical, mental, and emotional growth in the early years of life. Time spent watching television is time taken away from more healthful activities that nurture growth and development.

• Children who watch a lot of television during their early years are at risk for childhood obesity, poor social development, and aggressive behavior. They often have trouble adjusting to preschool or kindergarten. According to a study by Yale Family Television Research, teachers characterized children who watched excessive television as less cooperative, less imaginative, less enthusiastic about learning, and less happy than those who watched little or no TV.

You may have noticed that all of these points demonstrate the negative aspects of letting babies and toddlers watch TV, and you're wondering when I'm going to list the positives. There *are* a few, but I'll be honest: I had to be very creative to come up with this list, since published research doesn't demonstrate many good points for putting a young child in front of a television. Even so, we need to be realistic and acknowledge that most of us aren't going to put our TVs in the closet until all of our children start school.

So I'll discuss the good side of TV for young children, and then I'll help you come up with your own decision about when and how much TV should be in your baby's life. Here are some of the good points of television for children:

- *Quality* children's programming can teach your child basic academic skills, such as the ABCs, counting, addition, science fundamentals, basic language skills, manners, and even early reading skills.
- Your child can view things she might not otherwise see in daily life: exotic animals, distant lands, musical instruments, historical places, and diverse lifestyles. Your child can learn about the world beyond her home and neighborhood.
- Your child can learn basic social skills from watching wholesome programming—for example, how to play with other children and how to use good manners.
- If you use extraordinarily careful selection and restraint, a little bit of television can provide a parent with much-needed downtime or time to catch up on tasks that need adult-only attention.

TV-Watching Tips

The following tips may help you minimize the negative and maximize the positive effects of television watching for your little one:

- Hold off introducing television—even videos—to your baby for as long as possible. If you wait until your child's second birthday, you can consider yourself incredibly successful in starting your little one off well and with the kind of real-life interaction that is so important for a child's development. If you decide to allow TV before your child turns two, choose programming carefully, limit viewing time, and skip days when possible. The less time, the better! Set a goal, such as no more than thirty minutes or an hour per day, or one favorite show, so that you'll not be tempted to turn the TV on too frequently.

• Watch programs yourself before you allow your baby or toddler to watch them. Just because a network markets a show to young children doesn't mean it will reflect your own family's morals and values. You will be amazed to discover that many programs aimed at children contain violence or topics that are inappropriate for your child. Don't assume that your baby can pick out the moral message from a program that features violence or conflict on the way to an important lesson.

• Pay attention also to commercials. Surprisingly, an excellent children's show will sometimes feature commercials that depict the exact things you don't want your little one to see!

• Choose programs that are developmentally appropriate for your child. For *you*, this means slow, boring, and probably goofy! But choose from your child's perspective, not your own.

• Invest in a collection of appropriate and educational videos for your child so that you won't be confined to network programming schedules when you are ready to let your little one watch something.

• Watch along with your child when you can so that you can monitor your child's reactions to what he's seeing. Invite questions, and discuss what you are watching so that you can understand your little one's take. To get the most out of educational TV, point things out and talk about what is being taught. You may even follow up with some lessons afterward.

• Avoid keeping the TV on when no one is actively watching. Many people do this and are used to the background noise the set generates. However, your child will almost surely be exposed to programming that is inappropriate for her.

• Make a conscious decision about how you will use television in your family. Don't watch it by accident or default.

Thrush
(*Candida albicans*)

See also: Breastfeeding Your Newborn; Breastfeeding Your Toddler

What are the signs of thrush? How do we get rid of it?

Learn About It

Thrush (*Candida albicans*) is a common yeast infection that occurs in a baby's mouth and diaper area and on a nursing mother's nipples. It is almost always harmless, but because it thrives in these warm, moist places, it is extremely stubborn and difficult to eliminate. In addition, it can be very annoying because it is quickly and easily transferred back and forth from mother to baby, until both are totally clear of it.

The Signs of Thrush in the Baby

Your baby may have all of these signs, some of them, or even none. If you suspect thrush, review both the signs for a baby and the symptoms that you have. The following are typical signs of thrush in a baby:

- White or gray spots or patches on the inside of your baby's mouth, gums, or on the tongue (unlike a milk coating on the tongue, it does not wipe off easily)
- An opalescent shine on your baby's lips or inside the mouth
- Red face, particularly on the cheeks
- Persistent diaper rash that doesn't respond well to usual remedies
- Fussiness that appears worse during or after feeding
- Bleeding of the mouth or gums in severe cases

Signs of Thrush in the Mother

The following are typical signs of thrush, but many of these can signal other problems as well. If you review the list for yourself and that for your baby and suspect thrush is the problem, call your health care provider, lactation consultant, or La Leche League leader.

- Pain in the nipples or breasts during or after feedings that may persist between feedings
- Deep pink, red, or purple discoloration of the nipple and areola
- A shiny glow on the areola
- Dry, peeling nipples
- Rash or white spots on the nipples
- Itching or soreness that indicates a vaginal yeast infection

Note: You are particularly susceptible to thrush infection following the use of antibiotics, as these medications kill off not just "bad" bacteria, but the "good" types that keep candida under control.

Treating the Family

If you suspect a thrush infection, both you and your baby will need treatment simultaneously until all signs of thrush are gone. If you are also nursing an older child, you will have to treat her, too. In some cases, your partner or other members of the family may shows signs of thrush (athlete's foot, severe dandruff, jock itch, vaginal yeast infection) that will have to be treated to prevent the recurrence of thrush in the family.

Treating the Baby

Many babies with thrush show little response to the yeast infection. For others, it is painful and prevents proper nursing. In that case, the infection should be treated promptly and aggressively so that your baby's growth is not compromised. It's important that you talk to your baby's doctor, who may prescribe a topical medication that can be applied directly to your baby's mouth for pain relief and to clear up the infection. The most common medication is a prescription antifungal cream. A homeopathic doctor can talk with you about using a tincture made of usnea lichen, mugwort, rosemary, or unsweetened yogurt with active cultures.

An alternative treatment is 1 percent gentian violet solution, painted with clean cotton swabs onto affected areas once a day before breast-feeding. These areas include your baby's mouth as well as your nipples and areolae. It's very messy and will turn your baby's lips and your nipples purple for a few days, but it is often very effective. (Watch your baby's mouth carefully for any signs of negative reaction, such as sores, from the treatment. Too much of the solution can burn the skin's surface. If anything seems amiss or if no relief occurs within four days, stop treatment and visit your doctor.)

In addition, the following measures may help your baby feel better, speed up the eradication of the infection, and prevent it from recurring:

- Change diapers immediately when your baby is wet or soiled.
- Coat Baby's bottom with a diaper ointment between changes.
- Avoid using diaper wipes with ingredients that may cause stinging.
- Let your baby's bottom dry thoroughly before rediapering, and allow your baby to be naked for a time during the day.
- Avoid using plastic diaper covers. Instead, use coverings that allow air to circulate, or go without a cover if you're not expecting a big poop anytime soon.
- Wash cloth diapers, cloth wipes, towels, and washcloths in very hot water to remove all traces of the yeast. A vinegar rinse will complete the disinfecting process.

Treating the Mother

Talk with your doctor or lactation consultant about your suspicion of a thrush infection. She will confirm the diagnosis and prescribe a medication to clear up the thrush and any accompanying vaginal yeast infection. As mentioned earlier, if thrush is confirmed in the mother, the baby must be treated also, or the infection may continue to be passed back and forth between you. The following suggestions also can be helpful when treating thrush:

- Take an over-the-counter medication, such as acetaminophen (for example, Tylenol) or ibuprofen (for example, Advil), for breast pain. Alternatively, try chamomile, skullcap, or low doses of valerian.
- To reduce pain, place ice packs on the nipples before feeding.
- Massage the breasts to stimulate letdown before attaching your baby to the breast.
- Start feeding sessions on the least painful side.
- Take extra care in ensuring a proper latch when nursing.
- Position your baby tummy-to-tummy with you for feeding to create a straight latch position and reduce pulling on the nipple.
- Break the suction with your finger to gently detach Baby from your breast.
- Go braless or topless, or keep the flaps down on your nursing bra to allow your nipples to air dry.
- Avoid using breast pads, as these create a warm, moist place for yeast to thrive.

How to Prevent Recurring Infections

Here are some ways to keep a thrush infection from developing or returning:

- Clean and sterilize all pacifiers, teethers, and bottle nipples after each use.
- Let nipples dry after breastfeeding before covering them with clothing.
- Avoid letting your baby suck for long periods on a bottle or pacifier.
- Discard breastmilk that was expressed and stored during a thrush infection.
- Maintain diligent hygiene with frequent hand washing after breastfeeding, diapering, and using the toilet. Pay attention to underneath the fingernails, too. Wash your baby's hands frequently.
- Avoid excess sugar; that applies to you *and* your baby.
- Add plain yogurt to your diet (and to your baby's diet if she is eating solid food). Look for the "live and active cultures" description on the label.

- Avoid fermented foods, such as cheese, beer, and wine.
- Wear clothing that allows the skin to breathe, and avoid synthetic fabrics.
- Use regular hand soap instead of antibacterial soap. Antibacterial soap kills beneficial bacteria that control yeast growth.
- Disinfect toothbrushes and mouth appliances regularly with a bleach and water solution, or wash them in the dishwasher. Also, replace toothbrushes after starting treatment for thrush.
- Wash dishes in very hot water.
- Discard solid deodorants used during a thrush infection.
- If the thrush infection isn't going away, have other family members and even pets checked to see if they are carriers.

Thumb Sucking

· · · · · · · · · · · ·

See also: Breastfeeding Your Newborn;
Breastfeeding Your Toddler; Pacifiers

*My baby found his thumb a week ago, and he has become an
ardent thumb sucker. At first, I thought it was cute, but now I've
started to wonder if it is the start of a bad habit. Should I worry
about his thumb sucking?*

Learn About It

Babies need to suck to survive, and they begin learning how to suck
before they are even born. Some parents are treated to the sight of their
unborn baby practicing this skill during an ultrasound. Other future
thumb suckers may not discover the thumb until a few weeks or months
after birth. Often, it goes like this: Your baby's natural instinct is to find
everything possible to suck on, so first his whole hand goes in his
mouth. Then he figures out that it is easier to get two fingers in.
Finally—blissfully, as far as the baby is concerned—he finds a perfect-
sized, always warm, easily available object: his own thumb. Thumb
sucking soothes and calms your baby, pleasantly stimulates nerve endings in his mouth, and gives him some control over an environment that
must occasionally seem overwhelming.

But parents are often not quite as happy about thumb sucking as
babies. They worry that thumb sucking will lead to orthodontic problems or speech issues. They worry that it signals insecurity. They worry
about what their parents and grandparents will say.

What Do Professionals Say About Thumb Sucking?

Most experts (doctors, dentists, and psychologists) say parents shouldn't worry so much about young babies sucking their thumbs. There are potential problems as a baby gets older, but the large majority of children gradually and voluntarily give up thumb sucking between the ages of two and four. The American Dental Association has stated that thumb sucking should stop by the time a child's permanent teeth come in, which is usually around age five or six. At least at that point, you can explain to the child why continued thumbsucking is problematic and perhaps use incentive charts and positive reinforcement to change the habit.

What to Do About Thumb Sucking

You do need to make sure that your thumb sucker is getting enough breast or bottle time, as sucking can provide so much satisfaction for your baby that she may not drink as much milk as she should. You can determine this by monitoring your baby's development. Ensure that your baby continues to grow well and has plenty of wet diapers.

The next most important thing for you to do is not to get worked up about your baby's thumb sucking, as it is a perfectly normal self-comforting habit. Many happy, contented, and secure babies suck their thumbs. In the middle of the night, when your baby is able to soothe himself back to sleep by putting his thumb in his mouth, you will start to see one advantage of your baby's new habit.

Since thumb sucking is usually harmless in the first year, any measures a parent uses to stop the habit might wait until your baby is around a year old and should be gradual, gentle, and emotionally supportive. Negative treatments, like applying a bitter-tasting substance to the thumb, often are unsuccessful and can be harmful to the child's self-esteem. You can help your baby to learn other ways to comfort himself, so that he doesn't spend an excessive amount of time with his thumb in his mouth:

• If you are a breastfeeding mother, let your baby nurse a bit longer to ensure that he knows his primary source for sucking—and comfort—is Mom's breast.

• Be careful that you give your talented self-soothing baby the cuddles and carrying that he needs. Thumb suckers are not emotionally deprived, but they are often able to soothe themselves better than babies who don't master this handy practice, so it can be tempting to leave them in an infant seat or swing, when they need instead to be cuddled and carried.

• Distract your baby occasionally from thumb sucking by giving her a toy to play with, a book to manipulate, or a round of hand games like patty-cake. She may enjoy the new activity so much that she will temporarily "forget" her thumb.

• Introduce another comfort object, perhaps a blanket, stuffed animal, or rag doll. This may or may not become a replacement for thumb sucking. In fact, it could lead to the comfort object becoming associated with thumb sucking (your baby holds the blanket in one hand, and then automatically pops his thumb in his mouth). But this can work to your advantage later because the blanket can't go everywhere with your child, and if he doesn't have the blanket, he may not suck his thumb. If you can wean him gradually from taking the blanket everywhere you go, you may also wean him from thumb sucking.

• Some professionals suggest that you consider giving your baby a pacifier. Pacifiers have their own problems with continuous, prolonged use throughout early childhood (*see* Pacifiers), and both types of sucking can lead to dental and orthodontic problems. However, some dentists prefer the pacifier to the thumb because, unlike the thumb, the pacifier can be taken away if it begins to present a problem. Some pediatricians prefer the thumb to a pacifier for various reasons. To be honest, there is no true consensus among professionals in the pacifier-versus-thumb debate. As with many issues where babies are concerned, what is best for your baby is your call as the parent.

Toothbrushing

See also: Baby Bottle Tooth Decay; Teething

> *I hate to admit it, but I don't brush my baby's teeth very often. Bed-time is challenging enough without the battle I have to fight to brush his teeth! I have to hold him down, and he cries and screams the entire time that I have a brush in his mouth. I figure that baby teeth just fall out anyway, so it's not a big deal, right?*

Learn About It

Actually, it *is* a big deal. Even though baby teeth aren't permanent, they do have a permanent effect on your little one's health and development. The minute that first tooth pops out—whether your baby is four months old or fourteen months old—it's important that you brush your baby's teeth. Some dentists even recommend cleaning the gums before any teeth erupt. Here's why baby teeth are so important:

- Baby teeth act as placeholders that ensure proper spacing and alignment of permanent teeth as they come in.
- Baby teeth are an important part of language development, ensuring proper jaw and tongue development and movements for speaking.
- Healthy baby teeth enable a child to eat the healthful foods so necessary for development.
- Proper daily care of baby teeth prevents the possibility of childhood tooth decay or periodontal disease.
- Improper care of baby teeth could cause early loss of those teeth and problems with the permanent teeth that replace them.
- Baby teeth are often not completely replaced by permanent teeth until age thirteen or fourteen. That's a long time for your baby to use the first set!

Toothbrushing Tips

Given the importance of baby teeth, brushing them every day is vital to your child's health. To make the task less stressful—maybe even pleasant—try some of the following ideas:

- Make toothbrushing a part of your routine. Do it at the same time every night, such as right after putting on pajamas, and as part of your morning routine, such as right after you get dressed.
- Use a small brush. While using a bigger brush may seem more efficient, it's the equivalent of sticking a hairbrush in your mouth: big and overwhelming. Instead, opt for the special tiny brushes made especially for babies and toddlers. Choose a soft-bristled brush to prevent hurting your baby's gums. If even a baby toothbrush seems to be too much (such as for a very small baby or a baby who sprouts teeth very early), simply use a piece of gauze or a wet cloth to wipe the teeth and gums. You can also purchase a baby finger brush (it looks like a finger off a rubber glove with bristles).
- Use only a tiny swipe of toothpaste. Too much can be unpleasant (and unhealthy) for your baby, and a tiny bit does the job.
- Use a tooth cleanser made especially for babies. Such products are gentle on baby teeth, pleasant tasting, nonfoaming, and safe to swallow. If you don't have baby toothpaste, use a very tiny spot of regular toothpaste. Products that contain fluoride should not be swallowed, since they can cause white spots on teeth, and your child won't learn to spit until much later (well, I mean learn to spit *toothpaste* out until much later).
- Experiment with different types of toothbrushes and toothpastes. Search out colorful, musical toothbrushes or those with playful designs. Try an electric or battery-powered brush made especially for children. These do a great job of cleaning teeth, and your little one may enjoy the buzzing sound and tingly feeling. If you have several brushes, let your little one choose which brush to use each time.

Parent Tip

"Let your baby brush his teeth in the bathtub (before soap and shampoo are in the water, of course!)."

—Aaron, father of Nathan (15 months)

• Be creative:

- Pretend the toothbrush is a train, and the teeth, a track. Make enthusiastic train noises.
- Give the toothbrush and teeth voices, and have them talk to each other.
- Pretend to be hunting for bits of food from the day, and make a big production about each speck you find.
- Make up a toothbrushing song, or use a variation of a favorite: "This is the way we brush our teeth . . ."; "The bristles on the brush go up and down, up and down, up and down . . ."; "Twinkle, twinkle little teeth . . ."
- To take your child's mind off the process, tell a story that is completely disassociated from the toothbrushing: "Once upon a time, a little boy named Coleton went to the beach . . ."
- Brush your child's teeth while she's watching her favorite video movie or TV show.

• After you brush Baby's teeth or before you get started, let your little one do it himself. He'll most likely just chew on the brush, but it will help him feel he has some control over the situation. It also will help him get used to having the brush in his mouth. Don't let your baby walk around with a brush in his mouth, though—he could fall and injure himself.

• Brush together, and take advantage of your little one's desire to imitate your actions. You might even take turns brushing each other's teeth.

• Try moving the toothbrushing routine to the changing table, and handle the event while your baby is lying down. (Put something under her head so she's not lying flat, and use a tiny amount of water so she doesn't gag or choke.) Another position that may work is with you sitting on the floor and your child sitting on your lap or lying with her head in your lap.

• Try brushing in front of a mirror so that your baby can see what's happening. Letting your little one sit on the bathroom counter and look into the wall mirror is often exciting enough to keep him from squirming too much.

• If your tooth-care routine has been really unpleasant, scale back to a shorter toothbrushing time. Then gradually increase the length of brushing time as your baby becomes more comfortable with it.

• The American Academy of Pediatric Dentistry recommends that your baby's first visit with a dentist occur within six months of the appearance of Baby's first tooth and no later than Baby's first birthday. In the meantime, your pediatrician can check your baby's teeth during regular appointments. You might also add the "dentist" game to your play from time to time so that your little one won't be so frightened at that very first dental appointment.

• The bottom line is, just do it. If none of these ideas seems to help, you'll just have to hold your baby in your lap and be thankful that she cries with her mouth open! I know that sounds awful, but the displeasure you have to deal with over toothbrushing is infinitely less than that of watching your toddler in the dentist chair screaming while she has cavities filled or, worse yet, suffering through surgery because of decayed teeth.

For More Information

Websites

American Academy of Pediatric Dentistry
aapd.org

American Dental Association
ada.org

The Canadian Dental Association
cda-adc.ca

Toys

See also: Independent Play

I'm not sure what kind of toys, or how many, my baby should have. I hear conflicting advice that runs from one extreme to another! It's either, "Don't give your baby toys; he'll be spoiled," or, "Give your baby lots of toys; they develop his brain." So which is it?

Learn About It

Both sides of this debate have valid points. A baby does indeed learn from the things she plays with, and the more things she has access to, the more she can learn. With this in mind, many parents spend a fortune buying toys. However, many toys hold a child's attention for three or four days, only to be relegated to the bottom of the toy box or back of a shelf.

Babies learn about their world by using all five of their senses: sight, hearing, taste, smell, and touch. Toys engage and refine these senses by doing several things:

- Helping babies learn how to control their movements and body parts
- Helping babies figure out how things work
- Showing babies how they can control things in their world
- Teaching babies new ideas
- Building babies' muscle control, coordination, and strength
- Teaching babies how to use their imagination
- Showing babies how to solve simple problems
- Helping babies learn how to play by themselves
- Setting the foundation for learning how to share and cooperate with others

Experts agree that babies need a variety of toys to enrich their lives and encourage learning. While your baby can learn from expensive store-bought toys, she can also learn from a crumpled piece of paper, a set of measuring spoons, an empty box, or a leaf. Everything is new and interesting to a baby, and if you open your eyes to the many wonders in our world, you'll see that you don't have to spend a fortune to keep your baby happy, interested, and learning.

What "Home-Grown" Toys Are Best?

As you view the whole world as a bottomless toy box, here are some tips to consider:

• Search for items of different weights, materials, textures, flexibility, sizes, shapes, colors, and smells. (Most store-bought baby toys are primary-colored plastic. That's why your metal keys on a leather key ring are so very appealing; they're different!)

• Babies are generalists. Your little one will apply what she learns from one object to any other that is similar. Therefore, don't give her an old book or magazine to scribble in unless you want *all* of your books to be potential notepads. A sealed bottle may look fun, but your baby may then think she can play with your pill bottles.

• Take a closer look at the things you consider "trash." Some objects may be valuable toys! Empty boxes, egg cartons, and tin containers are just a few examples of everyday castoffs that, once cleaned, can provide endless hours of play.

Parent Tip

"I made a great set of blocks for my daughter by collecting an assortment of empty boxes from regular household products and covering them with contact paper. They are colorful, lightweight, and many interesting shapes and sizes."

—Yu-ting, mother of Shu-Lin (3)

- Your kitchen is overflowing with baby toys! Once your little one begins to crawl, it's time to rearrange the kitchen. Put all your baby-safe items, such as plastic containers, pots and pans, pot holders, and canned goods, in your lower cabinets, and let your baby know where his "toys" are. You'll have to relax your housekeeping standards and deal with disorganized cabinets for a while, but the play potential is so fantastic that it's worth it!

- Young children love water play, and a bowl or pan of water along with spoons and cups of various sizes make a fabulous source of fun. You can put your baby in her high chair, sit her on the floor on a beach towel, or take her outside in a shady spot if the weather's warm. I guarantee she'll be soaked when she's done, but that will be after a very long and happy play session. In the winter you can bring in a little snow and put it in a pan for some indoor snow fun! (Remember to never leave your baby alone when she is having water play.)

- Containers to fill and empty are lots of fun for a baby. You can safely fulfill your older baby's desire to manipulate small things by filling a large bowl with a variety of colorful children's cereals (nothing hard or ball-shaped) and supplying spoons, measuring cups, and other containers. Since you're using cereal pieces, it's OK if some end up in Baby's mouth. *Don't* try this with beads, seeds, macaroni, or other items that pose a choking hazard.

What Store-Bought Toys Are Best?

A while ago, I went to the toy store to buy my youngest child, Coleton, a toy that my older three adored when they were babies. It was a simple pop-up toy with various buttons, levers, and dials, designed for toddlers. I found a bewildering variety of this kind of toy, but to my dismay, every single one in the store was electronic. They made sounds, played music, had blinking lights; they just about played by themselves! I finally had to order the prized toy from a specialty catalog offering "back to basics" toys.

Sure, electronic toys can be exciting—for a while—but they can also stunt your baby's developing ability to imagine and manipulate (and let's face it, those repetitive electronic sounds can get annoying). If a toy does everything by itself, it loses its potential as a tool for developing creativity. Also, if your little one gets used to these toys, then simple pleasures like wooden blocks seem boring by comparison because your baby expects the blocks to play *for* him. In contrast, simple toys are among the very best for baby playtime.

As you shop for your baby, look for these qualities:

- **Long-term play value:** Will this toy hold your little one's attention for more than a few weeks?
- **Durability:** Will it hold up when sat on, thrown, jumped on, mouthed, or banged?
- **Solid simplicity:** Babies don't need complicated toys.
- **Challenge:** Look for toys that teach but do not frustrate.
- **Appropriateness:** Does it match your baby's thinking, language, and motor skills?
- **Interest:** Will it encourage your baby to think?
- **Stimulation:** How does this toy foster creativity and imagination?
- **Interactiveness:** Does it engage your child or just entertain her as she watches passively?
- **Versatility:** Can your baby play with this in more than one way?
- **Washability:** Well-loved toys tend to get very dirty!
- **Fit with your family value system:** Does this toy reflect your family's particular values? For example, is the toy friendly to the environment? Does it promote diversity? Are you comfortable with what the toy represents?
- **Novelty:** Is this toy different from others your baby already has? You don't want a toy box filled with thirty different kinds of rattles!
- **Fun appeal:** Is it something that *you* will enjoy playing with, too? Toys that encourage you to play along with your baby are ideal.

Best Toys for Young Babies

Board books
Foot or hand puppets
Musical toys

Rattles

Small, lightweight, easy-to-grasp toys

Squeaky toys

Teething rings

Toys with high-contrast graphics, bright colors, or black-and-white
patterns

Best Toys for Older Babies

Activity boxes (with levers, buttons, dials, hinges)

Balls

Beginning puzzles (two or three large pieces; knobs are helpful)

Blocks

Cars and trucks

Chunky small people and accessories

Dolls and stuffed animals

Hammering toys

Large interlocking beads

Modeling dough

Musical toys

Nesting cups

Peg boards

Picture books

Plastic animals

Pop-up toys

Push or pull toys

Shape sorters

Stacking rings

Toy versions of everyday items (telephones, cooking utensils, doctor
kits)

Toys you still remember from your childhood (the classics endure
and are always a good bet)

Washable crayons or markers and blank paper

Playtime

As you give your baby new things to play with, keep in mind that there is no right way to play with toys. For example, a puzzle is not always for "puzzling." The pieces make great manipulative characters, can be sorted or put in boxes, and make interesting noises when banged together or against an empty pot. Children learn through play, so any toy they enjoy playing with is, by definition, educational.

Toy Safety Information

Always consider well the safety aspects of *anything* your baby is going to play with. Here are a few ways to keep playtime safe:

• Discard any plastic wrapping, plastic bags, packaging, or tags before giving a toy to a baby.

• Always watch for choking hazards. Anything small enough to fit inside your baby's mouth has the potential for danger. Watch for pieces that may become loose from a larger object, too. Make sure that no small parts can be pulled off or chewed off the toy.

• Check the paint or finish on the toy to make sure it is nontoxic, since babies put everything in their mouths.

• Check toys for sharp points, rough edges, rust, and broken parts.

• Always abide by the age rating on the package. No matter how smart your child is or how wonderful the toy, don't second-guess the manufacturer, since age rankings often are related to safety issues. If you choose to purchase a toy with an older age recommendation, make certain that the toy is used only when you are playing with your baby, and that it is stored where your baby can't get to it without your supervision.

• Remove rattles, squeeze toys, teethers, stuffed animals, and other small toys from the crib or bed when your baby goes to sleep for naps or bedtime. The exception here is a specialty made-for-baby toy that has been carefully created to be a safe sleeping lovey.

• Avoid pull toys with long cords that could wind around your baby's neck. Pull toys for babies should have either very short strings or rigid handles.

• Make sure toys are properly assembled, with no loose parts.

• Beware of excessively loud toys. Babies tend to hold things close to their faces, and you want to protect your baby's sensitive ears.

• Buy mobiles or crib toys from reputable manufacturers, and make sure they attach to the crib without dangling strings. Remove mobiles and other crib toys once your baby can sit up.

• Make sure that toys are never left on stairs, in doorways, or in walkways.

• Your baby's toy box should have a special safety lid (or no lid at all) to prevent it from slamming on your baby's head or hands or trapping your baby inside. There shouldn't be any hinges that could pinch little fingers.

• Never give a baby a balloon, Styrofoam, or plastic wrap as a toy. These present a serious choking hazard, since they cannot be expelled using the Heimlich maneuver.

• If a toy is secondhand (whether purchased from a secondhand store or garage sale or given to you by a friend or relative), give all of the preceding rules extra consideration. If you have any doubts, always err on the side of safety and discard the toy. Don't let your baby play with a paint-finished toy that appears to be older than a few years. The paint may be lead-based, which poses serious hazards to a baby who touches or mouths it.

• Keep toys (and parts of toys) designed for older children out of the hands of babies. Your baby may like to play with toys belonging to an older sibling or friend, but in terms of safety, these are geared to older kids and are not safe for little ones to use without very close supervision.

Travel by Airplane

· · · · · · · · · · · ·

See also: Breastfeeding in Public; Car Seat Crying; Grandparents, overzealous; Grandparents, reluctant; Sunshine; Swimming; Travel by Car; Unwanted Advice; Visiting Other People's Homes with Your Baby

We're about to take our first airplane trip with our one-year-old. We flew quite a bit before she was born, but now we're not sure what to pack or how to make this trip successful.

Learn About It

Even if you racked up your share of frequent-flier miles before your baby was born, forget what you know of travel so far. Flying with a little one is a whole different story.

If you fear turning into one of those families we've all met aboard planes—those with squalling, unruly, squirming children who tend to bring out the same traits in their fellow passengers—take heart. My oldest child, Angela, was just fourteen days old when she took her first flight, and since then, I've taken many more trips with my four children. I *know* you can travel with your little ones and enjoy the process. Forethought and preparation are the keys.

Planning the Trip

The details of your trip often can mean the difference between success and disaster. Keep these ideas in mind as you plan:

• Examine all aspects of the journey when you book your flights. Aim for direct flights so you can avoid changing planes. If you have to make a change, avoid short layovers that give you too little time to get from gate to gate, and conversely, avoid long layovers that require lots of idle time in airports.

• When you make your reservations, give the agent the ages of all passengers. You may learn some important rules such as these:

- FAA regulations allow only one lap-child per adult. If you are traveling with two children and only one adult, one child will require a seat of his own. (Not that you would want to travel with two children on your lap!)
- Some airlines do not allow newborns to fly, so check on age requirements.
- Some airlines offer discounted prices for children's tickets.
- Most airplanes have only one *extra* oxygen mask in each row, which means you can only seat one lap-child *in each row*. If two adults are traveling with two children, consider sitting across the aisle from each other, or two behind two.
- Some airlines count car seats and strollers as extra baggage.

• If your child falls asleep easily and stays asleep, try scheduling travel for during your child's nap or sleep times. If you have a finicky sleeper, on the other hand, avoid traveling during usual sleep times, as your baby may just stay fussy and awake.

• Reserve your seats in advance to be sure your entire party sits together.

- If you have an infant, ask for the bulkhead (front row), and request a bassinet.
- Contrary to popular advice, I think it's best to avoid the bulkhead with older babies and toddlers, because these seats offer neither under-seat space nor seat pocket, so you'll have to store all your toys and supplies in the overhead compartment. Also, in the bulkhead, the food tray pops up from the armrest, effectively trapping you in your seat when your table is laden with food.
- Don't put your child in the aisle seat, as the food cart and passengers carrying luggage could injure your child.

• Ask what special features your airline offers for families. Some companies offer children's meals, bassinets, gate check for strollers, or early-boarding privileges.

• If you can afford to, buy a seat for your child, and take along her car seat. Your baby is used to being buckled into her car seat, and the familiarity may make it easier for her to sit still and even sleep. (This only works, though, when your child is able to fit comfortably in the tight seat compartments. A toddler with long legs will be scrunched between her seat and the seat in front of her.) The added benefit of taking a car seat is the safety feature of having your child in a protective seat on the airplane. Make sure your car seat bears a sticker that says it's FAA approved for air travel, so that it's not turned away at the gate. You'll need that seat anyway to get to and from the airport at home and at your destination. (Car seat rentals are available through car rental agencies and rental service stores, but they are typically expensive and availability is often limited.)

• Visit your baby's pediatrician a week or two before your trip to be sure your little one isn't harboring an ear infection or other illness. If possible, avoid exposing your child to other children the week before the flight so he's less likely to catch one of those many kid-carried bugs.

• If you will be visiting relatives at your destination, make a family photo album and "introduce" your baby to these new people via their pictures before they actually meet.

• If your baby will be taking any medication on the day of the trip (such as a decongestant or pain reliever), be sure to test it out *before* the day of travel to gauge any side effects.

• Decide if you'll need a stroller at your destination. If you don't think you'll need a conventional one, at least consider taking a lightweight portable type for use in airports; this will give you a free hand as you tend to tasks such as luggage check-in and pickup, while keeping your child safe and close by. If you opt to take your regular stroller, you can usually check it at the gate or right at the door of the airplane.

• In place of a stroller, a sling or soft-pack carrier can be very helpful if your child still likes to be carried and is light enough for you to carry this way for long walks through the airport.

• Dress yourself and your child in comfortable layers of clothing. Airplanes are often cramped and hot, but sometimes they are too cold.

• Use the following "Carry-On Checklist" (and make lists of your own) to ensure that you don't forget anything.

Packing Your Carry-On

The right carry-on bag can be a lifesaver. Make sure that your bag is easy to lift or roll and that it falls within the airline's size limitations. Pack an organized bag that carries the items in this checklist.

Carry-On Checklist

☐ **Lots of diapers:** Plan for an unexpected layover or delay.

☐ **Baby blanket:** This is good for multiple uses (covering, napping, swaddling, creating privacy, and even for play, such as peekaboo).

☐ **Diaper-changing pad:** This is essential in case you end up changing your baby on the floor or on a dirty changing table.

☐ **Plenty of snacks:** Snacks are a great distraction for a bored or antsy child. Often the only snacks on airplanes are peanuts, which are a major choking hazard for babies. Even if you've ordered a child's meal, it might show up when your child is asleep or isn't hungry, or your child may not like the menu. Also, if your flight gets delayed or canceled or you miss a connection, you'll be glad you didn't rely on the airline for food. Here are a few ideas for easy-to-tote snacks:
  • Baby food
  • Dry cereal
  • Pretzels
  • Crackers
  • Bagels
  • Bread or rolls
  • Dried fruit
  • Lollipops (without a gum or chewy center)

☐ **Drinks:** Carry along favorites in a sippy cup, drink box, or bottle. You may even want to pack these in a soft lunchbox cooler.

☐ **Infant pain reliever:** Take along a few doses of the pain reliever you usually give Baby in case of ear pain or other discomfort. (But don't try anything new. Make sure it's something your baby has tolerated well already.)

☐ **Toys:** Fill the available space in your carry-on with lots of new toys or old favorites that have been hidden for a few weeks. Avoid noisy toys that will annoy fellow passengers. The following are great travel toys:
  • Crayons and a small pad or sticky notes
  • Stickers and sticker books (stickers that come in a book are reusable if stuck on their specially surfaced pages, whereas a sticker placed on paper is there for good, so a sticker book prolongs the activity)
  • Building toys like Lego or Duplo blocks
  • Paperback books
  • Puppets
  • Plastic animals, cars, or dolls
  • Playing cards (Go Fish or other games that feature interesting cards)
  • Tape or CD player with earphones for kid music or books on cassette or CD

☐ **Bib:** Bring one or two of these to protect Baby's traveling clothes from inevitable spills.

☐ **Pacifiers and lovey:** Even if your flight isn't during a normal naptime or bedtime, Baby may need rest and comfort. Carry extra pacifiers or your baby's lovey, special blanket, or toy.

☐ **Something for you:** Include a book, magazine, or activity for you when Baby is sleeping or playing, should you be lucky enough for that to occur!

☐ **First-aid supplies:** Pack a small medical kit with bandages and other supplies.

☐ **Wet wipes:** You'll need these for diaper changes and cleaning Baby's hands and face.

☐ **Empty plastic bags:** You never know where you'll need to change Baby's diaper, so carry a few plastic bags for soiled diapers. (But be sure to keep them away from your baby.)

☐ **Bottlefeeding supplies:** If your baby uses a bottle, pack several bottles. It's usually easiest to carry premeasured powdered formula and small bottles of water for mixing.

☐ **Extra clothing:** Spit-up and spills happen, so pack a complete change of clothes for Baby and an extra shirt for you.

☐ **Toothbrushing supplies:** Carry a toothbrush and toothpaste for unexpected layovers.

☐ **One carry-on per adult:** If you're traveling as two adults with two children, divide up the children's supplies into two separate bags in case your seats are separated on the airplane.

☐ **Child's backpack:** Consider packing toys in a small child's backpack for any child old enough to carry one.

☐ **Belt-bag or fanny pack:** A small belt-bag (fanny pack) is handy for tickets, ID, and cash. Wear it on the front of your body, not the back.

Before you leave, test your bag to be sure it's not too heavy!

Tips for Air Travelers

Besides packing everything you'll need, you can do a lot to cope with the demands of traveling. The following suggestions will help you make air travel pleasant for everyone involved.

The Night Before the Trip

- Get a good night's sleep so that you can be more relaxed during your trip.

- Pack all of your bags and put them in the car or near the front door so you're not scrambling when it's time to leave.
- Review your checklist.

At the Airport

- Get to the airport early. (Call your airline or visit its website to determine the airline's recommended time for arrival—and add at least a half hour to this.)
- Check as many pieces of luggage as possible. Avoid overloading yourself with things to carry.
- Keep in mind that most airport rental carts have to be unloaded to go through security and that your child may have to be taken out of the stroller or backpack when you go through the metal detector.
- When you check in, tell the desk attendant that you are traveling with a baby. Let this person know if you have a stroller or car seat with you.
- Change your baby's diaper immediately before boarding the airplane.
- Avoid breastfeeding or bottlefeeding your baby just before boarding, as he may fall asleep and wake up crying as you struggle to carry him and your belongings to the gate. Wait until you are seated and unloaded, then feed him, and maybe you'll be lucky and he'll take a nap!
- Avoid giving your little one snacks just before boarding. Save food and drink for when you're on the airplane, as these carry great entertainment value.
- Consider taking your stroller to the gate and checking it there. This way, you can carry Baby, the car seat, and all your belongings right up to the airplane gangway. Smaller strollers can be taken on the plane as carry-ons, and an attendant will take bigger strollers as gate-checked items. (Find out where to retrieve these.)
- If traveling with two adults and multiple children, ask at the desk if one adult can do the early boarding and set up your carry-on bags and car seat(s). Usually the preboarding time is extremely

short, and you'll have to rush to get the car seat secured and carry-on items organized before all the other passengers begin to board. This arrangement will also allow your little ones some last-minute exercise before boarding with the second adult.

- If you have a connecting flight, go straight to the gate upon landing. Sometimes it takes longer to walk from gate to gate than you expect. Any waiting time is best done closer to your next gate.

On the Airplane

- To help your baby's ears adjust to changes in cabin pressure, encourage swallowing during takeoff and landing. You can do this by breastfeeding or offering a bottle or pacifier. Toddlers can take a drink, nibble on crackers, or suck on a lollipop. (Look for lollipops without a gum or chewy center, which can present a choking hazard.) Use the feeling in your own ears to determine when to give your baby something to swallow, or feed your baby when you see the flight attendants preparing the cabin for takeoff or landing. But if your baby is sleeping soundly, don't feel you need to awaken her; she'll be fine.

- Flying in an airplane can cause dehydration, which occurs much more quickly in a child than in an adult. Keep your baby well hydrated with water, juice, or milk.

- Changing diapers can be a real challenge. Some airplanes have changing tables, but these are typically very small. While great for newborns, they present a tricky challenge for bigger babies. You can ask the flight attendant where the best place for changing is. A small baby can be changed on your lap or on the pull-down tray table. (Be sensitive to the people seated near you if you do this.) Some airlines will allow you to use the flight attendant's jump seat; some will let you change your baby on the floor near the galley or in the bulkhead area. If you have an older baby, consider using pull-up disposable diapers on the flight, as these can be pulled up with your little one standing. Use a plastic bag from home or the airsickness bag for disposal in the bathroom trash. Remember that, since flight attendants handle food, they can't handle dirty diapers (and probably don't want to, either).

- The flight attendant will usually heat a bottle for you. Be sure that you shake it well and test it thoroughly, as the galley system often makes things very hot.
- If your baby is unhappy and begins to cry, take a deep breath and focus your attention on your baby. Fellow passengers who are unhappy about the disruption may forget that you have as much right to be on the airplane as they do. They also may not know or may forget how difficult it is for a baby or young child to be patient during a long flight. Your best defense against an unpleasant stranger is to say with a smile, "I'm doing the best I can." And then tend to your baby.
- Unless you have to, don't rush off the plane. Let your child play until most of the passengers have disembarked. This will prevent you from standing in the slow-moving line in the aisle while carrying an armload of luggage and trying to keep your baby happy.

International Travel

- If only one parent is traveling, make sure you carry a letter of permission from the other parent. This should be signed and assert that the parent gives permission for the child to leave the country. You may not need this, but it's an easy document to take along just in case.
- Get passports for all travelers. It's easy to obtain a passport for a baby. Passport application forms and instructions are available at your local post office. Plan ahead, though, as obtaining a passport can take weeks after making application.
- Take advantage of the room available in a larger airplane by going for walks with your baby when it's safe to move about the cabin.

At Your Destination

- Determine in advance where your baby will sleep, and find out if you can rent or borrow a crib, if you need one. If you plan to co-sleep, you may need to move the furniture around or even pull the mattress off the bed to make a safe sleeping situation. (Most hotel housekeeping staff will help with this if you ask politely.) Other equipment such as car seat, stroller, high chair, and safety gates often can be rented or borrowed.

- Find out if your brands of diapers and formula are available at your destination. If not, send a box ahead of time.
- Ask if your accommodations have been childproofed. If not, take along some outlet protectors and a roll of duct tape for on-the-spot childproofing.
- Pack a child-safe night-light to make those middle-of-the-night potty runs and diaper changes safe.
- Make sure that the vehicle you'll be picked up in or that you are renting has enough seatbelts for everyone, plus room for luggage and your stroller.
- Upon arrival, you might want to collect your luggage and then send one adult for the car while the other stays at the curb with the bags and children.
- Remember to keep your carry-on bag organized, including snacks, for your return flight home.

For the Frequent Flier

Make a master list of the items you typically take along. Be sure to include those you're more apt to forget. Keep your list on your computer, if you have one, so it's ready to print out when it's time to pack.

Travel by Car

· · · · · · · · · · ·

See also: Breastfeeding in Public; Car Seat Crying;
Grandparents, overzealous; Grandparents, reluctant;
Sunshine; Swimming; Travel by Airplane; Unwanted Advice;
Visiting Other People's Homes with Your Baby

*To Grandmother's house we go! And we'll be in the car for five
whole hours—how can we make the trip enjoyable with a baby
along?*

Learn About It

There's no question: Marathon car trips with a baby on board take a
good amount of planning and organization. But it can be done—and,
yes, it can even be fun!

Planning the Trip

In the hustle that precedes a trip, it can be easy to *let* things happen,
instead of *make* things happen. Be proactive in making your trip decisions. Contemplating these questions and coming up with the right
answers can help make your trip more successful:

• **Does your baby sleep well in the car?** If yes, plan your travel
time to coincide with a nap or bedtime so your baby can sleep through
part of the journey. If not, plan to leave immediately after a nap or upon
waking in the morning. Don't fool yourself into thinking your baby
will behave differently than usual in the car just because it's a special
occasion.

- **Is it necessary to make the trip all at once, or can you break it up with stops along the way?** The longer your baby is strapped in the car seat, the more likely he'll become fussy. Planning a few breaks can keep everyone in a better frame of mind.
- **When estimating an arrival time, have you factored in plenty of extra time for surprises?** A diaper explosion that requires a complete change of clothes and a baby whose inconsolable crying requires an unexpected twenty-minute stop are just two of the setbacks that can easily happen.
- **Do you have everything you need to make the trip pleasant?** Here are some of the items that experienced parents have learned to use:

  - Window shades to protect your baby from the sun and create a darker, nap-inducing atmosphere
  - A cooler for cold drinks; a bottle warmer if needed
  - Plenty of toys that are new or forgotten favorites saved just for the trip
  - Baby-friendly music on tape or CD
  - A rear-view baby mirror to keep an eye on Baby (unless a second person will be sitting with your little one)
  - Books; have a passenger read to your baby

Preparing the Car

Take plenty of time to get the car ready for your trip. If two adults are traveling, consider yourself lucky, and arrange for one person to sit in the backseat next to the baby. If you are traveling alone with your little one, you'll need to be more creative in setting up the car, and you'll need to plan for more frequent stops along the way.

Here are a few tips for making the car a traveling entertainment center for your baby:

- Use ribbon or yarn and safety pins or tape to hang an array of lightweight toys from the ceiling of the car over your baby. An alternative is to string a line from one side of the car to the other with an array of toys attached by ribbons. Bring along an assortment of new toys that can be exchanged when you stop the car for a rest. Just be sure to use small toys and keep them out of the driver's line of view. Also be sure Baby doesn't pull down the yarn and become entangled in it or choke on it.

• Tape brightly colored pictures of toys on the back of the seat that your baby will be facing.

• If no one will be sitting next to your baby and your child is old enough to reach for toys, set up an upside-down box next to the car seat. On top of this box, place a shallow box or tray. Fill this with toys that your baby can reach for by herself. You might also shop around for a baby activity center that attaches directly to the car seat.

• If you plan to have someone sitting next to Baby, then provide that person with a gigantic box of toys with which to entertain the little one. Distraction works wonders to keep a baby happy in the car. One of the best activities for long car rides is book reading. Check your library's early-reading section; it typically features a large collection of baby-pleasing titles in paperback, which are easier to tote along than board books.

• Take along an assortment of snacks and drinks for your older baby who's regularly eating solids, and remember to carry food for yourself, too. Even if you plan to stop for meals, you may decide to drive on through if your baby is sleeping or content, saving the stops for fussy times.

• Carry books on cassette or quiet music for the adults for times when your baby is sleeping. The voice on tape may help keep your baby relaxed, and it will be something you can enjoy.

• If you'll be traveling in the dark, take along a battery-operated night-light or flashlight.

• Bring coffee, gum, or mints for yourself to help you stay alert while driving.

• Use the following Car Travel Checklist to make sure you haven't forgotten anything.

Car Travel Checklist

☐ Well-stocked diaper bag (*see* "Diaper Bag Checklist" under Diaper Bags)

☐ Baby's blanket and car seat pillow or head support

☐ Window shades (sun screens)

☐ Change of clothes for your baby

☐ Enormous box of toys and books

☐ Music or books on cassette or CD

☐ Baby food, snacks, and drinks for your baby

☐ Sipper cups

☐ Snacks and drinks for the adults

☐ Cooler

☐ Wet washcloths in bags, or moist towelettes

☐ Empty plastic bags for leftovers and trash

☐ Bottle warmer

☐ Cell phone

☐ Baby's regular sleep music or white noise (plus extra batteries)

☐ First-aid kit, prescriptions, medications

☐ Jumper cables

☐ Wallet or purse with money and ID

☐ Medical and insurance information, emergency phone numbers

☐ Maps and driving directions

☐ Baby carrier, sling, or stroller

☐ Camera and film

☐ Suitcases

During the Journey

If you've carefully planned your trip and prepared your vehicle, you've already started out on the right foot. Now keep these suggestions in mind as you make your way down the road:

• Be flexible. When traveling with a baby, even the best-laid plans can be disrupted. Try to stay relaxed, accept changes, and go with the flow.

• Stop when you need to. Trying to push "just a little farther" with a crying baby in the car can be dangerous, as you're distracted and nervous. Take the time to stop and calm your baby.

• Put safety first. Make sure that you keep your baby in the car seat. Many nursing mothers breastfeed their babies during trips. This can be dangerous in a moving car, even if you are both securely belted: You can't foresee an accident, and your body could slam forcefully into your baby. Instead, pull over and nurse your baby while he's still in his car seat. That way, when he falls asleep, you won't wake him up moving him back into his seat. (This takes some creativity and practice.)

• Remember: *Never, ever leave your baby alone in the car, not even for a minute.*

On the Way Home

You may be so relieved that you lived through your trip to your destination that you sort of forget the other trip ahead of you: the trip home. You'll need to organize the trip home as well as you did the trip out. A few days in advance, make certain that all your supplies are refilled and ready to go. Think about the best time to leave, and plan accordingly.

In addition, think about what you learned on the trip out that might make the trip back even easier. Is there something you wish you had packed but didn't? Something you felt you could have done differently? Did you find yourself saying, "I wish we would have . . ."? Now's the time to adjust your original travel plan so that your trip back home is pleasant and relaxed.

Twins

· · · · · · · · · · · ·

See also: Baby Blues; Baby Carriers; Breastfeeding Your Newborn; Breastfeeding Your Toddler; Breastfeeding with Bottlefeeding Supplements; Crying; Postpartum Depression; Sleep, newborn; Sleep, four months and over; Strollers

I just found out that I am expecting twins. Help! How am I going to cope?

Learn About It

The number of parents with twins and higher-order multiples has increased dramatically in recent years. Now one out of every forty births results in twins, and there are more than 125 million sets of twins in the world! About 70 percent of twins are fraternal, having grown from two separate eggs that were fertilized by two separate sperm. The other 30 percent are identical, arising from a fertilized egg that split in two in the initial days after conception. Fraternal twins have no more in common genetically than any two siblings have, but they share so many life experiences that they have a special bond. Identical twins have the same genetic makeup. They are always the same gender, and they have the same hair color, eye color, and blood type. However, there almost always are slight physical differences that enable family members to tell them apart (although most other people will see them as identical). And as is true with all human beings, twins can have significantly different personalities.

How to Cope with and Enjoy Your Baby Twins

The first thing you need to do is to accept that life is going to be a challenge for a while. Twin pregnancies are physically hard on the mother, and there is the constant worry about prematurity. Also, twin births are often difficult, with a high rate of cesarean sections. And after all that, you have two tiny babies to feed, dress, change, and bathe. But think about that: You have two tiny babies—two improbable miracles to love.

Daily life with a newborn is a challenge; daily life with twin newborns can seem completely overwhelming. In the beginning, you may feel lucky just to have made it through another day. The best approach, in fact, is to take life day by day. And when you go to sleep each night, give yourself a pat on the back because you are doing an amazing job in circumstances that would challenge any person.

"It will get better" is the mantra of many twins' parents, and it is indeed true. Until then, here are some specific tips about how to survive the first year with twins:

- **Prepare as much as possible before the twins arrive.** Get books on twins and see what they recommend in terms of clothes, baby equipment, and strollers (*see* Strollers). Join your local parents-of-multiples club, and ask for advice from experienced parents about what you need to do and buy before the babies arrive. Contact La Leche League or a lactation consultant, and ask for advice about breastfeeding twins, so you can start with a good store of knowledge. Stock your freezer full of premade meals for the hectic early days. Set up the babies' room, and wash and fold all their clothing. Buy diapers, carriers, and other supplies. And then sleep, read, and relax while you still have the chance!

- **Endeavor to breastfeed your twins.** Breastfeeding can take some time to establish with a singleton (*see* Breastfeeding Your Newborn), and it can be a challenge to start off with twins. Still, the basic facts about breastfeeding apply: Breastmilk is not only best for your babies; it's best for your wallet, too! Breastfeeding can be much easier than bottlefeeding, because you avoid dozens of daily bottles and complicated simultaneous bottlefeeding positions. A breastfeeding mother can learn to feed both babies at the same time and still have two free hands available for burping one of the babies—or even reading a book! Keep in mind that a mother of twins needs a tremendous amount of support to properly establish breastfeeding, so search out that support from the start. Some mothers of twins breastfeed and later, when the babies are a little older, add one or two bottlefeeding supplements to give the mother a bit of a break (*see* Breastfeeding with Bottlefeeding Supplements).

• **Get help.** Take advantage of *all* offers of help from friends and family. Make a list of the things that people can do for you: They can bring or make a dinner, fold some laundry, pick up groceries, or take the babies for a walk while you sleep. Realize that most people really do like to help, and if they offer, say *yes*! Even with help from family and friends, many parents of twins feel that it is worth the money to hire someone to come to their home in the early days and weeks. If a professional is too expensive, try hiring a "mother's helper" college or high school student, who could at least provide you with an extra pair of hands.

• **Keep track of your babies.** This may sound strange, but when you are completely exhausted, telling them apart can be very difficult. Many twins' parents keep the hospital bracelet around one baby's ankle for the first weeks, or they color code their babies' clothing. It can also be easy to lose track of when each baby was last fed or changed. A log can be very useful for jotting down feeding, changing, and sleeping times, and it can help you to develop a "flexible schedule" with as many simultaneous feeding and sleeping times as possible.

• **Go into survival mode.** In addition to taking care of your babies, your basic priorities are sleeping and eating. Your babies depend on a strong, healthy mother and father. Sleep when the babies do. Turn off the phone, and answer calls on your own schedule. Skip all but the most essential chores. Follow the suggestions in this book for helping your babies sleep better (*see* Sleep, newborn; Sleep, four months and over). Simplify meal preparation by using a slow cooker, frozen meals, ordering takeout, and using paper plates and plastic utensils.

• **Have a daily outing with your babies.** Getting two babies ready to go out can be extremely time-consuming, but the fresh air does wonders for your spirits and theirs. The more you do go out, the easier it will become. Mothers of twins are especially at risk for baby blues and postpartum depression (*see* Baby Blues; Postpartum Depression); a healthful walk outside or at the mall can help with this. Be ready for lots of admiring glances from strangers. Yes, you will get the usual comments—"better you than me," "double trouble," and "boy, *your* hands are full"—but instead of getting annoyed, just enjoy the extra attention and realize that people are fascinated by twins!

• **Talk to other twins' parents.** Because they have unique insight into what you are experiencing, other parents of twins can give you a tremendous amount of emotional support and practical advice. Search out parents of twins. Contact your local Mothers of Twins Club (MOTC), approach the mother you see walking with twins in the park (she'll love to talk to you, too!), or join one of the excellent message boards that are available online for parents of twins.

• **See your twins as individuals.** Make sure that you take separate photos of your babies, and don't always call your babies "the twins." Instead, get in the habit of calling them by their names. Try to give each baby some individualized attention every day, but don't feel guilty when you can't. Even parents of nontwin siblings struggle to find time for personalized attention to each child, but a little bit goes a long way.

• **Enjoy your babies.** Many twins' parents feel that the first year goes by in a blur, and they regret that they "miss out" on their babies' infancy. Because life is so hectic for these parents, they need to be especially aware that this is a unique time in their lives and to enjoy the wonder of these two amazing human beings. Savor the special moments. And when the going gets tough, the tough cultivate a sense of humor!

Parent Tip

"I started reading books to my twins when they were newborns, thinking that this was one thing I could do right for them, as they didn't get the individual attention a singleton would. This has paid off handsomely. Not only do they *love* books now, there have been few things so extraordinary in my life as the warm feeling I get when I read a book to my babies with their two little heads on my chest."

—Alice, mother of Patrick (6), Carolyn (4), and twins Rebecca and Thomas (2)

For More Information

Books

Gromada, Karen Kerkhoff. *Mothering Multiples: Breastfeeding and Caring for Twins or More*, rev. ed. Schaumburg, IL: La Leche League International, 1985.

Laut, William, Kristin Benet, and Sheila Laut. *Raising Multiple Birth Children: A Parent's Survival Guide.* Worcester, MA: Chandler House Press, 1999.

Tinglof, Christina Baglivi. *Double Duty: The Parent's Guide to Raising Twins, from Pregnancy Through the School Years.* Chicago: Contemporary Books, 1998.

Website

National Organization of Mothers of Twins Clubs
nomotc.org

Umbilical Cord Area

· · · · · · · · · · · ·

See also: Bathing

How should I take care of my baby's umbilical cord area?

Learn About It

After your baby is born and the umbilical cord is cut, a small piece remains attached to the belly. This piece dries and falls off, leaving the area to heal into your child's belly button.

Keeping the Area Clean

The most common method for cleaning the umbilical cord stump is using rubbing alcohol on a cotton ball, gauze pad, or cotton swab. A newer recommendation is to clean with clear water, which may work as well or even better. Ask your doctor for a recommendation.

Many new parents are afraid of hurting their baby, so they just dab the top, but this doesn't give a thorough cleaning and can result in an infection. For proper cleaning, push the stump up slightly and clean around the base. Don't tug on it, but do get below it for a thorough cleaning. You can then use a dry cotton ball or washcloth to dry the area, fan it with your hand, or blow gently. Clean the area three or four times a day, or just make it a routine part of every diaper change for an easy way to remember. Continue this cleaning ritual for a few days after the cord falls off to ensure complete healing.

Letting the Air In

When you diaper your newborn, be certain to turn down the front waistband of the diaper so that the cord area is exposed to air. This helps the healing process and prevents any irritation from the diaper rubbing on the area.

What About Bath Time?

Traditionally, parents were cautioned against submerging their babies in water until after the cord fell off and healed. Many health professionals now believe that a tub bath is fine as long as you don't let Baby linger in the water too long and you dry the area when Baby is out of the water. But if your doctor advises a sponge bath, follow these steps (*see also* Bathing):

- Be sure the room is warm and free of drafts.
- Lay a towel on a flat surface such as the changing table or kitchen counter.
- Fill a bowl or sink with warm water.
- Have baby's clothing, a new diaper, and lotion or powder set up within arm's reach.
- Lay your baby on the towel and undress her, keeping the areas you aren't cleaning covered with a small towel, and the diaper area covered.
- Wash and dry each part of her body with a warm, wet cloth.

Parent Tip

"I saw my baby's umbilical cord stump as a beautiful reminder of the physical joining that used to exist between us."

—Kavya, mother of Mohan (6 months)

What About Infection?

If you suspect that your baby's umbilical cord wound is infected, have your health care provider take a look. The following are signs of infection:

- Drainage from the cord area
- Foul smell
- Redness surrounding the cord
- Active bleeding

What if the Cord Doesn't Fall Off?

The cord will fall off sooner or later! Usually this happens within three to four weeks after birth, but it can take a few weeks longer. Don't ever pull the cord off; let it come off naturally. Occasionally, when the cord falls off, it will leave a piece of pink scar tissue that takes a few more weeks to heal. Just continue to clean the area with alcohol, and have your pediatrician check it out at your next well-baby visit.

Sometimes a baby develops an umbilical hernia. This isn't a result of how the cord was cut or how much your baby cries; it has to do with the size and shape of your baby's umbilical cord opening. If your baby has a hernia, you'll see a noticeable bulge that gets bigger when your baby cries and often disappears when he is lying down. It looks unusual but doesn't cause any pain. In most cases, this hernia shrinks and goes away without any treatment by the time your child is three years old. Methods of compression, such as banding or taping, are not effective in promoting healing and can even cause an infection, so it's best to let nature take its course. Your doctor will check your baby's belly with each office visit and will let you know if anything needs to be done.

Unwanted Advice

. . . .

See also: Breastfeeding in Public; Grandparents,
overzealous; Grandparents, reluctant

> *I'm getting so frustrated with the endless stream of advice I get
> from my mother-in-law and sister! It seems that no matter what I
> do, I'm doing it wrong. They are not just happy to explain it to me
> but anxious to present an entire lesson on the topic of the day. I
> love them both, but how do I get them to stop dispensing all this
> unwanted advice?*

Learn About It

The underlying concept here bespeaks love and concern more than it
does mean-spiritedness: just as your baby is an important part of your
life, your baby is also important to your mother-in-law and sister. Most
often, family members and close friends dispense advice from a position of love and caring for your baby. People who care about your baby
are bonded to you and your child in a special way that seems to invite
counsel. Knowing this may not make the advice any easier to tolerate,
but it may give you reasons to handle the interference gently, in a way
that leaves everyone's feelings intact.

Regardless of who is giving the advice, how many times they give
it, and why, it is about *your* baby, and in the end, you will raise your
child the way that you think best. Creating a world war over a well-
meaning person's advice is rarely worth the cost, no matter how unhelp-
ful the advice may really be.

You can respond to unwanted advice in a variety of ways. The
method you choose for each situation will depend on your personality,
mood, and relationship with the advice giver.

Listen First

It's natural to feel defensive if you perceive that someone is judging the way you are parenting your own child. Sometimes this defensiveness gets in the way of really hearing someone else's idea. Chances are, you are not being criticized; rather, the other person is sharing what she feels is valuable insight. Try to truly listen to the person giving the opinion; you may just learn something new and valuable (and maybe not!). Unless you listen with an open mind, you may miss something helpful. Sometimes, reining in our own pride can result in learning something of great value.

Disregard

If you know there is no convincing the other person to change her mind, the most helpful response may be to disregard the comments. For example, suppose you receive advice from a sister who has already raised her baby and is imparting advice along the lines of "I did it this way, and you should, too." Simply smile, nod, and make a noncommittal response, such as, "Interesting!" Then go about your own business in your own way.

Agree

You may be able to pick one point out of the advice that you agree with. If so, jump into the conversation with wholehearted agreement on that point, and take the conversation in that direction. If you can acknowledge the bit of advice that you value, you can shift the focus away from the other bits with which you disagree.

Pick Your Battles

Picking your battles is a matter of perspective. If your mother-in-law insists that your baby wear a hat on your walk to the park, go ahead and pop a hat on his head. This won't have any long-term effects except that of placating your mother-in-law. However, you don't have to capitulate on issues important to you or your child. If she insists that your three-month-old should be eating solid food, then resort to the other options for handling unwanted advice that follow.

Steer Clear of the Topic

If your best friend is pressuring you to let your baby cry it out, but you know you neither could nor would do that, then don't complain to her about your baby getting you up eight times the night before. By bringing up the topic, you invite her to share her opinion! If the other person brings up the topic, then diversion or distraction is definitely in order: "Oh! Would you like a muffin? I just bought them, and they're incredible. And how about a cup of coffee? Now, where did I put that bag . . . ?"

Educate Yourself

The more secure and confident we are in our parenting decisions, the easier it is to let other people's comments slide by without concern. Knowledge is power. Protect yourself and your sanity by reading up on your parenting choices, and rely on the confidence that you are doing your best for your family.

Educate the Other Person

If your "teacher" is imparting information that you know to be outdated or outright wrong, you might choose to share some of what you've learned on the topic. If you do it delicately, you may be able to open the other person's mind about the topic. Quote experts, or refer to a study, book, or report you have read. The more complete data you can cite, the more credible you will appear. For example, if Grandma is suggesting that you give your three-month-old a bowl of baby cereal before bed to help him sleep through the night, you can quote some of the information in this book (*see* Solid Foods, introducing) on the medical reasons for why it's best to wait. Remember that Grandma is basing her opinion on information that was considered valid when she was raising her children, so a polite update on current scientific and medical thinking can help her understand your way of doing things.

Quote a Doctor

Many people accept your point of view if a medical professional has validated it. If your own pediatrician agrees with your position on the topic, simply say, "My doctor said to wait until she's at least six months before starting solids." If your own doctor doesn't back your view, then refer to another doctor—perhaps the author of a book about baby care, such as Dr. William Sears or Dr. Jay Gordon. Then you can say, "The doctor says to wait until she's at least six months old before starting solids."

Better yet, present your "adviser" with one or two of the books that have most influenced your parenting philosophy so she can weigh the issues for herself based on current thinking. Don't *throw* the book; simply say, "I know the way I do things mystifies you. But I've read up on [insert issue in dispute here], and I've made my decisions based on what I believe to be good information. Here—see what you think of this. You'll be surprised at how much the advice has changed over the years!"

Be Vague

If you are aware that your position on a particular topic is opposite the other person's and you know that any discussion would just lead to a heated battle, you can avoid confrontation altogether with an elusive response to any question or comment. For example, if your sister asks if you've started potty training yet (but you know your baby is many months away from even starting the process), you can answer, "We're moving in that direction." Then change the subject.

Parent Tip

"If someone is giving me advice that is far from anything I'd ever even consider, then I simply pretend I didn't understand the meaning of what was said. I start talking about an entirely different topic."

—**Linda, mother of Victoria (15 months)**

Ask for Advice!

I'm sure that your friendly counselor is an expert on a few issues that you can agree on. Search out these points, and invite guidance. Your mother-in-law might be a pro at swaddling, while you can't seem to get the blanket tight enough to stay shut. Your sister might be an expert at making her own baby food, since she's done it for her three children. Go ahead and encourage them to teach you in these areas. They will be happy that they are helping you and that you're actually listening, and you'll be happy because you found a way to avoid a showdown about topics that you know you don't agree on. Plus, you just might learn something useful!

Memorize a Standard Response

Here's a great one-line comment that can be said in response to almost any piece of advice or criticism: "This may not be the right way for you, but it's the right way for *me*."

Be Honest

If someone you care about is becoming a true annoyance to you because of constant advice or criticism, consider being honest and direct about your feelings. Pick a time when distractions are at a minimum, and choose your words carefully. You might say something like, "I know how much you love little Harry, and I'm glad you get to spend so much time with him. As much as you think you're helping me when you give me advice about his sleeping habits, though, I'm really comfortable with my own approach, and I'd really appreciate if you'd understand that."

Find a Mediator

If the situation is putting a strain on your relationship with the advice giver, you may want to ask another person to step in for you. For example, if your mother is pressuring you on a particular topic, you can ask your sister, brother, or father to step in on your behalf and gently explain your feelings.

Search Out Like-Minded Friends

Join a support group or an online club with people who share your parenting philosophies. Talking with others who are raising their babies in a way that is similar to your own can give you the strength to face friends and family members who don't understand your viewpoints. (If you complain about your Ann Landers Wannabe counselors to your group, you'll probably have plenty of camaraderie on that point!)

Use Humor

If you are the kind of person who can pull off a quirky comeback with a smile on your face, then try warding off the advice with a joke. If your mother-in-law asks, "Are you ever going to wean that baby?" you can shrug and say, "Of course not! I figure it'll keep us close when he's in high school." If your sister says, "How long are you going to breast-feed that baby?" just smile and say, "About fifteen more minutes on this side."

Do unto Others

When the time comes for *you* to be the one giving the advice, remember to present your idea in a way that you'd like to receive it!

Vegetarian Baby

• • • • • • • • • • • •

See also: High Chairs; Homemade Baby Food;
Solid Foods, introducing

*I've been a vegetarian for about ten years, and now I'm pregnant.
I would love to start my baby off as a vegetarian. My mother has
expressed concerns that this won't give my baby enough protein
and other nutrients. I feel that I eat a well-balanced and healthful
diet. Would the same basic rules that I follow for myself apply to
my baby? Can a baby be raised from the start on a vegetarian diet?*

Learn About It

Yes, you can raise your baby as a vegetarian, right from the start—with
time and thought. But do you know what? Feeding your baby properly
according to *any* type of diet takes time and thought!

First Food for Your Vegetarian Baby

The ideal first food for a vegetarian (or *any*) baby is human milk. When
you breastfeed your new baby, you provide the best and most nutritious
food right from the start (*see also* Breastfeeding Your Newborn). Today's
experts recommend breastfeeding a baby for at least twelve months and
for as long after that as mutually desired by mother and baby. In fact,
the World Health Organization recommends that mothers nurse their
babies for two years or more. By following this guideline, your baby
will have the best possible nutrition leading up to and past the time
when he is eating at the table with you.

While research has proved that breastmilk is best for your baby, certain circumstances may make it necessary for you to feed your baby formula instead. If dairy products are not on your family's menu, a variety

of suitable commercial formulas are available that are made from soy-beans instead of cow's milk. Look to these products, *not* regular soy milk, and don't try to prepare your own baby formula. Soy milk alone has too much protein and not enough fat for a baby. Manufacturers of commercial formulas carefully develop soy baby formulas to meet the specific nutritional needs of babies. The ingredients of these formulas differ among brands, so read the labels to make an informed choice, or ask your pediatrician for a recommendation.

Creating a Healthful Vegetarian Diet for Your Baby

Following a *vegetarian* diet does not automatically mean having a *healthful* diet. Vegetarians, just like nonvegetarians, can eat a diet full of high-fat, high-sugar, low-quality foods, and they can also eat an unbalanced diet low in protein, iron, calcium, or other important nutrients. As for babies, vegetarian little ones run the risk of insufficient caloric intake, which might impede healthy growth and development. So it's important to do your homework and create a complete, healthful meal plan for your baby. Talk to your pediatrician about the right foods and vitamin supplements for your baby; these will include calcium, iron, zinc, vitamin D, and vitamin B_{12}.

The Food Groups, Vegetarian Style

Whether you raise your baby on a semivegetarian or a totally plant-based vegan diet, you must include foods from all the food groups and make sure your baby is getting enough calories and vitamins. The following list shows the five basic food groups for vegetarian children, along with the serving goals once your child's diet is made up entirely of solid foods. Your baby's tummy is about the size of his fist, so keep this in mind when determining serving sizes for your baby. Serving counts and sizes will vary if your baby is still breast- or bottlefeeding.

Breastmilk and/or Fortified Soy Formula

These are the best choices for the first year to ensure that your baby gets a healthy start. If you can extend breastfeeding into the second year, that's even better.

Vegetables (2 or more servings)

Provide a variety of vegetables, focusing on dark green (such as broccoli), dark yellow (squash), and orange (carrots and sweet potatoes).

Whole Grains (5 or more servings)

Focus primarily on grains that are rich in fiber and complex carbohydrates, such as brown rice, oats, barley, and corn.

Legumes, Nuts, and Seeds (2 or more servings)

Beans, peas, lentils, and nut butters are excellent sources of protein, iron, fiber, calcium, and other vitamins. Tofu and tempeh, which are made from soybeans, are excellent choices for children. (Nuts are high on the list of choking hazards and are highly allergenic, too, so avoid these until your baby is older.)

Fruit (2 or more servings)

A variety of fruit provides your baby with many vitamins, such as vitamin C. When possible, choose whole fruit over juice. Dried fruits can add extra calories when needed; just be cautious not to feed your baby small, hard pieces that may be choking hazards.

Fats (2–4 servings)

Aim for high-quality fats, such as those from avocados, soy products, and nut butters. (Remember to watch for allergic reactions to nut butters.)

Dairy Products and Fish

Dairy products, such as yogurt and cottage cheese, and fish are often added to these food groups by lacto-ovo or pesco-vegetarians.

For More Information

Books

Moll, Lucy. *The Vegetarian Child: A Complete Guide for Parents.* New York: Perigee, 1997.

Yntema, Sharon K., and Christine H. Beard. *New Vegetarian Baby: An Entirely New, Updated Edition of the Classic Guide to Raising Your Baby on the Healthiest Possible Diet.* Ithaca, NY: McBooks Press, 1999.

Websites

The North American Vegetarian Society
navs-online.org

Toronto Vegetarian Association
veg.ca

Vegetarian Baby and Child/Veg News
vegnews.com

The Vegetarian Pages
veg.org

The Vegetarian Site
thevegetariansite.com

Vegsource
vegsource.com

Visiting Other People's Homes with Your Baby

• • • • • • • • • • •

See also: Breastfeeding in Public; Restaurants, taking your baby to; Travel by Airplane; Travel by Car; Unwanted Advice

> We just spent the weekend visiting relatives. We've always enjoyed our visits there, but this time it was a disaster! My baby is crawling, and he was everywhere he wasn't supposed to be. He wouldn't eat the food that was served, and he wouldn't sleep. Do we just have to stay home for the next year, or is there a way to visit other people and actually enjoy the process?

Learn About It

No doubt about it, babies change your life in a multitude of ways. A simple visit to a relative's home is no longer simple! Yes, you *can* go visiting with your baby, and you *can* enjoy it, but not without addressing many new considerations. Instead of trying to force things to be as they were, it's better to acknowledge this new phase in your life and plan ahead to make future visiting experiences smooth and pleasant.

Keeping Baby Happy and Occupied

Babies love new places! There is so much to investigate, and there are so many new things to touch. However, many people aren't too happy to have your little one crawling or toddling freely about the house, exploring everything in sight. While you think it's adorable that your baby found the Tupperware, your host may not think it's so cute that her clean, tidy cabinet has just been rearranged by sticky baby hands. Of course, a host with young children—or a big heart—may let you know that your baby's exploring is perfectly OK. But even then, you run the risk of your baby breaking or losing something along the way. A better choice is to plan ahead.

When you know you'll be visiting someone's home, whether for an evening dinner or an overnight event, the best thing you can do is take along a bag of brand-new toys to seize your child's attention. You can purchase new items or dig through all your baby's older toys to put together a collection of forgotten favorites. Avoid bringing any loud or mechanical toys that may annoy other people, and try to find some that will have long play value so that they hold your baby's attention (*see* Toys).

Carry Your Own Supplies

Think about the things that most help you keep your baby happy and peaceful at home or in the car, and take along as many of these as possible. These might include your sling or baby carrier, a favorite blanket, your nursing pillow, favorite toys, or a special lovey. If you are prepared, then your baby will be more content, you'll be more peaceful, and your visit will go smoothly.

Call Ahead

If your visit is for an overnight stay, call ahead and talk with your host about a few things, such as sleeping details. You can always ask if they have a crib, high chair, or stroller you can borrow so you don't have to lug these along.

Think About Health and Safety

For longer visits, consider how you will handle awkward situations, such as how to mix a crawling baby and your relative's rambunctious cocker spaniel, or how to protect your baby from your grandfather's cigar smoke, or how to keep your baby from playing with your aunt's delicate china collection.

Safety is an important aspect of visits. Longer visits with a mobile baby are very tricky, especially if you're visiting a home that isn't child-proof. The point of a visit is to spend time with someone you don't see often, so if you want to avoid physically shadowing your baby around the house for your entire stay, take along a few extra safety tools. Examples include a few outlet plugs for areas where your baby will play and a folding baby gate to section off open stairways. When you arrive, assess the area where your baby will be playing, and very politely ask if chemicals, medications, or fragile vases can be put away during your visit. Most people are willing to help on these issues. Please remember, though, that you're certain to miss some hazards, so keep a close eye on your baby and the surroundings during your entire visit.

Food and Eating

Whether your baby is new to solid food or has been eating it for quite a while, carrying a supply of your baby's favorites is a great idea. I can guarantee that if you don't take snacks with you, your baby won't touch the dinner that's served and will be asking for her favorite peanut butter crackers. To avoid this situation, carry a bag or small cooler full of essentials. In any case, don't feel you must push your baby to try something new to the point of a temper tantrum. Politely requesting something simple like toast or cheese and crackers is perfectly OK and will be welcomed more than a loud and tense test of parent/child wills.

What if You're Breastfeeding and Your Baby Is Hungry?

If your baby is hungry, do what comes naturally: Feed him! Breastfeeding is the most natural way to feed a baby. If your hosts aren't used to seeing someone breastfeed, then you're doing our world a favor by introducing one more person to the beauty of baby feeding. Be thoughtful and courteous about other people's feelings, though. This doesn't mean you need to hide out of shame. Rather, your efforts to be discreet are a simple courtesy for those around you who may not be comfortable with the idea of a naked breast (*see* Breastfeeding in Public). Once you become skilled at discreet breastfeeding you can manage to nurse a baby easily while staying fully covered. As an example of this, when Coleton was a few months old, we were visiting the home of a business acquaintance and were all sitting in the living room. At one point, my colleague mentioned that if I wanted to nurse the baby, I was welcome to use one of the bedrooms. I thanked him but then informed him that I had just *finished* feeding the baby!

Changing Diapers

Of course, you'll need to change your baby's diapers while you are visiting. Your host knows this but probably isn't very excited about the idea. It's best if you come fully prepared, but if you aren't, a few polite requests should be met with accommodation.

Where to change? Take a changing pad on which to lay your baby; this will protect the surface you're using. If you don't have a pad, ask your host for a bath towel. I've seen people change babies in the middle of a living room party, but not everyone is comfortable with a public diaper changing. Ask where your host prefers that you change the baby. Some people, especially those who have children themselves, will offer the bed or a sofa. Childless folks may be less comfortable or sensitive to parental issues such as these, but you can suggest a location: "Do you mind if I lay a towel on your bed to change the baby?"

Take along (or ask to use) a few zipper-type plastic bags in which to store messy diapers. If you use cloth diapers, dump the contents in the toilet, and make sure the used diapers are properly sealed so they don't create odors. If you use disposables, put used diapers in a sealed bag and offer to take the bag outside to the trash. Not many people care for stinky diapers in their bathroom garbage can.

Sleeping and Napping

Preparation is again the key to the tricky issue of getting your baby to sleep in an unfamiliar place. Obviously, you can't use the exact same routines that work for you at home, but you may be able to create a *similar* place for your baby. If your little one sleeps in a cradle or crib, for example, you may want to take along a portable cradle or folding crib and ask if you can set it up in a bedroom.

But what if you don't have a portable crib? What if you co-sleep at home? This is a time when "anything goes." If your baby will sleep in your arms while you visit, then go ahead and let him enjoy an in-arms nap. If your baby is more flexible, try putting a blanket on the floor near you and setting up a little sleeping nest. Don't leave your baby alone, though, since the area probably isn't babyproofed.

A great nap solution is to bring your car seat into the house, tilt the seat back as far as it goes, and strap your baby in securely. Again, keep your baby close by or check on her frequently.

If you are spending the night at someone's home and don't have a portable crib, you can fashion one from a large box or an empty drawer from a dresser. For co-sleepers, your first order of business is to create a safe sleeping place for your baby. Check out the room where you will be sleeping, and look at the furniture placement. If you know that pushing the bed against the wall would make the situation safer for your baby, then politely explain to your host. Let her know that you'll move the bed back to its original position before you leave—and then remember to do so. Don't be afraid to ask (*see also* Co-Sleeping, making it work).

Be Prepared for Anything

Life with a baby is filled with surprises. You'll learn soon enough to always have an extra outfit or two on hand for the inevitable spit-up or spilling mishaps. Your usually happy snoozer may suddenly decide that a nap is out of the question and that being crabby for the entire visit is much more interesting.

Often, you can set the tone of your visit. If you are relaxed, take things in stride, and do your best to make the visit pleasant, then your host will likely enjoy the visit as well. Take a deep breath, and do your best to keep your baby content. And if things don't go as well as you'd hoped, remind yourself, "This, too, shall pass."

Show Your Appreciation

If you had an overnight stay, if your hosts were accommodating and helpful, if you rearranged your hosts' home, or if you made special requests during your stay, be sure to mention these special efforts in the thank-you note that you send afterward.

Vomiting

See also: Burping; Colic; Reflux; Spitting Up

> What should I do for my baby? She has vomited several times today.

Learn About It

In deciding how to care for a baby who has vomited, it is important to know how to distinguish vomiting from spitting up and reflux. These three reactions are similar, but they have differences that can determine your course of action. Nearly every baby "spits up." This is the dribbling or spitting back of breastmilk or formula after drinking during the first few months of life. If a baby who is otherwise healthy, happy, and gaining weight spits up a similar amount after most feedings, this is considered normal. The professionals, believe it or not, would call a baby like this a "Happy Spitter." A baby with reflux spits up regularly and more forcefully and shows signs of feeling gassy and uncomfortable after eating. "Vomiting" refers to the bringing up of a large amount of stomach contents and is situational, typically happening as part of another problem, such as an illness.

What Causes a Baby to Vomit?

If your baby is actually vomiting, not spitting up, it may be due to one of these things:

• **A stomach virus:** This is the most common cause of vomiting. The vomiting may be accompanied by diarrhea or fever. The most critical concern for a baby sick with a virus is the risk of dehydration, so you need to keep your baby well hydrated (*see* Dehydration; Fever).

- **Infection:** On occasion, a respiratory or sinus infection can cause a baby to vomit as a reaction to swallowing excess phlegm.
- **Response to a medication:** If your baby is taking a new medication and vomits in response to it, talk to your doctor or call the hospital before giving him any more doses.
- **Intense coughing:** A baby who has a cough due to croup (*see* Croup) or allergies (*see* Allergies and Asthma) may respond to a long bout of coughing by vomiting.
- **Excessive crying:** A hard crying spell may cause your baby to vomit. This may be nature's way of telling us that young babies shouldn't be left to cry for long periods of time. Of course, for a baby with colic, the crying spells are difficult to quell, so just soothe your baby in the best way that you can (*see* Colic).
- **Food allergies:** If your baby is vomiting in response to feeding, it may be due to a food allergy (*see* Food Allergies).
- **Overfeeding:** A baby who throws up after a particularly large feeding but then seems fine may have had an overfull stomach.
- **Food poisoning:** Babies put all kinds of things into their mouths. If a baby picks up spoiled food or a nonfood item off the floor, a table, or the ground, ingesting it may cause vomiting. If your baby is vomiting without any other signs of illness, you might suspect that he's eaten something he shouldn't have. Look around for any signs (such as an open cabinet with cleaning supplies), smell your baby's breath, and think about what you've done in the past few hours. If you suspect poisoning, call your local poison control center for instructions.
- **Shaken-baby syndrome:** If your baby was shaken by someone and, in addition to vomiting, is having difficulty breathing, is lethargic, or has a seizure, seek immediate medical care. If you or your partner have shaken your baby, this is a sign that you are severely overstressed; you need to seek help immediately. Please read about this problem (*see* Shaken-Baby Syndrome) and talk about your feelings to a trusted adviser, such as a doctor, minister, or friend.
- **Head injury:** If your baby has taken a seemingly inconsequential fall or accidentally hit her head and then begins to vomit, take her to an emergency room immediately. She may be suffering a concussion.

When Should I Call the Doctor?

When your baby is vomiting, review the following list of signs to watch for. If you observe any of these signs, you should call your pediatrician. This is just a guide, as you should always trust your own parenting instincts when it comes to your baby. If you think you should call the doctor, then do so without hesitation.

- There is blood in your baby's vomit.
- The color of the fluid is dark yellow or green. (This is bile and can signal a blocked intestine.)
- Your baby's stomach is distended, swollen, or hard to the touch.
- The vomiting is forceful and frequent.
- Your baby has a convulsion.
- Your baby is under two months old and is vomiting.
- Your baby shows signs of dehydration (*see* Dehydration).

Walking

· · · · · · · · · · ·

See also: Babyproofing; Crawling; Milestones of Development; Shoes

When should my baby start walking independently?

Learn About It

Should is a word we need to outlaw when it comes to babies! The important milestones in a baby's life, such as walking and talking, occur at such completely different times for each baby. Parents tend to worry themselves sick if their babies don't adhere to a chart or schedule that tells them when their baby "should" reach a particular milestone. Independent walking, like many other milestones, occurs within a wide range of normal ages. Some babies begin to walk at ten months, and others wait until they are eighteen months old or even longer—and it's all perfectly normal.

Walking and Physical Development

In regard to your baby's physical development, what's most important is a gradual forward progression of skills. When you take your baby to the pediatrician for regular well-baby checkups, your doctor will ask about your baby's emerging skills and will keep track of these. While babies have their own unique ways of approaching the physical milestones that lead to walking (and some are known to skip some steps completely), the following list shows the common process of progression of physical development from birth to walking:

- Holds up head
- Lifts head, shoulders, and upper body when lying on tummy
- Rolls over

- Sits with support
- Sits unsupported
- Moves self around on the floor (rolling, squirming, scooting)
- Stands when supported
- Crawls or finds some other method of moving from place to place
- Pulls up to a stand
- Cruises by holding on to furniture
- Walks with hand-holding support
- Walks independently
- Runs

Why Do Babies Walk When They Do?

A baby who is a proficient crawler may be so satisfied with his ability to get around that he doesn't even try to walk. A content and quiet baby may be much more interested in developing his small motor skills than walking. A chatterbox may be expending so much energy talking that there isn't any left for walking. A happy in-arms baby may so enjoy being toted around by family members that he's in no rush to get on the floor and go. These are just a few of the possible reasons a baby may wait until he's a little older to begin walking. There is just as much speculation about the *early* walker, too, such as a desire to keep up with siblings or an eager, energetic personality. For every theory as to why babies walk when they do, though, there's a gaggle of babies who defy it!

Professional Tip

"No matter which baby in the neighborhood walks first or wins the speed race, the age of walking has nothing to do with eventual intelligence or motor skills. Baby walking, both the timing and the style, is as unique as personality."

—Dr. William Sears in *The Baby Book*
(Little, Brown and Company, 1993)

How Can I Encourage My Baby to Walk?

The best device for encouraging a baby's physical development is a big, empty floor in a safe room, coupled with lots of free time to explore. Research shows babies do best in bare feet, since they use all of their muscles for grip and balance. (When it's time to head outside, learn about appropriate footwear; *see* Shoes.) You also can encourage your baby's natural inclination to get up and move by having stable pieces of furniture available for him to pull himself up on. Beyond this, cheer your baby's attempts at walking, and just let nature take its course.

What About Baby Walkers?

A walker holds a baby upright and gives her the ability to move around, but it may actually hinder a child's natural physical development and can delay the attainment of physical milestones. In addition, a baby walker can put your baby in dangerous situations, since it allows a level of mobility for which the child is neither physically nor intellectually ready. Many babies are injured when they fall down stairs in walkers or when they are raised up to the level of hazards, such as hot pans on the stove, that they would not otherwise be able to reach.

What About Swings, Bouncers, and Jumpers?

There's no doubt about it—many babies love their swings, bouncers, and jumpers. These can keep a baby entertained and happy while a parent makes dinner or catches up on paperwork. Like walkers, though, these do not enhance development or encourage walking. An excess of time in these toys and in infant seats and strollers can actually delay physical development. The key is to use these devices for what they are: pure entertainment for your baby and a safe place for her when she's not in your arms or rolling around on the floor.

When to Be Concerned

You know your baby better than anyone else. Closely monitor your baby's development to verify that there is progress along whatever path

Baby is on (*see* Milestones of Development). In addition, your pediatrician will be tracking your baby's development during regular exams. Your scheduled well-baby visits are routine exams that have several purposes, one of which is to evaluate physical development. The American Academy of Pediatrics recommends exams at these intervals: after birth, two to four days after birth, and at the ages of two to four weeks, two months, four months, six months, nine months, and twelve months. If you feel that your baby isn't following a regular, sequential progression of development, talk this over with your pediatrician at your next visit, or before. This information can help your doctor find and address any problems early.

Weaning from Bottlefeeding

See also: Bottlefeeding; Breastfeeding Your Newborn; Breastfeeding Your Toddler; Breastfeeding with Bottlefeeding Supplements; Drinking from a Cup; Solid Foods, introducing; Weaning from Breastfeeding

> I've read that a baby should be weaned around his first birthday. I've seen two-year-olds with bottles, so why should I worry about it with my fourteen-month-old baby? If I do decide to wean him from his bottle, how should I go about it?

Learn About It

Whether you should wean your baby from bottlefeeding depends on a number of factors. Pediatricians typically recommend that you begin the bottle-weaning process around your baby's first birthday if any of these conditions apply to your child:

- Your baby carries around a bottle and sips from it throughout the day. If this is the case, your child is bathing his teeth in sugars all day long, which increases the risk of tooth decay.
- Your baby uses the bottle for comfort beyond the need for food. When this is the case, babies often drink more milk and juice than is necessary, which takes the place of solid food and disrupts the balance of a healthful diet. But please note that this doesn't apply to breastfeeding, which can proceed as long as mutually desired, due to its many benefits (*see* Weaning from Breastfeeding).
- Your baby is over a year old and refusing to eat solids because he prefers drinking from the bottle.

- Your baby is always holding a bottle, so her hands are constantly full. As a result, the bottle is getting in the way of productive playtime, learning how to pull up to a stand, and learning to walk.
- Your baby has baby bottle tooth decay or cavities due to constant use of a bottle.
- Your baby sleeps with a bottle in the crib all night, which puts her at risk for baby bottle tooth decay.

If none of these situations apply to your baby, and your baby is using the bottle only two or three times a day, then you have more flexibility on when to start the weaning process.

How to Approach Weaning

Weaning from a bottle isn't only about a method of feeding. It's about saying good-bye to a piece of babyhood and a familiar comfort object. Because of this, weaning shouldn't happen suddenly. The cold-turkey approach may only confuse your baby and make him miserable. A more loving and gradual process is much easier on your baby and on you, too.

The Right Timing

It helps to begin weaning at the right time in your baby's life. Think about the following issues, which may signal that it's better to wait a bit before you start the weaning process:

- Is your baby younger than nine months old? Before this age, most babies aren't ready to take in all of their nourishment from solids and a cup.
- Is your baby sick or having a hard time with teething? Wait until your baby feels better before attempting to make this big change.
- Are you late in pregnancy, or has a new sibling recently joined the family? If so, it's better to avoid any other changes in your child's life right now.
- Is a major event looming in your household, such as a move, a new day-care arrangement, or a vacation? Adding weaning may just

complicate matters; consider waiting until things have settled back to normal.

Is your baby ready for weaning? If the answer is yes to the following questions, now may be the perfect time to get started:

- Is your baby eating a wide assortment of solid foods?
- Can your baby use a sipper cup well?
- Can your baby use a regular cup?
- Does your baby seem emotionally ready to give up the bottle?

How to Wean Your Baby from the Bottle

Once you've decided to go ahead, use some of these ideas to make the change. Keep in mind that unless there's a reason to rush this process, it's better to handle the change gradually, over the course of several months. Give your baby plenty of time to adjust to this milestone.

- Teach your baby to use sipper cups. A wide assortment of toddler cups with handles and spouts is available. These can smooth the transition from bottle to cup in a fun—and, if you get the right kind of sipper, also a spillproof—way (*see* Drinking from a Cup).
- Don't automatically reach for a bottle to quiet your fussy baby. Instead, take a moment to cuddle her. You may be surprised how well it works!
- Try offering your baby a cup at the times he normally would have a bottle, such as when he first wakes up in the morning.
- Create a rule that your baby must sit or lie down when having a bottle, instead of letting her walk around with it. She may become bored and leave the bottle behind so she can go off to play.
- If your baby asks for a bottle, try distracting him with an activity and a snack. Busy toddlers can be convinced to think about something else fairly easily.
- Gradually water down the liquids in her bottle while providing undiluted liquids in the cup; give both to your baby at the same time. Since the full-strength liquid will taste better, she may pre-

fer the cup. Over time, reduce the amount of liquid in the bottle so there are just a few sips there while a full cup awaits.

- If your baby is used to going to sleep with a bottle of milk, add a little more water to each nightly bottle over a period of weeks until it becomes 100 percent water. Or try substituting a pacifier instead.

When Weaning Is Working

Since your baby will be giving up some calories and nutrition when he gives up his bottles, you must be vigilant that he gets enough food and drink in his diet for continued healthy growth (*see* Solid Foods, introducing). Every baby is different, but most children around one year of age need sixteen to twenty-four ounces of milk or a dairy product substitute every day. Babies also need three meals plus two or three nutritious snacks every day. Think of offering your baby something to eat every two to three hours so that he doesn't get hungry.

If your baby is giving up bottles before his first birthday, continue to give him breastmilk or iron-fortified formula in his cup—not cow's or goat's milk—until he's at least a year old.

Weaning from Breastfeeding

See also: Breastfeeding Your Newborn; Breastfeeding Your Toddler; Breastfeeding with Bottlefeeding Supplements; Weaning from Bottlefeeding

I'm thinking of weaning my sixteen-month-old breastfed daughter. What's the best way to wean?

Learn About It

Your baby is now over a year old, so you've accomplished breastfeeding for more than the minimum amount of time recommended by the American Academy of Pediatrics. That's truly wonderful. Your baby has received the incredible benefits of breastfeeding, such as increased immunities, better health, solid emotional attachment, higher IQ potential (the list goes on and on), and you've enjoyed the beautiful closeness that breastfeeding your baby allows. These benefits, though, don't stop just because your baby has celebrated her first birthday and taken her first step! The phenomenal benefits of breastfeeding continue for as long as you choose to breastfeed your baby. So, before we talk about *how* to wean, let's talk about *why*.

How to Decide if You Should Wean Your Baby

Many mothers set a weaning time in their minds long before weaning happens. They may start out with the thought, "I'm going to breastfeed for a year," and before they know it, they're planning that first birthday party. When your predetermined time arrives, though, instead of accepting it as a given, treat it as a time of introspection. This is a time to ask yourself, "Why?"

There is no one right time for weaning; it is very different for every mother and baby. And there is no one standard reason for weaning. Rather, the reasons are as varied as the mothers themselves and the children they are breastfeeding. Every one of your children will require a separate weaning decision. I breastfed two of my children until they were fifteen months old; my third child was two and a half; and the fourth—well, he just turned three and he's still breastfeeding, although we're now taking slow steps toward weaning. Life situations are different with each child, and each baby deserves her own well-thought-out plan for weaning, even if that plan is to wait until your baby leads the way when she's ready.

So, before you read the rest of this section on *how* to wean, I strongly suggest that you take a few days to figure out the whys. And when you're clear about your answer and ready to take the steps to weaning, then come back here and read the suggestions on how to proceed.

Professional Tip

"There is no exact and universal age at which babyhood and nursing must end."

— **Norma Jane Bumgarner in *Mothering Your Nursing Toddler***

Slow Is Best

Unless there is some compelling reason to rush weaning, it's best to take your time. If you allow the process to happen gradually over a period of months, your baby and your body will adjust as they should, making the process as painless and easy as possible for both of you.

The First Step Toward Weaning

An excellent way to begin the weaning process is to test the waters and edge in the direction of weaning. This is often referred to as "don't offer, don't refuse." As the phrase implies, this means that you will continue to nurse your baby when she requests, but you won't assume the need for nursing, and you'll hold back from offering. Many nursing mothers do automatically offer the breast at typical times, such as when their babies first wake in the morning, right before naps or bedtime, or when their babies are fussy or unhappy. What surprises many nursing mothers is that, if their babies are as ready as the mothers are to begin the weaning process, they will be open to a new routine that doesn't include breastfeeding.

Distraction Works!

Babies are active little people, and they live busy lives. You can take full advantage of this when you want to move the weaning process along. When your baby expects or asks to nurse, try first to distract him into thinking about or doing something else. For example, if your baby usually nurses immediately upon waking, you can greet him as he wakes up with a fun toy or by opening the window shade and looking for birds outside. The first few times you try this, your baby may be confused and may fuss to nurse, but don't give in immediately. Try the distraction route for five minutes or more, and if your little one-track-mind can't be persuaded, then go ahead and nurse. If you continue the distraction method over a period of weeks, your baby will surprise you one day by waking up and asking you to open the window so he can find the birds. This same approach works for daytime nursing and can even have an impact on the bedtime session. An older baby will often enjoy a bedtime story with a promise to nurse afterward—and if your story is long enough, he may be asleep before the ending.

"In a Minute": The Delay Tactic

A similar approach is the delay: "You can have milk after I fold the laundry." Of course, by then your baby will be busy doing other things!

Do nurse after the laundry, though, if your baby still desires to. This builds trust and shows your baby that you are not ignoring her needs. You might even try postponement: "Let's wait until naptime (or bedtime)." This can sometimes be an effective way to reduce the number of daily nursing sessions.

Replacing Breastmilk with Solid Foods

Another approach to weaning involves offering your baby more solid food. If your baby is enjoying table food, he'll want to breastfeed more for comfort than for nutrition. When this happens, you can begin to substitute other forms of comfort and attention for breastfeeding—for example, reading books, cuddling, or playing with toys together.

Avoid Your Usual Nursing Spots

Most mothers have one or two places where they typically nurse their babies—maybe a rocking chair or favorite sofa. When you want to encourage the weaning process, refrain from sitting in these seats, even if you're doing something entirely different, such as reading a book. The familiar spot can trigger your baby's desire to nurse, so for the time being, find a different place to settle, and combine this with the distraction tips previously discussed.

Shorten Your Nursing Sessions

Another step toward weaning is to breastfeed for shorter amounts of time whenever you do breastfeed. If you usually nurse about fifteen minutes on each side, shorten this to ten. If you usually let your baby nurse for as long as he wants, try ending the session yourself with a distraction.

Substitute Playtime for Nursing Time

Sometimes mothers (even without realizing it) use breastfeeding as a way to find some quiet uninterrupted time with their babies. Make a conscious decision to replace the nursing with play. Read your baby some books, or sit on the floor and play with toys together. You might plan playtime for a time you typically breastfeed, and your baby may be so pleased just to have you as a playmate that she won't even ask to nurse.

Get Your Partner to Help

Since Mommy equals milk, it can help to have your partner tend to your baby during those times when you would usually breastfeed, such as when your baby first wakes up or before sleep. This requires a little more patience and finesse, but it can be a great way to create new patterns in your baby's day that don't involve breastfeeding.

The Weaning Dance

Don't be surprised if your baby seems to sense your desire to wean and suddenly wants to nurse like a newborn. This is a natural response to a big change in his life. If you give him a day or two to nurse, this will usually pass, and you can proceed in the direction of weaning again. Usually the progression from full-time breastfeeding to weaning isn't a straight line; it's more like a dance. But if you lead with care and sensitivity, you will end up dancing to the tune you've chosen.

For More Information

Books

Bengson, Diane. *How Weaning Happens.* Schaumburg, IL: La Leche League International, 2000.

Bumgarner, Norma Jane. *Mothering Your Nursing Toddler*, rev. ed. Schaumburg, IL: La Leche League International, 2000.

Worship Services, attending with your baby

· · · · · · · · · · · ·

See also: Breastfeeding in Public

Our faith is very important to us, and we have always gone to services every week. However, since our baby was born, we've hardly been able to make it out the door for church. Then, when we finally get there, it's a disaster! The baby is noisy, and I end up walking the hallways during the entire service. Should we just stop going?

Learn About It

Having a baby doesn't mean you need to give up worship services. It does mean you'll need to modify your expectations because your experiences at religious services will be very different for a while. It's very natural to find that you're not paying as much attention as you used to or coming away with a cohesive message. Take heart, though: As your child gets older and more mature, learns what kind of behavior is acceptable, and even starts to enjoy going to worship services himself, you'll see that it's a wonderful time of connection and strength for your family.

Making It Through the Service

Here are a few ideas for making attendance at your religious service with your baby an enjoyable experience for all concerned:

• **Even though it may be difficult, try to keep (or start) going to services from the time your baby is born.** Your baby will get used to going every weekend and will get used to the place, the people, and the way your service works. That way, you're not suddenly struggling with a toddler who's never been to worship services before. Try not to fall into the trap of leaving the baby with a sitter or family member. Over time, this may sound like much more fun to your child than going to services, and you'll have a hard time convincing him to go later on!

- **When your child is still an infant, sit toward the back of the room so that you can slip out if necessary.** As an option, many places of worship offer a special section or room specifically for parents with babies. If your place of worship offers this, then enjoy the privilege. Not only can you attend with your baby, you can share this chapter in your life with other parents like you.

- **When the baby gets old enough to observe what's going on, try sitting in the main section, and even sit up front so the baby can see the proceedings.** Being able to see the service may keep your baby from getting bored.

- **If your nursing baby gets hungry, go ahead and breastfeed him.** Even if you are completely comfortable with nursing in public, keep in mind that some people at a place of worship may be extra sensitive to observing breastfeeding here. If you feel that others seated near you fall into this group, you can use a blanket or other covering to be extra discreet, or find a less visible place to sit. On the other hand, you may find a religious congregation the most accepting "audience" you've yet experienced. A little practice, and you'll get the hang of nursing discreetly while sharing a beautiful part of motherhood with others who may never have the chance to see a nursing mother. Also, keep in mind that nearly everyone would rather have a quietly nursing baby than a noisy, crying one!

- **Bring a few quiet toys for your baby** (not your keys!). A few good choices are teething toys, stuffed animals, and soft picture books. If you can find a baby's book about your faith, all the better!

- **Try feeding Baby just before leaving, or give her a snack in the car on the way there.** If different times are available for your services, plan on going to one right after your baby's nap, so she's not fussy, or during her nap if she'll sleep while you're there. A lovely nap in your arms is a wonderful way for both Baby and parent to enjoy a service.

- **Take snacks (as a last resort).** You may not want to start a hard-to-break habit of having snacks at worship services every time you go, but be realistic: Snacks can be effective at preserving the peace. Pack a sippy cup of juice or water and a small, quiet snack, and provide these if your other methods of encouraging quietness aren't working.

• **Don't skip services if you can help it.** Children thrive on routine, and as your baby gets a little older, she'll automatically expect this to be a part of her week.

• **Try to evaluate which service your child will enjoy the most.** Is there a children's choir at one service? Or is one service quieter, with less singing, and better suited to a baby who's easily overstimulated? Does your baby do better when she's bright-eyed for a morning service, or does she prefer to sleep to the sounds of the evening sermon?

• **Once your baby is a little older, experiment with the special classes and areas for kids.** Some congregations offer outstanding programs for children. If your baby suffers from separation anxiety, you can begin by joining her; offer your services as a helper. Once she is comfortable with the routine, try leaving after she's settled. But don't go too far too quickly. She may become upset, and you'll need to slip back into the room for a time. Over a few weeks (or even months for more sensitive children), your child eventually will be comfortable enough to attend the children's class without you. If you feel you've missed too much of the service, arrange to attend a later or earlier one on your own, join a weekly study group, or do your own study at home. Your goal is to help your little one enjoy and look forward to weekly services and to build a relationship with God, and your patience is a key to success. This adjustment period is short in the overall picture of your family's spiritual life.

Parent Tip

"The way I have always seen it, some babbling and cooing during service is acceptable. I've never seen a sign on the door that says, 'No Children Allowed.'"

—**Becky, mother of Joshua (13), Karissa (11), Sarah (5), and Melissa (2)**

• **Consider starting another tradition, like making a big brunch after your worship service, going out for breakfast, having friends over, or having fun family time together.** This shows your children that these are special days and gives them lots to look forward to.

• **If your place of worship provides services on weekdays, think about attending those.** Midweek services usually are much shorter than the main weekly service and will give your child an opportunity to get used to the service.

• **Teach your child the songs, gestures, and prayers used.** As they become familiar, your child can show off these new skills during services.

• **Talk about your faith often, and make it an integral part of your life.** Whatever religion you may be, your faith is made of much more than what you do for an hour or two each week.

Index

About the Author

Parenting educator Elizabeth Pantley is president of Better Beginnings, Inc., a family resource and education company. Elizabeth frequently speaks to parents in schools, hospitals, and parent groups, and her presentations are received with enthusiasm and praise.

She is a regular radio show guest and frequently quoted as a parenting expert in magazines such as *Parents*, *Parenting*, *Woman's Day*, *Good Housekeeping*, *McCalls*, and *Redbook* and on over fifty parent-directed websites. She publishes a newsletter, *Parent Tips*, that is distributed in schools nationwide, and she is the author of four previous parenting books, available in nine languages:

- *The No-Cry Sleep Solution: Gentle Ways to Help Your Baby Sleep Through the Night*
- *Hidden Messages: What Our Words and Actions Are Really Telling Our Children*
- *Perfect Parenting: The Dictionary of 1,000 Parenting Tips*
- *Kid Cooperation: How to Stop Yelling, Nagging and Pleading & Get Kids to Cooperate*

She is also a contributor to *The Successful Child: What Parents Can Do to Help Kids Turn Out Well* (Little, Brown and Company), a joint effort with Dr. William and Martha Sears. Elizabeth is currently working on her next book, *Gentle Toddler Care*.

She and her husband, Robert, live in the state of Washington with their four children, Grama (Elizabeth's mother), and assorted family pets. She is an involved participant in her children's school and sports activities and has served in positions as varied as softball coach and school PTA president.

For More Information

You can write, call, or go online to obtain a free catalog of parenting books, videos, audiotapes, and newsletters; request information about lecture services available by Elizabeth Pantley; or contact the author.

Write to the author:
5720 127th Avenue NE
Kirkland, WA 98033-8741

E-mail the author:
elizabeth@pantley.com

Call the toll-free order line:
1-800-422-5820

Visit the website:
www.pantley.com/elizabeth